"Interpersonal Psychoanalysis is by far the most distinctive and specifically American contribution to psychoanalysis. Sullivan has persuasively been described as the "Psychiatrist of America," and interpersonal psychoanalysis has clearly absorbed and exemplifies such core American values as pluralism, pragmatism, concrete experience, and interactionism. Donnel Stern and Irwin Hirsch's *The Interpersonal Perspective in Psychoanalysis, 1960s–1990s: Rethinking transference and countertransference* provides the most solid introduction to this unique American school and it includes a scholarly and cogent historical introduction to the overall tradition as well as to each of the vintage papers and major contributors represented. This will remain a classic collection of psychoanalytic papers for many years to come."

—**Lewis Aron, Ph.D.,** Director, New York University Postdoctoral Program in Psychotherapy and Psychoanalysis.

"This is an important book. It is also an exciting adventure. A reader can "feel-into" the psychoanalytic meaning of *interpersonal* as the context of co-existence—a context in which the creative freedom intrinsic to the analyst/patient dyad shapes a *process* of personality growth that is its "outcome." The essence of interpersonal is not communicated through theory but through its commitment to empowering *psychoanalysis as psychotherapy*. One could argue that if psychoanalysis is to assure its future relevance it must uniformly earn the privilege by making the same foundational commitment. This volume should be an essential treasure in any library."

—**Philip M. Bromberg, Ph.D.,** Training and Supervising Analyst, William Alanson White Psychoanalytic Institute; Adjunct Clinical Professor of Psychology, NYU Postdoctoral Program in Psychotherapy and Psychoanalysis.

"This book locates and pays homage to the origins and early development of the interpersonal perspective but really does so much more than simply historiographical duty. In examining key voices over several generations of interpersonalists, we actually see and feel the radical vision. For some the birth narratives offer up Ferenczi (Wolstein, Searles), for others, it is Sullivan (Hirsch, Stern), for others still post modernism and post structuralism (Levenson), for others it is in the power of examining psychotic process (Searles, Barnett) and for others it is the unsettling of technique (Wolstein, Greenberg). We can see a variety of two person readings of early object relations (Bromberg, Stern). This book is a brilliant re-reading of the interpersonal worlds in which the editors Hirsch and Stern are prominent members of a current generation. In so many unique idioms and voices and stances, we are urged to loosen our grip on certainty, to face the harrowing experience of patient's suffering without retreating from our own. This collection gives us a half-century of wisdom, as useful for the mature as for the novice analyst."

—**Adrienne Harris,** New York University, Editor of the Relational Perspectives Book Series.

The Interpersonal Perspective in Psychoanalysis, 1960s–1990s

North American psychoanalysis has long been deeply influenced and substantially changed by clinical and theoretical perspectives first introduced by interpersonal psychoanalysis. Yet even today, despite its origin in the 1930s, many otherwise well-read psychoanalysts and psychotherapists are not well informed about the field. *The Interpersonal Perspective in Psychoanalysis, 1960s–1990s* provides a superb starting point for those who are not as familiar with interpersonal psychoanalysis as they might be. For those who already know the literature, the book will be useful in placing a selection of classic interpersonal articles and their writers in key historical context.

During the time span covered in this book, interpersonal psychoanalysis was most concerned with revising the understanding of the analytic relationship – transference and countertransference – and how to work with it. Most of the works collected here center on this theme. The interpersonal perspective introduced the view that the analyst is always and unavoidably a particular, "real" person, and that transference and countertransference need to be reconceptualized to take the analyst's individual humanity into account. The relationship needs to be grasped as one taking place between two very particular people. Many of the articles are by writers well known in the broader psychoanalytic world, such as Bromberg, Greenberg, Levenson, and Mitchell. But also included are those by writers who, while not as widely recognized beyond the interpersonal literature, have been highly influential among interpersonalists, including Barnett, Schecter, Singer, and Wolstein.

Donnel B. Stern and Irwin Hirsch, prominent interpersonalists themselves, present each piece with a prologue that contextualizes the author and their work in the interpersonal literature. An introductory essay also reviews the history of interpersonal psychoanalysis, explaining why interpersonal thinking remains a coherent clinical and theoretical perspective in contemporary psychoanalysis.

The Interpersonal Perspective in Psychoanalysis, 1960s–1990s will appeal greatly to psychoanalysts and psychoanalytic psychotherapists wanting to know more about interpersonal theory and practice than can be learned from current sources.

Donnel B. Stern is Training and Supervising Analyst at the William Alanson White Institute in New York City and Adjunct Clinical Professor of Psychology on the New York University Postdoctoral Program in Psychotherapy and Psychoanalysis. He is the founder and editor of the Routledge "Psychoanalysis in a New Key" book series and author of many psychoanalytic articles and books, the most recent of which is *Relational Freedom: Emergent Properties of the Interpersonal Field.*

Irwin Hirsch supervises and/or teaches at the Manhattan Institute for Psychoanalysis; the William Alanson White Institute; the NYU Postdoctoral Program in Psychotherapy and Psychoanalysis; and the National Institute for the Psychotherapies, National Program. He has authored over 80 journal articles and book chapters and two books: *Coasting in the Countertransference: Conflicts of Self-Interest between Analyst and Patient*, winner of the Goethe Award; and *The Interpersonal Tradition: The Origins of Psychoanalytic Subjectivity.*

Psychoanalysis in A New Key Books Series
Donnel Stern
Series Editor

When music is played in a new key, the melody does not change, but the notes that make up the composition do: change in the context of continuity, continuity that perseveres through change. Psychoanalysis in a New Key publishes books that share the aims psychoanalysts have always had, but that approach them differently. The books in the series are not expected to advance any particular theoretical agenda, although to this date most have been written by analysts from the Interpersonal and Relational orientations.

The most important contribution of a psychoanalytic book is the communication of something that nudges the reader's grasp of clinical theory and practice in an unexpected direction. Psychoanalysis in a New Key creates a deliberate focus on innovative and unsettling clinical thinking. Because that kind of thinking is encouraged by exploration of the sometimes surprising contributions to psychoanalysis of ideas and findings from other fields, Psychoanalysis in a New Key particularly encourages interdisciplinary studies. Books in the series have married psychoanalysis with dissociation, trauma theory, sociology, and criminology. The series is open to the consideration of studies examining the relationship between psychoanalysis and any other field—for instance, biology, literary and art criticism, philosophy, systems theory, anthropology, and political theory.

But innovation also takes place within the boundaries of psychoanalysis, and Psychoanalysis in a New Key therefore also presents work that reformulates thought and practice without leaving the precincts of the field. Books in the series focus, for example, on the significance of personal values in psychoanalytic practice, on the complex interrelationship between the analyst's clinical work and personal life, on the consequences for the clinical situation when patient and analyst are from different cultures, and on the need for psychoanalysts to accept the degree to which they knowingly satisfy their own wishes during treatment hours, often to the patient's detriment.

For a full list of all the titles in the Psychoanalysis in a New Key series, please visit the Routledge website.

RECENT TITLES IN THIS SERIES:

Vol. 33 *Needed Relationships and Psychoanalytic Healing: A Holistic Relational Perspective on the Therapeutic Process* Steven Stern

Vol. 32 *The Age of Perversion: Desire and Technology in Psychoanalysis and Culture* Danielle Knafo and Rocco Lo Bosco

Vol. 31 *Unknowable, Unspeakable and Unsprung: Psychoanalytic Perspectives on Truth, Scandal, Secrets and Lies* Edited by Jean Petrucelli and Sarah Schoen

Vol. 30 *Trauma and Countertrauma, Resilience and Counterresilience: Insights from Psychoanalysts and Trauma Experts* Edited by Richard B. Gartner

Vol. 29 *The Purloined Self: Interpersonal Perspectives in Psychoanalysis* Edgar A. Levenson

Vol. 28 *On the Lyricism of the Mind: Psychoanalysis and Literature* Dana Amir

The Interpersonal Perspective in Psychoanalysis, 1960s–1990s

Rethinking Transference and Countertransference

Edited by Donnel B. Stern and Irwin Hirsch

Routledge
Taylor & Francis Group
LONDON AND NEW YORK

First published 2017
by Routledge
2 Park Square, Milton Park, Abingdon, Oxon OX14 4RN

and by Routledge
605 Third Avenue, New York, NY 10017

Routledge is an imprint of the Taylor & Francis Group, an informa business

British Library Cataloguing in Publication Data
A catalogue record for this book is available from the British Library

Library of Congress Cataloguing in Publication Data
Names: Stern, Donnel B., editor. | Hirsch, Irwin, editor.
Title: The interpersonal perspective in psychoanalysis, 1960s–1990s : rethinking transference and countertransference / edited by Donnel B. Stern and Irwin Hirsch. Other titles: Prequel: Pioneers of interpersonal psychoanalysis.
Description: Abingdon, Oxon; New York, NY : Routledge, 2017. |
Articles previously published in various sources. |
Includes bibliographical references and index.
Identifiers: LCCN 2016040965 |
ISBN 9780415714280 (hardback : alk. paper) |
ISBN 9781138281936 (pbk. : alk. paper) |
ISBN 9781315471976 (e-book) Subjects: |
MESH: Psychoanalytic Therapy | Transference (Psychology) |
Countertransference (Psychology) | Interpersonal Relations |
Psychoanalysis–history | Collected Works Classification:
LCC RC500.5 | NLM WM 460.6 | DDC 616.89/17–dc23
LC record available at https://lccn.loc.gov/2016040965

ISBN: 978-0-415-71428-0 (hbk)
ISBN: 978-1-138-28193-6 (pbk)
ISBN: 978-1-315-47197-6 (ebk)

Typeset in Times New Roman
by Out of House Publishing

Dedication from Donnel Stern: For Allan Cooper
Dedication from Irwin Hirsch: For Dilan, Theo, Ana and Aurelie

Table of Contents

Acknowledgments

Donnel B. Stern: I am deeply grateful to my analyst, my supervisors, and my teachers at the William Alanson White Institute. They helped me make a life in psychoanalysis, and in interpersonal psychoanalysis in particular, which has come to mean everything to me. I thank my wife, Kathe Hift, also a psychoanalyst, for her continuous support and encouragement over so many years. I also want to thank my co-editor, Irwin Hirsch, without whom this project would not have gotten off the ground, and my friends and editors at Routledge, especially Kate Hawes, for their reliability and dedication.

Irwin Hirsch: Thank you to my friend, colleague and co-editor, Donnel Stern, who initiated this project, and to my wife and fellow psychoanalyst, Willa Cobert, with whom I share a deep connection to the Interpersonal tradition, and from whom I continue to learn. I also wish to acknowledge Erwin Singer and Benjamin Wolstein, the teachers and supervisors who most influenced my clinical work during my formative years as an analyst, and Harold Searles and Edgar Levenson, whose writing and thinking was the most significant to me in those years, and beyond.

The editors thank Wolters Kluwer Health – HRLP for permission to reprint the following article:

Searles, H. F. (1967). The "dedicated physician" in the field of psychotherapy and psychoanalysis. In R. W. Gibson (Ed.), *Crosscurrents in Psychiatry and Psychoanalysis*. Philadelphia and Toronto: J. B. Lippincott, pp.128–143.

The editors thank Guilford Press for permission to reprint the following articles:

Schecter, D. E. (1980). Early developmental roots of anxiety. *Journal of the American Academy of Psychoanalysis*, 8: 539–554.

Wolstein, B. (1975). Countertransference: The pyschoanalyst's shared experience and inquiry with his patient. *Journal of the American Academy of Psychoanalysis*, 3: 77–89.

The editors are indebted to Kenneth A. Frank, who granted permission to reproduce the following book chapter:

Singer, E. (1977). The fiction of analytic anonymity. In K. Frank (Ed.), *The Human Dimension in Psychoanalytic Practice*. New York: Grune & Stratton, pp. 181–192.

The editors are grateful to Taylor & Francis, LLC for permission to reprint the following articles:

Barnett, J. (1980). Interpersonal processes, cognition, and the analysis of character. *Contemporary Psychoanalysis*, 16: 397–416.
Bromberg, P. M. (1994). "Speak! that I may see you": Some reflections on dissociation, reality, and psychoanalytic listening. *Psychoanalytic Dialogues*, 4: 517–547.
Ehrenberg, D. B. (1982). Psychoanalytic engagement – the transaction as primary data. *Contemporary Psychoanalysis*, 18: 535–555.
Gill, M.M. (1983). The interpersonal paradigm and the degree of the therapist's involvement. *Contemporary Psychoanalysis*, 19: 200–237.
Greenberg, J. (1981). Prescription or description: The therapeutic action of psychoanalysis. *Contemporary Psychoanalysis*, 17: 239–257.
Levenson, E. (1978). Two essays in psychoanalytical psychology: Psychoanalysis: Cure or persuasion? *Contemporary Psychoanalysis*, 14: 1–17.
Mitchell, S. (1988). The intrapsychic and the interpersonal: Different theories, different domains or historical artifacts? *Psychoanalytic Inquiry*, 8: 472–496.
Stern, D. B. (1990). Courting surprise – unbidden perceptions in clinical practice. *Contemporary Psychoanalysis*, 26: 452–478.

The editors thank the Association for the Advancement of Psychoanalysis for permission to reprint the following article:

Hirsch, I. (1990). Countertransference and participant-observation. *American Journal of Psychoanalysis*, 50: 275–284.

Introduction

Interpersonal psychoanalysis: History and current status

Donnel B. Stern

When I began my psychoanalytic training at the William Alanson White Institute, I had read some of the work of interpersonalists Harry Stack Sullivan and Frieda Fromm-Reichmann, who had been among the small group who founded the White Institute; and, like most reasonably well-educated people at that time, not only those inside the field but outside it as well, I was aware of the work of Karen Horney and Erich Fromm (Fromm was another founder of White). I had also read Ernest Schachtel and Rollo May, writers from the second generation of interpersonal psychoanalysts. Schachtel (1959) was well known among his peers for his articles on psychoanalytic developmental themes; and May (1984), like Fromm, brought existentialism to psychoanalysis, and psychoanalysis to the wider public.

But I had never heard of so many of the other interpersonal psychoanalytic contributors to the literature from the 1930s to the 1970s. Here is a partial list of those people whose work I came to know during the late 1970s and early 1980s: Sabert Basescu, Joseph Barnett, Harry Bone, Walter Bonime, Hilda Bruch, Gerard Chrzanowski, Clay Dahlberg, Ralph Crowley, Marianne Horney Eckardt, Darlene B. Ehrenberg, Lawrence Epstein, Leslie Farber, Arthur H. Feiner, Maurice Green, Edgar A. Levenson, Ruth Moulton, Janet Rioch, David Schecter, John Schimel, Erwin Singer, Rose Spiegel, Edward Tauber, Clara Thompson, Edwin Weinstein, Earl G. Witenberg, Benjamin Wolstein, and Herbert Zucker. Even this list gives short shrift to the contribution of psychoanalysts from the institute founded by Karen Horney (the American Institute of Psychoanalysis), whose work bears a close relation to the work of the interpersonalists.

So why had I never heard of this body of work? And (as I was soon to discover) I was not alone: although the situation has changed for the better in our current era, many people in the field of psychoanalysis have never come across most of this literature, nor do they know most of the interpersonal psychoanalytic literature that has been written between then and now. When I travel to cities and countries outside the Northeastern United States and Eastern Canada to lecture and teach, and I identify myself as an interpersonal and relational psychoanalyst, colleagues very often ask me what "interpersonal" means. Sometimes they are a little hesitant to ask the question – perhaps because they have heard the term and feel that they should know more about it than they do. But often enough the question is asked with complete innocence.

I had a lovely lunch recently, right here in New York City, the home of interpersonal psychoanalysis, with a well-known senior Freudian psychoanalyst from one of the three institutes in this city that have always represented the psychoanalytic mainstream, reflected in their longtime membership in the American Psychoanalytic Association. This analyst, who is active in the intellectual life of the field, has been part of the psychoanalytic world for five of the eight decades during which interpersonal psychoanalysts have been writing and publishing. And yet, despite having lived and worked for all those decades in the same city with the interpersonal psychoanalysts I have just named, when the theoretical and clinical differences between us came up in conversation, and she asked me the names of interpersonal writers from the 1960s to 1980s, she did not recognize even one of them. Not Ernest Schachtel or Ruth Moulton; not Edgar Levenson (that one surprised me) or Benjamin Wolstein; not Joseph Barnett, Larry Epstein, or Leslie Farber.

There are very good social/historical reasons for this ignorance, reasons that are familiar to all interpersonalists and probably to most mainstream analysts, as well. And that brings me to the reason for this book.

Several years ago, thinking about how to remedy this problem, I decided that editing a collection of articles exemplifying interpersonal psychoanalysis over recent decades would be a good idea. But there was too much material for one volume; the project justified two. And that is what I proposed to my publishers at Routledge, who agreed to do it.

But one thing after another kept coming up, and somehow the project did not get off the ground. One day I was talking to my good friend and colleague Irwin Hirsch, one of the most prominent of today's interpersonal psychoanalysts, and I happened to mention this project and my frustration about its progress. Immediately in tune with the same impulse that had animated my original decision, Irwin proposed that we do it together.

This was a very good idea. Irwin is the best person I could have imagined for this job. He is steeped in the interpersonal psychoanalytic literature, and he has probably done more than anyone else to make sure that this literature is recognized by other psychoanalysts (see Hirsch, 2015).

I had selected articles to be reprinted in the books, but Irwin and I rejigged the selection to reflect both our sensibilities. I had originally thought I would write contextualizing introductions for each article. It was Irwin's idea that he take over those introductions in this first volume, an idea to which I readily agreed, since that would ensure the project's completion. I agreed to write this general introduction, and we each reviewed and edited the work of the other.

The authors represented in this book and its companion volume, *Further Developments in Interpersonal Psychoanalysis, 1980s–2010s: Evolving Interest in the Analyst's Subjectivity* (Stern & Hirsch, in press), are those whose work has been most significant in the modern history of interpersonal psychoanalysis. A number of first- and second-generation interpersonal writers are not included in either of these compilations: Harry Bone, Ralph Crowley, Leslie Farber, Erich Fromm, Frieda Fromm-Reichmann, Janet Rioch, Ernest Schachtel, John Schimel, Harry Stack Sullivan, Edward Tauber, and Clara Thompson. The work of these writers appeared in an earlier edited collection, *Pioneers of Interpersonal Psychoanalysis* (Stern, Kantor, Mann & Schlesinger, 1995), which was dedicated to the work of the first generations of interpersonalists.[1] That book should be considered a prequel to these two volumes. But there are other significant interpersonal writers who we regret were not included in *Pioneers* or either of the two volumes of this series. We would like to have included their work: Sabert Basescu, Walter Bonime, Hilde Bruch, Gerard Chrzanowski, Margaret Crastnopol, Rebecca Curtis, Jack Drescher, Kenneth Eisold, Tess Forrest, Roger Frie, Richard Gartner, Mary-Joan Gerson, Emmanuel Ghent, Alan Grey, Maurice Green, Elizabeth Howell, Ruth Imber, Emily Kuriloff, Jay Kwawer, Robert Langan, Marylou Lionells, Paul Lippmann, Ruth Moulton, Dale Ortmeyer, Robert Prince, Jerome Singer, Rose Spiegel, Paul Trad, Paul Wachtel, Cleonie White, Warren Wilner, and Earl Witenberg.

Our criterion for deciding who was to be considered an interpersonal psychoanalyst was self-identification. If writers considered themselves interpersonal, we did also. Almost all of those we have included in these two volumes are interpersonal psychoanalysts in these terms. We regret not being able to include those authors who would not necessarily identify themselves as interpersonal psychoanalysts, but whose work is consistent with that designation.

That is the genesis of the book you hold in your hands, *The Interpersonal Perspective in Psychoanalysis, 1960s–1990s: Rethinking Transference and Countertransference*.

It is the first of two volumes, organized very roughly according to chronology. Articles in the present volume are drawn from the 1960s through the early 1990s. The second book, *Further Developments in Interpersonal Psychoanalysis, 1980s–2010s: Evolving Interest in the Analyst's Subjectivity* (Stern & Hirsch, in press) is composed of articles drawn from the contemporary era.

At the request of our publisher, as a means of differentiating the two books, each volume is distinguished not only by a time period but also a thematic subtitle. When we were asked to think about how the content of interpersonal psychoanalysis has been different in the overlapping eras covered by the books, we settled on different, but closely related themes, which in turn developed from the themes that had animated the work of the founders of interpersonal psychoanalysis. The founders – Sullivan, Fromm, Thompson, Fromm-Reichmann, Schachtel, and others – established the interpersonal perspective as an interpretive scheme based on interpersonal relations. In the era covered by the first of our two volumes – the 1960s to the 1990s – the theme of the interpersonal literature seems to us to have revolved around the development of a characteristically interpersonal theory and practice of transference and countertransference. That is, the emphasis was less on the theory of interpersonal relations as an interpretive scheme and more on how thinking that way affected clinical praxis, particularly the way we work in and through the analytic relationship. As time passed, and interpersonal psychoanalysis entered the contemporary era – the 1980s to the 2010s, the time during which the articles in our second volume were published – the focus seems to have shifted to the very closely related topic of the subjectivity of the analyst.

That is, now, in addition to the earlier interpersonal emphasis on the unconscious aspects of analytic relatedness, there is a particular interest in what can be learned via the examination of the analyst's experience. In what way is the nature of the analyst's (affective) involvement with the patient, especially including whatever can be gleaned about his unconscious involvement, clinically informative?

In the remainder of these introductory remarks, I first offer an account of the inception of interpersonal psychoanalysis. The history will help to explain the isolation and widespread ignorance of the interpersonal contribution, a subject to which I have already alluded. I will then briefly address the question I have already mentioned: What distinguishes interpersonal psychoanalysis today?

The beginnings

Interpersonal psychoanalysis was not actually called by that name until Maurice Green invented the term as the title of the book he edited of Clara Thompson's (1964) selected articles. (Thompson, one of the founders of the White Institute, was its first director, from its inception in 1946 to her death in 1958.) Prior to 1964, the ideas that were eventually referred to as interpersonal psychoanalysis were known as "interpersonal relations" (Harry Stack Sullivan's term) or the "cultural orientation" in psychoanalysis. "Cultural psychoanalysis" was meant to be an alternative to drive-based psychoanalysis, the word "cultural" indicating the primacy of meanings borne of systems of human social living rather than predetermined biological processes.

This kind of disagreement (i.e., between drive theorists and those others who emphasized the formative properties of culture or society) was familiar in early psychoanalysis. We can see it to some degree in Jung's and Rank's disagreements with Freud, and very much in Adler's and Ferenczi's. By the 1920s, according to Thompson (in press), there were three "outstanding rebels" in European psychoanalysis: Rank, Reich, and Ferenczi.[2] At the same time, in the United States, Sullivan was independently developing ideas that were similar to Ferenczi's. Thompson met Sullivan in 1923 and says he was "a more influential factor in my psychiatric life than any other person." On Sullivan's recommendation, Thompson traveled to Budapest to be in treatment with Ferenczi for several long periods between 1928 and 1933, the year of Ferenczi's death. Thompson found that Ferenczi

> thought very much the way we did and, in fact … he could not believe that Sullivan had developed a way of thinking that was so close to his own, without any collaboration. I really think that he thought I was not telling him the truth for a long time about that.

At the time, a close association between the ideas of Sullivan and Ferenczi, because of Ferenczi's rejection by the Freudian mainstream and the tarring of his reputation with the absurd implication that he was psychotic (apparently invented by Ernest Jones (1957) in his hagiographic biography of Freud), meant to Thompson (and anyone else who knew about the correspondence of their views) only that "we [interpersonalists] were really controversial; that what we were thinking was anathema…." Today, given the ongoing rehabilitation of Ferenczi's reputation as a highly original thinker and clinician (e.g., Harris & Kuchuck, 2015), the similarity of Ferenczi's views and Sullivan's has become, if anything, a badge of honor for both.

But, of course, there were many years in-between. And they were not good years for the relationship between interpersonal psychoanalysis and mainstream psychoanalysis – which, in those days in the United States, meant classical ego psychology. In 1934, Horney, who had moved to Chicago from Berlin in 1930 to become the assistant director of the Chicago Institute, moved to New York, became a training analyst at the New York Psychoanalytic Institute, and in 1936 convinced Thompson to move from the Baltimore Washington Society to the society of the New York Psychoanalytic Institute (NYPI). Horney was very popular with the students there, who "flocked" to her classes and supervision, according to Thompson. This began to concern certain people at NYPI (again, according to Thompson), because of Horney's emphasis on "cultural" factors. There was "a landslide of anger" when Horney's first book appeared; and this led to the New York Psychoanalytic Institute "starting its system of getting people out of power." Horney's students, says Thompson, ceased graduating; they just didn't pass the required tests; they were told that what they were doing was not psychoanalysis. The students became rebellious.

Then, according to Thompson, Horney's status as a training analyst was taken from her, and she was no longer allowed to supervise candidates' clinical work. At this point, Thompson tells us, five senior analysts and fourteen of their students resigned from NYPI and, with William Silverberg and Erich Fromm, established the American Institute of Psychoanalysis, headed by Horney and devoted to the freedom to think, talk, and teach any psychoanalytic idea at all. (It may be hard to grasp today how precious and rare this freedom was.) A number of other analysts who Thompson knew from the Baltimore Washington Institute joined this group.

But according to Thompson, although Horney, Thompson, and Fromm were the three original training analysts in the new institute, new students were soon assigned only to those closely associated with Horney. And then the same thing that had happened to Horney happened again: on the basis that his ideas were bad for the new institute, Thompson tells us that Fromm's status as training analyst was taken from him. At that point, Thompson and Fromm and their students, who comprised half of the American Institute's members, left the new institute. Thompson says she brought in Sullivan (from Washington) at that point, and in 1943 this group established the New York Division of the Washington School of Psychiatry. (The original Washington School, according to Ortmeyer [1995, p. 23], had been formed in 1936.) The date given for the establishment of the William Alanson White Institute is also usually 1943, because the Washington School in those days, says Thompson, is what metamorphosed into the White Institute over the coming years. (The Washington School of Psychiatry continues to exist, but has not been connected to the White Institute since those early days.) Ortmeyer (1995, p. 15) tells us, in fact, that the New York Division of the Washington School of Psychiatry became independent in 1946 and at that time changed its name to the William Alanson White Institute of Psychiatry, Psychoanalysis, and Psychology.

Most of these events took place in the middle of World War II, which meant that there were many fewer men than women in civilian life; and despite the relatively greater presence of women, because it was a different time, there were relatively few women in psychoanalysis to take over the teaching duties. Teachers were therefore at a premium. Partly for that reason, the Washington School could open its New York Division only by sharing the available teachers between the two institutions.

But the Washington School of Psychiatry had been denied membership in the American Psychoanalytic Association (APsaA), which meant that all those who belonged to the Washington School, if they wanted to be members of APsaA, also had to belong to the Baltimore Washington Institute, which was a member institute of APsaA despite the fact that it was well known at that time to be the most liberal institute in the country, according to Thompson, and dominated by Sullivan. And so those who taught at the New York Division of the Washington School (what would become the White Institute) were members of the Washington School when they taught there, and they were members of the Baltimore Washington Institute for the purposes of dealing with APsaA.

Thompson opines that APsaA became alarmed that the Baltimore Washington Institute was really operating a "culturally oriented" school in New York; and for that reason (Thompson conjectures), in 1946, APsaA began for the first time to require that anyone who wanted to be a member of APsaA had to be individually approved. Prior to that time (and later on, when this controversy had ceased to be a thorn in APsaA's side), anyone who graduated from an institute that belonged to APsaA was automatically granted membership in the national organization.

Perhaps things would have worked out, says Thompson, except that the war ended, and the GI Bill (the legislation intended to ease the transition of servicemen and women into civilian life after the war by funding educational and other opportunities) then made it possible for many people to go into the field of psychiatry. Many of those people wanted to become psychoanalysts. So instead of a small group of dissident analysts, APsaA was suddenly faced, in the Washington School of Psychiatry and its New York Division, with "a large and flourishing institution" operated by people with ideas about psychoanalysis that were not what the leaders of APsaA believed was properly psychoanalytic.

Only some of those analysts affiliated with the Washington School and its New York Division were also members of the Baltimore Washington Institute; those who were not members of the Baltimore Washington Institute were therefore not members of APsaA. And so the New York Division of the Washington School (again, the group that would become the White Institute) continued to apply for APsaA membership. The New York school received encouragement and assurance of sponsorship from the Baltimore Washington Institute; but the New York application materials to APsaA and supporting documentation were routinely misplaced or found to be inadequate. Eventually, says Thompson, these clerical problems turned out to be due to reasons other than mere inefficiency. Apparently, at least one member of the relevant APsaA committee told Thompson that the New York group's (the White Institute's) application to APsaA would never be accepted, because of widespread disapproval among APsaA members of the ideas being taught there. In a recent article, Arnold Richards (2013) describes what happened. Perhaps, as Richards's account might suggest, the person who told Thompson that the White Institute would never be accepted into APsaA was Merton M. Gill, the widely known ego psychologist who eventually (many years after all this) created a theory closely related to interpersonal psychoanalysis (Gill, 1982) – and whose work is represented in this book. Here is Richards's account:

> [D]espite APsaA's rigidity with regard to medical exclusivity, for a while after 1946 it seemed to be open to a certain amount of ideological diversity. After all, the Sullivanian/Interpersonal analysts of the William Alanson White Institute (WAW) were members of APsaA by virtue of WAW's complicated relationship with the Baltimore Washington Institute (see Mosher & Richards, 2005, for more on this). But when that relationship ended – another complicated story – so did the hope for diversity within APsaA. The WAW analysts who were members of APsaA sought independent affiliate status for WAW in the Association, and a committee was formed at BOPS [the Board on Professional Standards, the group in the American Psychoanalytic Association charged with defining principles and standards of psychoanalytic education] to consider their application. The deliberations dragged on for years. Finally Merton M. Gill, who was a member of the BOPS committee, told the WAW members that it would never happen, and they withdrew their application. Gill made it clear that the issue was more their ideology than the other old bone of contention, analytic frequency. This decision had fateful consequences for the American Psychoanalytic Association. It more or less closed the door on the possibility of amicable ideological differences, and doomed analysts who diverged from BOPS's view of orthodoxy to the status of dissidents at best, and heretics at worst. (2013, pp. 9–10)

With this sequence of events the die was cast, and the relationship between the White Institute and APsaA, and – more important for the present purpose – between interpersonal psychoanalysis and mainstream North American psychoanalysis, was set in the mold it would take for the next sixty years.

Recently, however, this relationship has changed: the White Institute was invited several years ago to join APsaA, and after two years of internal debate, the White Institute accepted the invitation in 2014. But even given this new development, interpersonal psychoanalysis cannot be understood without contextualizing it in the intellectual, clinical, and political issues that came before (Stern, 2015a).

Interpersonal psychoanalysis and classical American ego psychology

For that reason, I begin with the point that interpersonal psychoanalysis in its early years was partly defined by its conflict with ego psychology. This conflict worked in both directions. That is, while mainstream analysts did isolate and exclude the interpersonalists, necessitating the development of their own, independent institutes, professional societies, and scholarly journals, it is also true that the interpersonalists were proud of their iconoclasm, and rejected the theories and practices of the mainstream. And so interpersonal psychoanalysis was defined both in distinction to the mainstream and in opposition to it (Hirsch, 2015).

Today, and increasingly, the oppositional part of this definition of interpersonal psychoanalysis is relevant primarily for historical reasons. I will take up some of these historically significant reasons in a moment. I want to emphasize, though, that the question that really matters in today's world is not answered by pitting interpersonal psychoanalysis against any other psychoanalytic group. Because the ideas and practices of the early interpersonalists have been so widely adopted by the rest of the North American psychoanalytic world, the problem that really matters today is to identify what it is about interpersonal thought and practice that continues to distinguish the work of this group from the rest of psychoanalysis. What is unique about interpersonalism? What makes it a living, developing tradition in the present-day world?

And so the primary focus of what I want to say here does not fall on the oppositional self-definition of interpersonal psychoanalysis. I do nevertheless want to summarize briefly that part of the history before moving on.

In the 1930s, and extending through the 1970s and into the 1980s, ego psychology was hegemonic in the United States. As Hirsch (2015) and others have pointed out, we have no adequate explanation of the fact that a substantial proportion of the European analysts who relocated to the United States just before World War II, and during it, quickly became the leaders in their new country's burgeoning psychoanalysis and rigidified their psychoanalytic principles to such an extent that mainstream psychoanalysis in North America is only now recovering from those decades. Many young analysts and candidates were drawn to interpersonal thinking because of its rejection of this rigid interpretation of human living. The list of the ideas they rejected is familiar at this point: the inevitable centrality of the Oedipus conflict; the inevitability of the transference neurosis; the insistence on defining psychoanalysis as the application of a single, standard technique in which the analyst as a particular individual should make no difference, resulting in rigid conceptions of psychoanalytic neutrality and anonymity, and a definition of psychoanalysis that depended on concrete matters such as frequency (four times a week or more) and the use of the couch; the belief that experience unfolds more or less exclusively from the intrapsychic world; the death instinct; penis envy; drive theory in general, with its internal, biological emphasis, and its de-emphasis on the "real" experience with "real" people that interpersonalists stressed;[3] and the resulting biologized understanding of psychological development, with its theories of libido and inevitable, rigidly unfolding psychosexual stages.

Today most of these positions are more or less discredited, even in the psychoanalytic mainstream. The Oedipus conflict is still acknowledged, of course, but it is no longer understood as the be-all and end-all that it was fifty years ago; the concepts of transference neurosis and standard psychoanalytic technique, including rigid definitions of analytic neutrality and anonymity, seem quaint; the matter of frequency and the use of the couch have been discredited as litmus tests;[4] the theory of psychosexual stages and the resulting theories of psychopathology (outmoded accounts of obsessive-compulsive neurosis, hysteria, and narcissism) are just plain dead; and drive theory, penis envy, and the death instinct, while they continue to be addressed in the mainstream literature, are discussed in a way that is so much less concrete and foundational, and so much more sophisticated and integrated with subtler understandings of their place in clinical relatedness, that interpersonalists, even if we cannot comfortably embrace them, can often live with them.

In the meantime, while ceasing to use many of the ideas with which the early interpersonalists most strongly disagreed, mainstream American, Freudian analysts have also leavened their use of intrapsychically-oriented ideas with a much greater acceptance of the significance of the contemporary psychoanalytic interaction and the personal participation of the analyst, particularly her unconscious personal participation. (For accounts of this process, and the lack of recognition of the pre-existing interpersonal literature by the mainstream analysts of the 1980s and 1990s who began to embrace the importance of psychoanalytic interaction and the analyst's personal participation, see Hirsch, 1985, 1996, 1998a; Stern, 2015a.)

And so, while there are certainly important differences of emphasis remaining between interpersonal and mainstream Freudian psychoanalysis in the United States, these differences have moderated; and psychoanalytic culture has changed enough that the disagreements that remain can more often be openly discussed rather than contemptuously rejected (by both groups). Interpersonal psychoanalysis no longer finds much of its identity or meaning in its conflict with American ego psychology.

Interpersonal psychoanalysis and relational psychoanalysis

In 1983, two interpersonally-trained analysts, Jay Greenberg and Stephen Mitchell, published an immensely influential work of comparative psychoanalysis, *Object Relations in Psychoanalytic Theory*. That book, along with Mitchell's (1988) *Relational Concepts in Psychoanalysis*, birthed the new, big-tent theory, relational psychoanalysis, which by the early to mid-1990s had begun to influence all of American psychoanalysis (see Harris, 2011). Mitchell always said that interpersonal psychoanalysis was the primary theoretical source of relational theory. But along with interpersonal theory, Mitchell included in his understanding of "relational" the work of the English object relations writers and Kohut's self psychology. In fact, one of the seminal moments in the creation of relational theory was the desire of Mitchell and several of his colleagues (Philip Bromberg, Emmanuel Ghent, James Fosshage, and Bernard Friedland) in the mid-1980s to teach courses on Winnicott, Fairbairn, Guntrip, and others in NYU's Interpersonal-Humanistic (I-H) Track.

In those days, there were two tracks in the NYU Postdoctoral Program, The I-H Track and the Freudian Track, each of which tended to protect its own turf. (That territorial rancor is no longer part of the institution.) The I-H Track turned down the request by the group wanting to teach object relations theory (they are said to have felt that object relations thinking was too intrapsychically oriented), which eventually resulted in the creation of a new track. In discussing what to call it, the founders hit upon "relational," a word they took from Greenberg and Mitchell's 1983 text, in which "drive/structure" models were distinguished from "relational/structure" models.

If the I-H Track had been more hospitable, perhaps this book would not be necessary, because perhaps what became relational psychoanalysis would never have been conceived to be something other than an expansion of and elaboration on interpersonal thought. Whether melting these two groups together would have been good or bad is something we will never know. But because history unfolded as it did, interpersonal and relational psychoanalysis came to be referred to separately, however closely related they were understood to be; and in some quarters they also came to be understood as separate sets of ideas.

We need to understand whether this difference is only political, or also substantive. Are the relational analysts who are also interpersonalists different in some definable way from the relational analysts who do not define themselves as interpersonalists? If the justification for considering interpersonalism as a separate point of view is to remain viable, and not just historical, interpersonalists must distinguish their ideas not only from contemporary Freudian theory, but also from the ideas held by their relational brothers and sisters.

This is a difficult task, perhaps especially for someone like me, because I am one of those analysts who identifies as both interpersonal and relational. I (Stern, 2006) have written elsewhere that relational psychoanalysis, with its emphasis on the unconscious and the relationship of interpersonal life with the intrapsychic world, is what I hoped (during my training in the 1970s) interpersonal psychoanalysis would become. I suggested in that article that relational psychoanalysis was interpersonalism's contemporary face.

I remain sympathetic to that view. But I also think that interpersonal/relational analysts can be meaningfully differentiated from other relational analysts. There are differences, that is, but these are differences within a family.

There have been attempts in the literature to differentiate interpersonal and relational psychoanalysis (Aron, 1996; Crastnopol, 2006; Ehrenberg, 2006; Frankel, 1998a, 1998b; Hirsch, 1997, 1998b, 2006; Levenson, 2006; Stern, 2006). Some of these attempts have been inspired by critical attitudes, i.e., not only how one view is different than the other, but how it is better; other writers have tried more even-handedly to describe the difference.

But it has been ten years since even the most recent of these entries in the literature. Ten years is a long time for an issue that has only been alive for twenty or twenty-five years. My own views have changed over these last ten years, and I imagine the views of others have too. And so in these brief introductory remarks, I will not summarize the literature I have just cited, but simply present what makes sense to me today.

THE THEMATIC COHERENCE OF INTERPERSONAL PSYCHOANALYSIS

I think that what interpersonal writers have in common, and that differentiates them from other relational writers, is a commitment to a radical form of field theory and a particularly deep sympathy with existential-humanistic values. I will argue that defining interpersonal psychoanalysis in these terms reveals interpersonal thought to be a thematically coherent body of work.

Field theory

Despite its centrality in interpersonal thought, field theory was seldom addressed explicitly by interpersonal writers, including Harry Stack Sullivan.[5] This was true despite the fact that Sullivan, the person most responsible for the centrality of field theory in interpersonal psychoanalysis (he preferred the term "interpersonal relations") wrote contemporaneously with Kurt Lewin (1935, 1936), the inheritor and elaborator of the *Gestalt* field theory of Koffka (1935) and Köhler (1929). Lewin was recognized in his own time as an important innovator in academic psychology. Yet as far as I know, Lewin did not cite Sullivan at all, and Sullivan only cited Lewin once, briefly, in a footnote.

But intellectual historians often trace influence in other ways than citations. In this vein, we can imagine that closer investigation might reveal more relationship in the case of Sullivan and Lewin than meets the eye. Despite the absence of references to one another's work, in other words, the two men may very well have influenced one another, directly or indirectly. Actually, it is hard to imagine that they didn't. They even used some of the same terminology ("tension" and "tendency," for example), although of course both writers may have adopted the terms from general usage of the period, or from some third writer.

While the opportunity to introduce interpersonal psychoanalysis in this book prompted, for me, a new consideration of these issues, this introductory essay is not the place to lay out the kind of detailed, scholarly case for the relation of interpersonal psychoanalysis and radical field theory that the issue deserves (but see Stern, 2015a). For the purposes of this volume, I merely want to offer a context in which the chapters to come can be read; and so I intend only to argue that interpersonal psychoanalysis makes a distinctive contribution to psychoanalysis, and then to outline, in broad strokes of the brush, how this contribution has been made.

Lewin and others

For Lewin,

> as far as content is concerned ... we no longer seek the "cause" of events in the nature of a single isolated object, but in the relationship between an object and its surroundings. It is not thought then that the environment of the individual serves merely to facilitate or inhibit tendencies which are established once and for all in the nature of the person. One can hope to understand the forces that govern behavior only if one includes in the representation the whole psychological situation. (1936, pp. 11–12)

Lewin then turns to the "situation," which he defines as the momentary state of the "life space," which is, in turn, "the totality of facts that determine the behavior of an individual" (p. 12). Lewin's most revealing characterization of the situation is the following description, which lands close to the heart of those many psychoanalysts, myself among them, for whom conviction is most often aroused not only by case histories but also by fiction (see also Buechler, 2014). It has been eighty years since Lewin wrote these words, but there is every reason for us to feel now as he felt then:

> The most complete and concrete descriptions of situations are those which writers such as Dostoyevsky have given us. These descriptions have attained what the statistical characterizations have most notably lacked, namely, a picture that shows in a definite way how the different facts in an individual's environment are related to each other and to the individual himself. The whole situation is presented with its specific structure. This means that the single factors of the situation are not given as characteristics which can be arbitrarily combined in a "summative" way. (p. 13)

I think Lewin's field theory helps us to specify the nature of interpersonal psychoanalysis. In both these views, the influence of the past is not contained in separate aspects of mind like unconscious fantasies or repressed memories, separate mental items that are brought to bear on the present and play a role in constituting it. Instead, the character's past is "there" in the way he lives in the present, as in fiction. In fiction, the present, we could say, is "always already" constituted by the influences of the past. Just as, in *Crime and Punishment*, Raskolnikov's situation – the influence of Raskolnikov's past included – is conveyed in Dostoyevsky's portrayal of the moments in which Raskolnikov commits the murder, so, too, the experience of our patients and ourselves in the clinical situation can be described also in the present tense – with all the reverberations of the past built right into those present moments. The past is not shorted in such accounts; it is instead represented in the total situation of the present. As Lewin puts it elsewhere, "only the present situation can influence present events" (p. 34). But Lewin does not minimize history. He writes that,

> One could argue that psychological facts are intrinsically of a historical nature. As a matter of fact the structure of the person and psychological characteristics of the environment at each moment and in each point are in a decisive way dependent upon the previous history.... However, this influence of the previous history is to be thought of as indirect in dynamic psychology: From the point of view of systematic causation, past events cannot influence current events. Past events can only have a position in the historical causal chains whose interweavings create the present situation. This fact has often not been given enough consideration.... (p. 35)

Lewin wrote these words many decades ago, and so while much of what he had to say remains timely, psychoanalysts of most schools have taken this point to heart. I think that very few psychoanalysts would argue today, as the experimental psychologist Wundt did in the nineteenth century, that the past *causes* the present.

On the other hand, I do think that interpersonal psychoanalysis is distinguished by its integration of the past *in* the present. The case histories of interpersonal psychoanalysis do not focus on explanation; instead, they focus on creating narrative thrust. The point of these cases is the story they tell, not the explanations they offer. They share this orientation with Bion (1962), who argues that psychoanalysis should not focus on discovering causes, but on noting events that occur in relation to one another, events that can be understood to be a function of one another, what he calls "constant conjunctions."

Lewin, too, takes this perspective, as is conveyed by the quotation with which this section began. In that passage, remember, Lewin argues that, "One can hope to understand the forces that govern behavior only if one includes in the representation the whole psychological situation" (p. 12).

This perspective is reflected, it seems to me, in the fact that the only psychoanalytic writers who have explicitly taken issue with the traditional concept of unconscious fantasy, as far as I know, have all been interpersonalists (Bromberg, 2011b; Levenson, 1981, 1982, 1985, 1988; Stern, 2010, 2014).

Part of what these writers on unconscious fantasy have in common, besides their interpersonal commitment, is their position that the past does not maintain an existence in the mind independent of the present. That is, like Lewin, they take the position that what matters is not to "facilitate or inhibit tendencies that are established once for all in the nature of the individual"; what matters instead is the person in context – a context that, in the consulting room, very much includes the analyst. Unconscious aspects of the analytic relationship maintain central importance for these analysts, but these unconscious aspects are not conceived as unconscious fantasy. Instead, unconsciousness is understood to be built into present-day relatedness. The expressions of the unconscious are configurations or patterns of relatedness, and they are not banished to the unconscious mind, as unconscious fantasies are said to be, but remain to be discovered in what is present but selectively inattended – as in Levenson's (1987) metaphor of Poe's incriminating purloined letter, which sat on the table in plain sight. Or, as Levenson (1982) said in the terms of a different metaphor, turning the issue on its head but making the same point, "the therapist listens to the patient's story, gets a background, looks for what are essentially the lacunae – the holes in the Swiss cheese, the gaps in the continuity and coherence of the patient's life story" (p. 9). In both cases, the crucial data is not unconscious fantasy, but data from the present that are missing – for all the wrong (or right) reasons. Fantasy remains significant in Levenson's (1981, 1982, 1988) view, but as mystified experience, as the attempt to come to terms with something poorly understood. Fantasy is not the template for experience, an endogenous motivational source, or a long-preserved representation of early experience, but the result of what Levenson

(1983) once called "semiotic incompetence." Levenson has been the most frequent and articulate proponent of this conception of fantasy, but it has been elaborated on and endorsed by a large enough group of interpersonal writers that it should be considered the consensus view of interpersonalists (see Stern, 1995).[6]

One of the best expressions of this interpersonal theme of the past embedded in the present appeared many years ago in a volume of essays on the work of Sullivan. In the following passage, Murphy and Cattell were writing about Sullivan's field theory soon after Sullivan's death:

> Strictly speaking, the past as such is not properly used in the formulation of field events; the past has, so to speak, its surrogate, its aftermath, in the present; we cannot mix past events as such in the field forces which are the determination of each individual's conduct. Sullivan was aware of the problem and termed it "the most difficult element in the field theory of interpersonal relations." (1952, pp. 174–175)

These authors felt that field theory in psychotherapy, up to the time of their article in 1952, had "failed to clarify the fact that it is only the present – rich as it is in heirlooms from the past – *only* the teeming present that counts" (p. 175).

I could not have expressed any better the theme I am trying to capture. This idea persevered in the systems theory of the 1960s and 1970s, and today it appears in nonlinear dynamic systems theory (e.g., Coburn, 2013; Galatzer-Levy, 1995, 2002, 2004, 2009; Seligman, 2005; Thelen & Smith, 1994). In that frame of reference, systems, which can be conceived to exist in the elements of almost any imaginable kind of phenomenon (e.g., cell assemblies, individual minds, dyads, social groups, etc.), are self-organizing. The process by which systems develop, while lawful, is not linear, but emergent, because that developmental process depends on the interaction of the present state of the system with factors that perturb the system from outside it; and because of that interaction, system development is often nearly impossible to predict. The patterns or configurations that are system constants, on the other hand, like unconscious relational configurations in psychoanalysis, are discoverable.

And then consider what the field concept does to our understanding of the analytic relationship. The field, that is, is the smallest meaningful unit of human experience. There can be no such thing as the individual in anything but the physical sense, because any consideration of the individual mind must take account of the fact that all psychic phenomena take place between people, even if one of those people is sometimes imaginary, internal, or otherwise present in the mind, although physically absent. Emmanuel Ghent (1995) put it this way: "We have come to recognize that not only is there no such thing as a baby, there is no such thing as an individual, only matrices of individuals in constant interactive flux" (p. 480).[7] And *that* means that, in the consulting room (and often enough outside it), the analyst and the patient are always, inevitably, conclusively, part of one another's experience, consciously and unconsciously. The analyst's subjectivity, in other words, is always relevant to the patient's experience, just as the patient's subjectivity is understood to continuously affect the analyst. Analyst and patient are playing on a level field on which they cannot and should not be differentiated as sick and healthy, or crazy and sane. The analyst does have expertise: she knows something about how to conduct an exploratory psychoanalytic treatment; but this is not an expertise that creates a status hierarchy between patient and analyst. This position lies at the heart of interpersonal psychoanalysis.

Existential-humanistic values

The experiential immediacy of the interpersonal field (remember Murphy and Cattell: "it is only the present – rich as it is in heirlooms from the past – *only* the teeming present that counts" [p. 175]) is consistent with another defining characteristic of interpersonal psychoanalysis: its existential orientation. If the interpersonal field was the creation of Harry Stack Sullivan, the existential-humanistic orientation of interpersonal psychoanalysis was the invention of Erich Fromm, the other primary contributor to the beginnings of the interpersonal perspective.

Let me hasten to say, though, that by "existential" I mean to refer less to the philosophical position of that name – which also inspired a group of important psychoanalytic theorists (for an overview, see Frie, 1997), some of whom identified themselves as interpersonalists (e.g., Basescu, 2010; May, 1984) – than to a set of existential-humanistic clinical values that led a much broader group of interpersonalists to work in the here-and-now, to emphasize the patient's agency, and to acknowledge their own personal and unconscious involvement in the clinical process, long before that emphasis was as widely recognized as it is today.[8] Those values included the analyst's spontaneity and authenticity, and a direct, affectively alive, democratic, I–Thou (Buber, 1957 [1970]) engagement with the patient, resulting in what Fromm called "core-to-core" or "center-to-center" relating. Let me offer an expression of this orientation from the work of Fromm (1960), who, after suggesting that Sullivan "may not have gone far enough" when he suggested his clinical model of participant-observation, writes the following:

> The knowledge of another person requires being inside of him, to *be* him. The analyst understands the patient only inasmuch as he experiences in himself all that the patient experiences; otherwise he will have only intellectual knowledge *about* the patient, but he will never really know what the patient experiences, nor will he be able to convey to him that he shares and understands his (the patient's) experience. In this productive relatedness between analyst and patient, in the act of being fully engaged with the patient, in being fully open and responsive to him, in being soaked with him, as it were, in this center-to-center relatedness, lies one of the essential conditions for psychoanalytic understanding and cure. The analyst must become the patient, yet he must be himself; he must forget that he is the doctor, yet he must remain aware of it. (p. 112)

This attitude is apparent in the articles gathered in this volume and its companion, beginning with Searles and Singer, and continuing through the work of Buechler (2004, 2008), Ehrenberg (1992), Fiscalini (2004), and Hirsch (2015).[9] Levenson elaborated Sullivan's field theory into one of the mainstays of interpersonal psychoanalysis; Wolstein (Hirsch, 2000; Shapiro, 2000) did the same for Fromm's existential-humanistic orientation.

The clinical passage quoted above is unusual for Fromm; his published work was primarily social criticism. Yet he was a devoted and passionate clinician. The exhortative tone he adopts in this passage seems to have been represented not only in his few clinical writings, but also in his clinical supervisory work, which was considerable. In fact, there is reason to believe that he was the most significant clinical influence on the generation of interpersonal clinicians at the White Institute he helped to train (Stern, 2015a); and their clinical impact on the interpersonal analysts that came after them has perpetuated this influence.

The clinical work of some earlier interpersonal psychoanalysts was sometimes criticized for being too confrontational and taking too little account of patients' needs for emotional safety. More than we would today, Fromm and some of his students probably confronted patients with their responsibility for the nature of their own unconscious participation in the creation and maintenance of the kinds of interpersonal transactions that resulted in their own unhappiness. In this, it seems that Fromm and those of his students who practiced this way embraced a sense of responsibility similar to that advocated by Sartre (1957) in his conception of "bad faith." Sartre's conception of the unconscious did not take account of the psychoanalytic understanding that unconscious experience is not simply created by an individual's unwillingness to acknowledge responsibility for his own conduct and experience, but rather exists in the borderland between choice and compulsion.

All of us are vulnerable to practicing clinical excesses that are made more likely by our particular theoretical commitments; different excesses tend to be associated with different theories (Stern, 2015b), and these excesses tend to be closely related to the strengths of the perspective. In the case of interpersonal psychoanalysis, excessive confrontation may have had its source in the otherwise salutary emphasis on the analyst's spontaneity and authenticity, the patient's responsibility for his unconscious life, and the patient's agency in enacting it.[10] To whatever extent confrontational excesses might have been committed by interpersonal psychoanalysts in the past, though (and I think the extent was limited), no interpersonal psychoanalyst has advocated this kind of practice since, in the late 1970s and the 1980s, Levenson and Wolstein elaborated the work of Sullivan and Fromm in a way that directed attention toward the continuous, unconscious, mutual involvement of analyst and patient.

There are other points that might be used to distinguish interpersonal psychoanalysis. The wide use of the concept of dissociation and the multiple self, rooted in the work of Sullivan, but pioneered in their modern forms by Philip Bromberg (1998, 2006, 2011a), come immediately to mind. But today these ideas have been widely absorbed by relational analysts; and there are interpersonal analysts who do not subscribe to them. For my present purpose of specifying how interpersonal psychoanalysis remains distinctive and coherent, it makes most sense to focus attention on aspects of theory and clinical practice that are characteristic of all, or almost all, interpersonal psychoanalysts.

And so in answer to the question I posed for myself earlier, I am suggesting that what distinguishes interpersonal-relational analysts from other relational analysts is what I have just said about the prominence in interpersonalism of existential-humanistic values; and about the consequences for interpersonalism of its longtime embrace of radical field theory. The work of many interpersonal writers goes beyond these features, yet is nevertheless rooted in them. Bromberg, whom I have just mentioned in another context, is a prime example. I have argued that radical field theory leads to a number of outcomes: a de-emphasis on unconscious fantasy and repressed memories as templates for conscious experience; an emphasis on fantasy as mystified experience; a correspondingly greater emphasis on the embeddedness of the past in the forms of the present; and, most of all, the continuous, unconscious, mutual influence of the subjectivities of analyst and patient on one another. It goes without saying, though, that the last of these points – continuous, unconscious, mutual influence – while it did originate in interpersonal psychoanalysis (Hirsch, 2015), is shared today by all relational analysts. When this point is combined with the positions I have outlined about fantasy, memory, and the-past-in-the-present, and the existential-humanistic sense of the emotional immediacy of the psychoanalytic situation, the result is what I believe is a coherent psychoanalytic perspective. It is our hope that this view will inform your reading of the essays that follow.

Notes

1 *Pioneers of Interpersonal Psychoanalysis* was not the only reference work on interpersonal psychoanalysis to be published in 1995. It was not even the most significant. In that same year an encyclopedic compendium on the subject appeared: *The Handbook of Interpersonal Psychoanalysis* (Lionells, Fiscalini, Mann & Stern, 1995). In this book appear summaries of all aspects of the literature of interpersonal theory and practice up to the time of its publication. Despite the passage of time, this volume remains essential today for anyone seriously interested in interpersonal psychoanalysis.

2 This quotation, along with any other unattributed facts in the next several paragraphs, and the quotation that follows this one, are from a history of the White Institute by Clara Thompson (in press), presented to the Harry Stack Sullivan Society (the society of psychoanalytic candidates at the White Institute) in 1955, and soon to be published for the first time in *Contemporary Psychoanalysis*, with several contextualizing commentaries from present-day analysts.

3 I use the word "real" here, along with the early interpersonalists, as a contrast with now-anachronistic forms of drive theory, in which the external world was largely a scaffold on which the fantasies and drive derivatives of the intrapsychic world were projected. But I print the word "real" in quotes because constructivists believe that, while reality does exist, and supplies constraints on what can validly be claimed as real or true, its final form remains to be articulated in any particular instance, so that there is no single truth that exists in isolation from subjectivity. Explicit conscious experience is preceded by "unformulated experience" (Stern, 1983, 1997) or an "essential ambiguity" (Mitchell, 1993) that is articulated by emergent, nonrational processes of the interpersonal field.

4 There remains general agreement that frequency is significant, because it is often true that the more time is available, the greater the emotional intensity that can develop in the treatment. The use of the couch can be helpful, too, because it can focus patients on their inner lives. But the claim that concrete treatment factors such as these can be clinically important is quite different from the larger claim that they must be present in order to consider a treatment psychoanalytic.

5 For quotation of the passages in which Sullivan most explicitly discussed the interpersonal field, see Stern, 2015a, 2015b.

6 This is not the occasion to take up the complex general problem of unconscious structuring influences on conscious experience. I (Stern, 2014) have taken up that problem elsewhere, arguing that any psychoanalytic theory requires some kind of conceptualization of such influences. In my conception self-states, which I understand to be configurations of identity no more or less rational (or nonrational) than unconscious fantasy, serve this structuring function. Other unconscious relational configurations that could be cited here, among many, include Sullivan's (1953) "personifications," Bowlby's (1973) "internal working models" (IWMs) of attachment, and Daniel Stern's (1985) "representations of interactions that have been generalized" (RIGs). To me, the concept of unconscious fantasy is defined by its primarily endogenous origins, even if in the hands of modern writers such fantasies also take on aspects of the external world (e.g., LaFarge, 2014). Unconscious relational configurations, on the other hand, are internalizations. For me, then, unconscious fantasies and unconscious relational configurations, despite the fact that both kinds of conception provide unconscious structuring influences, do not otherwise belong in the same category.

7 Other interpersonalists represented in this volume, more influenced by Erich Fromm's existentialism than Harry Stack Sullivan's empiricism (see the next section of the text), disagree with this point of view. Erwin Singer (e.g. 1965) and Benjamin Wolstein (e.g. 1983, but the theme saturates most of his later work) are among these writers. But consider Wolstein's (1959) early recognition that the transference and the countertransference inevitably "interlock" with one another – by which I believe Wolstein meant something like what I have just written in the text. Later, though, Wolstein championed the unique individuality of both patient and analyst. The issue will remain complex for any student of Wolstein's work.

8 As I mentioned earlier, the NYU Postdoctoral Program originally had two "tracks" of training, the Freudian and the "I-H," or Interpersonal-Humanistic. "Humanistic" was (and is today) meant to refer to the kinds of values described in the text. This use of the word testifies to the significance of existential-humanistic values in interpersonal psychoanalysis.

9 The work of Buechler and Fiscalini is represented in the forthcoming volume, *Further Developments in Interpersonal Psychoanalysis, 1980s–2010s: Evolving Interest in the Analyst's Subjectivity* (Stern & Hirsch, in press).

10 Freudian analysts, because of their embrace of the ideal of analytic neutrality and restraint, may more easily than other analysts commit an excess of emotional distance. Self psychologists, at least those of an earlier era, because of their continuous pursuit of an empathic appreciation of the patient's experience, may be more prone than other analysts to miss aggression, both their patients' and their own. And so on.

References

Aron, L. (1996). *A Meeting of Minds: Mutuality in Psychoanalysis*. Hillsdale, NJ: Analytic Press.

Basescu, S. (2010). *Sabert Basescu: Selected Papers on Human Nature and Psychoanalysis*. New York: Routledge.

Bion, W.R. (1962). *Learning from Experience*. London: Heinemann.

Bowlby, J. (1973). *Attachment and Loss, Volume 2. Separation: Anxiety and Anger*. New York: Basic Books.

Bromberg, P. M. (1998). *Standing in the Spaces: Essays on Clinical Process, Trauma, and Dissociation* Hillsdale, NJ: Analytic Press.

Bromberg, P. M. (2006). *Awakening the Dreamer: Clinical Journeys*. Hillsdale, NJ: Analytic Press.

Bromberg, P. M. (2011a). *The Shadow of the Tsunami: And the Growth of the Relational Mind*. New York: Routledge.

Bromberg, P. M. (2011b). "Grown-up" words: A perspective on unconscious fantasy. In *The Shadow of the Tsunami: And the Growth of the Relational Mind*. New York: Routledge, pp. 145–163.

Buber, M. (1970). *I and Thou*, trans. W. Kaufmann. New York: Charles Scribner's Sons.

Buechler, S. (2004). *Clinical Values: Emotions that Guide Psychoanalytic Treatment*. New York: Routledge.

Buechler, S. (2008). *Making a Difference in Patients' Lives: Emotional Experience in the Therapeutic Setting*. New York: Routledge.

Buechler, S. (2014). *Understanding and Treating Patients in Clinical Psychoanalysis: Lessons from Literature*. New York: Routledge.

Coburn, W. (2013). *Psychoanalytic Complexity: Clinical Attitudes for Therapeutic Change*. Hove: Routledge.

Crastnopol, M. (2006). Untangling views of self in interpersonal and relational theories. *Contemporary Psychoanalysis*, 42: 529–533.

Ehrenberg, D. B. (1992). *The Intimate Edge: Extending the Reach of Psychoanalytic Interaction*. New York: W. W. Norton.

Ehrenberg, D. B. (2006). The interpersonal/relational interface. *Contemporary Psychoanalysis*, 42: 535–550.

Fiscalini, J. (2004). *Coparticipant Psychoanalysis: Toward a New Theory of Clinical Inquiry*. New York: Columbia University Press.

Frankel, J. B. (1998a). Are interpersonal and relational psychoanalysis the same? *Contemporary Psychoanalysis*, 34: 485–500.

Frankel, J. B. (1998b). Reply to Hirsch. *Contemporary Psychoanalysis*, 34:539–541.

Frie, R. (1997). *Subjectivity and Intersubjectivity in Modern Philosophy and Psychoanalysis: A Study of Sartre, Binswanger, Lacan, and Habermas*. New York: Rowman & Littlefield.

Fromm, E. (1960). Psychoanalysis and Zen Buddhism. In D. T. Suzuki, E. Fromm & R. DeMartino (Eds), *Zen Buddhism and Psychoanalyis*. New York: Grove Press, pp. 77–141.

Galatzer-Levy, R. M. (1995). Psychoanalysis and dynamical systems theory: Prediction and self similarity. *Journal of the American Psychoanalytic Association*, 43: 1085–1113.

Galatzer-Levy, R. M. (2002). Emergence. *Psychoanalytic Inquiry*, 22: 708–727.

Galatzer-Levy, R. M. (2004). Chaotic possibilities: Toward a new model of development. *International Journal of Psychoanalysis*, 85: 419–442.

Galatzer-Levy, R. M. (2009). Finding your way through chaos, fractals, and other exotic mathematical objects: A guide for the perplexed. *Journal of the American Psychoanalytic Association*, 57: 1227–1249.

Ghent, E. (1995). Interaction in the psychoanalytic situation. *Psychoanalytic Dialogues*, 5: 479–491.

Gill, M. M. (1982). *The Analysis of Transference*, Volume 1. New York: International Universities Press.

Greenberg, J. R. & Mitchell, S. A. (1983). *Object Relations in Psychoanalytic Theory*. Cambridge, MA: Harvard University Press.

Harris, A. (2011). The relational tradition: Landscape and canon. *Journal of the American Psychoanalytic Association*, 59: 701–735.

Harris, A. & Kuchuck, S. (Eds) (2015). *The Legacy of Sandor Ferenczi: From Ghost to Ancestor*. New York: Routledge.

Hirsch, I. (1985). The rediscovery of the advantages of the participant observation model. *Psychoanalysis and Contemporary Thought*, 8: 441459.

Hirsch, I. (1996). Observing participation, mutual enactment, and the new classical models. *Contemporary Psychoanalysis*, 32: 359–383.

Hirsch, I. (1997). The integration of the interpersonal school into the psychoanalytic mainstream: A review essay on *The Meeting of Minds: Mutuality in Psychoanalysis* by Lewis Aron. *Contemporary Psychoanalysis*, 33: 656–668.

Hirsch, I. (1998a). The concept of enactment and theoretical convergence. *Psychoanalytic Quarterly*, 67: 78–101.

Hirsch, I. (1998b). Further thoughts about interpersonal and relational perspectives: Reply to Jay Frankel. *Contemporary Psychoanalysis*, 34: 501–538.

Hirsch, I. (2000). Interview with Benjamin Wolstein. *Contemporary Psychoanalysis*, 36: 187–232.

Hirsch, I. (2006). The interpersonal roots of relational thinking. *Contemporary Psychoanalysis*, 42: 551–556.

Hirsch, I. (2015). *The Interpersonal Tradition: The Origins of Psychoanalytic Subjectivity*. New York: Routledge.

Jones, E. (1957). *Sigmund Freud: Life and Work,* Volume 3. *The Last Phase 1919–1939*. London: Hogarth Press.

Koffka, K. (1935). *Principles of Gestalt Psychology*. New York: Harcourt.

Köhler, W. (1929). *Gestalt Psychology*. New York: H. Liveright.

LaFarge, L. (2014). Psychoanalytic controversy: How and why unconscious phantasy and transference are the defining features of psychoanalytic practice. *International Journal of Psychoanalysis*, 95: 1265–1278.

Levenson E. A. (1981 [1991]). Facts and fantasies: On the nature of psychoanalytic data. In A. H. Feiner (Ed.), *The Purloined Self: Interpersonal Perspectives in Psychoanalysis*. New York: Contemporary Psychoanalysis Books, pp. 97–110.

Levenson E. A. (1982 [1991]). Playground or playpen. In A. H. Feiner (Ed.), *The Purloined Self: Interpersonal Perspectives in Psychoanalysis*. New York: Contemporary Psychoanalysis Books, pp. 127–133.

Levenson, E. A. (1983). *The Ambiguity of Change*. New York: Basic Books.

Levenson E. A. (1985 [1991]). The interpersonal (Sullivanian) model. In A. H. Feiner (Ed.), *The Purloined Self: Interpersonal Perspectives in Psychoanalysis*. New York: Contemporary Psychoanalysis Books, pp. 151–165.

Levenson, E. A. (1987). The purloined self. *Journal of the American Academy of Psychoanalysis and Dynamic Psychiatry*, 15: 481–490.

Levenson E. A. (1988 [1991]). Real frogs in imaginary gardens: Facts and fantasies in psychoanalysis. In A. H. Feiner (Ed.), *The Purloined Self: Interpersonal Perspectives in Psychoanalysis*. New York: Contemporary Psychoanalysis Books, pp. 211–223.

Levenson, E. A. (2006). Fifty years of evolving interpersonal psychoanalysis. *Contemporary Psychoanalysis*, 42: 557–564.

Lewin, K. (1935). *A Dynamic Theory of Personality: Selected Papers of Kurt Lewin*. New York: McGraw-Hill.

Lewin, K. (1936). *Principles of Topological Psychology*. New York: McGraw-Hill.

Lionells, M.-L., Fiscalini, J., Mann, C. M. & Stern, D. B. (1995). *The Handbook of Interpersonal Psychoanalysis*. Hillsdale, NJ: Analytic Press.

May, R. (1984). *The Discovery of Being: Writings in Existential Psychology*. New York: W. W. Norton.

Mitchell, S. A. (1988). *Relational Concepts in Psychoanalysis: An Integration*. Cambridge, MA: Harvard University Press.

Mitchell, S. A. (1993). *Hope and Dread in Psychoanalysis*. New York: Basic Books.

Mosher, P. W. & Richards, A. (2005). The history of membership and certification in the APsaA: Old demons, new debates. *Psychoanalytic Review*, 92: 865–894.

Murphy, G. & Cattell, E. (1952). Sullivan's field theory. In P. Mullahy (Ed.), *The Contributions of Harry Stack Sullivan: A Symposium on Interpersonal*

Theory in Psychiatry and Social Science. New York: Hermitage House, pp. 161–179.

Ortmeyer, D. (1995). History of the founders of interpersonal psychoanalysis. In M.-L. Lionells, J. Fiscalini, C. Mann, & D. B. Stern (Eds), *The Handbook of Interpersonal Psychoanalysis*. Hillsdale, NJ: Analytic Press, pp. 11–27.

Richards, A. (2013). The American Psychoanalytic Association's long march to inclusion. *Bulletin of the Association for Psychoanalytic Medicine*, 48: 4–16.

Sartre, J.-P. (1957). *Being and Nothingness: An Essay on Phenomenological Ontology*, trans. H. Barnes. London: Methuen & Co.

Schachtel, E. (1959 [2013]). *Metamorphosis: On the Conflict of Human Development and the Development of Creativity*. New York: Routledge.

Seligman, S. (2005). Dynamic systems theories as a metaframework for psychoanalysis. *Psychoanalytic Dialogues*, 15: 285–319.

Shapiro, S. A. (2000). Publications of Benjamin Wolstein. *Contemporary Psychoanalysis*, 36: 361–367.

Singer, E. (1965). Identity vs. identification: A thorny psychological issue. *Review of Existential Psychology and Psychoanalysis*, 2: 160–175.

Stern, D. B. (1983). Unformulated experience: From familiar chaos to creative disorder. *Contemporary Psychoanalysis*, 19: 71–99.

Stern, D. B. (1995). Cognition and language. In M. L. Lionells, J. Fiscalini, C. Mann & D. B. Stern (Eds), *The Handbook of Interpersonal Psychoanalysis*. Hillsdale, NJ: Analytic Press, pp. 79–138.

Stern, D. B. (1997). *Unformulated Experience: From Dissociation to Imagination in Psychoanalysis*. Hillsdale, NJ: Analytic Press.

Stern, D. B. (2006). States of relatedness: Are ideas part of the family? *Contemporary Psychoanalysis*, 42: 565–576.

Stern, D. B. (2010). Unconscious fantasy versus unconscious relatedness: Comparing interpersonal/relational and Freudian approaches to clinical practice. *Contemporary Psychoanalysis*, 46: 101–111.

Stern, D. B. (2014). A response to LaFarge. *International Journal of Psychoanalysis*, 95: 1283–1297.

Stern, D. B. (2015a). The interpersonal field: Its place in American psychoanalysis. *Psychoanalytic Dialogues*, 25: 388–404.

Stern, D. B. (2015b). *Relational Freedom: Emergent Properties of the Interpersonal Field*. New York: Routledge.

Stern, D. B. & Hirsch, I. (Eds). (in press). *Further Developments in Interpersonal Psychoanalysis, 1980s–2010s: Evolving Interest in the Analyst's Subjectivity*. New York: Routledge.

Stern, D. B., C. Mann, S. Kantor & G. Schlesinger (Eds). (1995). *Pioneers of Interpersonal Psychoanalysis*. Hillsdale, NJ: Analytic Press.

Stern, D. N. (1985). *The Interpersonal World of the Infant: A View from Psychoanalysis and Developmental Psychology*. New York: Basic Books.

Sullivan, H. S. (1953). *The Interpersonal Theory of Psychiatry*. New York: W. W. Norton.

Thelen, E. & Smith, L. (1994). *A Dynamic Systems Approach to the Development of Cognition and Action*. Cambridge, MA: MIT Press.

Thompson, C. M. (1964). *Interpersonal Psychoanalysis: Selected Papers of Clara M. Thompson*, edited by M. Green. New York: Basic Books.

Thompson, C. M. (in press [1955]). The history of the William Alanson White Institute. *Contemporary Psychoanalysis*.

Wolstein, B. (1983). The first person in interpersonal relations. *Contemporary Psychoanalysis*, 19: 522–535.

Chapter 1

The "dedicated physician" in the field of psychotherapy and psychoanalysis (1967/1979)

Harold F. Searles

Harold Searles was not part of the first generation of interpersonal psychoanalysts who studied and taught at the Washington School of Psychiatry and the William Alanson White Institute, but his thinking, his conduct, and his spirit were interpersonal. Certainly we, the editors of this book, have felt a theoretical and clinical kinship with Searles during our entire careers. He has always been an interpersonalist to us. But let Searles speak for himself:

> I never met Sullivan personally, and do not consider myself to be a Sullivanian. But the early years of my analytic training took place in a Washington strongly influenced, if not dominated, by him and his ideas; I was a student in 2-1/2 of the courses he taught (he died midway through the last of these); and I have acknowledged in earlier writings my debt to him. His term, "participant observation", seems to me well and succinctly to capture the spirit of the analyst's functioning *vis à vis* the patient. (1977, p. 67)

Despite the fact that, as Searles says, he was "not a Sullivanian," a case can be made that, more than any other psychoanalytic writer, Searles carries forward Harry Stack Sullivan's credo that analyst and patient are each much more human than otherwise, i.e., that by virtue of the humanity that they have in common, their subjectivities have equal value and their ways of being in the world are equally flawed. The quality and depth of Searles' writing about analytic work with schizophrenic people expresses a passion of Sullivan's that no one besides Searles has ever matched. Few people today view psychosis, as did Sullivan, as a human process – a function of internalized, real experience with significant others. The current prevailing wisdom places schizophrenia and other varieties of psychosis in the realm of biology and/or neurology, thereby instantiating in our present day Searles' picture of the clinical hierarchy of his own era. Searles felt that many therapists of his time believed themselves to be healthy and the troubled people they treated to be afflicted with illnesses that made them "less-than" their doctors. Today's clinical hierarchy may be even more extreme than the clinical hierarchy Searles blisteringly denounced in his own day. Searles skewers the attitude of condescending therapists who create in themselves a feeling of well-being by convincing themselves of their devotion to their patients, who are, in turn, routinely characterized as "egoless" and therefore less human than their therapists. To the extent that analysts deny their own troubled and darker affective and motivational states in order to be protective, hovering rescuers, all that is bad and weak is attributed to the patient. From the moment that Sullivan introduced the term "participant-observation," it should have become clear to all who embraced the developing tradition of interpersonal psychoanalysis that the flawed analyst and flawed patient inevitably co-participate with one another, each possessing a wide range of conscious and unconscious affective states. To the extent that countertransference subjectivities are denied or otherwise not experienced, these are invariably acted-out to the detriment of the patient, who will inevitably be perceived as having all of the bad or troubled personal qualities.

Any therapist who views himself as simply a kind and well-meaning healer to an afflicted patient will miss the strengths of the patient; the adaptive nature of the patient's way of being; and the patient's wish to heal his troubled family – and in the transference, his troubled analyst. Such a therapist or analyst is also quite likely to deny his self-interest in maintaining a hierarchy in which one person is strong and benevolent at the expense of the other, who, unfortunately, may embrace the role of being the receiver of supplies from the "healthier" psychotherapist or analyst. With equal misfortune, such supplies will never help, since some of the analyst's genuine motives – to aggrandize himself – are never embraced; and as a result the patient is likely to feel more and more like a fragment of a human being.

In the tradition of interpersonal psychoanalysis, Searles views all psychological development as a function of internalized experience with key others. Perhaps more than any psychoanalytic writer he illustrates the clinical significance of understanding that, for therapists and analysts, not just for patients, the most important part of the experience of the therapeutic situation is deeply affective. To recognize and acknowledge this point is to dismantle the destructive parts of clinical hierarchy. It is no longer clear that one participant in the treatment is weak and the other strong, that one is ill and the other well. No one has ever written more clearly about the degree to which the analyst's subjectivity fully interacts with and influences that of the patient – and is influenced by the patient. Searles' unique openness to his own experience, not only about his subjectivity but his personal flaws, set the bar for future interpersonal and relational analysts. Very few of us meet that standard even now.

Reference

Searles, H. (1977). The analyst's participant observation as influenced by the patient's transference. *Contemporary Psychoanalysis*, 13: 367–370.

The "dedicated physician" in the field of psychotherapy and psychoanalysis (1967/1979)

Harold F. Searles

Psychiatric patients, and above all schizophrenic patients, cause one to doubt one's capacity to love, and to feel that one's devotion is meaningless or, worse, malevolent. When I used to see a hebephrenic woman, with whom I had been working for ten years, walking about on the hospital grounds appearing vague, disheveled, bleakly unloved, I felt her to be a kind of living, ambulatory monument to my cruelty and neglect. Even though I had not forgotten that I had been subjected to something like 2000 hours of her reviling me, ignoring me, sexually tantalizing me, making heart-rendingly unanswerable appeals to me either mutely or in largely undecipherable words, and so on, I still winced at the sight of her. It was as though the Methodist hell of my boyhood yawned widely for my thus-proved un-Christ-like soul.

A year or two previously, on one of the rare days when she had her wits sufficiently about her to be considered able to come with me to my office, about 100 feet away, she stood in confused helplessness while an ostensibly kind, loving, gentle female aide, who (as I later came to realize) busily infantilized all the patients, was putting shoes on this woman's feet. I felt remorse because I did not feel at all like doing so – because I was feeling, at that moment, nothing toward the patient except impatience, contempt, and hatred.

My papers have chronicled my finding, to my mingled relief and self-deflation, how able schizophrenic patients are not merely to endure but to turn to therapeutic benefit one's expressions of deepeningly intense feelings of all kinds. But the events of my final year at Chestnut Lodge showed that I had underestimated to the last, nonetheless, these patients' strengths. I gave notice, one year in advance, of my intention to leave the Lodge; such notice was required by my contract, which in turn, of course, was based on clinical and staffing necessities. Regarding it feasible to go on working with no more than two of my six patients after I would leave there, I was now faced with the immensely difficult matter of which two, among six persons with whom I had been working intensively for years, I would go on seeing. With one of these persons, I had worked for nearly six years; with each of four, between ten and 11 years; and with one, for 13 ½ years.

My ambivalence toward each of these individuals, like his or her own toward me, of course, knew no bounds. I wanted utterly rid of the whole lot of them, yet felt almost unbearably anguished at the prospect of losing any one of them. A passage from my last staff presentation at the Lodge, just before I left, expresses something of what I had come to learn of the strength that each of these persons possessed:

> The one biggest lesson … I have learned in working with schizophrenic patients in my last year here has been to see how very tough they are … I can say that I have, in this last year, burdened or battered, or what-not, each of these six patients with all the sarcasm, harshness, contempt, and just general resentment and reviling that I'm capable of and they've all survived it fine, see, just fine, and I have felt that I have just barely been operating in their league – just barely been qualifying to be in the major leagues. When I start this with Edna she is soon on the offensive again; she can take all I've got and she can go on for more.
>
> Another way that I conceptualize it is, the work is so god-damned difficult that we cannot do it if we deny ourselves certain parts of our armamentarium. We can't do it with one hand tied behind our back. So this has been something memorable to me; this I'm going to keep using with patients. I am.

My experiences with colleagues over all these same years, as a supervisor or a consultant in their work with their schizophrenic patients, have shown me, similarly, with what toughness, tenacity, and sadistic virtuosity their patients tend to coerce these therapists into the ever-alluring role of the dedicated physician treating the supposedly weaker patient. Typically, to the extent that one feels bound by the traditional physician role, one feels wholly responsible for the course of the patient's illness, and believes it impermissible to experience any feelings toward the patient except kindly, attentive, long-suffering, and helpful dedication. The psychiatric resident, in particular, relatively fresh from the dedicated-physician atmosphere of the medical school and general internship, is often genuinely unaware of feeling any hatred or even anger toward the patient who is daily ignoring or intimidating or castigating him, and unaware of how his very dedication, above all, makes him the prey of the patient's sadism. It has been many years since a young schizophrenic man revealed to me how much sadistic pleasure he was deriving from seeing a succession of dedicated therapists battering their heads bloody against the wall of his indifference, and I have never forgotten that.

In general, if the patient's illness is causing more suffering to the therapist than to the patient, then something is wrong. But it is not at all easy, technically, to become more comfortable than the patient. With many schizophrenic patients, one tends to feel like a butterfly, pinned squirmingly in their live-butterfly collection, without any reliable way of drawing blood from the pinner, the invulnerable patient. It is our omnipotent self-expectations that, more than anything else, pinion us and tend, as well, to stalemate or sever the therapeutic relationship. The obnoxiously behaving paranoid patient cannot help wondering what ulterior motives make us so concerned to *keep him in therapy*; instead of our becoming aware of our angrily wanting rid of him, we act out our repressed desires to reject him by manifesting an omnipotence-based, devouring, vampire-like devotion that understandably frightens him away from treatment. And the suicidal patient, who finds us so unable to be aware of the murderous feelings he fosters in us through his guilt-and-anxiety-producing threats of suicide feels increasingly constricted, perhaps indeed to the point of suicide, by the therapist who, in reaction formation against his intensifying, unconscious wishes to kill the patient, hovers increasingly "protectively" about him, for whom he feels an omnipotence-based physicianly concern. Hence it is, paradoxically, the very physician most anxiously concerned to *keep the patient alive* who is tending most vigorously, at an unconscious level, to drive him to what has come to seem the only autonomous act left to him – suicide.

The therapist's functioning in the spirit of dedication that is the norm among physicians in other branches of medicine, represents in the practice of psychotherapy and psychoanalysis an unconscious defense against his seeing clearly many crucial aspects of both the patient and himself – for example, his sadism. He does not see how much sadistic gratification the patient is deriving from his anguished, tormented, futile dedication. He does not realize that, as I overheard one chronically schizophrenic man confide to his therapist, "The pleasure I get in torturing you is the main reason I go on staying in this hospital." I had heard this therapist say that for many months he had never known, when he went into this man's room on the disturbed ward, whether to expect a blow or a kiss from the patient.

Further, the dedicated therapist does not see how much ambivalence the patient has concerning change, even change for the "better." He does not see that the patient has reached his present equilibrium only after years of thought and effort and the exercise of the best judgment of which he is capable. To the patient, change tends to mean a return to an intolerable preequilibrium state, and the imposition on him of the therapist's values, the therapist's personality, with no autonomy, no individuality, for him. He resents the therapist's presumption in assuming that the patient is pitiably eager to be rescued, and equally humiliatingly that the intended help is all unidirectional, from therapist to patient.

A dozen years ago, I reached the conviction that it is folly to seek to rescue the patient from the dragon of schizophrenia: the patient is both the maiden in the dragon's grip and the dragon itself. The dragon is the patient's resistance to becoming "sane" – resistance that shows itself as a tenacious and savage hostility to the therapist's efforts.

The heart of this resistance springs from the fact that, since early childhood, the patient's own *raison d'être* has been as a therapist, originally to the parent whose unwhole integration he, the child, was called upon to complement, in a pathologic and unnaturally prolonged symbiosis. He was given over to this therapeutic dedication, as a small child, for the most altruistic of reasons – he lived in order to make mother (or father) whole – as well as for reasons of his own self-interest, so that he would have a whole parent with whom to identify, for the sake of his own maturation. But he failed in his therapeutic dedication; and, more hurtfully, his dedication was not even recognized by the parent, who incessantly hurt, disparaged, and rejected him. Now, as an adult schizophrenic patient in treatment, he takes vengeance on this rival, "official" therapist of his, and causes his therapist to feel as anguished, futile, and worthless or malevolent an intended healer as he had been made to feel by his mother or father. Only insofar as the therapist becomes able to see and respond to the patient's genuinely therapeutic striving toward him and, earlier, toward the parents, will the patient himself be receptive to therapy. Among my feelings during the final year at Chestnut Lodge was, prominently, grief at various of my patients' having refused to identify sufficiently with my healthier aspects and, by the same token, at my own having failed to help them do so. I surmise that such grief is of a piece with the patient's own repressed grief, stemming from early childhood, at proving unable to save the sick parent through encouraging him to identify with the healthier aspects of the patient as a growing child.

We therapists tend to feel frightened away from seeing how concerned our patients are to help us, partly for the reason that the transference-distortions, in which this therapeutic striving of theirs is couched, are very great. That is, our patient tends to see us as being not merely somewhat depressed today, but as being his deeply, suicidally despondent father; or he perceives us as being not merely somewhat scatterbrained today, but as being his insane, hopelessly fragmented mother.

Patients' specific therapeutic aims, and their individual techniques in pursuing those aims, are manifold. As examples, various of my patients have rescued me from periods of withdrawal and depression by presenting themselves as being in such urgent need of rescue that I have felt it necessary to bestir myself, come out of myself, and thus cast off the chains of my depression in order to save them. Others, by presenting themselves as being infuriatingly, outrageously undisciplined, have eventually "made a man of" me – by impelling me into becoming a stern disciplinarian, have made me into the kind of man that they had been unable to make their wishy-washy father into.

Their therapeutic techniques are outwardly so brutal that the therapeutic intent is seen only in the result. One apathetic, dilapidated hebephrenic patient of mine received considerable therapeutic benefit from a fellow patient, newly come to the ward but, like him, a veteran of several years in mental hospitals, who repeatedly, throughout the day, gave my patient a vigorous and unexpected kick in the behind. From what I could see, this was the first time in years a fellow patient had shown any real interest in him, and my patient as a result emerged appreciably from his state of apathy and hopelessness.

As for the many crucial aspects of himself in relation to the patient, against which the therapist is unconsciously defending himself with his physicianly dedication, I have already touched on some. He is unaware of how much he is enjoying his tormenting the patient with his dedication, of which the patient, who feels himself to be hateful and incapable of giving anything worthwhile to anyone, feels so unworthy. He is unaware, similarly, of how much scorn his own "dedication" is expressing. I asked a female colleague, who was describing her work, a very actively dedicated and ostensibly maternally loving work with a deeply regressed woman, how much ego she felt the patient to have.

The therapist replied, as though this were obvious, "None." Such unconscious scorn for the patient – for the patient's own strength and for his ability to reach out, himself, for help from the therapist without the therapist's having constantly to keep pushing the help at him – seems to me to betray much self-contempt on the part of the therapist. If the therapist is convinced that he himself is a worthwhile person, with something useful to give – with something, that is, that this fellow human being, the patient, can be relied on to discern and to admire and want – he will not need to try, anxiously and incessantly, to persuade the patient to accept his help.

Further, the "dedicated" therapist, who feels under such intense pressure to cure the patient, goes on oblivious of his placing, through his dedication, equally great pressure on the patient. I can offer here a vignette from my own work. A paranoid schizophrenic woman whom I have been treating for years has come, in recent months, to spend many sessions wet-eyed, describing in verbose detail her life-experience, current and past, in terms that imply that there is an ocean of grief in her, but never with any frank outpouring of tears. Finally, at the end of one such session, I confided to her, with mixed feelings of guilt and exasperation, that at the end of such an hour as this, as many times before: "You always make me feel remiss in not having said or done something that would enable you to weep." To my surprise, she instantly responded with something that evidently had been on her mind for many sessions: "And *you* always make *me* feel remiss for not weeping."

The supervision of other therapists gives one a chance to see these things more objectively and, of course, with less harsh narcissistic injury to oneself. Specifically, one can clearly feel how sadistic are the demands on oneself, week after week, of the so-dedicated therapist who is agonizedly eager to cure his patient. One such therapist, chronically depressed and long-suffering about the work with his patient but chronically "dedicated" to the latter, would tell me, week after week, of his patient's asking him, "What do I do? What's the right thing to do?" He himself was passing along to me much this same kind of draining and unanswerable demand by implicitly asking me, throughout each supervisory session, "Doc, what do I do to relieve my suffering at the hands of this patient who is crucifying me?"

Our "dedicated physician" way of relating to the patient serves not only to act out our sadism toward him but also to express our unconscious determination to maintain the status quo – to preserve the patient's present, immature level of ego-functioning in order to ensure the inflow of deniedly-cherished supplies from him. Thus, the loosening of the stalemate requires that the therapist becomes aware of not only his sadism and other negative feelings toward the patient but also his cherishing what the latter has been providing him.

In other words, an intensely pressuring, dedicated therapeutic zeal denotes an unconscious determination, on the part of the therapist, to protect and preserve, for reasons of his own psychic economy, the patient's present level of psychotic or neurotic ego-functioning, because of various narcissistic and infantile gratifications that the therapist is receiving from the patient, who represents at one level a transference-mother who is feeding him, and because the patient's illness serves to shield the therapist from seeing clearly his own illness.

So, unconsciously, the therapist is bent on maintaining the patient in an infantilized state, and is opposing that very individuation and maturation to which, at a conscious level, he is genuinely dedicated. I, for one, tend dedicatedly to remain immersed in a rescue-effort toward the "fragile" patient, in order to avoid seeing him or her as being stronger, or potentially stronger, than myself. For example, one hebephrenic woman, from whose incredibly low levels of ego-functioning I derived many fascinating data about the schizophrenic patient's subjectively "prehuman" identity (data included in my monograph on the nonhuman environment), finally told me, in vigorous protest, "I can't stay down forever!" This woman would evidence, from time to time over the years of our work, remarkable forward surges in her ego-functioning, and unfailingly I would find that my rejoicing in this development was outweighed by an upsurge of my feeling inadequate. I had been feeling despair at how grievously ill she was; but now I would find her manifesting an appearance of blooming physical health that made me feel old and jaded, and I would be reminded, ruefully, too, that she was physically taller than I. In the same process, she would reveal a kind of effortless *savoir faire*, in matters both interpersonal and cultural, traceable to an upbringing far richer in social and cultural "advantages" than my own. In short, I would feel her to be an all-around hopelessly larger person than myself. Then, as if quickly detecting that I still couldn't take it, she would soon be, again, her deeply fragmented, "hopelessly ill" hebephrenic self, and I was once more in my comfortable role of the long-suffering Christ trying to heal this wounded bird.

Even more embarrassingly, I found my feelings toward another long-schizophrenic woman oscillating, often session by session for months on end, from my viewing her as a hopelessly confused mental patient who, clearly incurably ill, would undoubtedly be spending the rest of her life in psychiatric hospitals, to my viewing her as a predominantly well, wonderfully warm, intelligent, and witty woman for whom I felt greatly tempted to give up everyone and everything else in my life, but who, I had anguishedly to realize, recurrently, could never practicably be mine. At this point, incidentally, it should be abundantly clear that, among the needs for which the "dedicated" therapist is obtaining gratification are his masochistic needs.

The more deeply one examines the psychodynamics of the dedicated-physician therapist who is unconsciously devoted to preserving the status quo, one finds that he holds, at an unconscious level, split images, one an idealized image and the other a diabolized image, of himself and of the patient as well, and that he is dedicated, unconsciously but tenaciously, to preserving these split images and preventing their coalescence, with the leaven of reality, into realistic images of himself and of the patient as two fellow human beings, each possessing both strengths and limitations on his strengths, each capable of hating *and* loving.

As a function of his unconscious effort to preserve these split images, the therapist represses the ingredients of his diabolized self-image – his hatred, his rejectingness, his subjectively nonhuman unfeelingness, and so on – and projects these on the patient. At the same time that he is placing intense though unwitting demands on the patient to emerge in such a healthy way as will enable the therapist to realize his idealized self-image as an all-loving and omnipotent healer, he is unconsciously holding at a safe distance, or driving progressively deeper into autism, this patient who personifies the diabolized, unacceptable, and therefore vigorously projected aspects of his own self-image. Thus the therapist's dedication becomes, from this vantage point, an anxious, deeply ambivalent effort both to make contact with and to keep safely at a distance the projected components of his *self*.

To describe this a bit further. How well it serves the therapist's unconscious rejectingness for the patient to become progressively withdrawn. Consciously, he is dedicated to making contact with the patient and helping him to join him in the "real world"; unconsciously, he wants rid of the disappointing, frightening, and otherwise unsatisfactory patient – the patient who by any standards is so, and all the more by reason of the therapist's unconscious image of him as presently diabolical, no matter how much the therapist clings also to the unconscious hope that the patient may one day fit an ideal image. In still other terms, the therapist is trying consciously to help the withdrawn patient to materialize, while unconsciously he wants to make him disappear. In proportion as the patient becomes able to evidence love, the therapist's projected image of himself as diabolical comes home to roost, and he tends to perceive himself as subhumanly bad, malevolently obstructing the full liberation of the patient's supposedly supra-humanly good self. What makes this so formidable a difficulty, in therapy, is not so much that the therapist is unadulteratedly neurotic, but rather that the chronically schizophrenic patient contributes to the maintenance of these processes of splitting a degree of intensity and tenacity of which the therapist's own stake in the matter is a relatively small sample. But it is the therapist's own dawning recognition of his "countertransference" – his own contribution to these stalemating processes – that provides the best handle for his effecting a change in the therapeutic relationship; that is why I dwell here on the therapist's contribution to the difficulties.

We tend, thus, to make the patient feel both idealized and diabolized by us, with a hopelessly unbridgeable gulf between these two so-different creatures we are calling on him to be toward us. At the same time that we are unwittingly calling on him to fulfill our diabolized image of him, we are unconsciously looking to him to provide our life with its central meaning, to give us a *raison d'être*, to make real our idealized self-image. I want to emphasize that it is no pernicious thing *consciously* to regard the patient as supremely important and meaningful to oneself. For us consciously so to relate to him can only enhance his self-esteem and help him to become whole. The pernicious thing is that we repress both our idealized image and our diabolized image of him, hide both from ourself and at the same time act out both these toward him, by inappropriately employing, in psychotherapy and psychoanalysis, the traditional dedicated-physician-treating-his-patient approach that, however conventionally accepted in the practice of medicine generally, congeals and reinforces the wall between patient and doctor when we employ it in this field.

Paradoxically, the withdrawn patient is likely to be identifying with the very therapist who is consciously devoted to a diligent and even desperate attempt to help him emerge from the withdrawal, but many of whose feelings are actually withdrawn from his conscious attitudes toward the patient. That is, the patient, in seeking the isolation of the seclusion room, may well be identifying with those increments of the therapist that are secluded from access to the therapist's conscious ways of viewing and relating to the patient. This is one variety of what I have termed, in an earlier writing, delusional identification, on the patient's part, with his therapist. In general, these are instances in which the most tenacious, treatment-resistant aspects of the patient's craziness are found based on his exaggerated and distorted identifications with real but unconscious aspects of the therapist's own personality and ways of functioning in the treatment relationship.

In discussing now the phenomena marking the resolution of these dedicated-physician stalemates – phenomenas of which I have already hinted – I have in mind the form this resolution takes in one's work with the schizophrenic patient on the one hand, and with the depressed patient on the other; but there are many patients, of course, who show prominently both these varieties of psychopathology.

In any case, as the therapist becomes aware of the whole gamut of his feelings toward the patient, he comes to see that the patient is a real and separate person, afflicted with an illness that is also a part of genuinely outer reality for the therapist, rather than its being the product of the therapist's heretofore repressed, subjectively omnipotent hatred and infantile demands.

As we become free from our previous compulsive "dedication" and able now with our new objectivity to view the patient and our relationship with him, we no longer assume a wholehearted, dedicated interest on our part as a *given* in the situation, and can notice in our interest toward him fluctuations, often fostered by him, of much transference-significance. For example, I have seen that, with various of my patients, just as we get to working closely and most constructively together, the patient will do something (such as making a last-minute, inconsiderate and impersonal cancellation of a session) that cools my interest in him, thus revealing to me his fear of closeness with me, his fear of my strong, sustained and deepening interest in him, which I would not have detected had I gone on holding myself totally responsible for maintaining an unflagging interest in helping him – had I gone on feeling guilty whenever I found myself not interested in him and not caring whether he might elect to continue with our work. This is but an example of how, in analytic terms, a therapist's physicianly, compulsive "dedication" interferes with the kind of free-floating objectivity that is so necessary an ingredient of the analyst's effective functioning.

As our previous, compulsive dedication loosens its grip on us, we become aware – lo and behold – of a keen esthetic appreciation of that very illness in the patient which heretofore we have felt so desperately and guiltily responsible for curing. Several years ago, I found myself having to face the fact that I seemed to find much more fascinating the schizophrenic, rather than the more conventional and healthier, aspects of my patients' functioning. At first, I felt deeply troubled at this discovery, for I believed that it must mean that I am dedicated more to the causation and preservation of severe and exotic illness than to the fostering of health in my patients. But then I began to see that my preference was not so unnatural, after all. Keeping in mind the point I made earlier – that the schizophrenic patient is not only the maiden in the dragon's grip but the dragon also – let me ask you which of these you find more fascinating: the relatively pallid and conventional lady, or the exotic and colorful dragon?

I have been deeply reassured to find, as time has gone on, that this very esthetic appreciation is a form of scientific interest that, in contrast to my early anguished therapeutic dedication, enables me to be of maximal use to the patient. For example, I used to feel, for years, desperately and urgently concerned to relieve the indescribably severe confusion of one of my chronically schizophrenic patients, and it was with guilt bordering on self-loathing that I began to realize that I was actually fascinated by the vivid, intricate, so-unconventional nature of her confusion itself. At first, my interest in this felt unclean, perverse, unworthy of any physician; but gradually I came to feel that I was facing a genuine work of creative art, which is, as I now clearly see, the product of the highest forms of the patient's intelligence and creative originality. As for her, she shows every evidence of finding much more useful my appreciative, unanxious and unguilty studying of her confused verbalization, than she used to find my desperate attempts somehow to shut them off.

Along with such esthetic-scientific interest, one comes to feel, as one becomes freer from omnipotent guilt about the patient and his illness, companion gratifications in the realm of humor and playfulness – all necessary ingredients of the phase of the mutually enjoyable therapeutic symbiosis that I have described in a number of writings. Time after time, I have found that the patient benefits most from our sharing humorous, playful moments together. When I can leave off my deadly serious dedication, and be amused at the patient's craziness, he can come to laugh with warm and loving amusement at the delightfully crazy foibles of his mother, whom he had been desperately dedicated, heretofore, to curing, at an introjected level, in his own tragic craziness. When one is working in this new spirit with the patient, one is very close to him, openly showing how much one likes and enjoys being with him. His formerly maddening symptoms are now only part of the background music in an atmosphere of contentment.

As the therapist becomes aware of how much gratification the illness is providing to him as well as to the patient, he becomes free of his infantile omnipotence-based guilty feeling of *having to cure* the patient. The patient genuinely is faced now, not simply at one crucial juncture but ongoingly, session after session, with the choice of whether he himself wishes to cling to the gratifications of remaining ill or to accept the therapist's *also*-offered assistance in becoming a healthy adult.

Conclusion

Briefly, three points. First, it seems impossible – and perhaps it would be untherapeutic if it were possible – for a therapist to have at the beginning of his work with any one patient, and to maintain throughout the treatment, a realistic as opposed to an omnipotence-based feeling of dedication. It would be unclinical to postulate that there is *one* most therapeutic attitude as regards dedication that the therapist should have at the beginning of the therapy and maintain throughout it, beyond his dedicating himself as fully as possible to becoming aware of whatever thoughts and feelings are being called forth, in the treatment process, in himself as well as in the patient. It seems inescapable that we shall go through torments of feeling omnipotently responsible for each of our patients, that we shall repress our sadism and project it on the patient, that we will come to develop split images of ourself and of the patient, and so on; and it may well be that our becoming thus enmeshed, for a time, in the patient's illness is necessary to the therapeutic process. But I suggest that the considerations discussed here will facilitate our going through this evolution and emerging to a more realistic experience of ourself in relation to the patient. I suggest, in other words, that these considerations will help us to avert, or at least to shorten, such covertly sadomasochistic stalemates as are familiar clinical experiences to all of us.

Second, we see that the kind of therapist-devotion characteristic of such stalemated situations is a genuinely "selfless" devotion, but selfless in a sense that is, in the long run, precisely antitherapeutic. That is, so many of the therapist's own unconscious ingredients are being projected onto the patient that he is in a real sense selflessly submerged in the patient's narcissism. In this sense, the therapist is deriving the unconscious gratification of functioning without the responsibility for having a self and thus, paradoxically, in his "selflessly dedicated" functioning is burdening the patient with a total responsibility for the whole relationship. Such "devotion," which temporarily supports the patient's narcissistic world-self, inevitably must be revealed one day as a lie. This disillusioning discovery, now, that the therapist after all is a separate person with a self and a self-interest of his own, after the patient has been led for so long to assume otherwise, will repeat for the patient his bitter childhood experience that, as one schizophrenic woman put it, "People are interested only in themselves," and as a borderline schizophrenic man phrased it, "Kidding your children for 20 years that you love them and want them – this is what I'm bitter about, I guess; Mother has *pretended* that she put me first, and it's just been her little game. It's not been true – she's more interested in herself, in her neurosis...."

The paranoid individual is especially prone to assuming that if the therapist proves not to be wholeheartedly devoted to his welfare, then the therapist must be bent on sabotaging and destroying him. This assumption seems referable to the patient's experiences as a child, in which the parents maintained a "wholeheartedly devoted" demeanor toward him, in a reaction-formation against their largely unconscious, more sinister feelings toward him – their hostility toward him, their wishes to be free of him. Hence he will remain suspicious, and with good reason, if we endeavor to submerge, from the beginning of his treatment, our self-interest in his "welfare."

Third, in earlier papers (Searles, 1965) I have described the therapeutic symbiosis, which implies a degree of selflessness on the part of the therapist as well as patient, as marking the most essential aspect of the treatment. But this stands in the most direct contrast to the kind of "dedicated-physician selflessness" that this paper is questioning. Where the latter is a defense against hatred and other "negative" emotions, this former kind of merging between patient and therapist can occur only after all emotions, of whatever variety and in either participant, have become so unthreatening that these need no longer be defended against by the maintenance of a "self," a structure which, in light of the processes at work in this stage of the treatment-evolution, could serve only as a hindrance to the therapeutic forces that are streaming toward new and deeper patterns of individuation for both patient and therapist, patterns at this point unpredictable and therefore all the more exciting and fulfilling.

Reference

Searles, H. F. (1965). *Collected Papers on Schizophrenia and Related Subjects*. London: Hogarth Press and Institute of Psycho-Analysis; New York: International Universities Press.

Chapter 2

Countertransference

The psychoanalyst's shared experience and inquiry with his patient (1975)

Benjamin Wolstein

In a democratic and anti-hierarchical spirit reminiscent of both Sullivan and Searles, Benjamin Wolstein (1977) argued for the existence of what he called psychic symmetry in the analytic encounter. For Wolstein, transference and countertransferece are equivalent in the sense that each represents one participant's unconscious involvement with the other. Patient and analyst are conceptualized as co-participants in the analytic inquiry, and the patient is encouraged to observe and inquire about countertransference with the same freedom with which analysts comment on and inquire about transference. Analysts are viewed as just as subjective and consumed with affect as patients. Analysts hold no special status as experts or objective observers of patients' experience. Wolstein was among the earliest to recognize that patients can detect even the most subtle and nonverbal of the analyst's moods or attitudes. Neither the couch nor silence can conceal analysts' participation.

Since both analysts and patients are commonly unaware of much that is significant in their experience, Wolstein finds it necessary to encourage patients to be direct about what they perceive within the analyst, just as analysts attempt to read patients' unconscious processes. Wolstein challenges the notion of the weak and helpless patient and has no interest in encouraging patients' submission to analytic authority and expertise. Again like Sullivan and Searles, Wolstein believed that excessively hierarchical relations in the treatment exacerbated psychopathology. He took the position that symmetry in the status and power relations of the analytic relationship was a factor in the healing potential of psychoanalysis and psychoanalytic psychotherapy.

Wolstein eschewed prescribed analytic technique. His credo was: each patient is unique, each analyst is unique, each dyad is unique. He opposed metapsychology and the prescription of technique, considering both these phenomena to be inauthentic and superficial forms of relatedness – what he called personas (Wolstein, 1974). Theories of psychopathology, metapsychology, and technique encourage analysts and patients to diverge from what Wolstein idealizes as direct relatedness, by which he means the willingness of each co-participant to communicate his or her experience of the other in an uninhibited manner.

Wolstein's freedom to speak from his psychic center (ibid), by which phrase Wolstein meant to describe speaking freely, authentically, and with minimal inhibition – encourages patients to do the same. This freedom facilitates a sense of agency and a gradual discovery by the patient of what has been inhibited about his experience of himself and others. Wolstein had enormous admiration for Ferenczi and was influenced by his own analyst, Clara Thompson, who had a brief analysis with Ferenczi. But despite these influences, and despite Wolstein's championing of egalitarian values in psychoanalysis, Wolstein did not advocate Ferenczi's "mutual analysis" (Wolstein, 1997)). Wolstein did sometimes write in that vein, but unlike Ferenczi, he acknowledged that the analytic relationship was also inherently asymmetrical (ibid).

Wolstein's rejection of metapsychology led him away from explanations and interpretations as significant mutative factors. Useful insight, for him, emerged from the analyst's countertransference observations, often shared with the patient. This kind of insight was meant to provide increased awareness to patients about how they and others perceived one another. Wolstein engaged with his patients in a way that was meant to facilitate their ability to see themselves and others with increased freedom and clarity, and to help them embrace an image of themselves that included the psychic strength reflected in such an enhanced ability.

References

Wolstein, B. (1974). "I" process and "me" patterns: Two aspects of the psychic self in transference and countertransference. *Contemporary Psychoanalysis*, 10: 347–357.

Wolstein, B. (1977). From mirror to participant-observation to coparticipant inquiry. *Contemporary Psychoanalysis*, 13: 381–386.

Wolstein, B. (1997). The first direct analysis of transference and countertransference. *Psychoanalytical Inquiry*, 17: 505–521.

Countertransference

The psychoanalyst's shared experience and inquiry with his patient (1975)

Benjamin Wolstein

From all that has been said about countertransference during the last 70 years, I have selected for discussion a theme that has not received the full attention it deserves; that of countertransference as part of a field of experience and inquiry, belonging as much to that field for shared experience and inquiry as, for example, the patient's transference. And this, of course, applies not only to countertransference but also to counterresistance and counteranxiety, not only to transference but also to resistance and anxiety.

I do not mean to refer only to the psychic symmetry of the psychoanalyst and his patient as two human beings in therapeutic relation to each other, but, more importantly, to indicate that psychoanalytic therapy does, in fact, take place precisely because the two coparticipants can treat transference and countertransference within a coequal frame of reference and within a shared field of experience and inquiry.

The principle that their relatedness is symmetrical rather than coordinate, or that their frame of reference is coequal rather than hierarchical, derives from some relevant social and cultural philosophies of our time, especially for those psychoanalysts and patients who believe systems of value rooted in humanism, science and democracy, such values as individuality, truth and freedom.

But the principle of psychic symmetry in psychoanalysis, however, does not express a mere preference in social and cultural philosophy. It reflects, instead, the unity underlying all psychic process. It points up the essential condition of the human psyche, whoever possesses it, in whatever environment of biology and geography, history and sociology, beliefs and values, as simply human psyche striving to realize itself.

Since the psychic data of psychoanalysis are investigated by the methods of direct psychological inquiry, they remain, by the same token, symmetrical data. From this principle we derive, in addition, the clinical theorem that countertransference, as psychic experience undergone during psychoanalytic therapy, is no different from transference, or from other psychic processes and patterns of any two coparticipants in psychoanalytic therapy.

The important clinical application of this principle of psychic symmetry is that the psychoanalyst cannot ascribe to himself special status for his social or ego-interpersonal role with his patient. Nor can he claim it by virtue of the symbols of power and prestige ordinarily ascribed to his expertise and professionalism. From beginning to end, his psyche is uniquely present in psychoanalytic process with his patient's for better or worse, until the two reach some accord about termination.

To do psychoanalysis in this experiential field of therapy, it is necessary to redefine its actual target of inquiry into transference and countertransference. There is, for example, no point to viewing them as either patient-oriented or psychoanalyst-oriented. The particular patient and his psychoanalyst, to the extent of their respective capacities and capabilities, really *make* their therapeutic inquiry.

Just as the study of transference is no longer a patient-centered process – with the psychoanalyst hidden behind an impersonal and authoritarian facade of professional expertise, and therefore assumed to be capable of conducting an inquiry he is not part of – so the study of countertransference within the actual psychoanalytic inquiry is no longer a psychoanalyst-centered process, with the patient, this time, hidden behind a facade of submissiveness, long-suffering neurosis, character disorder, schizoid personality and more, and therefore assumed to be capable of producing insight for an inquiry he is not part of.

The point, of course, is that the very opposite is true. In psychoanalytic therapy viewed as a field of shared experience and inquiry, the study of unconscious aspects of transference centers on the psychoanalyst, since if genuinely unconscious, they are beyond the patient's scope of awareness. And all things being equal, the study of unconscious aspects of countertransference centers on the patient, since they are beyond the psychoanalyst's scope of awareness. He cannot treat the unconscious aspects of his own countertransference until, with the help of another, he manages to penetrate his defensiveness and distortions about them. It may even be his patient who might, in this instance, be able to openly discuss them with him in a constructive way.

This is obviously not the most comfortable view for the psychoanalyst who prefers a hierarchical position of authority, or for the patient who prefers a submissive position of dependency. But uncomfortable as it may be, the unconscious aspects of the analyst's countertransference are greatly involved in the therapeutic experience; distinct and unavoidable, emergent and waiting to be observed and defined, transformed and explained, interpreted and metapsychologized.

It is these very unconscious resources of thought and feeling however, that if not evaded nor covered up, may, as countertransferred, become sources of enlightenment and healing for the patient who can see how and why the psychoanalyst, within his own psychic limits, works through the patient's resistances and anxieties in order to obtain a better grasp off his transferences. Such understanding of his coparticipant, among all the other things therapeutic taking place between them, may only arise from the patient's open observation of countertransference.

The way a particular psychoanalyst deals with his patient's reactions to countertransference, however, depends on the many private and uniquely individual factors that cannot be subsumed under any simple rule of general procedure. A psychoanalyst's reaction to his patient's reaction to countertransference depends on his given resources of affective and cognitive experience in response to that particular patient's transference, resistance and anxiety, love and hate, anger and self-pity, hostility and manipulation – or more generally, in response to the qualities and traits of the patient's relatedness in therapy.

How a psychoanalyst relates to the traits and qualities of his patient's relatedness, in turn, determines what that particular psychoanalyst can do about transforming them out of his own uniquely individual psychic resources. But he cannot possibly know how he will finally relate to any particular patient in advance of the actual therapeutic involvement. He may, at best, only work outward from the inner experience he can cultivate within that particular field of therapeutic inquiry.

If he were, on the other hand, to behave according to the pattern of some colleague's procedure – as taken over, for example, in supervision – that would lay an impersonal, self-estranging procedure on the outside of his experience, covering it with a behavioral facade that imperceptibly moves him one step further away from his uniquely individual capacities of working directly from his own psyche with that patient.

And finally, if he cannot get through that surface behavior of procedure, into the unconscious aspects of his patient's psychology manifested in transference, resistance and anxiety, then he and his patient will enter into a dry and fallow period – an impasse, plateau, stasis – in which nothing of psychoanalytic moment can take place for either coparticipant.

In this event, the two gradually become trapped in an interlocking experience of their own making, in an inquiry so jammed that neither can pursue it fully on his own. Neither one is, in fact, able to do it without the other. And if both fail to accept their mutual dependency for living and working through it, then nothing of deeper therapeutic import can happen, and their therapeutic inquiry gradually comes to a standstill.

Whether or not they terminate the formal context of their relatedness, if neither is open to the other's hunches and intuitive moves and tentative hypotheses about their interlocking of transference and countertransference (notice that either the patient or the psychoanalyst may innovate these efforts) their therapeutic work arrives inevitably at its terminal phase. It has nowhere else to go.

At such a point, the integrity of the psychoanalyst's training and the solidity of his psychic relatedness are important determinants of what happens next. As a well-trained psychoanalyst, whose sense of personal worth and therapeutic capability does not depend on success or failure with any one particular patient, he is prepared to throw that interlocking of transference and countertransference open for shared inquiry. He may even consider turning a de facto into an actual termination, if both he and his patient have seriously attempted to explore the whys and wherefores of their particular failure at shared inquiry.

This therapeutic effort itself, pursued with intelligence and openness from both sides, may, in fact, prove to be of great benefit, because transference and countertransference, when sensitively treated, become most critical for moving the psychoanalytic inquiry forward. If insensitively treated, however, it may lead most directly to its premature failure.

This terminal phase, if not bungled through defensiveness and distortions on either side, may prove to be the most illuminating phase of the entire therapeutic experience. Aside from what the psychoanalyst may learn about his contribution to the interlocking of transference and countertransference, the patient may learn some important things about himself in conflict, about himself relating to individuals with psychic structures like his own or his psychoanalyst's, or something important about all three.

The psychoanalyst who openly accepts the therapeutic impact of his countertransference may invoke its changing processes and patterns in order to guide and integrate the experience of both himself and his patient for the ongoing and future conditions of their work together. This, inevitably, makes the available evidence for countertransference part of his psychoanalytic inquiry with every patient, potentially involving all his thoughts and feelings, intuitions and marginal hunches, and, of course, his basic beliefs, values and ideals.

It raises, moreover, the fundamental question of how to be both a psychoanalyst behaving as professional expert and a person experiencing a unique psyche. From a common-sense point of view, he is obviously both. But he is, I think, even more than that. For being a person is only his social and egoic or interpersonal mask, providing for gross characterizations of the subtle aspects of his inner psyche extending outward, since as its Latin derivation would suggest, the individual's persona is nothing more, nor less than the model of performance as in a play or a game. In this sense of the notion of the person, then, there is no discrepancy between being a psychoanalyst and being a person because, from the point of view of his being the uninvolved professional expert, both terms refer to his outward social and ego-interpersonal presence in the therapeutic field.

And his persona is not the same as his psyche. The differences between the two may be summarized thus: the persona refers to the objective, ego-interpersonal "me" patterns of the surface self observed and interpreted by others without, however, indicating how subjective, first-personal "I" processes express the inner self, or the deeper resources of the psyche.

This relation of the psyche to the persona, then, reveals the extent to which a psychoanalyst may become involved in therapeutic relatedness with his patient, for the nature of his involvement depends, finally, on how real and full he can become with his patient, on how deeply probing and exploratory he can become, on how capable he is of immersing himself in the serious psychological problems of another.

Every psychoanalyst, as he moves through a series of shared experiences with a wide variety of patients, has to discover for himself the critical boundaries of his therapeutic awareness. And he has to discover them for himself because no two psychoanalysts do, in fact, possess the same uniquely individual psyche.

The attempt, however, to organize this knowledge into the structure of psychoanalytic inquiry is a different issue. For this purpose, it is necessary to formulate the rules or definitions governing the observation of transference and countertransference, resistance and counterresistance, anxiety and counteranxiety, as well as their transformation, explanation and interpretation. This structure of inquiry maps the overall limits and possibilities of the therapeutic experience available in psychoanalysis.

But again, every psychoanalyst engaging in the clinical work of therapy, not unlike the physicist or biologist engaged in experimental work in the laboratory, has to find within himself the best way to fit that structure of inquiry to the unique resources of his own individual psychology.

The structure of psychoanalytic inquiry, of course, provides a base of support for the psychoanalyst who would be himself with his patient, risking himself to his patient's transference of hostility and criticism, manipulation and destructiveness, and eventually to the full experience of his patient. For only by exposing himself with his patient to the pain and dread and misery beyond those transferences can he practice his healing art.

But if he did not seek this experience, and instead worked over the patient from the outside of his defensive and power operations, the patient then could not, in turn, invite him to work under him from the inside of that burden of loneliness and terror, distorted though that has now become as a result of long-standing repression. And if the patient cannot become aware of it directly with his psychoanalyst, there is, no doubt, little that he may expect to do about it in any other way, in therapy or elsewhere. The acceptance of this psychic pain and misery into therapeutic awareness is an essential condition for any successful psychoanalytic therapy.

The psychoanalyst may, therefore, discover the best fit for the structure of his inquiry within himself only as he is willing, at the same time, to share the uniqueness of his psyche openly with his patient. From this shared uniqueness, he also opens the moving center of his inner experience to those same intimations and realizations of the uniqueness of his patient's psyche. In this way, the psychoanalyst who shares his unique individuality can see his therapeutic inquiry extending outward from his affective and cognitive resources. And also see how his being a psychoanalyst, and his having a persona, arise from common roots in those selfsame inner resources of his psyche.

On the other hand, the psychoanalyst who falls back on the role of expertise presents his patient with a professional persona or trained facade. By putting up this sort of front, although he engages the patient's defensive and power operations, he is, in effect, trapped by the limits of a manipulative device of his own making.

And he also sets the stage for the patient's performance of his own suffering persona and dependent facade. But the patient's performance is simply a response to his psychoanalyst's performance and not for the purposes of furthering the inquiry. The patient is only putting up a front of defense and engaging in power operations in realistic response to his psychoanalyst doing the same with him.

The reality of this experience cannot be washed away by simply appealing to ad hoc interpretive principles, since, as Freud long ago taught and we now know well, metapsychology is like the mythical witch whose services we call upon whenever observation and inference, or logic and reason fail to support our preferred point of view. That is, if a patient responds to the professional facade a psychoanalyst covers himself with, the psychoanalyst cannot, then, turn around and claim neutrality with respect to that particular response, which, in his interpretive judgment, merely echoes the patient's experience in infancy or childhood. For the patient is responding to something real, here and now, and in that measure his response cannot be judged as being simply distorted. The psychoanalyst, whatever else he would do about it, has to treat it at least as such.

If the psychoanalyst comes on like a professional expert, and the patient tries to counter him in kind, for example by becoming testy or submissive or even combative, the psychoanalyst creates serious question about his capacity, afterward, to be the healer. For how, in truth, can an expert in procedure also heal psychic wounds? Not without relating directly to them, which he does not allow himself to do.

The psychoanalyst who plays the role or enacts the persona of expertise, in effect, interposes an egoic or interpersonal boundary between his creative inner resources and the problems of his patient's psychology, and in so doing, also pushes the patient's creative inner resources one more step backward into himself. But if that is the way the psychoanalyst works best, and relates best, he should, of course, do it directly and straight-forwardly, although the patient, as a result, may have the added problem of getting at his own original resources with a psychoanalyst twice-removed from the resources of the psyche, once from his own and once from his patient's.

If the psychoanalyst is truly expert, however, he need only demonstrate that with the calm and depth and integrity required for the study of inner experience. And if he is not the expert he professes to be, enacting a professional facade – in therapeutic fact, a fictional facade – will not misguide or deceive his patient very long.

Aside from traces of faulty training, which every seasoned psychoanalyst overcomes in due course, another reason for enacting a social and ego-interpersonal facade is his conscious decision to cover up such countertransference problems as detachment and loneliness, hostility, sadism and destructiveness. And he probably covers them up on the judgment that they could, if opened to therapeutic inquiry, interfere with the patient's confrontation of his own problems within himself.

The psychoanalyst should not, on principle, withhold such countertransference problems from open and ongoing transaction with his patient, but in his best psychoanalytic judgment of himself, he still cannot integrate them with another on a conscious basis. He may, of course, be wrong in his judgment, and could require it as a rationalized cover for his counterresistances and counteranxieties. But that, in any event, does not automatically set any limiting conditions to his patient's awareness. It is a well-known fact that regardless of his psychoanalyst's professional facade, the patient, if he is capable of such perception, gradually comes to perceive aspects of his psychoanalyst's unconscious experience whether or not the psychoanalyst would wish it, or cooperate in it.

As with transference, countertransference may also be explored as it occurs in the experiential field of therapy. This effort to study its manifestations in the original field of its occurrence with the patient is the most important advance in the psychoanalysis of countertransference in the past 20 years. The direct study of it, as a rule, intensifies the psychology of the inquiry as experienced: instead of having, at such points, to turn awareness toward the more practical concerns of behavior, the further inquiry into countertransference within its original field of occurrence, in fact, deepens the movement of the therapy into unconscious experience as well, and does so for both coparticipants.

As the premise for this innovation of procedure, I have already indicated that the psychoanalyst's psyche and persona are as fully part of the therapeutic inquiry in countertransference, counterresistance and counteranxiety as the patient's are in transference, resistance and anxiety. And this premise, furthermore, signifies other important changes in the therapeutic relatedness of the psychoanalyst and his patient.

Consider its development in the following perspective. From Freud's (1943) and Ferenczi's (1959) mirror of id impulses, to Hartmann's

(1958) and Sullivan's (1940) expert in ego-interpersonal relations, to the contemporary coparticipant in shared experience and inquiry, the psychoanalyst has gradually moved more deeply into the immediate context of his unconscious experience directly with his patient. And, in so doing, he has also learned to let go of absolute commitments in metapsychology; for its many special metaphors – such as instinctual dialectics (Freud 1943), struggle for power (Adler 1917), archetypes of the collective unconscious (Jung 1927), absolute will (Rank 1947), and so on – no longer distinguish his work as psychoanalyst. He has, in this movement, increasingly focused therapeutic inquiry on the psychology of his relatedness with his patient rather than the metapsychology of the abstract reasons for his patient's experience and behavior, and for his own as well.

This therapeutic focus is consistently set on the relations of conscious and unconscious experience as the domain of human psychology best explored in psychoanalysis, and on pursuing that exploration to the point where the patient's unique individuality engages his psychoanalyst's in direct exchange. In the overall structure of psychoanalysis, the focus is now, rather, on the pluralism of its perspectives on metapsychology, to be seen not only from the interpretive standpoint of sex and egotism, money and power, satisfaction and security, and so on, but also from the empirical standpoint of what two particular coparticipants find unconscious, and make conscious.

In this new experiential field of therapy, the psychoanalyst's direct response to his work is affective and cognitive – liking and disliking, trusting and suspecting, hurting and pleasing, and so on – as he lives and works through the appointed sessions with his patients. He does, of course, perform a service as he applies his expertise, but he cannot possibly do that without both consciously and unconsciously living through his sessions with his various patients. He obviously is and does what he can be and do, only as capable of being there with them in therapy as he is with others elsewhere.

And this leads to the substantive question about the basic meaning of the psychoanalytic experience. Each experience, I would propose, acquires its own meanings in terms of its own ends. That is, as motive and consequence, as relatedness and significance, as live and ongoing stream of consciousness. Its basic meaning is, therefore, larger than the pragmatism of any transitional goals and purposes, and larger than the idealism of any absolute beliefs and values. But even larger than these is a psychic sense of living and becoming a uniquely individual person, a psychic sense of direction pulsating through the experience and inquiry shared by the particular psychoanalyst and patient.

Once the patient gets to the center of his first-person singular, active dimension of self – to his psychic "I" processes by which he relates to his ego-interpersonal "me" patterns – the psychoanalyst can no longer turn him aside, or off, with some arbitrary notions of procedure, such as being only a mirror, or only a professional expert in interpersonal relations when, in fact, his patient is now quite capable of perceiving uniquely individual aspects of personality, his psychoanalyst's as well as his own.

No less than ego psychologists such as Hartmann (1958) and A. Freud (1946), and interpersonal relationists such as Thompson (1950) and Sullivan (1940) who, by the late 1930s, took the distinction of psyche and instinct seriously, in order to study social and cultural aspects of personality, we, today, take the distinction between psyche and culture seriously, in order to study the uniquely individual aspects of each patient's affective and cognitive resources.

But psychoanalysis, for its successful undertaking, does not require the psychoanalyst or patient to accept any one single system of beliefs and values, or myths and metaphors, nor any single interpretive meta-psychology. It depends, instead, on a disciplined and intensive study of the recurrent and invariant processes and patterns of each patient's uniquely individual psyche. This exploration of experience is no more an alternative to, nor defense against, the modification of behavior, than the modification of behavior is an alternative to, or defense against, the exploration of experience. The two are not mutually exclusive. But psychoanalytic inquiry, as its name implies, is essentially the analysis of the psyche becoming directly available as processes of experience before producing patterns of behavior.

At this point, it may be appropriate to summarize the definition of countertransference deriving from a field theory of psychoanalysis. What sort of processes and patterns may be referred to in defining these terms? Countertransference, in its most general sense, arises from the psychoanalyst's coparticipation in therapeutic relatedness to the fullest range of experience and inquiry he is capable of undergoing with any particular patient. This, finally, places his psychology as deeply into the actual psychoanalytic therapy as his patient's.

Of course, not every psychotherapy becomes a psychoanalytic therapy. In the select instances that do, the psychoanalyst may, finally, involve himself to the point of no return in a transference–countertransference neurosis, complex or interlock, in which the two coparticipants have to make the psychic effort to work through their therapeutic relatedness to another base. They do not, otherwise, obtain a better understanding of their mutual contributions to the particular shape of its development.

And furthermore, this convergence of transference and countertransference makes it necessary to place greater emphasis on the psychoanalyst's capacity to generate the inner psychic resources of affective and cognitive experience, as distinct from his ability to distribute the outer social and ego-interpersonal patterns of behavior. So his countertransference, as it involves his patient's transference, may become live, real, spontaneous instead of remaining stilted, mechanical, manipulative.

The psychoanalyst, unlike the therapist who modifies behavior, engages his patient essentially as a psychological explorer who would learn something new about the psychology of two humans experiencing each other, and whose patient is then free to decide how he will behave this new knowledge in relation to others. The psychoanalyst becomes what his name literally depicts him to be, an analyst of the psyche rather than the adaptive consensus of behavior by which he or his patient, at any given phase of the development of culture, is to experience and behave his psychic resources. He, of course, is interested in his patient's behavior, but not primarily so. He studies it essentially as a source of observation and inference about inner experience, but not with the objective of modifying behavior. In this therapeutic inquiry, it is the patient who, finally, is responsible for both the course and consequence of his behavior, and no psychoanalyst, unless he is quite irrational, can assume any more responsibility for a patient's life than the patient does for it himself.

But while the psychoanalyst may be interested in the ongoing modifications of his patient's behavior, since he obviously cannot get closer to the private sources of a patient's behavior than the patient himself, he cannot actually modify his patient's behavior or its effects. If anyone is going to do that, and do it with some sense of freedom and dignity, it is the patient himself.

For this psychoanalytic frame of reference, we may define countertransference in the widest sense of its psychological meaning. That is, to refer to all the experience and behavior relating the psychoanalyst's psyche to a particular patient's, in so far as its processes and patterns may be observed to occur as a function of his counterresistances and counteranxieties. The important point, here, is that the psychology of countertransference may be taken to cover both his real and his distorted reactions to any particular patient.

The extent to which countertransference is real or distorted cannot be measured by antecedent perspectives on metapsychology. It is, from my point of view, a question to be decided on the basis of subsequent psychoanalytic inquiry, if at all, and finally at the terminal phases of the work. My view, here, differs from those that sharply distinguish countertransference from real feeling, real thought, real relationship, or real whatever toward the patient. And I take this view because it points up that countertransference does not arise in psychoanalytic inquiry fully packaged and defined, with a label on its wrapper indicating how much is real, distorted, etc.

There are several reasons for taking this view. First, it is better psychology because it unifies the psychoanalyst's transfer of his uniquely individual processes and patterns with the rest of his psyche. In actual clinical inquiry, the patient may, therefore, also observe his psychoanalyst countertransferring both the real and the distorted aspects of his experience and behavior.

Second, it frees the psychoanalyst to immerse himself unselfconsciously in therapeutic inquiry with his patient in order to discover whether, and in what measure, his reactions are in fact both real and distorted, the realism and distortedness of his countertransference also being a question to be answered by further inquiry.

And third, it is a constant reminder that the psychoanalyst can never shed his psychological skin and transcend the given limits of his unconscious experience, not, at least, while he lives his life under the natural conditions of human experience. So long as his experience and behavior are governed by this distinction between the conscious and the unconscious, it is naive – or perhaps more simply, even self-serving – to expect that he can ever become so completely real as to be perfectly free of distortion, but rather that he is a searching, changing, growing mixture of the two, and should always expect to be.

References

Adler, A. (1917). *The Neurotic Constitution*. New York: Moffat, Yard.

Ferenczi, S. (1950). *Further Contributions to the Theory and Technique of Psychoanalysis*. London: Hogarth Press.

Freud, A. (1946). *The Ego and the Mechanisms of Defense*. New York: International Universities Press.

Freud, S. (1943). *A General Introduction to Psychoanalysis*. Garden City, UT: Garden City Publishing.

Hartmann, H. (1958). *Ego Psychology and the Problem of Adaptation*. New York: International Universities Press.

Jung, C. (1927). *Contributions to Analytical Psychology*. New York: Harcourt Brace.

Rank, O. (1947). *Will Therapy, and Truth and Reality*. New York: Knopf.

Sullivan, H. (1940). *Conceptions of Modern Psychiatry*. Washington, DC: W. A. White Psychiatric Foundation.

Thompson, C. (1950). *Psychoanalysis*. New York: Hermitage.

Chapter 3

The fiction of analytic anonymity (1977)

Erwin Singer

Erwin Singer reflects the radical qualities of interpersonal psychoanalysis in the 1960s and 1970s. He seemed to delight in turning conventional analytic thought on its head. Singer, like Searles, believed that purportedly ill and dysfunctional people are often anything but weak and pliable. Instead, the reasons disturbed people in that era were homebound or incarcerated in hospitals reflected their effort to preserve the well-being of their troubled loved ones, an effort that Singer, Searles, and others felt was often actually heroic (see, for example, Levenson & Feiner, 1968). Therapists who believe their caretaking grows from having greater strength than their patients do their patients no service, although holding such beliefs does often help the analyst feel potent, kind, benevolent, and humane.

Searles and Singer both make it quite clear that therapists and analysts, being more simply human than otherwise, are motivated not only by the desire to help, but also by a range of self-interests, some of which are ultimately harmful to patients. Both writers illustrate the irreducibly subjective nature of all human interaction, including psychoanalytic co-participation; and both provide evidence supporting Sullivan's model of participant-observation, still radical in that era, as an alternative to valorizing the analyst's objectivity.

In 1977, when Singer published this article, there was almost universal acceptance in mainstream psychoanalysis of the idea that the well-analyzed analyst should be able to exert control over his subjectivity. Patients were routinely understood to be blind to the analyst's sentiments, attitudes, beliefs, biases, and personal problems. The collapse of hierarchy in the consulting room, largely initiated by the participant-observation model, did not even begin to take hold in mainstream psychoanalysis until the 1980s. That it happened at all was due in no small measure to work like Singer's, which, like the thinking of Wolstein and

Searles, was iconoclastic in this regard. All these writers exploded the myth that the analyzed analyst invariably functioned at a high level and was better put-together than his patients. Like Heinrich Racker (1968), writing in South America during the same era, Singer recognized that such claims, including the unjustified belief that only one of the two analytic participants was able to see the qualities of the other, undermined the patient. For Singer, the fiction of analytic anonymity protected analysts from recognizing that they are exposed and prevents intimacy between the analytic partners. Perhaps most harmful of all, the fiction of analytic anonymity unnecessarily pathologized and infantilized patients by creating the perception that patients are blind and insensitive to the other.

References

Levenson, E. & Feiner, A. (1968). The compassionate sacrifice: An explanation of a metaphor. *Psychoanalytic Review*, 55: 552–573.

Racker, H. (1968). *Transference and Countertransference*. New York: International Universities Press.

The fiction of analytic anonymity (1977)

Erwin Singer

Some years ago, while discussing Goethe, Santayana (1910), in one of his essays, fully acknowledged Goethe's shortcomings. Such criticism, justified as it was, is a rare literary event. But Santayana also pointedly portrayed Goethe as the "philosophical poet" of inner turbulence and flux and of the insights attending familiarity with internal turmoil. This knowledge led the most prominent of all German writers to a highly moral position, yet a stance singularly devoid of the banalities of moralizing. I have chosen to introduce my essay with his aphorism because it harbors profound implications for the excruciating task of the psychoanalyst, even though it was penned long before formalization of his therapeutic art came into existence. Indeed, only he who risks experiencing the poet's world and in doing so admits familiarity with it can meet the poet fully. But he who chances to expose himself *by* bearing truly his fellow's anguish and ecstasy can hope to be met equally exposed by him. In any genuine meeting, both participants stand equally bared before each other, and the moral fiber of such an authentic encounter precludes the trivia of moralizing.

From their very beginnings the psychoanalytic literature and institutes dedicated to the training of psychoanalysts have insisted that a person seeking preparation for the practice of this art must be willing to be a patient himself, must be a person prepared to scrutinize himself in infinite detail. And *willingness* to do so is all one may rightfully expect; we may ask if anyone can claim with honesty that he is really eager to face his own abyss of affect and associated agonies. Originally Freud (1937 [1953]), and many since him who also deemed it essential that future analysts engage in self-examination before they try to aid others in such efforts, thought of this process as "training analyses," procedures designed to familiarize candidates in firsthand fashion with methods and techniques of the endeavor. Simultaneously, they expected that in the course of a "training analysis" and subsequent periodic reanalyses the analyst would develop so profound a familiarity with his own up-to-then unconscious promptings that it would help him recognize similar unconscious tendencies in his patients. And furthermore, it was hoped that this self-investigation would free him to meet turbulent passions in others, unworried about their potentially touching upon aspects of his own inner flux. After all, it was reasoned, an analyst aware of his inner life is not too much in need of avoiding those affective realities of his patients that parallel his own struggles. Clearly, it was implied, the higher the analyst's level of consciousness, the less he will be tempted to selectively dissociate communications likely to bring to awareness previously unconscious material. There will be less need to avoid the patient in order to avoid himself. When Sullivan (1947) exclaimed, "We are all simply more human than otherwise," he restated succinctly both Goethe's insight that only efforts to travel through seemingly unfamiliar lands enable one to meet the poet and Freud's recognition that only self-confrontation may bring in its wake the possibility of courageously encountering other fellow human beings.

All this makes perfectly good sense and has been for years part and parcel of that credo which analysts of all persuasions feel free to support. And yet for some years now the suspicion has grown within me that this deep insight advanced by Goethe and others before him and by Freud and Sullivan and their epigones since contains, paradoxically it may seem, the key to understanding one of the most troublesome stumbling blocks of the psychoanalytic process. In a previous paper (1968), I have suggested that analysts often appear peculiarly reluctant to comment insightfully and incisively on their clients' communications lest their remarks reveal all too well that they have grasped the patient's subtle message. They seem fearful that their insight would make self-evident that the analyst, too, "has been there," at least at some point in his life. Their empathic grasp, they correctly sense, would betray pointedly that the basic precondition for empathic communion is given, that is, personal knowledge of the experience under scrutiny – or as common language has it, "it takes one to know one."

The obvious thought suggests itself that our insights about ourselves resemble the only windows available to us for contemplating and understanding the world outside. Genuine understanding of another person's life becomes inevitably a function of intimate contact with one's own existence, and, I might add parenthetically, these windows of self-recognition represent the only valid escape route from the horrors of loneliness. It follows that nobody can ever talk about anybody but himself or herself, even though, perhaps especially when, they are engaged in penetrating discussion of others. The process I have had occasion to call "expansive projection," (1970) as juxtaposed to what is usually referred to as "defensive projection," makes itself immediately heard. This process is at one and the same time the foundation, the vehicle, and the expression of all intimate exchange. Therefore, neither I nor anybody else may rightfully say, "You are..." or "She is...." I may imply only, "In your presence *I* tend to feel..." or "When you do what seems to *me* ... then *I* think...." Apparently, what analysts so fondly think of as interpretations are neither exclusively nor even primarily comments about their clients' deeper motivations but first and foremost self-revealing remarks. If the analytic process represents a series of situations in which all the patient's acts, be they commissions or omissions, reveal him if we had the courage to grasp the revelations' meaning, then exactly the same must be true about the analyst. The crucial difference between the two rests in what is hopefully the analyst's less defensive posture and his fuller realization that both participants inevitably reveal themselves to each other, were they willing to see and hear what is to be seen and heard.

Of course, I am not talking about the analyst merely sharing with the patient events or facets of his life, although this, too, undoubtedly happens at times, and such sharing may not be as destructive to the process of inquiry as some seem to think. No, I am talking about a much more subtle process in which the patient, in exposing the structure and content of his concerns, simultaneously reveals what Fromm (1950) once called the person's private religion or the genuine hierarchy of values by which he lives no matter what fancy pretenses he may cherish or proffer. And similarly, the structure, focus, and content of the analyst's response to the patient reveals the analyst's private religion, no matter what his pretenses to himself and others. Let me illustrate with a clinical excerpt.

Quite some time ago, while working with a young woman whose mode of communication was so confusing to me that I could grasp the meaning of her statements only on the rarest of occasions, she related one day in language and organization of material much more comprehensible to me an episode of years gone by. It was an instance in which her father – a man of whom she had always felt ashamed, whom she rejected whenever the opportunity arose, and whom she had denigrated and humiliated mercilessly – had shown her unusual kindness and tenderness. Somewhere in the middle of relating this episode and the devotion clearly reflected in the father's actions, she began to restructure and shade the events so as to belittle his efforts on her behalf. Oh, she allowed, he really had not done all that much for her, and furthermore he had looked and smelled dirty while laboring for her, and besides all this he seemed so clearly outside the much more "refined" rest of her family.

As she spoke, two things happened. She became progressively agitated, rambling, and returned to her usual rather incoherent manner of speech; and I, preoccupied with the image of the touching scene she had described, felt deeply moved by the man's efforts to comfort his daughter. Suddenly I felt forced to comment, "Did you feel so guilty then and even now that you must talk that way?" As if quite startled and struck by surprise, she bolted up in her chair, looked straight at me, and asked in what was for her an unusually serious vein, "How do you know this?" I did not answer but merely returned her gaze. After a while she sat back, nodded her head, and simply added," I know how you know." I felt exposed – I *was* exposed. Years later, when we terminated our work, she returned to this moment of meeting, musing about how she had experienced, at least temporarily, a sense of liberation brought about by her recognition that I, too, must know the burden of having betrayed and the unbearable length to which one will go to deny guilt associated with betrayal.

I am not insisting on the validity or the appropriate timing of my comment. It would also be easy to imagine that in the course of the episode she had described, the little girl had been sexually aroused, and one might therefore be inclined to focus the inquiry on this potential aspect of the events. Certainly, some of her descriptive terms, her references to her father's looks and his smell, her increasing anxiety while relating the story, leading once again to disorganized speech lend themselves readily for the development of such inferences. I merely insist that if the analyst's comments are to be relevant rather than "correct" or "deep" – though obviously I maintain that relevance is synonymous with genuine precision and depth – then they must unavoidably touch upon his experiential realm. In their relevance the analyst's comments must willy-nilly expose him to the patient as much as the patient is exposed to him.

Hand in hand with this recognition there has grown over the years another realization within me. I now know that I am in urgent need of sharp self-examination when I catch myself working very hard to be "accepting and understanding" of the patient. I have grown suspicious that my working so hard to help the patient feel accepted reflects my distrust of his willingness to accept *me* and that somehow I have grasped some inclination on his part to be rejecting of *me*. By such a rejection I do not mean his refusal to enter analysis in a formal way with me. Such rejections are easy enough to take and not infrequently denote the person's unconscious sense that our particular interaction may be too burdensome for both of us and therefore not as fruitful as one might hope it to be. No, I mean by rejection here a process potentially much more devastating: the likelihood that the patient may reject me as a human being and that he may, in a critical, controlling, and derisive manner, deny the reality of my experience – that I am of consequence. At such moments, I seem to fear an undermining and rejection of my reality because, contrary to psychoanalytic folklore, patients are not the only ones concerned with acceptability as human beings – analysts are also, or at least this analyst is. Again, let me illustrate with a clinical example.

I was once consulted by a man who, before seeing me, had "interviewed" three other analysts but claimed somewhere in the middle of our meeting that he had decided to work with me. He explained that he wanted to work with a nonmedical person and the other three had been physicians. When I inquired how this entered into his decision, he said something about physicians being too "clinical and cold." This remark did not impress me as valid, particularly since I knew all three quite well as genuinely concerned, empathic, kind, and highly competent analysts. And so I commented along these lines. Well, he said, he had been in analysis before, in another city, with a medical analyst, and he insisted that his experience with this man had been disastrous. There was not enough time left to investigate what he had found so "disastrous," but the thought crossed my mind that even if that were true, it reminded me of a man who, once having had a tough piece of roast beef, had decided to become a vegetarian. Indeed, a strange reason for such a decision. But I did not express this thought, somehow "concerned" that the man was not "prepared" or "ready" for such a comment and that he might feel "put down" or "rejected" by it. I let it go with a skeptical expression on my face, a puzzled shrug of the shoulders, and slightly raised hands suggesting we would have to see what this is all about. I recommended that we meet in a few days again, allowing each of us some time to reflect on our meeting and to exchange on that occasion notes on our thoughts and reactions. To this he readily agreed.

That evening I ruminated about our conversation. In the course of the double session – I usually meet for initial consultations in a double session – he had told me a good deal about his reasons for having sought help earlier and why he was contemplating renewed analytic exploration. Among them, he mentioned some rather superficial suicidal gestures, some verbal expressions of violence toward members of his family, and his wasting his life as a dilettante by dabbling in various artistic pretensions in the hope of impressing most anyone he met. His family's considerable wealth, which he considered his own, allowed him to indulge himself haphazardly in his fancies. But time was passing by. Now, at the end of his thirties, he knew he had contributed nothing. And while he did not put it this way – indeed at one point he resented my use of the term bitterly – he did think of himself as some strange type of lounge lizard.

While reflecting on our meeting, things became clearer. I had felt flattered and thereby controlled, and I had to ask, had this perchance been his intent. Hadn't he tried to control others by feigned violence against them or himself? And clever fellow that I thought he was, wouldn't he prefer working with a psychologist who, he could imagine, would feel professionally more insecure than a psychiatrist – ergo, more capable of being intimidated and controlled than one of his medical confreres?

The picture seemed rather obvious, for clearly there had been enough time to at least start exploring at its edges. Yet I had to let it go. Why? No doubt it was unpleasant and disappointing to reencounter childish competitive feelings in myself, tendencies that I liked to think of as long past and buried. But disappointment with oneself is, at least in part, the inevitable lot of the analyst – that much I know and accept – and had I not caught these silly neuroticisms easily enough in the evening, why had I avoided them during the session? Sadly, I had to face the fact that investigations along these lines would have revealed me (and heightened my anxiety quite early in our contact) as one who knew about the desire to control, to manipulate, and to intimidate and about the devious ways such desires can take, including the use of flattery and playing on the insecurities of others. How else would these possibilities come to my mind? Was *I* ready to stand exposed this way; would the patient accept me as one who knew about such devious motives and maneuvers? It had never been a question of his being ready and his need to be accepted. Much more it was a question of my anxieties along these lines.

Once again I feel forced to repeat that our insights about ourselves – perhaps I ought to say more modestly, my insights about myself – represent to me a double-edged sword. They potentiate my insight into the patient, but this insight, in turn, potentiates his deeper knowledge of me. They make me realize that relevant comments about him are inevitably revealing of myself, and therefore my courage to bare myself via pointed reflections and the posing of pertinent questions is constantly tested, for the therapist's question, "Will the patient accept me if he knows me?" always hovers in the background.

This brings me to three related themes central to our therapeutic concerns. I believe that the preceding discussion bears implications for aspects of our theory of psychopathology, for our notions as to what is therapeutic in psychotherapy, and for our theoretical ideas concerning termination of analytic work. Let me take one issue at a time, using as my point of departure a complaint every analyst must have heard all too often. One of the most common laments of patients insists, "I feel so exposed and embarrassed and angry. You know so much about me, and I know nothing about you. It isn't fair."

To the first issue, the question of a theory of psychopathology: it seems to me that a patient's "ignorance" about the analyst, unless it is a conscious ploy, a somewhat psychopathic fake and pretense employed for whatever manipulative reasons, depicts precisely what is wrong with him – indeed, it describes the very nucleus of *all* psychopathology. It reflects that the patient has abandoned a birth right and a fundamentally given human capacity: to hear what can be heard, to see what can be seen, to grasp what can be grasped. Those among us who maintain a vision in which psychological well-being is defined by the courage to know oneself rather than by adherence to prescribed behavioral norms always understood psychopathology as a form of cowardliness, its particular modes of expression, and their often disastrous consequences. Hopefully, we have stated this understanding without pompously preaching courage when we encounter an example of the universal human propensity to look away when passing the mirror. I think that among those who broadly define themselves as "depth psychologists" there are no crucial differences in their acceptance of this definition. All of them apparently view this all too human avoidance of self-confrontation and self-recognition as the hub of psychopathology, various syndromes simply describing the spectrum of maneuvers and avenues available to all of us in our quest for self-deception. Where psychoanalytic schools of thought, of course, do differ is on the question of precisely what human beings so studiously avoid noticing about themselves and what is responsible for the development of such cowardliness and its specific manifestations. In brief, their arguments are not about the definition of psychopathology but about their respective metapsychologies.

If it is true that through self-knowledge and self-recognition analysts become capable of grasping the essentials of their patients' lives, and if, conversely, it is also true, as I have argued, that through their newfound or rediscovered self-knowledge patients grasp the essentials of their analysts, then psychoanalytic success seems to me readily definable. It expresses itself in the patient's ultimately becoming as conversant with the analyst's personal visions, his psychological operations, and his hierarchy of values – including the discrepancies between what he professes and by what he truly lives – as the analyst, hopefully, has become conversant with these central aspects of his patients' lives. Therefore, I feel inclined to comment, when listening to the lament of the patient that he knows nothing about me, "That's your trouble. You could know as much about me as I know about you. Yet it seems as if you do not want to know, either about yourself or about me." Of course patients do not *actually* know details of their analysts' lives, such details ranging from food preferences through favorite leisure time activities to idiosyncratic sexual practices. But in themselves these data are as inconsequential as all data *qua* data happen to be. They are merely trivial bits of information. For data are of significance only to the extent to which they illuminate broad issues and phenomena. In our discipline, bits of historical, behavioral, and reactive data are of consequence only if they illuminate and thereby help the participants grasp by direct experience and/or inference aspects of their own or the other person's character. While patients have quantitatively less data to draw upon, there is a wealth of qualitatively significant and poignant information about their analysts at their disposal – if they were only courageous enough to avail themselves of it. I say "courageous enough" because I have insisted that to know about the other in depth requires penetrating confrontation with oneself. And therefore a patient's ability to grasp the meaning of the analyst's life denotes a rather heroic achievement, a remarkable willingness to know oneself and thereby know the other. Growth to such a point may well denote that termination is around the corner.

As the title of this paper and the discussion suggest, I am convinced that the whole notion of analytic anonymity is fictitious. I would be tempted to call it a myth were it not that this term in the context of our work has been preempted brilliantly by Szasz (1960). It seems to me that this anonymity is an artifact carefully maintained by an analytic *folie à deux*. It minimizes the rawness but also the excitement that a full encounter will bring. Obviously Freud, too, was not overly impressed by the substantiveness or importance of "analytic anonymity" – all protestations to the contrary not with-standing – if we are to lend any credence to the Wolf-Man's (1971) account of his work with Freud. Furthermore, even a superficial reading of Freud's description of some of his work (1905 [1953]) makes it quite clear that he was never an "anonymous" analyst. Incisive mind that he was, he must have realized that try as one may, one cannot be anonymous, that one's very effort to be that would in itself be most self-revealing. And, finally, how could he have thought otherwise? Didn't he recommend an evenly hovering attention as the analyst's most productive orientation when in session with his patient so that his own reactions and associations may freely come to the fore, eventually to be communicated to the patient in what he called "interpretations" (1912 [1953])?

I would like to add a brief postscript to this part of the discussion, even though I have touched upon the issue in an earlier paper (1971). I believe that the warnings offered there bear repeating. Self-evidently, neither the inevitability of the analyst's self-revealing behavior nor the derivative recognition that "analytic anonymity" is a fiction can be construed as license for his engaging in self-important chatter, self-indulgent ruminations, or intrusive diversions, no matter how tempting such digressions may be. I suspect that the temptation for such "time out" is always with us and in it we recognize how difficult our work is and how eagerly we therefore may look for a respite. Disciplined opposition to such temptation and careful examination of its meaning is part and parcel of the daily struggle the analyst must suffer, but in his self-discipline and self-examination, he reveals to the patient that he, too, must struggle, that the struggle against primitive narcissistic indulgences is always with us, and that it can be carried on, at least at times, successfully.

But to return to the mainstream of the discussion, not only do I think that psychopathology equals self-imposed ignorance about oneself and therefore about others, and not only do I believe that the patient's courage to know himself is often strikingly reflected in his courage to know the analyst, but to me of even greater theoretical and practical importance is the recognition that the patient's profound and realistic knowledge of the analyst as a representative of his fellow men – past, present, and future – enables him to live authentically, in mutuality, in solidarity, and in communion. The development of such intimate personal knowledge represents to my mind the true meaning and the glorious promise of the dissolution of the Oedipus complex and of paratactic distortions. This realistic sense and grasp of the other's life line offers us the chance to "forget," not in a repressive sense but in the sense of designating as old business what indeed is past history; only such knowledge enables us to forgive, perchance with sadness – not to maintain grudges in madness – and to resolve – again in sadness rather than in madness – that the suffering we have caused others need not be perpetuated. This willingness to forgive, to put aside, and to resolve demands has as its foundation the recognition that the analyst – as were our elders – is potentially as limited, as pathetic, and as heroic as we are. This recognition then enables us to contemplate in sadness and perhaps with bittersweet humor our shared destiny of folly, shortcomings, and courageous heroism; and it reduces the power of the neurotic banner of self-righteousness.

Obviously, this process does not lead to happiness in the conventional sense of the word but leaves us indeed sadder, perhaps even tormented, and yet I shrink from saying wiser and substitute instead more conscious and alive. This sadness, which seems to me the inevitable outcome of any searching self-investigation and therefore of any successful therapeutic encounter, must not be mistaken for or equated with depression. Unfortunately, this question is all too common in the superficial use of language, observations, and concepts that can be noted all around us. Indeed, I have the firm conviction that sadness and depression are mutually exclusive states. If depression is understood as a sense of total futility engendered by injured narcissism, that is, by injury to a fictitious though highly cherished (because presumably very impressive) self-image, not by injured self-love from Fromm's (1956) sense (for how could true self-love ever be inured?), then sadness may be understood as the exact opposite: as a burst of rich and authentic affect, albeit sorrowful in nature, brought about by the realistic though painful recognition that life has been wasted and destroyed.

I am not in the habit of making promises to people who consult me, even when they pressure me to do so. When such pressure is exerted, I am much more inclined to inquire about their tendencies to test my sincerity. Experience has taught me that the more intense this pressure, the more the patient knows that I have nothing I rightfully may promise other than my efforts and hopefully some skill in conducting a joint inquiry about his life and the premises on which he has built it. Yet I must ask myself, if our efforts were to be fruitful, what may the person facing me expect? And I must reply, fewer illusions but less depression as I have defined it; also more sadness, yet with it more aliveness and hope; more separation and with it, paradoxically, more intimacy and less loneliness and isolation.

In two beautiful essays, Ehrenberg (1974, 1975) has discussed what she calls the fine edge of therapeutic intimacy. If the growth of one's capacity to develop intimate knowledge of personal experience and, through it, comparable knowledge of the experience of others, if this growth represents our aim, then the very nature of the analytic exchange must be the starting point for this growth. The nature of such a growth-producing exchange demands first and foremost that the analyst divest himself most strenuously from all exercise of what Laing (1960) so pointedly calls "mystification," without engaging in equally debilitating intrusiveness. Not that one can really practice mystification on people unwilling to be treated in this way; as I have said earlier, we are all rather transparent to those who want to see. But to repeat, patients, perhaps all human beings, are not too eager to see. And so I must conclude that the nature of the therapeutic effort in the analytic encounter is the nurturing of therapeutic intimacy furthered by the absence or at least the minimization of efforts in mystification, even when the patient tempts us – indeed, as is so often the case, even when the patient persistently tries to seduce us into being mystifiers, when he tries to "transform" us, as Levenson (1972) has it, into what are to him psychologically familiar characters. Implicit in Levenson's presentation is the thought that one need not worry about the development of transference; it is always all too much with us and so is that patient's attempt to force countertransference upon us. The steadfast refusal by the therapist to be transformed in this fashion and his continued authentic self-revelation through the pursuit of his thoughts and reactions as they are triggered by the patient represents to me the therapeutic effort of psychoanalytic work. This process may, of course, acquaint the analyst with unpleasant truths about himself, and these unpleasant truths will become apparent to his patient, too. This may seem embarrassing to some, but in the genuine spirit of our work, it is exciting and rekindles hope.

I cannot close without inserting a note of caution. Our efforts to avoid mystification, with the attending likelihood of increasing clarity about and awareness of inner and outer reality, may, perhaps inevitably does, lead to some at least temporary sense of unreality and disorientation in the patient. The unreality of our patients' lives has become all too often their reality. A shift in relatedness to oneself and the outside world as represented by the analyst, if based on authenticity, turns the patient's world upside down, reduces his neurotic hope for certainty, and is therefore invariably anxiety provoking. These are the moments that test the analyst's convictions. They require that he reveal himself even more than he has done up to now by resolutely desisting from offering reassurances and similar operations. In desisting from such reflexive follies and by pursuing the exploration, with its inevitable and mutual denouement, he reveals that he, too, knows the agony of uncertainty, that he, too, is subject to common sorrows, but that he also deems it possible to go on despite them.

References

Ehrenberg, D. (1974). The intimate edge in therapeutic relatedness. *Contemporary Psychoanalysis*, 10: 423–437.

Ehrenberg, D. (1975). The quest for intimate relatedness. *Contemporary Psychoanalysis*, 11: 320–331.

Freud, S. (1905 [1953]). *Fragments of an Analysis of a Case of Hysteria*, Standard Edition 7. London: Hogarth Press.

Freud, S. (1912 [1953]). *Recommendations to Physicians Practicing Psychoanalysis*, Standard Edition 12. London: Hogarth Press.

Freud, S. (1937 [1953]). *Analysis Terminable and Interminable*, Standard Edition 23. London: Hogarth Press.

Fromm, E. (1950). *Psychoanalysis and Religion*. New Haven, CT: Yale University Press.

Fromm, E. (1956). *The Art of Loving*. New York: Harper.

Laing, R. D. (1960). *The Divided Self*. London: Tavistock.

Levenson, E. A. (1972). *The Fallacy of Understanding*. New York: Basic Books.

Santayana, G. (1910). *Three Philosophical Poets*. Cambridge, MA: Harvard University Press.

Singer, E. (1968). The reluctance to interpret. In E. F. Hammer (Ed.), *Use of Interpretation in Treatment*. New York: Grune & Stratton.

Singer, E. (1970). *Key Concepts in Psychotherapy*. New York: Basic Books.

Singer, E. (1971). The patient aids the therapist. In B. Landis & E. S. Tauber (Eds), *In the Name of Life*. New York: Holt, Rinehart and Winston.

Sullivan, H. S. (1947). *Conceptions of Modern Psychiatry*. Washington, DC: William Alanson White Psychoanalytic Foundation.

Szasz, T. S. (1960). The myth of mental illness. *American Psychologist*, 15: 113–118.

Wolf-Man. (1971). *The Wolf-Man*. New York: Basic Books.

Chapter 4

Psychoanalysis

Cure or persuasion? (1978)

Edgar A. Levenson

Edgar Levenson was one of the first psychoanalytic writers to describe and explicate the continuous subjectivity of the analyst's participation in the clinical encounter. Since the early 1970s, he has been situating the analyst's observations in the context of clinical interaction. Levenson has shown that the analyst's experience and conduct are inevitably situated in, and related to, the context of each idiosyncratic analytic moment, embedded in who the analyst is and how he/she is engaging with each individual patient in any given moment. Although he has recently begun to adopt a more accepting attitude, he has been critical of metapsychology during much of his writing life, arguing that theories encourage their adherents to understand patients in ways that merely validate their ideas. Levenson has also eschewed explanations of clinical process on the basis of theories of development. All our theories, he believes, those about development and those about therapeutic action, make good sense, but no one of them is necessarily better than the others. But the extent to which we cherish them leads us to use them in a way that turns them into little more than self-fulfilling prophecies. From Levenson's perspective "persuasion" in psychoanalysis is the unwitting inclination to indoctrinate patients to embrace our formulations about human development and psychodynamics. He notes with a certain cynicism the degree to which analytic cure is defined in a way that reflects little more than the acceptance of the analyst's ideologies. While Levenson does recognize that theory-free psychoanalysis is impossible, he advises analysts to hold their belief systems lightly and to recognize that it is not patients' acceptance of these views that leads to change.

Levenson argues that the methods by which analysts arrive at their formulations are far more important than the theories that underlie these formulations. That is, the process of analytic exploration deserves more attention than its outcomes. We fall into confusing the results of historic analytic theorizing with truth, and we thereby lose track of the fact that truth is always discovered in context and anew. It is only the respect for the process of inquiry itself, and the particular interpersonal context in which it comes about, that can prevent analysts from unwittingly doing nothing more than persuading patients to believe what the analyst believes. Analytic benefit emerges from the subtleties of the way that the analyst is with the patient, independent of the rituals and interpretive conventions of any developmental theory or theory of therapeutic action.

Levenson, like Wolstein, postulates that the value of the analytic experience lies in the detailed examination of the unique, unfolding discourse between patient and analyst. As he has argued, the proper question for psychoanalysts is not what does this mean, but, what's going on around here? (Levenson, 1989). The examination of clinical relatedness itself has more value than the analysis of patients' verbal presentations. Perhaps the most significant of Levenson's insights is that the pattern or structure of the analytic relatedness is likely to be reflected in all the phenomena of the treatment and the patient's life: dreams, extra-transference relationships in the present, and the significant relationships of the past. The clarification of this repetitive patterning, and the mutual participation of analyst and patient in the enactments patterned in the same way, is the most likely way to facilitate change. The very recognition of this patterning in the here and now may create an awareness that opens the way for potentially new and expanded ways of being – in the transference-countertransference field and beyond.

Reference

Levenson, E. (1989). Whatever happened to the cat? Interpersonal perspectives on the self. *Contemporary Psychoanalysis*, 26: 537–553.

Psychoanalysis

Cure or persuasion? (1978)

Edgar A. Levenson

My most consistent interest has been the perplexing relationship between what the psychoanalyst *formulates* about what he does and what he *actually* does in therapy (Levenson, 1972). And, if the process of therapy does not follow straightforwardly, as I suspect it does not, from the theory, how does the therapist know how to do what he does, when he does it?

> When [psychoanalysis] becomes an institution, when it is applied to so-called "normal subjects," it utterly ceases to be a conception that can be justified or discussed on the basis of cases: it no longer cures, it persuades; it shapes for itself subjects who conform to its own interpretation of man. It has its converts and perhaps its rebels; it can no longer convince. Beyond the true and the false, it is a myth, and Freudianism thus degraded is no longer an interpretation, but a variant of the Oedipus Myth. (Lévi-Strauss, 1963, p. 196)

Certainly it must be agreed that therapists of different persuasions all get results they deem satisfactory. Are they doing different things, or the same thing in different ways? Are there different cures? If the treatment depends on the metapsychology of the therapist, is it not just an ideological conversion? Then, what one therapist calls "cure" is nothing more than a successful proselytization, i.e., the patient is now fine according to the therapist's scriptures.

This gap between practice and theory exists in any activity that can be performed and described. It is equally true of art, dance or skiing. In most activities, though, the theory is understood to be no more than a temporary manual of procedure on which to lean until the process becomes automatic. Theory, in these instances, may not help, but it does not hurt, either. As Frederick Crewes put it, "Freud wrote (in 'On Narcissism') that 'the whole structure' of psychoanalysis stands apart from metapsychological propositions, which 'can be replaced and discarded without damaging' that structure. Freud knew that high-level theory was an afterthought to the relatively direct inferences of the consulting room" (Crewes, 1976). But in psychoanalysis, the danger is that the theory becomes an ideological indoctrination *sui generis* and the patient becomes a disciple.[1]

Is there a psychoanalytic cure distinct from persuasion, a unique psychoanalytic process which is something more than, or better yet, other than, the therapist's molding the patient to his particular view of man? Is the therapist's vaunted system of meanings and interpretations merely a strategy to produce the change he deems necessary? Are we involved in persuading the patient to live better without letting him know we are doing so? There has been considerable confusion throughout the history of psychoanalysis about the relationship of its means to its ends, yet, how can one possibly do therapy without some system of beliefs, some structuring orientation, and simultaneously how can one avoid making psychoanalysis a technique of persuasion, of eliciting change in the direction selected by the therapist?

Whether the patient is seen as victim or wrong-doer doesn't much matter. Whether the therapy proceeds along principles of Martin Buber or Machiavelli doesn't much matter. Whether the therapist is nurturing or depriving doesn't much matter. Even if the therapist exercises the greatest possible restraint, he cannot fail to see the material according to his own categories of experience and belief. It is a neokantian imperative. There is no psychoanalytic neutrality be the patient upright or horizontal, be the therapist garrulous, or silent as the grave. If the therapist knows where the therapy should go and what the outcome should be, it is *pari passu* ideological and unavoidably persuasive. One may have a metapsychology that holds that the patient has been mystified by family experience. The goal of therapy becomes to lift the mystification, to let the patient see that he has learned not to "know what he knows he knows." But, I cannot see this as an emergent process. It is ideological conversion no matter what emphasis is put on transference. It is in the service of directed change; i.e., cure follows the patient's acceptance of the therapist's truth. Technique is the rhetoric of this process. Masud Khan (1969) has said facetiously that we obtain the patient's truth so that we can tell him the metatruth. Resistances to truth (proper meaning) are worked through, analyzed.

This often becomes a series of metacommunicational ploys much as Haley (1963) has described. Moreover, it has been claimed that manipulation of the patient, or the family milieu, is justifiable in terms of therapeutic ends. It is indeed this element of unabashed manipulation which makes some family therapy seem uncomfortably fascistic to the analytic therapist struggling to be neutral. The family therapist makes the decision about what constitutes relevant living and pushes the patient towards it. At the other end of the continuum, one finds those therapists who feel that such direction is a serious political contaminent to the therapy process; that the therapist must guard against even unconsciously coloring the therapy with what he thinks matters. And, of course, there has been a great deal of protest about the tendency of some therapists to politicize improvement, to define it in terms of their own value systems.

How then can a therapist maintain neurtrality? In this sense, what actually defines participant-observation? Is it possible to be an observer of a process in which one is a participant? Is there something operationally paradoxical in this concept? To restate the original question, is there a therapy independent of the therapist's beliefs? Is it possible to do therapy without subtly persuading the patient to believe what you believe? What it comes to is that unless the method of arriving at the truth is at least as relevant as the truth arrived at, then, I would claim, one is pressing ideology. In other words, *unless one examines the method at which one arrives at the truth and treats that as having an independent validity, separate from the truth arrived at, then one simply is indoctrinating the patient.*

This may be a quite benign operation as in the case of a patient who had quit her first therapist. The treatment was characterized by frequent serious suicidal threats. The therapist, existentially oriented, was accustomed to treasure his self-doubts as evidences of his authenticity. He was having a really difficult time dealing with this woman's threats, unsure whether he was treating her properly, and whether he was competent to contain her self-destructiveness. The patient quit therapy and went on to a second analyst, a Kleinian, who was able to stand rock-solid in the face of the patient's onslaught of suicidal threats. The patient kept threatening suicide, the analyst equally implacably, interpreted early deep dynamics. The patient recovered. Both the theoretical position of the therapist and his characterological unflappability (which may well have made the theoretical position initially sympathetic to him) combined to offer the patient the climate of conviction, and faith in change, that led to her improvement.

Surely there is some love affair between a theory and the characterological styles of both patient and therapist. The therapist in writing up this case report is very much impressed by the effectiveness of his deep direct interpretations. He feels quite sure that the truth of the interpretations triumphed. But one wonders, could it simply have been the different participation in the suicide threats? Both therapists believed they knew what mattered. Both had different conceptual frameworks. Both went about it differently. What is the explicit relationship then between their theory, their practice and the fact that an interpretation works or a patient gets better? What does that really say about the "truth" of what one tells the patient?

One must remember that an interpretation is not only a version of the truth or an understanding, but it is also a *participation*. There is no interpretation without participation. This was, after all, Harry Stack Sullivan's great contribution to operational psychoanalysis. Every participation is a metacommunication about the content of the interpretation. Every interpretation is a message, and a message about the message, as Bateson (1955) put it. But, additionally, *the metacommunication is an enactment of the content under discussion at the time of the interpretation.* This participation is as vital a part (but no more so) of the interpretation as the spoken message.

In short, two things occur in an interpretation. The therapist formulates a truth, and in the process of telling the truth, the therapist participates with the patient around the truth that he is telling the patient.

There is a much quoted case of Harry Stack Sullivan's (1954) wherein he sees in consultation a young man who has been rapidly sinking into a schizophrenic decompensation. On inquiry, Sullivan notes that the patient's parents are described as being quite perfect, beyond reproach; although they have obviously stifled every move towards independence the young man has attempted. Sullivan says to himself, "Oh yeah, it doesn't sound so good to me. It doesn't make sense. Maybe you've overlooked something." Does he say that to the patient? No way! What he does say is, "I have a vague feeling that some people might doubt the utility to you of the care with which your parents, and particularly your mother, saw to it that you didn't learn to dance." Then Sullivan reports, "I was delighted to see the schizophrenic young man give me a sharp look." This exchange, which I think is in language and style worthy of a Baker Street Regular, has been described as technique. Havens, for instance, has written a book about Sullivanian technique and describes this as a conscious decision on Sullivan's part to approach the young man obliquely so not to elicit excess anxiety (1973). In other words, it is a strategy of technique that is appropriate to Sullivan's concept of the schizophrenic dilemma.

But why such a strange crusty Edwardian indirection, so different than his first comment to himself? There are other ways of being oblique. Essentially Sullivan is making an interpretation of content. He is saying to the patient something of what he thinks the parents have done. But he is also making another interactional communication. He is saying to the patient: I am aware that you are aware that what you are saying about your parents' beneficence is sheer boloney. You do not believe it but you expect me to believe it because you think we are all hypocrites aligned against you. I'm not stupid enough to try to be friendly towards you because you would think I'm trying to butter you up, but I thought I would let you know that I'm in on the game. Now that sounds rather more like R. D. Laing and of course it may not be what Sullivan had in mind at all. But it seems to me it is equally as probable as the idea that he was simply trying to spare the patient anxiety by a studied indirection. In essence it is a very complex communication to the patient about the layering-upon-layering of awareness in his life, in Laingian paradox, about what he doesn't know he knows, about what he doesn't know he knows.

I'm claiming that in the psychoanalytic process there is an essential force for change that does not depend alone on the truth of the professed content, the metapsychology of the therapist. Nor does it depend on the therapist's participation with the patient, but rather on a dialectical interaction of both these elements. It feels "bigger than both of us" and gives both therapist and patient a feeling of being carried along by a current of change. It doesn't help the patient to arrive at what the therapist already knows although the therapist may well know what is wrong; nor is it exclusively a healing by encounter although both operations take place in therapy. What human function can mediate this paradox?

Like Oedipus confronting the Sphinx we are asked, what is inside us yet between us? What is intrinsically mine yet intrinsically yours? What is there given, yet made between us? The answer, of course, is language. And my claim is that *the psychoanalytic process, the healing process, is a language process which allows for, indeed requires, the synthesis of these two paradoxically oppositional aspects of therapy; the aspect of meaning and the aspect of experience*. Rather than calling it a language process, I think it might be more precise to refer to it as a semiotic process in the sense that it encompasses more than spoken language. It includes also sign systems, non-verbal cueings, distances, dispersions; the whole repertoire of interpersonal language.

Language obviates the hoary battle between inside and outside since language is, of course, both. There can be no communication without an intrapsychic language process and there can be no language without a recipient, even an imaginary recipient. Language also permits of an open resolution because the process is what can be called teleonomic, not teleological; i.e., there is no predetermined end goal although the process is goal-seeking; i.e., it is a process seeking out, by continuous exchange with the environment, optimum outcomes. That sounds like a mighty fine distinction, but it is the difference, as von Bertalanffy (1968) views it, between open system theory and its explanations of biological goal-seeking (the way an open system develops, say, in an evolutionary system or a genetic system), and the final cause explanations of religion.

Thus the patient develops in therapy a solution that is not his solution really and that is not the therapist's. Although it may or may not coincide with either one of their prior expectations, it is, in essence, a mutual solution, almost in the Gestaltist sense, a "best" configuration.

I am attempting a distinction between two kinds of interaction. One, that I'm going to describe in more detail, I shall label *discourse*; and the other, which I have described, admittedly pejoratively, as ideological indoctrination or persuasion. In an interesting book, Schwartz, an advertising executive, has defined the heart of persuasion (soft-selling) as what he calls "resonance" (1973). The main thrust of "resonance" is that the power of persuasion lies in reinforcing what people already believe. In other words, rather than coercing or cajoling the subject into believing something new, one picks up latent configurations and reinforces them. "The patient learns," as Lacan put it, "what the therapist knows, which is what the patient already knew." In essaying persuasion, one knows what one is after, what the *desiratum* is. In discourse, there is really no script at all. One proceeds quite differently. I think it is of relevance that in the earlier works on analysis, particularly the Wolf-Man, that when Freud and the patient were collaborators, explorers, not operating out of a formal structure, the therapeutic milieu seemed more spontaneous and possibly effective. It's once the Procrustean theory begins to come in, that the patient and the entire process is reified.

The perspective I'm going to describe has been the focus of the structural linguists; e.g., Barthes, Jakobson, Lévi-Strauss, De Saussure. It is of real significance that Freud can, and has been reinterpreted in structural linguistic terms.[2] Freud discovered structuralism before structuralism discovered Freud, since both Freud and the structuralists base their programs on the analysis of surface phenomena derived from underlying structures through the interposition of transformational rules. In Freud, distortions of dream work and ego defenses constitute the principal transformations. Barthes has said, "We are all trying with different methods, styles and perhaps even prejudices to get to the core of the linguistic pact so that every moment of discourse is both absolutely new and simultaneously absolutely understood" (1970). It is this dialectic between understanding and newness which I think makes for the core of the therapeutic discourse.

Note, for the moment, that I'm talking about the structure of discourse not the content *per se*. For instance, when a therapist listens to a dream, automatically he groups the data along two different lines. And, the two different groupings he uses are the same groupings used in ordinary speech, or which Lévi-Strauss uses to delineate cultural patterns. This is really a very difficult concept. First the therapist deals with what is true over time; with what is consistently meaningful and remains constant. Secondly, he deals with what is immediately and contextually true, what is, in Chomsky's phrase "structure-dependent", that is, the significance of any feature depends on its placement, its position in a structure; this is equally true of chess-pieces, words in a sentence, or tonal or expression changes: relevance *is* contextual location. One deals with what is consistently true and one deals with what is immediately relevant.

As a very simple clinical example: a patient has three dreams together. In one dream, he is dealing with his Chinese laundry man who is giving him trouble about getting his shirt back. In the second dream, he is in a restaurant and although he has a reservation he is being made to wait for his table. In the third dream, he is in a bank and he is trying to obtain a loan and he is being asked to pay some outrageous interest. The consistent theme running through all three dreams is the frustration at dealing with some functionary who is giving him a hard time. They express his difficulty with authority figures and his complex attitudes about frustration, disappointment and disapproval. But every analyst immediately hears something else in these dreams. He hears them as transferential dreams. Why? Because inscrutability, rigid unforgiving time and money arrangements are all three strongly characteristic of the psychoanalytic setting. Now this collation occurs automatically – but the two kinds of thinking processes that are involved are entirely different. The first axis is the axis of the story – the manifest content. One doesn't need to know the patient to hear the message: all three dreams are about someone who is having a lot of trouble with people who are supposed to be servicing him and are not. This first axis, the axis of what remains consistently true, is called the axis of *metaphor*. Metaphor meaning literally "to carry over." The second axis is considerably more obscure. One notes, in this case it doesn't come from the patient's associations at all. One doesn't need his association to laundry men and inscrutability. The associations could have come from him, but they are not his exclusive province. They are culturally shared by both therapist and patient; the meaning is determined by social *context*. We know the meaning because we know where it fits in the context of our mutual experience. This axis is called the axis of *metonymy*.

The two axes then are *metaphor* and *metonymy*.[3] Metonymy is a variant of another rather obscure word *synecdoche*, wherein a part is used to represent the whole. For instance, if one says "The Flag" one is using the flag in a synecdochic or a metonymic sense, which is to say one is not just talking about the cloth object, but about patriotism, country and all its implications. To restate, metaphor is always independent of time and space. It is always true. Metonymy is dependent on time and space. It is true only at the moment and in context.

Since, as Barthes (1970) has said, "Discourse is no more than one great sentence," this dialectical process is the same that goes on in discourse with the patient. It is an innate structure, given, not a matter of choice or preference, it is consistent with the structuralist ethos of trying to examine the way ordinary knowing occurs.

I am not attempting to present a way of doing psychoanalysis as a volitional inquiry; but rather attempting to examine what happens when therapy is done. We use language, much as we hum tunes, quite automatically. We do not know what we are going to say until we hear ourselves say it. I suggest that the process of therapy has much this same surface unselfconsciousness, and deeper intricate organization. In therapy, then, one listens to the material automatically along these two lines. One listens for the metaphor which remains constant all the way through. It is there that the therapist's metapsychology is validly appropriate because one can use a variety of imageries for the metaphor. As in Kafka's *Metamorphosis*, which can (and has been) given a Catholic interpretation, a Marxist interpretation, and a Freudian interpretation, the metaphor, the parable of metamorphosis, remains generally available. Metonymy, on the other hand, is the reservoir of the idiosyncratic and social experience of both the patient and the therapist. It is non-lineal, it doesn't tell a story and it doesn't increase understanding as much as it focuses temporality. It adds immediate relevance and quite often the real depth of affect.

Shifting from axis to axis is quite automatic. For instance, a dream in which a patient is struggling through mud to reach a perfect white house doesn't require much associative inquiry except to wonder why it emerges now. It's true of you as well as me, its message is evident in any patient who has the dream. It is a perfect metaphor. But if I dream of a bird with two heads and a yellow weskit one needs associations to make any sense of it. That is pure metonymy; without knowing the associations that dream is utterly without any kind of meaning. It is true also that this is not either/or; it is really two ways of looking at the same phenomenon. It is the Yin/Yang of symbolism. Schizophrenics, for instance, talk almost exclusively in the metonymic axis.[4] Much the same bipolarity can be discerned in literature and poetry.

I wish to emphasize that this is not another more complicated way of describing free association. Metonymy includes the associations of *both* therapist and patient, and covers both idiosyncratic associations and commonly shared cultural associations. Moreover, so-called free association implies an underlying truth which is going to be revealed by penetrating the defenses of the patient. Defenses scramble the truth, free association reveals the metatruth that is under the truth. In the structuralist perspective, the truth is never arrived at; rather it keeps changing as the process proceeds. One does not arrive at a static reductive truth, one simply deals with an emergent increasingly complex reality.

Let me use another dream as an example of this. This is a patient who dreams of eating his hat. I'll omit most of the details, but the point of the dream is that he is eating a hat which he describes as made of "polymer urethane." In the dream he thinks, "Funny, it doesn't taste like rubber." I've chosen this dream because it illustrates the different parameters of metaphor and metonymy and their overlap. There are many associative links: for example, he works for a chemical firm. There are even associations to chewing on his hat. But one need not know anything about this man to know that the metaphor for eating one's hat is some kind of an act of contrition, or losing a bet and paying off. Yet there are other metaphoric issues. Anybody old enough to remember the 30's, remembers it was a very common visual theme in the comic strips and movies. This man is visually oriented, he is old enough and quite witty. So one might think either the reference is somewhat anachronistic, it is not a term which people use much anymore, or perhaps it sets the time period of the relevant historical experience. But still more, examine the logic of the dream. He eats the hat, he tastes the hat and says to himself, "Funny, it doesn't taste like rubber." This is precisely the logic of the Mad Hatter's tea party when the Mad Hatter is trying to repair his watch with butter and Alice says to him, "You can't fix a watch with butter" and he dips it in the tea and comments wistfully, "But it was the very best butter."

Now those are not free associations nor are they even associations particularly relevant to the patient's private experience. But they are the kind of play I think most therapists do. Once one catches the zany Alice-in-Wonderland logic of the dream, the therapist suddenly realizes that he and the patient have been having exactly this kind of exchange; that it goes on all the time when one speaks with this man. He goes off in this funny kind of oblique, paralogical negativism. The metaphor of the dream then has meaning not just for the dream, but for its carrying over of its patterning into the transference, to the other areas of the patient's life. In other words, they are transforms of each other. The metaphor "carries over," which is what metaphors are meant to do. Moreover, once one has heard the metaphor and extended it with the metonymic associations the patient never seems the same again and one never hears what he is saying exactly the way one has heard it before. And what's more, one has absolutely no choice in the matter. Something has occurred in the therapy.

To recapitulate, metaphor is ideological, necessary but not sufficient; one must have some way of talking about things. Metonymy is totally contextual, either immediately personal or cultural, but it is equally necessary.[5]

If the therapist says I think you are afraid of having positive feelings towards your mother, the metaphor is clear enough. At least the coding of the message is clear. This occasion has a similarity to many others in your life. It is manifested by the same sequence of tentative offering of love, double-bind response, dissociation and then anger displaced to some other area. Transformationally, the same sequence occurs in the session, in your dream in which you were telling me about your husband, and now with me. But there is an additional message which can only be abstracted from the total semiotic context. Even a stenographic transcript won't give it to you. Let's suppose the therapist says all this in a kindly fashion, without accusation, with the firm conviction that he is not feeling rebuffed. This is a quite different communication than if he had arrived at the insight by first feeling distracted, bored, recognizing his own anger and then backtracking to realize that the patient had rejected his efforts to be responsive. It is the same metaphoric configuration of events but it is entered from a different direction and played out from a different starting point. Let's suppose as a third possibility that the therapist is really offended, doesn't contact his own anger but makes the same interpretation as a doctrinary gesture. The observer might see a different metacommunicational set. The therapist would be smiling kindly, but there would be a slightly icy tone to his voice: the patient would look vaguely uneasy. So, the full message requires not simply the knowledge of content, of the metaphor, of what the therapist is saying to the patient, but also the immediate contextual framework. The metaphor remains constant and moreover it is correct, even if the therapist says it out of pique, out of countertransference. The effect of the interpretation will differ, though, depending on *who* the therapist is in the transferential situation as he makes the interpretation. Bateson's "metacommunication" is, in the patient–therapist relationship, the metonymic clue to the posture of the therapist (therapist as good mother, bad mother, good father, sibling, etc.). Without this situation-dependent clue, the onlooker cannot know what the whole message is.

Interpretations of content without context degenerate into cliché or indoctrination. If one listens to a patient and simply interprets what one conceives to be the truth, an indoctrination results. Interpretations of context without content occur frequently in therapies concerned with authentic exchanges. I think that can be equally disastrous since, without being anchored into any system of explanations, one gets essentially spontaneous acting-out between the therapist and the patient not ever anchored in any structure of comprehension. If one believes in insight, or truth, one believes that the patient must hear the truth of what is being said to him about himself and that this truth must bypass or work through his defenses. Insight in the sense of sight into his own head is required. If one believes that immediacy is all, then one believes that it is the experience with the therapist which is healing. The words don't really matter as much as the quality and authenticity of the exchange. I think both these views are correct, but I think they are both actually incomplete. They are the Siamese twins of psychotherapy: inseparable and irreconcilable.

Viewed from this perspective, then, why do patients change in therapy? I'll put it the most condensed way first and then elaborate.[6] It is the transfer of data from the metonymic to the metaphoric axis which permits an open system to move and change. In other words, when what is contextual and immediate becomes transferred into permanent metaphor and integrated into the recurrent patterning of the patient, change has occurred. This has equivalence with what Piaget says in his concept of assimilation and accommodation. Assimilation and accommodation are really the same two axes of change. Changing the metaphor is changing the basic wiring of a person's self-system. I don't mean changing the imagery of the metaphor but its basic organization. One could use libido theory language or interpersonal language without changing the basic metaphor one bit. It would be really a matter of old wine in new bottles. For change to occur, material that emerges from the metonymic dimension must enlarge and change the metaphor. The metaphor is heard differently, as I stated about the dream with the hat. The therapist, hearing the meaning differently, changes his participation automatically. He *sees* the patient differently. His changed participation changes the metonymic axis which changes the metaphor which changes the metonymic axis; and so change hitches along, like an inch-worm.

Let me give an example of this: the patient is a man in his thirties. He is talking about his mother critically; complaining that she is an obsessive, humorless and self-righteous woman and how she irritated all the family by her dim devotion to large liberal causes. He sounds derisive and amused by her. This, one notes, was the tone of the family exchanges when she held forth, and he and his sister and father listened with amusement and contempt. Transferentially he is now talking to the therapist-as-father. The therapist is listening lightly, amused by his presentation. He is not blank, serious, appalled or even questioning the patient's derisiveness. The patient is saying how she collected reams of newspaper and magazine articles to bolster her continuous contentiousness. He says, "She collected in paper bags. For God's sake, *brown* paper bags," and he begins to laugh and laugh and laugh. The laughter gets out of control and begins to sound desperate. The therapist hears that "brown paper bag" is like the tip of an iceberg of metonymic meaning. The therapist sits solemnly now listening to the patient's increasing laughter. Suddenly, the patient begins to cry helplessly. Why? "I don't know. It just makes me feel terrible," he says. "Brown paper bags for Christ sake." The therapist says something like, "It sounds like you feel sorry for your mother." Which, by the way, may not be true, but it is essentially a sympathetic response to the man's crying. Now one could say about this, so what? The patient's feelings broke through his defenses of detached amusement. True, but it took a metonymic "brown paper bag" to do it. Not paper bag mind you, but *brown* paper bag; a condensation of "bag-lady," those derelict ladies in New York who haunt the garbage cans, carrying their belongings, and brown bagging, which was a phrase used for carrying one's lunch to school because one couldn't afford to buy it. If his mother had collected her data in a Bendel tote I don't think the tearfulness would have been precipitated. One notes that the metaphor was: I'm having a hard time getting away from my sticky, opinionated, castrating mother. The metonymic clue was brown paper bag. Note that the transference was at first, "You are daddy and we collude in making fun of mommy. We know what a pain she is." The therapist goes along. The metonymic clue, the subsequent change in affect, changes the therapist's participation. He now hears the message differently. He hears, "I am vulnerable to my feelings. I feel profoundly ashamed of, and very sorry for my poor mother who is the butt of our humor." If the therapist had laughed the material would have stopped, but hearing it differently changes his participation. He now fails to collude against the mother and says to the patient, in essence, it's all right, daddy is saying so, for you to feel sorry. It doesn't make you a sissy. See, I can show compassion and caring too. Thus the therapist's perception of the patient and his perception of himself interacting with the patient has changed. In other words, there has been a shift that doesn't have to be spelled out by either one of them. It has happened to both of them and I think one would be hard put to know exactly why "brown paper bag" precipitated the incident except that it is in some way a very specific, highly charged, metonymic cue. It doesn't have to do entirely with mechanisms of repression because one sees the same release of feeling and memory in Proust or Schachtel's work on childhood memory. What seemed to be very, very casual cues will set off a whole associative complex. This is more than just eliciting a dissociated affect or working through an anxiety-laden incident. The change persists because we have effected a change in our own metaphor and if we fail to do this we stay where we are. In a certain sense this isn't far from Harry Stack Sullivan's concept that the self-system is made up of reflected appraisals. The therapist is not in any sense a passive mirror for the reflected appraisals. It is much more of an active exchange between the two.

There are many other possible interpretations for that exchange with the therapist. There are many ways of getting at whatever the repressed affect was. Concern, shame, disgust, disappointment in the patient's mother could have been elicited in a variety of other ways. Therapists will automatically re-edit, correct, translate this vignette, perhaps seeing the right way to do it. But as far as I can see the therapist is never in the position of clearly knowing once and for all what anything means. This process of discourse as I have described it has one tremendous saving grace and that is as long as the process is proceeding the content is relatively unimportant. That is, starting with a variety of interpretations and metonymic cues we all arrive at some farther point along the developmental trajectories available to the patient. This is what von Bertalanffy (1968) called the principle of *equifinality*: open systems, no matter where one starts, if permitted to develop and move, will move along the trajectories available to them in terms of their own general programing. Therapists starting from different positions and with different interactions can elicit similar changes in the patient.

It is worth noting that affect is at the call of the metonyomic, not of the metaphoric. One usually trips the affect in the process of eliciting these iceberg-tip cueing exchanges. I think that is one of the limitations of metaphoric interpretation. It is very useful, inasmuch as it teaches the patient about the way he lives, but it doesn't have much emotional impact. It seems very likely that metonomy calls on a deeper more "analogic" process, with obscure but very pervasive connections. Metaphor is a more "digital" process, more lineal and intellectual. There are some interesting implications, playfully, at least, for the left brain (digital), right brain (analogic) – split brain theorists (Ornstein, 1972).

If we assume that psychoanalytic change depends on the specific truth and the relevance of the therapist's formulations or beliefs then I think we are on the razor's edge of ideology. Therapy technique then becomes technique for helping the patient arrive at insight which will be acceptance of the therapist's truth. What is this if not the art of persuasion? It may not be the truth arrived at as much as the manner of arriving at the truth which is the essence of therapy. This process of arriving at the truth has a structure which is linguistic in nature. With a therapist willing to listen in the most profound sense of the word, certain lines of inquiry will be followed. The therapist will identify patterns and configurations of events. He will pattern events, over time, across the present including his own interactions with the patient, in the transference, in dreams, in the history, in any other material the therapy encompasses. These patterns are endlessly repeated over and over again in larger and smaller events.[7] This constancy, this search for transformational sameness or metaphor is perhaps the most striking feature of human efforts to make sense of the world, from paleolithic scratchings on tusks, all the way up to the computer technology of the present. Heisenberg (1970) said that, "Patterns in our mind may reflect the internal structure of the world. The language of images, metaphors and similies is probably the only way to approach the one from wider regions." Simply put, the oldest of human endeavors is the search for constancy, for recurring patterns, for metaphor. But one also learns not to count on constancy if one wishes to survive. So one looks for shift, for changes, for novelty.

Metaphor, like myth, is a mnemonic device. It is a way for dealing with constancy. Metonymy is a device for dealing with change. So, the two faces of reality are constancy and change; or being and becoming; or truth and relevance; or code and context; or metaphor and metonymy.

I've been suggesting that analysis is in the mainstream of structuralist theory and its more popular offspring, in this country, general systems theory. It is a dialectical linguistic process and subject to the rules of that process. Human language and perhaps human survival is dependent on an integration of the search for timeless pattern and the detection of imminent change. It is this out-of-balanceness that makes for movement and keeps us neither as ephemeral as the May fly or as perfectly immutable as the shark. The same deceptively simple process motivates vast systems of biological and ecological change from genetics to evolution. Any analyst of any persuasion must follow this same dialogic process to be effective. Every institute has its idealogues and its hunch players, but, in the end, therapy really is the integration of both. There is a Sufi saying, "Don't learn, listen." It's not bad advice, but it's not easy either.

Notes

1 I would define ideology as a system of beliefs that explains the past, defines the present and predicts the future. Lévi-Strauss put it very nicely when he said that a myth is a "machine for the suppression of time." Ideologies, too, take out of life all the unpredictables, contingencies and tendency to novelty. Newtonian clockwork predictability reigns.
2 See Wilden (1972) for discussion of Lacan, Jakobson, Bateson and Lévi-Strauss.
3 Edmund Leach (1970) has an excellent exegesis of the different nomenclature used for these two axes in his little book, *Lévi-Strauss*.
4 See Wilden (1972) for discussion of schizophrenic metonomy.
5 There is some reason to believe there may be a neurological substratum for this description. Pribram (1971), Lurie and Jakobson have described two areas of the left brain, in the language cortex, each area of which roughly approximates one of these two different functions. And Jakobson has described a series of aphasias in which one of these functions is lost and not the other; for example, where the person knows the function of a coin but can't name it. Or can name it but doesn't know the function of it: the function of an object being essentially metonymic.
6 See Wilden (1972) for detailed presentation of open-systems change.
7 One can find the same patterns folded into any ten minutes of the therapy session. Many good therapists can take ten minutes of a session or a dream and explicate an entire experience with the patient from it.

References

Barthes, R. (1970). In R. Macksey & E. Donato (Eds), *The Structuralist Controversy*. Baltimore, MD: Johns Hopkins Press, p. 136.

Bateson, G. (1955). *The Message 'This is Play': Transactions of the Second Conference on Group Processes*. New York: J. Macy Foundation, pp. 145–242.

Bertalanffy, L. von. (1968). *General Systems Theory*. New York: Braziller.

Crewes, F. (1976). *New York Review of Books*, February 5, p. 34.

Haley, J. (1967). *Strategies of Psychotherapy*. New York: Grune & Stratton.

Havens, L. (1973). *Approaches to the Mind*. Boston, MA: Little, Brown & Co., p. 186.

Heisenberg, W. (1970). *Natural Law and The Structure of Matter*. London: Rebel Press, pp. 44–45.

Khan, M. (1969). *Introduction to Marion Milner: The Hands of The Living God*. New York: International Universities Press.

Leach, E. (1970). *Claude Lévi-Strauss*. New York: Viking Press.

Levenson, E. (1972). *The Fallacy of Understanding*. New York: Basic Books.

Levenson, E. (1976). A holographic model of psychoanalytic change. *Contemporary Psychoanalysis*, 12(1): 1–20.

Lévi-Strauss, C. (1963). *Structural Anthropology*. New York: Basic Books, p. 196.

Ornstein, R. (1972). *The Psychology of Consciousness*. New York: Viking Press.

Pribram, K. (1971). *Language of the Brain*, Englewood Cliffs, NJ: Prentice Hall.

Schwartz, T. (1973). *The Responsive Chord.* New York: Anchor Books.

Sullivan, H. S. (1954). *The Psychiatric Interview*, edited by H. S. Perry & M. I. Gawel. New York: W. W. Norton, pp. 21–22.

Wilden, A. (1972). *System and Structure – Essays in Communication and Exchange*. London: Tavistock, pp. 354–364.

Chapter 5

Early developmental roots of anxiety[1] (1980)

David E. Schecter

David Schecter addressed a different subject matter than most other interpersonal writers of his era. The spirit of his thinking is less radical, in the sense that he is more accepting than most of his interpersonal colleagues of the Freudian perspective of his day. Schecter was a developmentalist, and his concerns and his way of thinking are closely related to the mainstream of that era's psychoanalytical developmental thought. In Schecter's focus on anxiety, however, it is clear enough that Sullivan's work was a major influence on him.

Developmental theorists have been rare among interpersonal writers (although see the work of Ernest Schachtel [1959] for a major exception). Sullivan (e.g., 1953) did spell out a theory of development as well as a developmental way of understanding the origins of psychopathology, but most of those who were influenced by him, at least those who published, showed little interest in this element of Sullivan's thinking. Indeed, some writers representing other traditions have been critical of what they have felt was the paucity of developmental writing in interpersonal psychoanalysis (e.g., Frankel, 1998). In their view, Sullivan's developmental theorizing was simplistic and vague, and it inspired too little interest in these matters in those who came after him.

Among many of the most renowned interpersonal writers, there has been a sense that developmental theorizing does not contribute substantially to an understanding of clinical process, and even holds the potential to obscure it. Why? Because general developmental observations and theories, it has sometimes been thought, encourage grasping individuals as examples of broad developmental trends instead of encouraging the understanding of each person in a way that is itself unique. Since Erich Fromm and Clara Thompson, many interpersonal analysts have been wary of strong theory of any sort, rebelling against what they saw as the imposition on clinical understanding of the kind of stereotypical thinking that they felt was often characteristic of the then-hegemonic classical Freudian position. These interpersonal analysts criticized their Freudian colleagues for depicting patients in ways that varied too little from one person to another. (For example, everyone had Oedipal conflicts, castration anxiety, penis envy, sibling rivalry, etc.) Though it was recognized that it was impossible for analysts and therapists to avoid conceptual biases and predilections, efforts were made to make as few assumptions about psychodynamic development as possible.

Schecter's writing is the best of his era regarding interpersonal thinking about development. He is clearer and more specific about the developmental issues he discusses than Sullivan was, and so he presents Sullivan's ideas, and elaborates on them, in a way that is more experience-near and comprehensible than was Sullivan's own work. Schecter describes Sullivan's "self-system" (or personality structure) as a function of the lifelong pursuit of interpersonal security and the avoidance of anxiety. Anxiety, for both Sullivan and Schecter, results from the loss of love, or the threat of it; and the extent or degree of this anxiety is likely to determine the degree to which one can live a full life. Schecter tells us that the greater is one's anxiety, the more likely one is to retreat to rigid, self-protective, and limiting ways of engaging with others.

References

Frankel, J. (1998). Are interpersonal and relational analysts the same? *Contemporary Psychoanalysis*, 3: 485–500.

Schachtel, E. (1959). *Metamorphosis: On the Development of Affect, Perception, Attention and Memory*. New York: Basic Books.

Sullivan, H. S. (1953). *The Interpersonal Theory of Psychiatry*. New York: W. W. Norton.

Early developmental roots of anxiety[1] (1980)

David E. Schecter

Anxiety can be defined as the ego's reaction to or anticipation of danger (Freud, 1926). When the ego is overwhelmed or disorganized by the reaction to the danger situation we refer to the quality and quantity of anxiety as traumatic. By contrast, *signal anxiety* is a smaller dose of tension in anticipation of the danger situation, signifying "danger ahead." From a developmental point of view, it would make sense to refer to signal anxiety only when the ego has begun to develop the function of anticipation or foresight at around three to four months of age.

There are several areas that contribute to the individual's predisposition to anxiety: hereditary – constitutional factors, prenatal conditions, the birth experience itself, and early postnatal experience. However, at this point in our knowledge we know too little about the contribution of each of these areas to postulate anything beyond the general likelihood of their positive contribution to the predisposition and threshold to anxiety.

Benjamin (1963) notes a critical period in the infant at three to four weeks of age, when there is a rapid change in neurophysiologic maturation, especially in the area of "plugging in" of sensory modalities to central nervous system experience. There is EEG evidence of neurophysiologic change at this time. The mother must function as part of the infant's stimulus barrier, or protective shield, in order that he not be overwhelmed by the new connections of sensory experience from within and without. The variability in the adequacy of parenting in this critical period is probably another factor in the variability of predisposition to anxiety later on.

Benjamin describes a "fear of the strange" developing around four months of age. This includes strange sounds and sights while the infant is not able at the same time to see mother's face. This takes place at a stage in the infant's development when there is specific attention to facial expression. The infant can respond with negative affect – i.e. early anxiety – to even a frown on mother's face. Thus, mother's "forbidding gestures" (Sullivan, 1953) induce anxiety in the infant, a fact of great developmental and clinical importance. Other changes in mother's appearance – a new hat, hair curlers, sunglasses – will also induce "strange-mother" anxiety. My view on this form of anxiety is that it is due to the "perceptual dissonance" (Sandler, 1977) between the familiar and strange factors in mother who is thus *both* familiar and strange (Schecter, 1974). There is in these phenomena a combination of both stranger and separation anxiety.

Stranger anxiety

Let us now turn to the dramatic phenomenon of *infantile stranger anxiety* proper, which can begin between five and eight months and which has been called the "eight-month anxiety" by Spitz (1950). Both Spitz and Freud (1926) explained the phenomenon of stranger anxiety as being based on the experience of mother's absence – the presentation of the strange face gestalt when the familiar mother gestalt is expected. (We use the term "mother" to stand for "parenting one" since we now know that separation anxiety from father can be equally significant.)

Phenomenologically, the infant's reaction to the stranger's face runs the range of behaviors from no apparent reaction, to sobering of the infant's face, expressions of mild apprehension, or wide-eyed staring, a freezing (inhibition) of motor and expressive behavior, aversion of visual gaze, clinging, quivering of lips to outright screaming and panic behavior. Indelibly imprinted on my memory is a young toddler who froze upon the appearance of strangers, in an uncomfortable crouched position, for 20 minutes before he began to loosen up and become mobile.

Benjamin, in contrast to Freud and Spitz, described some intriguing differences between separation anxiety and stranger anxiety. Though stranger and separation anxiety are related dynamically and correlate positively, statistically there are babies who demonstrate high separation anxiety and low stranger anxiety as well as vice versa. Stranger anxiety can occur whether or not mother is present, whereas separation anxiety occurs in the absence of mother whether or not anyone else is present. Also, the average and peak times of onset are different for each type of anxiety, occurring somewhat earlier for stranger anxiety. We assume with Benjamin that stranger anxiety, though sharing a common root with separation anxiety – fear of object loss – has in addition a *relatively independent source of anxiety based on the infant's fear of the strange*, which is observable even earlier than the anxious response to the stranger per se. For example, the three-to-four month old may become apprehensive with strange objects or sounds or when he is handled in an unfamiliar manner.

An apprehensive response may also be aroused in the young infant by altering an anticipated gestalt pattern through the addition of unfamiliar elements or by the omission of some apparently crucial familiar element. For example, we have noted that for some infants the visual presentation of a smiling, nodding adult face without the accustomed accompanying vocalizations may evoke an anxious expression. When vocalizations are added the infants relax and smile, giving the impression of closure of the anticipated familiar gestalt. In a similar vein, humming or a falsetto voice excluding the visual presentation of the adult face could produce fearful reactions (Benjamin, 1963).[2]

The expression around the adult's eyes seems to be of particular importance to the infant, and this fits in with Wolff's (1963) observation of the infant's tendency to search out the eye area and make eye-to-eye contact before smiling at the face presentation. All these signs of increasing perceptual discrimination of alterations of facial gestalt, including the discrimination of adult negative affect expressions, predate and constitute the precursors to the appearance of infantile stranger anxiety in Benjamin's sense.[3]

From observation one can describe a range of experience in the infant from "strange" to "novel" to "familiar." If the infant is secure on mother's knee he may react to the strange toy as if it were merely novel and proceed to explore it. For this to happen mother is sometimes required to give the new toy her "magic blessing" by handling it, thus transforming the strange-forbidden into the novel-exciting in the sense that the child now handles the toy with curiosity. In a parallel way in psychoanalytic therapy the analyst through his mediation helps transform a frightening, strange area of experience into one that is now open to exploration with the curiosity characteristic of pursuit of the novel.

Anxiety by contagion

It now becomes possible to understand the relationship between stranger anxiety and *that form of anxiety that is induced in the infant by the anxiety of the mothering one*. Sullivan (1953) refers to the as-yet unknown mechanism which mediates the interpersonal induction of anxiety as "empathic linkage"; Escalona (1953) refers to the process with the felicitous word, "contagion." We are all familiar with the contagion of affects from clinical work and observation of normal families. It is our speculation that when mother is anxious or distressed she appears as *both familiar and strange to her infant*. We know that by six to seven months the infant has clearly come to discriminate mother (or father) from less familiar persons. We see this from the great eagerness of his smiling response to her at this time as well as his beginning separation protest. We assume that he has a positively endowed memory of a gestalt experience of mother, including her facial and vocal physiognomy, as well as the quality of her touch and probably body scent. We would speculate that the child through repeated pleasurable experiences anticipates seeing, hearing, and feeling the familiar "good mother" and is shocked, frightened and baffled when the strange elements of her anxiety – facial frown, tight lips, and vocal alterations – are all presented simultaneously with her recognizably familiar elements. Dan Stern's (1971) work on the "ballet" of eye-to-eye contact and aversion suggests a further mechanism by which anxiety is induced in the infant by the mothering one. I would speculate that observation would reveal a distinct change in the interpersonal rhythm and "choreography" in the area of eye-to-eye contact when mother is anxious. The loss of smooth, familiar visual rhythm would disrupt the euphoric quality of the relationship and contribute to the induction of anxiety.

Separation anxiety – the basic human anxiety

Separation anxiety is the basic anxiety of infancy and remains a fundamental anxiety throughout life. In childhood and adulthood separation anxiety becomes transformed into a fear of abandonment, an almost universal fear which is available to psychoanalytic inquiry. Whereas in the early months the infant may react with negative affect upon separation from any caretaker, by seven or eight months the anxiety reaction is specific to the parent to whom the baby is most significantly attached. A not uncommon finding is strong protest with crying and distress when mother leaves the room even if the child is left in the presence of a familiar person. A young mother I see in therapy describes a heart-rending daily departure for work to the accompaniment of the wailing of her infant, left in the care of a familiar babysitter. Through the use of empathic observation the observer notes the protest, rage, and fear expressed by the baby in the separation reaction. There is peak separation anxiety around eleven to twelve months and then again at eighteen months, lasting, in lessening degree, often until age three years, when object constancy becomes more consolidated (Mahler, Pine & Bergman et al., 1975).

Bowlby (1973) describes three important stages in the separation reaction. First there is angry, anxious *protest* in which the infant seems to be demanding the return of the disappearing mother.[4] (Interestingly, there is no separation anxiety expressed when the baby takes the initiative to leave mother. However, there is frequent checking back visually to assure him that mother is still available.) A second stage of the separation reaction, if separation is prolonged, is described by Bowlby as *despair*. The infant looks despondent, in grief and mourning, and may even regress in his ego functioning, e.g., a child who has been toilet trained may regress to wetting himself during this stage.[5] The third stage of a prolonged separation is described as *detachment*. The child is no longer manifestly anxious, angry, or despondent during this phase; however, he may actually avert his gaze from mother upon their reunion. Theoretically, the detachment defenses are crucial in understanding the development of *characterologic detachment*, which is seen not only in the schizoid character but as part of the defensive structure of a patient who may bear any diagnostic label (Schecter, 1978). Detachment is a protective defense against the painful effects of separation and also serves to withdraw the child or patient from a state of attachment to a significant figure.

The intensity of attachment, and of separation anxiety, is heightened by illness, fatigue, fear, a strange environment, a recent separation, or following a period of increased social stimulation, for example by a doting relative.

Although Freud did not use the concept of separation anxiety as the fundamental human anxiety, he did state (1926) that missing someone who is loved is the key to the understanding of anxiety. We wholeheartedly agree with this latter position. A later development in the fear of object loss (separation anxiety) is the anxiety that is triggered by the *loss of love*. This form of anxiety is so important that it will be considered separately from separation anxiety even though it can be regarded as part of a continuum of the separation reaction.

Aggressive feelings toward the beloved object-person serve to increase separation anxiety. Since angry, aggressive feelings are evoked upon separation, the makings of a vicious circle exist: separation–aggression–fear of abandonment–further anger, and so on. We have to consider the fact that angry, aggressive feelings can be projected onto the parent, after which a cycle of persecutory anxiety is set up. The child comes to feel abandoned because he feels hated by mother. We are now in a situation of "bad-mother" and "bad-me," a situation that can only be terminated upon the tender reunion of parent and child. However, probably starting from the second half of the first year, the infant begins to symbolize a "bad-mother" and a "bad-me" which become internalized objects or personifications characterized by structural constancy. This phase represents the end of the "Garden of Eden" bliss between mother and child. Concurrently, differentiation of self and mother proceeds apace during the individuation–separation phase (Mahler et al., 1975). Here we have the beginning splits of self as subject and object and, as object, the child begins to feel observed, evaluated and potentially ashamed. The experience of shame includes the anticipation of or reaction to the danger situation in which the child is failing a standard or ideal set up for him – a standard that will soon be internalized. Since shame involves the reaction to or anticipation of a danger situation, we can refer to the affect as *shame anxiety*, which is often accompanied by the dread of abandonment. Shame anxiety is so fundamental that it can affect *how* the self evolves – under constant scrutiny from within or without as against under relatively spontaneous conditions.

By the same token, when the child feels he has transgressed a forbidden boundary, he feels "bad" and experiences *guilt anxiety*. This occurs after the taboo area has been internalized by the child. Later on both of these forms of anxiety can be classified as *superego anxieties*. Both anxieties can be accompanied by a plummeting self-esteem that in itself can evoke severe anxiety.

It must be remembered that anxiety is highly contagious, so that if mother suffers high separation anxiety, she will induce anxiety in the infant around separation situations. This phenomenon is observable early in life and comes to the fore when the child separates regularly as in going to nursery school, kindergarten, etc.

There are also more subtle forms of separation anxiety. One example is found in the underresponsive mother who may be quite depressed or detached so that the infant experiences periodic breaks in the "refueling dialogue" (Sandler, 1977) that normally goes on in the healthy parent–child relationship. This form of deprivation surfaces frequently in analysis when the patient feels a lack of empathic responsiveness by the analyst.

In the older child – from age four years onwards – there develops the ultimate separation anxiety, namely, the fear of death. Once the child cognitively evolves the concept of eternity, i.e., "forever," he becomes prone to thoughts and fears about the death of those who are close to him as well as the notion of his own mortality. Life is never again the same for him once he is captured by the sense of its finitude. Developmentally this marks the beginning of what has been referred to as existential anxiety.

Anxiety through loss of love and security

In a healthy mother–child relationship there is a two-way flow of loving behaviors, a musical conversation, smiling faces, various forms of touch, cuddling, cooing, soothing, etc. These loving behaviors are available when the child needs them and this need is empathically sensed by the parent. However, if the parent is depressed or disapproving, the loving behaviors will be withheld or even replaced by a scolding voice or a frowning face. This experience of loss of love signals a danger situation for the child and hence he experiences anxiety. He cannot then count on a loving "refueling dialogue" and he symbolizes this situation as bad – "bad-me" and "bad-mother." Moreover, since the loving and soothing behaviors act as a kind of antianxiety protection, their withdrawal renders the infant vulnerable to experiencing anxiety from whatever source without the loving protective barrier:

> Love to the infant means the security of empathic responsiveness to his needs by the mothering one.[6]

Sullivan (1953) puts it this way: "The tension called out in the mothering one by the manifest needs of the infant we call *tenderness* and a generic group of tensions in the infant, the relief of which requires cooperation by the person who acts in the mothering role, can be called *need for tenderness.*" Winnicott (1965) uses the term "holding" to denote the total "environment provision" offered by the mothering one. "The infant exists only because of maternal care, together with which it forms a unit" (cf. Mahler's 1975 symbiotic unit). Winnicott goes on to describe how the infant develops means for doing without actual care. "This is accomplished through the accumulation of memories of care ... with the development of confidence in the environment" (cf. Erikson's 1950 basic trust). Further, Winnicott's holding environment has as its main function "the reduction to a minimum of impingements to which the infant must react with resultant annihilation of personal being" (p. 47). Winnicott sees anxiety in early infancy as related to the threat of annihilation, by which he means the cessation of the "continuity of being" caused by "reactions" forced by impingements on the infant. I agree with Winnicott's view that it is through *identification* of herself with her infant that the mother knows "what the infant feels like and so is able to provide almost exactly what the infant needs in the way of holding and in the provision of an environment generally."

I quote these authors in part to show that love, security and holding have very specific meaning to the infant and the loss of love can signal a major calamity for the infant. We can only mention here the security function of transitional objects (Winnicott, 1958) in maintaining security without the direct participation of the mothering one.

The anxiety gradient and the self-system of H. S. Sullivan

Sullivan (1953) describes learning by the "anxiety gradient" as learning to discriminate increasing from diminishing anxiety, with alteration of activity in the direction of the latter. I would suggest that one of the major ways that the child experiences loss-of-love anxiety is through the disapproval patterns of the parents – which is not to suggest that this is pathologic. To quote Sullivan: "This is the great way of learning in infancy and later in childhood by the grading of anxieties so that the infant learns to chart his course by mild forbidding gestures or by mild states of worry, concern or disapproval mixed with some degree of anxiety on the part of the mothering one. The infant plays ... the old game of getting hotter or colder, in charting a selection of behavioral units which are not attended by an increase in anxiety." Sullivan reminds us that anxiety is responsible in a basic sense for a great deal of what comes to the psychiatrist for attention. Although anxiety is not the motor of interpersonal relationships, "it more or less directs the course of their development."

Severe anxiety, unlike the anxiety gradient, is like a blow on the head. It causes confusion and little opportunity for recall or learning.

It is connected with uncanny feeling and the beginning personification of not-me which is experienced in nightmares or in the waking life of someone suffering from a severe schizophrenic episode. To quote Sullivan: "The *not-me* is a gradually evolving personification of an always relatively primitive character that is organized in unusually simple signs in the parataxic mode of experience and made up of poorly grasped aspects of living which will presently be regarded as 'dreadful' and which will still later be differentiated into incidents which are attended by awe, horror, loathing or dread." These are the uncanny *not-me* affects usually associated with intense forbidding gestures on the part of the mothering one.

By contrast, "*good-me* is the beginning personification which organizes experience in which satisfactions have been enhanced by rewarding increments of tenderness, which come to the infant because the mothering one is pleased with the way things are going." "Good-me" is the ordinary topic of discussion about "I." It should be noted that the pursuit of the good-me is not only in the service of adaptation but also of conformity. In this sense we can see how this pursuit in later infancy and later life can lead toward the structuring of the "false self" (Winnicott, 1965), a course that may be utterly required for the psychological survival of the child.

Bad-me is the beginning personification which organizes experience in which increasing degrees of anxiety are associated with behavior involving the mothering one. "Bad-me is based on the increasing gradient of anxiety and that in turn is dependent on the observation, if misinterpretation, of the infant's behavior by someone who can induce anxiety."

The dynamism of the *self-system* is purely a product of interpersonal experience arising from the general pursuit of satisfaction. The self-system is an antianxiety system – not the whole self – which functions as a compass to steer the infant away from experiences of increasing anxiety and toward maximum euphoria. The pursuit of "good-me" is maintained just as the moving away from "bad-me" is simultaneously pursued. Sullivan refers to the self-system as coming into being in late infancy as an organization of experience which will ultimately be "of nothing less than stupendous importance in the personality." The self-system gives the infant a structure through which it is possible to live with the socializing parenting person. Sullivan goes on to say, "The self-system is thus an organization of educative experience called into being by the necessity to avoid or minimize anxiety" (p. 165). This in turn frees the infant to pursue his needs for satisfaction since anxiety is a vector that pulls 180 degrees in the opposite direction from the pursuit of satisfactions. In fact, Sullivan implies that the self-system, with all its unfortunate consequences, comes into being "and can be said to have as its goal the securing of necessary satisfaction without incurring much anxiety." The self-system – in some degree parallel to Freud's ego defenses – is at the same time the principal obstacle to favorable change in the personality. Sullivan points out that there can be inculcated in the growing personification of "bad-me" and "not-me" "disastrous distortions" which will manifest themselves in the subsequent development of personality and with which the project of therapy will have to come to grips.

The self-system cannot necessarily contain a continuous flooding of anxiety that may be coming from the parenting ones. In other words there are limits to the success of the self-system's task of avoiding anxiety. With the failure of containment of anxiety by the self-system, mechanisms of defense are called forth to protect the infant from the raw experience of continuing anxiety. Two rather extreme defenses that Sullivan refers to are apathy and somnolent detachment, defenses for which the infant has to pay a high price, including severe constriction of his personality growth. If these defenses have to be in service frequently the infant will develop what I have called character detachment (Schecter, 1978), the extreme of which would be schizoid detachment.

Discussion

We can look at each form of infantile anxiety as constituting the beginning of a "development line" (cf. A. Freud, 1965) that runs through childhood into adulthood. By this we do not have in mind a simplistic, one-to-one, causal relationship between anxiety experience in infancy and that of childhood and adulthood. Important structuralization of the ego and its defensive system occurs not only in infancy but in later developmental stages as well. These structures can modify or heal, in varying degree, the quality and quantity of anxiety experienced in infancy. Nevertheless the particular quality of, let us say, separation anxiety in infancy acts as an *organizer* for qualitatively similar anxieties in later developmental stages. Psychoanalytic reconstruction, as shaky an undertaking as it sometimes may be, reveals to us that significant separation or "loss of love" anxieties have developmental consequences.

Our clinical training alerts us to the importance of detailed history-taking in the psychoanalytic inquiry. It is not uncommon, for example, for an adult suffering specifically from fear of abandonment to have a significant history of marked separation reactions or "loss-of-love" anxiety. I have in mind a 25-year-old architect whom I have seen periodically since age seven and who suffered severely from separation anxiety that consciously baffled him. His early hospitalizations for repeated surgery involved anxieties of separation, of strangeness and strangers, and of body mutilation. Nevertheless, it is the separation aspect of his anxieties that can be followed like a red thread throughout his childhood, adolescence and early adulthood. This developmental line, separation anxiety, has in part yielded to reconstruction in his analytic experience; it was a key without which his adult dread of abandonment could never have been understood. Similarly, his self-puzzling anxious reactions to strange new situations have been understood and largely worked through via the analysis of stranger and mutilation anxieties which also came to be organized early in life as separate developmental lines.

I would like to focus attention on the most neglected of developmental lines of anxiety, namely, that of stranger and strangeness anxiety. In a remarkably illuminating paper, Sandler (1977) describes a piece of psychoanalytic therapy with an adult woman related to the patient's fear of metabolizing anything new and strange in her self- and object-representations. Sandler emphasizes that the source of dissonance in self-image can be internal just as the source of dissonance (strangeness) can be external for object-representations. She states her hypothesis in the following way: "The child constantly and automatically also scans and has a dialogue with his own self to get refueling and affirmation through the perception of cues that his self is his old familiar self, that it is no stranger to him…." The child may attempt to protect himself from danger in a strange situation "through action in which he alters himself which makes his self-representation more affirming, more reassuring." He may grossly distort his attitudes and behavior in order to avoid the dissonance and panic which accompanies simply being himself, by creating varieties of "false self." This is often done by idealization of the self as well as the object. To quote Sandler: "Mrs. B's [reaction] to my comments was a kind of almost reflex-like panic which forced her to deny any internal emotional stress and cling automatically to some concrete island of security, based on denial and negation and the preservation of me as the 'perfect' object."

What was denied was any perception of the new and unfamiliar in the self, in the therapist, and in their relationship.[7] "Interpretations, however correct, aroused the danger that she might be faced with a strange and unfamiliar part of herself and of the object...." She made strenuous efforts to dissociate strange, threatening and unwanted thoughts, wishes and feelings from herself. With ongoing therapy the patient seemed to increasingly tolerate the dissonance of the strange.

When we think of Sandler's patient it becomes clear that much of what we call "resistance" in psychoanalytic therapy has to do with anxiety connected with the conscious discovery of strange, new, ego-alien aspects of the self, of significant object-persons and of their relationships. In this sense Sandler's description of her patient's fear of dissonance is the rule (resistance) rather than the exception in clinical psychoanalysis. A simple clinical illustration of the analysis of that which feels foreign is the analysis of aggressive and sadistic character tendencies in a person whose ideal self-image is one of gentleness and tenderness. Resistance often functions in the service of maintaining a sense of self-constancy and continuity, warding off a sense of discontinuity in one's identity.

The therapist's function in meeting such resistance parallels that of the mothering one of the child in some important ways. The therapist's gentle repetitions of the new and strange elements function as the "magic blessing" described earlier by the mother; the strange material is converted into the "merely" novel which can now potentially be faced with the zest of curiosity. The analyst represents the steady holding environment watching over the patient's struggle to look, together with the therapist, at the strange and ego-alien thoughts, wishes and feelings which gradually can be accepted as part of the self-representation.

Similarly, new elements can be looked at in the object-person who had often been idealized into perfection, and this includes transference figures. To see the self and other in their "suchness," e.g., without idealization, is an immensely liberating experience. One can now risk spontaneity and openness to the world because there is less stake in desperately maintaining an embedded familiar representation of self and other.

Change in therapy, as in life, involves the induction of anxiety that has to be endured in order for healthy development to proceed. The capacity to endure such anxiety is, of course, another variable that differs from person to person. The analyst offers a carefully titrated presentation of nonfamiliar aspects of the self so that the patient is not overwhelmed by the anxiety that is a necessary experience when nonfamiliar aspects of the self have to be metabolized.[8]

Summary

Our purpose has been to consider the early developmental situations that constitute a danger and hence an anxiety for the infantile ego. We have taken as our definition of anxiety "the ego's reaction to or anticipation of danger." Several "developmental lines" of anxiety are described in some detail: strangeness and stranger anxiety, anxiety by contagion, separation anxiety, and anxiety through loss of love or security. We have only mentioned the mutilation or castration anxieties, the fear of death, and the superego anxieties in the form of shame and guilt. From our study of anxiety we conclude that most types of early anxiety derive from some form of *disruption of a good "external" interpersonal relationship as well as of a good internal object relationship*.

The organization of experience by the anxiety gradient and the self-system (antianxiety system) is discussed as H. S. Sullivan's contribution to the understanding of the interpersonal and intrapsychic role of anxiety in infancy. The concept of "developmental line of anxiety" is presented and seen as an organizer of specific forms of anxiety throughout the life cycle. The developmental line of stranger anxiety is discussed as an example of the application of developmental line anxiety to psychoanalytic theory and treatment.

Notes

1 This paper was first given at the American Academy of Psychoanalysis on November 30, 1979. Until his death on July 12, 1980, Dr. Schecter was Training and Supervising Analyst at the William Alanson White Institute and Associate Clinical Professor at the Albert Einstein College of Medicine.
2 We have also noted that to both the face mask and the stranger the infant may be alternately sober, then apprehensive, smiling, and apprehensive once more. He may respond with apprehension to a variety of alterations of the facial gestalt such as placing pads over the eyes, the forbidding expression of a frown with vertical (as against horizontal) forehead creasing (Spitz, 1965) or with changes in mother's appearance.
3 Wells Goodrich (personal communication) has suggested that there may be a value in considering two types of stranger anxiety. One would be based on the stranger reaction before object constancy has been achieved. The second would occur after the achievement of object constancy, which would afford a more secure base from which the stranger is experienced.

4 This is an example of the adaptational value of the expression of anxiety.
5 It needs to be emphasized that prolonged separation or loss of love leads to anaclitic depression (Spitz, 1946).
6 When this empathic responsiveness becomes internalized by the child, we have the beginnings of that structure we call the Loving Superego (Schafer, 1960; Schecter, 1979). Paul Lippmann (personal communication) points out that the infant's *active* loving of the parenting one tends to be neglected in discussions of the infant's need for love *from* the parent.
7 By their very nature, transference and countertransference phenomena serve to make the therapeutic interactions feel familiar. The stranger analyst becomes the familiar parent. To the extent that transference expectations do not match the experience in the analysis, the latter comes to feel unfamiliar or even strange. The discrepancies of experience become material for analysis and clarify the nature of the transference.
8 As a footnote to the concept of stranger anxiety we should make note of the widespread fear of the stranger and nonfamiliar as seen in racism and xenophobia in general. However, the Bible commands love for the stranger – not only for the neighbor – and explains this command by saying, "For you were sojourners in the land of Egypt" (Deut. 10:19) (Fromm, 1966).

References

Benjamin, J. (1963). *Further Comments on Some Developmental Aspects of Anxiety, in Counterpoint, New York*. New York: New York University Press.

Bowlby, J. (1973). *Attachment and Loss*, Volume 2. *Separation*. New York: Basic Books.

Erikson, E. (1950). *Childhood and Society*. New York: W. W. Norton.

Escalona, S. (1953). Emotional development in the first year of life. In M. Senn (Ed.), *Problems of Infancy and Childhood*. New York: Josiah Macy Jr. Foundation.

Freud, A. (1965). *Normality and Pathology of Childhood*. New York: International Universities Press.

Freud, S. (1926). *Inhibitions, Symptoms and Anxiety*, Standard Edition 20. London: Hogarth Press.

Fromm, E. (1966). *Ye Shall Be as Gods*. New York: Holt, Rinehart and Winston, p. 83.

Mahler, M., Pine, F. & Bergman, A. (1975). *The Psychological Birth of the Infant*. New York: Basic Books.

Sandler, A. M. (1977). Beyond eight month anxiety. *International Journal of Psycho-Analysis*, 58: 195–207.

Schafer, R. (1960). The loving and beloved superego. *Psychoanalytic Study of the Child*, 15: 168–188.

Schecter, D. (1978). Attachment, detachment, and psychoanalytic therapy. In E. Witenberg (Ed.), *Interpersonal Psychoanalysis*. New York: Gardner Press.

Schecter, D. (1979). The loving and persecuting superego. *Contemporary Psychoanalysis*, 15: 361–379.

Spitz, R. (1946). Anaclitic depression. *Psychoanalytic Study of the Child*, 2: 313–342.

Spitz, R. A. (1950). Anxiety in infancy: A study of its manifestation in the first year of life. *International Journal of Psycho-Analysis*, 31: 138–143.

Spitz, R. A. (1965). *The First Year of Life*. New York: International Universities Press.

Stern, D. (1971). A microanalysis of mother–infant interaction, *Journal of the American Academy of Child Psychiatry*, 10: 501–518.

Sullivan, H. S. (1953). *The Interpersonal Theory of Psychiatry*. New York: W. W. Norton.

Winnicott, D. (1958). Transitional objects and transitional phenomena. In *Collected Papers*. London: Tavistock.

Winnicott, D. (1965). Parent–infant relationship. In *The Maturational Processes and Facilitating Environment*. New York: International Universities Press.

Chapter 6

Interpersonal processes, cognition, and the analysis of character (1980)

Joseph Barnett

Joseph Barnett wrote at a time when analysts identified as interpersonal were still trying to clarify the distinctions between their own thinking and the hegemonic classical Freudian tradition in the United States. Although Barnett used his own term, "post-Freudian," to identify his perspective, it is unmistakable that his work, with its existential, pragmatic, and phenomenological cast, developed within the interpersonal tradition. Intentionally distinguishing his thinking from the mainstream psychoanalysis of his day, Barnett emphasized what he called "experiential knowing," by which he intended to refer to the meaning that each individual gives to lived experience. Unconscious motivation grows not from drive and defense, as it did in the ego psychology of that time, but is instead the result of the way people internalize their experience of interpersonal interaction from the first moments of life. Barnett contrasted this relative priority of the exogenous over the Freudian emphasis, in that era, on endogenous origins of experience. In the Freudian frame of reference, sex and aggression, and the sanctions against these, led to a constellation of unconscious fantasy life that defined each person's motivational system and their view of the world of others. The Freudian unconscious of that time was largely composed of drive states, while Barnett's "post-Freudian" unconscious consisted of the meaning people give to lived experience with others.

To describe the process by which people give meaning to experience, Barnett used a term that was, in this context, unique to him – "cognition." Barnett used the term to refer to the conscious and unconscious processing of present-day lived experience on the basis of internalizations of previous experience. The regularities in the way in which the individual processes current experience of themselves and their worlds – cognition as analogous to a worldview – defines each person's essential personality or character. Character, therefore, consists of the particular ways in which the individual's cognitive organization transforms his encounter with the world into subjective, emotional meaning.

Extrapolating from Sullivan's conception of the "self-system," Barnett equated character with self. For Barnett, who shared Sullivan's optimism about the possibilities for change, self or character is fluid and subject to modification in the context of new life experience. The potential value of psychoanalysis is the opportunity it affords to integrate new external experiences into an existing self or character structure.

Addressing the scholarly controversies of his day, Barnett took issue with the positions of both Heinz Kohut and Otto Kernberg that neurotic psychopathology could and should be distinguished from what they called pathology of the self. In different ways, Kohut and Kernberg both argued that what they diagnosed as narcissistic character, in contrast to neurotic character, reflected an underdeveloped self based on deficient caretaking. They argued that different kinds of psychoanalysis, based on different developmental lines, are required for neurotic and narcissistic character structure. In contrast, Barnett believed that, because all self or character is shaped by internalized experience, in the same way by everyone (even if the nature of what is experienced is different), it is unnecessary and misleading to posit two distinct diagnostic categories or developmental lines. Barnett's position is consistent with the thinking of his interpersonal forbears, who believed that, because all of us are shaped by experience with others and are therefore more human than otherwise, clinicians could work with even psychotic people in the same basic way.

Interpersonal processes, cognition, and the analysis of character (1980)

Joseph Barnett

Post-Freudian psychoanalysis implied a shift from a psychology of drives in which meaning was seen as appetitive and motivations were defined as functions of drives, to a psychology of self and character in which meaning is experiential and both motives and intentionality derive from meaning and the organization of experience. In previous communications, I argued that this shift implicated cognition, conceived as experiential knowing, as the core phenomenon of mental life rather than as an epiphenomenal derivative of drives as envisioned by classical theory. This paper will outline my views on character and self as derivatives of cognition, which I view as the central organizing factor in mental life. In essence, the notion of character or personality represents the general theory of cognition and its organization, while the self can be seen as a special instance of cognitive organization involving the transformation of experience into subjective meaning.

The post-Freudian revisionists of the 1940s, in my opinion, were re-confronting an early problem in psychoanalytic theory development. While this problem had been addressed by others before them and is still being addressed by current revisionists, the post-Freudians offered a more radical solution than had many others who preceded them or who followed them. Freud, in his early work, saw meaning as being derived from actual experience. He interpreted the symptoms of his "hysterical" patients as symbolic expressions of repressed memories of actual childhood seductions. When, later, he discovered that these seductions existed only in the imaginations of these patients, he replaced his original theory with that of the libido theory. Sexual thoughts and wishes created the fantasies, and the sexual drive itself was implicated as the source of meaning of the symptoms.

By this shift, Freud was able to maintain his interest in the sexuality that was so abounding a preoccupation of Victorian Viennese culture, and so inevitably a major content of his patients' mental life. Libido theory, however, radically altered the implicit structure of his approach to meaning. Libido theory heralded the abandonment of the notion that meaning is derived from actual experience with the environment. It located the ultimate source of meaning in the individual's drives, and reduced the concept of motivation to drives, their aims, and defenses against them. Psychoanalytic psychology was locked into viewing the individual as the result of the organization of drive phenomena under the impact of environmental strictures. Not only meaning and motivation, but even personality and psychopathology were reduced to this basic model. Mechanistic and reductionistic though it was, the theory appealed because of its elegance, basic parsimony, and its resemblance to the concrete and highly successful theories of physics and mechanics that dominated the times.

As a direct outgrowth of libido theory, the structural theory of mind was developed, in which the structures of id, ego and superego were postulated to explain the source and eventual distribution of drive phenomena and instinctual energies, and to link all functions of mind to these drive phenomena. Structural theory furthered the commitment to drive explanations by implicitly structuring and institutionalizing the assumptions of drive psychology, and by reinforcing the atomistic approach to personality.

The tension created by this theoretical assumption and its collision with the growing clinical evidence that more holistic forces were at work in the individual has created problems since the earliest days of psychoanalysis, and there were many different attempts to resolve the dilemma, some of which still reappear in contemporary psychoanalytic revisions. The full history of this problem and the many attempts at its resolution is in itself a fascinating intellectual odyssey which unfortunately we do not have time to explore.

The resolutions of the problem offered by Fromm, Horney and Sullivan shared a rejection not only of drive theory, but of structural theory as well. This enabled them not only to readdress the problem of the relationship of meaning to experience, but to focus more on the holistic organizations of experience into structures of self and character which became central to their theories. This reorientation of theory to the organization of experience allowed for a more complex approach to meaning and its relationship to experience, a richer, more diverse understanding of motivation and intentionality, and a broader concept of psychic conflict than was afforded by the vicissitudes of the instincts and their fate in the process of socialization.

It seems to me that the basic issue between classical and post-Freudian theorists was and remains epistemic, and involves this issue of the nature of meaning. Post-Freudian revisions in theory were attempts to redefine and relocate the source of individual meaning to the world of experience, and to the person's cognitive interaction with that world. Fromm (1941), in his position that man is separated from the animals by his capacity for awareness of his own human condition, and his ability to conceive of his own death, exemplifies through generalization this shift of emphasis to a more explicit concern with cognition, and the attempt to shift meaning to experience. Horney (1950), in her concept of basic anxiety which sees the child as feeling isolated and helpless in a world conceived as potentially hostile, clearly derives meaning in relation to the world of experience, and uses such meaning in her development of the dynamics of personality. Horney's concern with and elaboration of a psychology of self, and Sullivan's (1953, 1956) examinations of the self-system illustrate this shift of emphasis to a concern with cognition and an organization of experience that is clearly related to concepts of character and personality unlimited to the defensive and structural model required by drive theory.

My own concern with cognition derives from my studies of Fromm, Horney and Sullivan, and my belief that they were dealing with an appreciation of cognition that far transcended the usual psychoanalytic interpretation of cognition as being limited to structures of the processes of thinking alone. Interpersonal theory especially, with its operational approach, its concern for the structuring effects of language, its detailed examination of the structure and organization of experience, and its insistence on defining the intrapsychic in terms of interpersonal experience, focused my approach to the central and architectonic nature of cognition in the study of psychoanalytic psychology.

I will begin this outline of my approach to the relationship between cognition and personality with an exploration of the self, both because most theoreticians explicitly or implicitly agree that the self is a cognitive structure and because the self is a concern directly and immediately involved with our patients' perception of their persons and their problems of living.

I view the self as the way the individual experiences his person and his relationship to the inner and outer world. The experience of self is the product of the cognitive apparatus that transforms actual experience into subjective meaning, and arises from the uniquely human capacity to organize experience in two different and interacting modes, the sensate and the syntactic. In previous communications in which I proposed that the designs of knowing and meaning are cognitive templates central to character structure, I indicated that I also view the self as a part of the cognitive system related to character (Barnett 1968, 1978, 1979, 1980b). I proposed that the self is a cognitive event, a bridging concept between the designs of knowing and meaning on the one hand, and action and behavior on the other. I further observed that the self is designed and limited by the cognitive templates of character.

The self refers to the experience of "I," "me," and "my." It is a system of constructs, implicit and explicit, formed by cognition which I have conceptualized as experiential knowing that includes sensate and syntactic forms existing at all levels of awareness or consciousness. The referent of self is always the person, as subject as well as object. The form and content of the self are provided by the impact of experience with the real world. The structure of the self is designed by the interaction of the person's cognitive system with external experience as well as by the internal organization of that system in the form of character. Our tendency to think of self as a fixed and static entity is related to our awareness of the substance and continuity of our bodies and the memory of the perceived continuity of our experiences in time and space. The self, however, is an holistic experience organized to integrate the constantly changing and growing experiences that arise from our evolving potentials for living and the way we interact with life. Although we tend to conceive of self as relatively monolithic, a conception that satisfies our need for meaning and significance, the self as experience is more fluid and inconsistent than we like to believe. Ideally the experience of self would be constantly growing and changing, reflecting in its dimensions and contradictions our manifold and developing potentials for living and our perceptions of our varied human responses to the constant change and flux of life. In essence the self is a quasi-fictive rendering of subjective experience and meaning. Drawing on one's historical life experience with the real and significant personal environment, the person constructs a fictive rendition in the attempt to integrate outer reality with the sense of personal existence and significance. The extremely varied, conflicting, and contradictory aspects of one's person and one's interaction with the complexities of living are difficult to organize into a coherent and consistent system. It is a task we respond to with a range of construction varying from the one extreme of the most conventionalized stereotypes to the other extreme of fantastic and idiosyncratic constructs which burst the bounds of reality. From a psychological point of view, the self is the person's major artistic and creative expression of his life and subjective experience. The wisdom and functional adequacy of the self involves the degree to which it reflects and integrates the person's sources of vitality and aliveness, the extent to which it is responsive to his potentials for living and to the complexities and ambiguities of life. The danger of the self involves the fact that an organized system of this sort can easily live our lives for us, and we can become constrained and confined to a sterile existence by the very system we erect in our search for meaning.

I find it convenient to divide the self experience into phenomenal aspects which I call the operational self and the representational self. This is obviously an heuristic and arbitrary division of what is an holistic experience of our person and our relationship to the world. The distinction is not absolute because static representations may be constructed about actions and operations, and actional concepts may be constructed from static representations. The utility of the distinction between operational self and representational self is that it focuses attention and distinguishes between constructs formed about the self as agent and self as essence. The tension between the operational self and the representational self is often the source of great ambiguity and confusion in living, and frequently defines the focal point of disorders of living.

The operational self corresponds roughly to James's (1892) notion of the self as subject, and to Sullivan's (1953) concept of the self-system. The operational self involves the perceptions and constructions about the person as actor or agent. It includes the organization of perceptions of one's ability to act, make choices, initiate or react to the environment and the ongoing process of living. The operational self implies both will and intentionality. It is the organization of what is conceivable to the individual of his own action and behavior, and of his functional roles with the environment. As the "I" of the experience of self, the operational self has its origins in the earliest sensate perceptions during infancy of one's actions in response to inner and outer sensations and perceptions. The operational self involves the growing sense of one's actional impact on the environment. It evolves into patterns created by the response of the environment to the child and by the sensations experienced by the child in the course of his actions and reactions. While Sullivan emphasized the structuring effects of anxiety, and the creation of an operational sense of self related to the tendency to avoid anxiety, which he called the self-system, other factors have been implicated in the development of the operational self. Schachtel (1959) discussed the existence of what he called activity affects, tension states which are pleasurable experiences orienting the child towards action. I consider these activity affects central to the development of the person's perception and organization of the operational self. Recent research by Stern (1977) and others has substantiated such a view of the patterning of the operational self by microanalytic observations on the impact of mother–infant play and interchange on the development in the child of patterns of interpersonal communication, a sense of the nature and timing of dialogic interaction, the development of expectational sets in relation to action and interaction, and even the development of affects and their expression. Yogman (1977), R. K. Barnett (1979) and others have extended these microanalytic observations to father–infant interactions as well, providing us with evidence of the earliest patterning of the operational self by experience with significant others.

The representational self corresponds roughly to James's notion of the self as object, Sullivan's conception (1953) of the personified self, and Horney's self-concepts (1950). As the "me" and "my" of experience, the representational self encompasses constructs about the perceived substantive aspects of the person, about the parts, qualities, nature and essence of the person perceived as the object of mental activity. It is the representational self, existing at different levels of cognitive organization and levels of awareness, that we usually refer to as self-images, self-concepts, self-representations, etc. The representational self involves the creation of referential systems that become the static, objectified, and eventually ideological reflections of one's perceived meaning and significance, as well as one's experience of others as seen through the filter of one's own perceived meanings. The representational self defines individual meaning in terms of static constructs and representations derived from the person's organization of experience with the real world. The constructs of the representational self, positive and negative, have special significance in that they become the source and reservoir of the dialectic of meaning which results in the person's self-regarding systems, the ultimate source of self-esteem and self-contempt.

The individual's self-regarding systems are a natural outgrowth of the complexities and ambiguities of the self as a product of the individual's cognitive system. The formulation of constructs about one's person inevitably creates a polarization of experience, in that it creates an implicit contrast with a construct perceived as its polar opposite. Both Sullivan and Horney implied as much in their explorations of the self. Sullivan's concept of the "good-me" and "bad-me," personifications of actional possibilities according to the gradient of anxiety evoked because of past experience with significant others, and Horney's observations about idealized and despised aspects of self, relating to the attempt to actualize grandiose images and concepts derived from past experience, both imply the polarization I believe is inevitable in self-construct formation. Since neither the environment nor the individual are neutral about the terms of one's polarized constructs, preferred and non-preferred constructs of the experience of self are designed. The evolving fictions and ideological premises of one's experience determine the judgments and evaluations of the self which are a central aspect of the self-regarding systems.

The dialogue of internal meaning about self not only reflects this tension between preferred and non-preferred constructs of the self, but involves also the ambiguity that often exists between constructs of the operational self and the representations of self as object. It is possible, as Sullivan pointed out, to construe one's actions and operations with the environment in a way that implies congruence with representations of self even when they are incongruent. It is equally possible to create representations which imply congruence with behaviors and operations which are in fact incompatible with existing self-concepts. The coexistence of incompatible behaviors and concepts leads to stress about the perceived unity and integrity of the self, and to conflict about self exposure, shame and self-contempt.

The development of self-regarding systems that structure self-esteem and self-contempt and determine the parameters of the internal dialogue of meaning, stimulates the evolution of two modes of self-expression, the presentational and private modes of self experience. Each mode includes elements of the operational self and the representational self which are organized according to the individual's perception of which aspects of self are most acceptable. The presentational mode and the private mode reflect the dominant fictional or ideological structure of the experience of self, its preferred and non-preferred aspects, and the attempt to organize that structure into a system of content and process. The presentational and private modes of self experience directly reflect, as Forrest (1978) has observed, the roles and functions the individual has had in his social and familial experience and the impact these roles and functions have on his sense of personal meaning. The presentational self includes those aspects of self which the person identifies with the roles and functions he has learned to accept as the dominant view of self that makes him meaningful to others. It reflects the structure of the person's perceived significance to the interpersonal world. The private mode is the counterpoint to the presentational mode, involving those aspects of self withheld because they might negate one's significance to others.

The problem of authenticity in the experience of self is a recurrent and complicated issue in the study of self. Various authors have proposed a concept of a real self, an authentic self as opposed to a false self, pseudo-self, or actual self. From our clinical experience, we can see where this tendency derives. Social and interpersonal factors, psychodynamics and psychopathology do warp and distort the person's sense of self. The person who, during the course of analysis, moves towards experiencing himself with a broader and more human repertoire of potentials for living than he was able to tolerate before, can be said to be experiencing himself in a more authentic way; a real self rather than a pseudo-self can be said to be emerging. It is probably more valid, though, to speak of authenticity of our moment-to-moment responses to living than to speak of a real self. The concept of a real self is problematic because it is idealistic, not existent, and tends to be ideological. A more central issue in any discussion of authenticity of self is the congruence of self-constructs with the person's capacities, talents, behaviors, values, way of living, etc., as well as the tension and ambiguities that exist between action and conception. It is difficult to conceive of an existent real self, first because the self is of necessity a limited and fictionalized view of a highly complex group of experiences, secondly because a real self would have to include the unfolding of potentials for living in the context of ongoing and even future experience, and finally because the very notion of a single self, true or false, arises out of our need for meaning and unity of experience. The idea of a single self reflects the attempts to organize what is, in effect, the variety of selves that characterize most people's lives, which have varying degrees of consistency with each other and varying degrees of congruence and incongruence with our actional relations to others. The capability of living a rich, full and varied life depends on the person's capacity to develop a sense of self that is not too narrowed by the twin forces of the social pressures of his past experience and his own cognitive organization of that experience.

My orientation is clearly towards the self as experience. It presupposes a shift from a psychology of instincts in which meaning is appetitive, derived from motivations which are functions of drives, to a psychology of knowing in which meaning is directly derived from experience, and in which intentions and motives stem from meaning. Post-Freudians, myself among them, prefer a psychology of self integrally interwoven with a psychology of personality or character to a drive psychology. We do not consider a psychology of self merely a second psychology for selected conditions, or an epiphenomenal appendage to a drive psychology. Post-Freudian theorists, and I include in this term all those who reject both libido theory and the structural theory of id, ego and superego which supports and institutionalizes drive theory and its assumptions, believe that all the classical syndromes of the disorders of living are understood more accurately and treated more effectively from a perspective of self and character. My own conviction is that such a perspective is essentially a cognitive one, and needs further explication of the cognitive and epistemic issues implicit in self and character. To accept the view proposed by recent theorists that a theory of self is required by a new group of disorders, the narcissistic or borderline personalities (Kernberg, 1975; Kohut, 1971, 1977), would, in my opinion, truncate the significance of self, character and cognition. For, in fact, we find in clinical practice that the notion of psychological disorder is synonymous with a disordered sense of self and disturbed self-regarding systems. Dysfunctional patterns of living, whether of hysteric, obsessional, impulse neurotic, paranoid or depressive nature, are without exception outcomes of damage to self-esteem and of a constricted and distorted sense of self. The study of the self, and the analysis of character, make untenable a division of pathology into transference neuroses in which distortions of meaning are libidinal and appetitive, and narcissistic neuroses in which distortions of meaning are self and experience related. It seems unlikely to me that two theories with contradictory implicit premises about meaning and motivation can comfortably coexist as explanatory systems. The study of both self and character indicates, I believe, that the central issues of mental life and of psychopathology are cognitive, having to do with the organization of experience and its fate in the process of socialization. What is called for is the reorientation of our concerns and our theories of therapy so that these issues are explicated as central rather than the peripheral phenomena they are envisioned to be by classicalist models of theory (Barnett, 1966a, 1980b).

I view the self, then, as a special instance of the organization of cognition, involving the architectonics of subjective experience and personal meaning which provides the psychological matrix and impetus for intentionality and motivation. The self is designed and confined by the cognitive templates of character, by the restrictive systems of knowing and meaning created by the impact of living, and by the systems of innocence established to protect the individual's sense of cohesiveness and significance. This position is based on an interpretation of character which views it as a central phenomenon of mental life rather than an epiphenomenon of ego serving defensive or at best adaptational functions. I propose that character is the general organization of cognition and meaning while self is a special instance reflecting the subjective organization of cognition and personal meanings. I would now like to sketch for you the relationship between self and character especially as we see it in the clinical situation, an outline of prominent themes in my understanding of the origin, organization and structure of the self experience as it is designed and influenced by the cognitive templates of different character structures. I have suggested that the neuroses in essence are cognitive disorders. Barnett (1966a, 1968, 1978, 1979) defined cognition as experiential knowing, derived from the human capacity to structure experience simultaneously in two interacting but distinct modes, the sensate and the syntactic. Sensate processes result in the apprehension of experience, commonly called feelings, while syntactic processes result in the comprehension of experience, commonly referred to as thought. Adequate systems of knowing involve a harmonious interchange between the sensate and syntactic modes of experience.

I have defined character as the central structural phenomenon of mental life whose design and formal attributes arise from the organization of experience in a person's life, and are reflected in his behavioral and cognitive operations. Character functions to determine the organization of ongoing experience, its perception and interpretation, the designs of meaning, of expectation and anticipation and the behavioral tendencies and interpersonal operations of the individual in relation to self, others and the inanimate world. Ideally, the state of cognition in character organization would be an expanding interchange between levels representing both sensate and syntactic structure, each enriching, complementing and renewing the other, and each dependent on the other for optimal functioning. This ideal model is that of an open-ended system in homeostasis with the environment, restricted only by the inherent limitations of the human organism.

In normal living, affective experience has both external and internal importance for the personality. Affect is used expressively for reaction and communication, and intrapsychically as data for thought and syntactic organization of experience. Affect thus normally gives rise to expression and impression. Expression involves the direct presyntactic communication of affects. Impression refers to the perception and storage of sensate data of experience which become important sources of experience for syntactic organization and comprehension.

Dysfunctional character organizations, the dynamic roots of neurotic living, have consistent areas of "not knowing" or innocence which function as predictable systems. These systems of innocence imply historically and dynamically created areas of difficulty in cognitive organization. Their effect is to block the interchange between apprehension and comprehension, to create closure of cognition, and to restrict opportunities for growth. Knowing is interfered with at various specific levels of cognition, and the creative interplay between apprehension and comprehension is limited by the confines of a rigid and dysfunctional template.

In the dysfunctional character formations affective experience is used either explosively or implosively and disorders normal cognitive organization. Explosion of affect is a cognitive dynamism in which a forceful ejection or voiding of apprehended experience takes place before adequate structuring or thoughtful integration of experience can occur. Implosion of affect is a cognitive dynamism in which affect is forced inward on the cognitive processes and disorganizes them. Both explosion and implosion interfere with normal cognitive ordering of experience, but differently. In affective explosion, there is an emptying of the apprehended data of experience before adequate syntactic structuring and comprehension can take place. Implosion of affect, on the other hand, disorganizes the very processes necessary for adequate organization, with the result that apprehended data is contained but left simply as raw data. These dynamisms are reflected in characteristic ways in the dysfunctional characters which give rise to neurotic living.

I have proposed that two basic types of dysfunctional character can be defined structurally, the explosive disorders and the implosive disorders. Explosion of affect is the dominant cognitive dynamism in the hysterical disorders, the acting-out personalities and the impulse disorders. Affective implosion characterizes the obsessional disorders, the paranoid character disorders and the depressive personality.

The utility of such an understanding of the dysfunctional character organizations is that it bears directly on issues of cognition central to the issues of neurosis, that it concerns itself with the epistemics of experience including the experience of self, and that it opens the way to a theory of therapy explicitly concerned with the psychoanalytic enterprise as an exercise in personal epistemology (Barnett, 1966b, 1972, 1978, 1979, 1980a).

The development and characteristics of self in those disorders of living I call the implosive disorders (i.e., the obsessional, the paranoid and the depressive character organizations) are organized around a central dysfunction in which systems of innocence about self are maintained dynamically to avoid further damage to self-esteem or confrontation with self-contempt. Because of the nature of the person's past experience, and of its effect on the organization of experience (described elsewhere at greater length), implosion of affects is utilized to create dysfunctions in interpersonal inference-making which prevent the syntactic organization and comprehension of self, others and relationships in specific areas determined by past experience with significant others. The threat is that such syntactic organization of experience might lead to perceptions of self that might challenge their literal view of their competence and expose their underlying and implicit sense of self-contempt and lack of significance (Barnett, 1966a).

The operational self of the patient suffering from an implosive disorder of living is severely constricted by the danger of interpersonal behaviors or transactions which might precipitate self-contempt by revealing non-preferred or dissociated aspects of self to oneself or to others. Their selective inhibition of activity in areas in which they need to maintain innocence leads to passivity which guards against the possibility of self-exposure and shame, prominent aspects of the dynamics and experience of these patients. Because of the interrelatedness of many aspects of intimate interpersonal integrations, irradiation both of guarding and inhibition and the resulting passivity may occur to the point that there appears to be no effective operational self in interpersonal situations other than that cued by the significant other in the relationship. Withdrawal, distantiation, and withholding patterns are all related to this inhibition of the operational self. In the most severe situations, an actional or operational self is only constructed in impersonal areas like business or the patient's profession in seeming contrast to the lack of actional constructs in intimate situations.

The sense of "I" as actor and agent in interpersonal situations is usually relegated to what I have called the secret life of these patients. Feelings, thoughts, fantasies and even actions which involve shame and fear of exposure are maintained in the private mode of self-experience, disowned as aspects of self and unavailable for adequate comprehension of the range of one's human responsivity.

The representational self of the implosive patient has a fixity, rigidity and stereotypy that belies its significance as a true reflection of an ongoing process of self-experience. As I have indicated, there is a dysfunction in the inferential processes that might organize syntactic comprehension of experience, and the representational self of these patients is often derived from the use of preferred labels from the past rather than ongoing constructions about self-experience. These labels reflect the interpersonal demands which were the conditions of acceptability to significant others in the past around which the earliest concepts of acceptability are organized. Being good, right, etc. are related, in effect, to role perceptions of the past, ignoring the realities of the patient's ongoing interaction with life.

Implosive patients show the widest discrepancies between their operational self and their representational self especially in intimate interpersonal relations. The need to maintain innocence of their intentions as well as the need to fictionalize self-representation in terms of the conditions of the past conspire to divorce action from conception in the most extreme manner. This gulf is perpetuated by a cognitive system organized to maintain obscurity, vagueness and lack of awareness especially in the area of self-experience. These discrepancies, as I have noted before, are of great importance to the therapeutic situation and to the problem of the development of effective insight in the patient, indicating the areas of cognitive repair essential before effective integration of insight can occur. The dichotomy between operational self and representational self in these patients also serves as a clue to the understanding and reaching of the private mode of self-experience which indicates the specific design of the patient's past experiences and the referential systems created by his family which are often obscured in their presentation.

Implosive characters all have nuclear problems of damage to self-esteem and the sense of self, not as accessory facts to supposedly central libidinal or Oedipal pathology, but as central issues in their organization of experience and their dysfunctional living. Covert yet central problems of narcissistic damage are the core of these neuroses and issues of narcissism are central to the organization of their experiences of self and others. The implosive character, in my opinion, shows a typical pattern in his use of narcissism in the structure of his personality (Barnett, 1971). I have described this typical relationship between narcissism and dependency as one in which the implosive character uses overt dependency in the service of his covert narcissism. The ambiguous referential systems of his past enable him to define love as service, and to be openly dependent in his covert search for approval and narcissistic repair. The formal restrictions in his sense of self, the areas of innocence, the need to maintain ambiguity and confusion about self in relation to others establishes an extensive vagueness about self especially in situations implying relative degrees of intimacy. Such patients often show increasing reliance on others for "self" definition as a substitute for the sense of self and approval as a substitute for self-esteem. The increment of such behaviors, especially in situations where self-esteem is damaged, even in the impersonal areas of living can lead to full-time preoccupation with narcissistic issues. In my opinion, implosive characters are often incorrectly called "narcissistic personalities" because of this preponderance of narcissistic themes.

The development and characteristics of self in those disorders of living I call the explosive disorders (the hysteric, the acting-out personalities and the impulse neurotics) are similarly organized around the cognitive disorders at the core of these character organizations (Barnett, 1971). The patient with an explosive disorder typically expels affective experience before it is adequately structured syntactically. Hyperemotionality or acting-out is used to void apprehended aspects of experience and consequently the impressions which provide the experiential data for refined syntaxis. The early history of such patients regularly reveals an affective overload in areas such as aggression or sexuality which results in a fear of the cognitive implications of affects and severe feelings of helplessness and isolation. The premature voidance of affectivity and lack of organization do not allow for the differentiation, nuances and ordering of the meaning of experience, and as a result the hysteric's comprehension of experience is simple and imprecise. Expelled and undigested affective experience is often used to form the over-generalizations, hyperbolic constructs and crude formulations that characterize the hysteric's transitory comprehension of experience, unrefined by the effect of impression.

In terms of self, the hysteric has suffered profound anaclitic damage. Affective overload has disturbed the basic dependent support and trust the child needs to adequately structure and organize experiences of self and others as separate and interacting entities. The resulting fused self-image leads to attempts to repair the anaclitic damage by the development of a surface narcissism geared to capturing dependent contact with others. In the explosive character organizations, overt narcissism is used in the service of underlying, covert and often denied dependency needs. The counterphobic quality of many explosive characters is related to the fact that their sense of self involves a presentational mode of narcissism and exhibitionism and a private mode of the more covert dependency needs of their fused self-image.

Patients with explosive disorders show a much greater latitude in the development of an operational self than do those with the implosive disorders. Indeed, they often seem addicted to affective expression and action. Among their greatest assets are their empathic sense of others, their expressive abilities, and their ability to chance action and commitment in living. In contrast to the inhibition, caution and circumspection of the implosive characters, one often gets the impression of recklessness or thoughtlessness in the actional and behavioral proclivities of the explosive characters.

It is in the area of the representational self that the crudities of the cognitive systems of the explosive characters take their greatest toll. Representations of self and others are hyperbolic and idealized, accounting for the rapid shifts between adoring idealization and hateful contempt and cynicism, both of self and others. These swings are not related to adequate self-constructs but to constructs reflecting their search for fusion and dependent contact. These patients believe that what they feel must be right. This breakdown between sensate experience and syntactic organization prevents adequate self-representation and mars the authenticity of self-experience.

You will undoubtedly have noticed, in this outline of my approach to the relationship between character and self, that my discussions of narcissism and (neurotic) dependency relate them at all times systemically to one another, and, indeed, imply different dynamic balances between narcissism and dependency in different dysfunctional character types. I have found this to be so important an observation clinically, both in the understanding of individual dynamics and in the clarification of interpersonal and transactional dynamics, that I would like to sketch my approach to characterological patterns of narcissism and dependency, leaving a more complete examination for another paper.

From a perspective that makes cognition and the organization of experience central to personality development, narcissism and (neurotic) dependency are inevitable accompaniments of dysfunctional character organizations and damage to the sense of self and self-esteem. In the everyday experience of psychoanalytic therapy, analysts constantly deal with organizations of self in which patterns of pathological dependency and narcissism are prominent. By and large, our theories have tended to isolate these patterns from each other, and to deal with them separately, implying they arise from discrete lines of development relatively unrelated to each other. This theoretical tendency has become especially marked in the work of recent theoreticians like Kohut and Kernberg, who see narcissistic disorders as disorders of self and neurotic dependency disorders as transference neuroses. They imply, therefore, that narcissism and dependency not only have unrelated sources of origin, but, indeed, are to be understood by different theories of the source of meaning and motivation, narcissism being self and experience related while dependency is drive and instinct related. Above and elsewhere (Barnett, 1980b) I have enlarged on my objections to this approach. Let me say here that I find this approach to theorizing both untenable and rather patchwork.

My observation is that narcissism and neurotic dependency always occur together and are systemically related to each other in pathology of the self, i.e., in all the dysfunctional character types. I have observed that narcissism is a pathological system arising from damage to self and self-esteem (Barnett, 1980b). Similarly, I believe that neurotic dependency is present in all neuroses as an attempt to solve problems of self-esteem and damage to the sense of self. Narcissism and dependency both reflect damage to the self structured by early experience. Both imply damage to the self in its potential for the development of autonomy and the creative evolution of the sense of uniqueness and completeness that might result from each individual's confrontation with life. Narcissism and dependency are aborted forms of the cognitive experience of self and involve the sacrifice and subversion of authentic self experience. Dependency sacrifices autonomy for care while narcissism sacrifices autonomy for approval. Dependency appeals through need for helplessness while narcissism appeals through performance. Both incorrectly identify approval with self-esteem, and both create operational systems inevitably bankrupt and evocative of still further damage to the self.

Where there is damage to the self, the options of attempting to repair the damage by dependent fusion or narcissistic performance are open to the developing individual. Experiential factors determine the use of dependency and narcissism and their interrelationship dynamically. Performance and need become polarized operational constructs at different levels of awareness in the person's attempts to achieve interpersonal security and a spurious sense of self contingent on others. In the presence of damage to self, approval is sought by utilizing both narcissism and dependency in different relationships to each other as flawed substitutes for a sense of significance.

In an earlier paper (Barnett, 1971), I described in detail the interpersonal and interactional dynamics that arose from systems of narcissism and dependency as they were seen in marriages between male obsessional patients and female hysterics. I found that, in the obsessional, dependency was overt and used in the service of more covert and central narcissistic demands in intimate interpersonal situations. Often this was reversed in impersonal areas of living. The hidden theme of the obsessional lay in his covert damage to self. Dependency became the tool for repairing narcissistic damage in personal living. The hysteric, in contrast, utilizes overt narcissism and exhibitionism in the service of more covert anaclitic damage. Surface narcissism is used to fill dependent needs for contact and care which are the hidden theme of the hysteric.

I have found that these dynamic systems are highly characteristic of the developing structure of personality in the implosive and explosive characters and lead to dynamic interactional systems that are highly predictable and characteristic. For me the systemic relationships of narcissism and dependency have provided an invaluable bridge between the psychodynamics of the individual and the dynamics of marital and familial dysfunctions. Narcissism and dependency provide an important guide in understanding the clash of subjectivities and the difficulties in communicating and relating that occur between people in their search for intimacy and interpersonal security. Above all, though, these systems aid in understanding the individual's organization of experience and its dynamic impact on the experience of self in the different character types.

In summary, then, I have outlined a view in which cognition and the organization of experience is the core of the development of personality and the root of the disorders of living that concern psychoanalysis. The concept of character becomes the general theory of cognition reflecting the design of cognitive templates which organize the experience of self, others and the inanimate world. Self is a special instance of cognition, reflecting man's capacity for the transformation of experience into personal subjective meaning, and providing the bridge between the organization of experience and action. As a subsystem of character, self is designed and confined by the cognitive templates of character structure, and always exists in intimate integration with character, its integrity and deformations. Narcissism and neurotic dependency are seen as inevitable accompaniments of dysfunctional character organizations and damage to the sense of self and self-esteem. They appear in all neurotic structures, and are systemically related to each other. Their relationship to each other provides important clues to the understanding of interpersonal and interactional dynamics in living.

References

Barnett, J. (1966a). On cognitive disorders in the obsessional *Contemporary Psychoanalysis*, 2: 122–134.

Barnett, J. (1966b). Cognitive repair in the treatment of the obsessional neuroses. *Proceedings of the IV World Congress of Psychiatry Excerpta Medica International.* Congress Series No. 150.

Barnett, J. (1968). Cognition, thought and affect in the organization of experience. *Science and Psychoanalysis*, XII: 237–247.

Barnett, J. (1971). Narcissism and dependency in the obsessional-hysteric marriage. *Family Process*, 10: 75–83.

Barnett, J. (1972). Therapeutic intervention in the dysfunctional thought processes of the obsessional. *American Journal of Psychotherapy*, 26: 338–351.

Barnett, J. (1978). Insight and therapeutic change. *Contemporary Psychoanalysis*, 14: 534–544.

Barnett, J. (1979). Character, cognition and therapeutic process. *American Journal of Psychoanalysis*, 39: 291–301.

Barnett, J. (1980a). Cognitive repair in the treatment of the neuroses. *Journal of the American Academy of Psychoanalysis*, 8: 39–55.

Barnett, J. (1980b). Self and character. *Journal of the American Academy of Psychoanalysis*, 8: 3.

Barnett, R. K. (1980). The father's role in early infancy: A case study of paternal paralanguage, Unpublished doctoral dissertation, Yeshiva University, New York.

Forrest, T. (1978). A synthesis of individual theory and therapy with family concepts. *Psychoanalytic Review*, 65(4): 507–521.

Fromm, E. (1941). *Escape from Freedom*. New York: Rinehart and Company.
Horney, K. (1950). *Neuroses and Human Growth*. New York: W. W. Norton.
James, W. (1892). *Psychology: Brief Course*. New York: Henry Holt.
Kernberg, O. (1975). *Borderline Conditions and Pathological Narcissism*. New York: Jason Aronson.
Kohut, H. (1971). *The Analysis of the Self*. New York: International Universities Press.
Kohut, H. (1977). *The Restoration of the Self*. New York: International Universities Press.
Schachtel, E. G. (1959). *Metamorphosis*. New York: Basic Books.
Stern, D. (1977). *The First Relationship: Mother and Infant*. Cambridge, MA: Harvard University Press.
Sullivan, H. S. (1953). *Interpersonal Theory of Psychiatry*. New York: W. W. Norton.
Sullivan, H. S. (1956). *Clinical Studies in Psychiatry*. New York: W. W. Norton.
Yogman, M. W. (1977). The goals and structure of face to face interaction between infants and fathers. Paper presented to the Society for Research in Child Development, New Orleans.

Chapter 7

Prescription or description

The therapeutic action of psychoanalysis[1] (1981)

Jay R. Greenberg

Jay Greenberg's "Prescription or description: The therapeutic action of psychoanalysis" is the first article in this collection to have been penned by a new and younger generation of analysts trained in the interpersonal tradition. The article was published in 1981, two years before Greenberg and Mitchell's *Object Relations in Psychoanalytic Theory* (1983), one of the most important books in the history of psychoanalysis. In the early 1980s comparative psychoanalysis was still a new way of thinking and writing. In keeping with this comparative project, Greenberg cites in this article a range of sources that were not commonly cited in the Freudian literature of that time – Kleinian (Grinberg, Racker), object relations (Fairbairn, Guntrip, Khan, Winnicott), and interpersonal (Bromberg, Epstein, Feiner, Kasin, Sullivan). He also recognizes new contributions developing within Freudian circles (George Klein, Holt, Schafer).

Jointly crediting Stephen Mitchell, Greenberg introduces in this article the distinction between what he calls the "drive/structure model" and the "relational/structure model." This distinction became the heart of *Object Relations in Psychoanalytic Theory*. Greenberg criticizes the classical model for its assignment of priority in psychological development to intrinsic drive states over lived experience and the meaning attributed to this interpersonal experience. He highlights the differences in the theories of therapy that result from these two ways of conceptualizing development. The heart of this difference lies in whether or not the analytic relationship, per se, plays a role in therapeutic change. Greenberg argues that if development depends more on interpersonal life than on inherent, biological drive, then the events of the analytic relationship, and the subjectivity of the analyst, are important influences in the outcome of psychoanalytic treatment. If drive comes first, on the other hand, the analyst's subjectivity is not crucial, and technique can be based on a prescribed technique characterized by neutrality and driven by "objective" interpretation.

Greenberg argues that mutual analytic interaction is not a strategy or a technique, but an inevitable consequence of any two people being on the same field of play. That is, try as one might, an analyst cannot not participate. Indeed, every gesture or mood, and certainly every interpretation, is a subjective and interpersonal participation. Nonparticipation can be prescribed but it cannot be lived out, and failing to take this into account perpetuates the illusion that interpretations in and of themselves are the exclusive factors leading to change.

Greenberg observes that early interpersonalists, and Sullivan in particular, contradicted themselves by characterizing the analyst as one who participates in all respects while simultaneously knowing the nature of this participation. Sullivan called this participant-observation, and described the therapist's grasp of his participation as the basis of his or her expertise. This criticism was eventually taken up by some relational analysts (Frankel, 1998). Greenberg also presents the corrective to this problem, created by the next generation of interpersonal thinkers. He refers to Edgar Levenson as the most articulate spokesperson for the view that the analyst's subjectivity is, in Renik's (1993) later terms, "irreducible." The analyst, that is, is hardly an expert on what is currently taking place in the analytic situation. Instead, the analyst's task is precisely to learn about the nature of his own unconscious involvement with the patient. This point of view eventually transformed Sullivan's interpersonal psychiatry into what Levenson (1992) and others considered contemporary interpersonal psychoanalysis.

References

Frankel, J. (1998). Are interpersonal and relational psychoanalysis the same? *Contemporary Psychoanalysis*, 3: 485–500.

Greenberg, J. & Mitchell, S. (1983). *Object Relations in Psychoanalytic Theory*. Cambridge, MA: Harvard University Press.

Levenson, E. (1992). Harry Stack Sullivan: From interpersonal psychiatry to interpersonal psychoanalysis. *Contemporary Psychoanalysis*, 28: 450–456.

Renik, O. (1993). Analytic interaction: Conceptualizing technique in the light of the analyst's irreducible subjectivity. *Psychoanalysis Quarterly*, 62: 553–571.

Prescription or description

The therapeutic action of psychoanalysis[1] (1981)

Jay R. Greenberg

My purpose today is to discuss this year's White Society theme, the interpenetration of interpersonal and object relations theories, from the perspective of its clinical implications. My focus will be on the broadest aspect of this issue, the theory of the therapeutic action of psychoanalysis. I am going to approach the problem through a back door, by pointing to some recent ferment within classical psychoanalysis. This approach will, I hope, illuminate some of the problems which come up in any discussion of the relationship between theory and practice.

The past five or ten years have seen an unprecedented outpouring of criticism directed against Freudian metapsychology by analysts who were trained in and who have contributed to the classical tradition. The modifications which have been suggested, although they differ significantly from each other, share a common directional thrust: each represents an attempt to substitute a psychology predicated on experience and meaning for one based on structure and mechanism. Thus, Kernberg (1976) retains the classical concepts of drive and structure, but describes each of these as derivative of the early experience of the self with others. In a more sweeping attempt at theoretical revision, Kohut (1977), in his "psychology of the self in the broader sense," retains the concept of structure itself, although not the concept of drive. Kohut substitutes a new structural unit, the bi-polar self, for the classical tripartite model. The justification for this change is that it brings metapsychology more into line with self experience, at least of narcissistic patients and probably of everybody. Perhaps the most radical critique of existing theory has been forthcoming from the colleagues and students of David Rapaport. Klein (1976), Schafer (1976) and Gill (1976), each in his own way, have questioned whether psychoanalysis needs metapsychology at all, and have proposed theories which remain closer to clinical data. As Klein states explicitly, this suggests a theory based on the meaning attributed by the patient to events in his life, and implies an emphasis on object relations.

These theoretical changes have been instigated by a number of developments within the field. Among these are: the burgeoning psychoanalytic observations of child development, with their elucidation of the importance of early interpersonal experience; the evolution of ego psychology, with its emphasis on reality relations in general; and pressures impinging from outside the classical tradition, specifically from the persistent questions raised by the American interpersonalists and the British object relations theorists. Perhaps the most important pressure, however, and the one which I wish to emphasize, derives from the data of clinical experience, and particularly from work with so-called "new," "more disturbed" psychoanalytic patients. The treatment of these individuals, as outlined in the work of analysts such as Modell (1968), Kernberg (1975) and Kohut (1977), involves methods or, I think more accurately, invokes sensibilities which transcend the classical conceptualization of the psychoanalytic situation. While different clinicians continue to work differently, there has been a convergence of opinion in the view that the patient's relationship to the analyst, as much as the technique of the analyst, bears decisively on therapeutic change. Moreover, this emphasis has been extended to include the relational aspects of the therapeutic action of psychoanalysis with all patients, not only those in the "new" diagnostic categories. Thus, the working alliance, which was originally postulated as a *sine qua non* of analytic work (Greenson, 1967), is now itself considered an analyzable aspect of the treatment situation (Settlage, in Scharfman, 1979). These ideas are not, of course, new. They have been around for years in the writings of Sullivan, Fairbairn, Guntrip, Fromm-Reichmann, Searles and others. What is new is their introduction into the theoretical framework of the classical school. Within this framework, it is radical change.

Because it is radical change, the new perspective has not been taken lightly by many analysts. Professional identities and loyalties are involved, and these are not given up easily. Too often, debate becomes dispute, a new understanding of what has gone on in clinical practice is argued over as if the analyst had done something different, and probably, therefore, something wrong. There are two major lines of attack in such discussion. According to the first, what the analyst says he has done is not really what he has done, and in fact he has done nothing that the rest of us haven't done all along. The second asserts that the analyst may have done something new, but that what he has done is "not-real-psychoanalysis," and whatever has happened to the patient is "not-real-psychoanalytic-change." In its extreme form this can become a matter of asserting that *no* change has taken place, because the analyst is working out of the wrong theoretical paradigm, and therefore no change could have taken place.

According to an old story, the laws of aerodynamics dictate unequivocally that the bumblebee is incapable of flight. The relationship between the bumblebee and the aerodynamicist is replayed constantly in our field, except that unlike the bee we can and do talk back to our critics, arguing that we damn well can fly, but that we are not so sure about airplanes. I think Antonovsky is pointing to this phenomenon when, in discussing clinical work, she states that "there are always some degrees of freedom within which we make a choice – to talk, e.g., about symbiosis and not about incest, or – à la Kohut – about narcissistic rage and not aggression" (1980, p. 208).

How little these degrees of freedom are studied in terms of their theoretical determinants and how much choice becomes a matter of institutional dispute is evident in the recent supplementary issue on technique of the *Journal of the American Psychoanalytic Association* (Blum, 1980). This contains a number of articles by leaders of the classical group that are written in response to Kohut's (1977) suggestion that the experience of mirroring and idealization, rather than the analysis of these aspects of the transference, is the curative agent in the treatment of patients with narcissistic personality disorders. This, of course, is a prime example of the sorts of modification in the theory of therapy that I mentioned earlier. Thus, Leo Rangell argues that the method advocated by Kohut is in fact nothing new. The idea that aspects of the transference should not be analyzed "is true at times in all cases, and for other transference mechanisms as well" (Rangell, 1980, p. 93). It is simply a matter of the timing of interpretations. But in the same issue, Valenstein (1980) criticizes Kohut for seeking to cure faulty development through "a corrective emotional experience in the setting of a full-fledged interpersonalization of the transference" (p. 124). One man's analytic timing is another's "corrective emotional experience"; one man's "nothing new" is another's "not-real-psychoanalysis." Neither author attempts to come to grips with what *happens* between Kohut and his patients, with how and why they get better, and with how the understanding of these questions relates to the broader issues of psychoanalytic theory.

These considerations bring me to one of the points suggested in my title, the relationship of prescription and description in discussions of psychoanalytic theories of technique. I believe that inter-institutional dispute over what the analyst *ought* to do leads to a neglect of the more interesting question of what he *has done*. Let me begin with the question: what is description? On its face, description is simply a statement of what has gone on. But, as any storyteller, literary critic, historian or psychoanalyst knows, such accounts are selective. Sullivan makes the point throughout his writings, and especially in "The Illusion of Personal Individuality" (1950), that insofar as one is a scientist one cannot talk about phenomena outside one's universe of discourse. In other words, the framework which determines one's particular selective criteria is one's theory. The act of description implies acknowledgment that one is organizing data on the basis of an underlying way of looking at things, and a particular description is always relative to that.

Psychoanalytic technique, however, is often presented in the imperative mode, as an injunction, a prescription, Thus, we are told that we should act like a blank screen, that we should be a participant with the patient, that we should establish a working alliance, create a holding environment, mirror the patient's grandiosity and so on.

There are any number of problems with attempting to prescribe psychoanalytic technique, of which I will briefly mention three. First, I doubt that technique can, outside of some very broad guidelines of the inculcation of rigidly doctrinaire points of view, be either taught or learned. This view, of course, is in accord with Freud's (1913 [1958]) famous analogy in which he compares psychoanalysis with chess: only the opening and the endgame have anything like established "rules"; the crucial middle is almost infinitely variable. Moreover, each of us has had the experience of conveying to a patient a wonderful interpretation that we have heard from our analyst or supervisor and having it fall utterly flat. The context is wrong, the tone of voice is wrong, the accompanying gestures are wrong and so on. Few prescriptions make very much sense outside of the unique relationship between a particular analyst and a particular patient.

A second difficulty arises from the fact that the privacy of the psychoanalytic situation makes it virtually impossible for any of us to know what others of us have actually done. This of course makes it difficult to generate a prescription, and next to impossible to verify that it has been carried out.

The third problem with prescription is, I believe, the most telling. The relationship between theory and prescription purports to be as follows: theory generates prescription; carrying out the prescription leads to a result; positive results confirm the utility of the prescription and the validity of the underlying theory. When we apply this schema to psychoanalysis, however, the plot thickens. Let me go through the sequence. How we talk about what we did is itself a description which, as I have said, implies a selectivity which is already based on theory. If we are classical analysts, for example, we may neglect to report having advised the patient about something, having expressed concern over an important situation in his life, even having smiled or frowned and so on, because our theory tells us that these are not salient aspects of the psychoanalytic situation. The next step in the sequence, the result, is another descriptive concept which rests on a theoretical orientation. Differences of opinion as to what constitutes psychoanalytic or even psychotherapeutic change are so commonplace that I don't need to spell this out. A third point, the connection we see between what we did and the change that took place, is again determined by theory. Does an accurate interpretation bring about change because it communicates information or because it communicates the analyst's empathy? Outside of psychoanalysis, I imagine the relationship between theory and prescription to be more straightforward. Controlled studies are possible (a pill can be administered uncaringly, a placebo can be given with kindness), and results are somewhat more accessible to consensual validation. In psychoanalysis the issue is more difficult because we can never leave our theory behind. And yet we continue to argue over prescription, as if we knew something beyond what our theories and our clinical experience (which contains the unique element of our selves, including our particular integration of theory) tell us.

I believe that many if not most psychoanalytic prescriptions are in fact descriptions, reformulated so as to reverse the relationship with theory. Prescriptions confirm theory (because the patient gets better); description depends on it. Let me cite several examples.

It is becoming increasingly clear in recent accounts by his patients of their analyses with Freud that he did not act like anything we might today consider a blank screen. Yet his technical papers are unequivocal on the subject. I would suggest that this follows from the fact that drive theory and the topographic model, with which Freud was working at the time of the technical papers, requires that whatever the analyst does he must be construed as a blank screen. Psychopathology is contained within the patient; regardless of his actions, the analyst is external to the neurotic process, and must be "factored out" of any description of the transaction; he must be understood as blank. Moreover, Freud's theory prior to the advent of the structural model contained scant framework for understanding the influence of relations with reality, of object relations. The theory, therefore, could not account for the therapeutic vicissitudes of what the analyst did except for interpreting, that is, making the unconscious conscious. Thus Freud could discuss literature and current events with his patients, he could offer advice and he could lend money, yet still, within the terms of his theory, consider himself a screen or a reflecting mirror. The blank screen concept is a descriptive, theory-bound construction rather than a prescription, although Freud's followers have not always or often acknowledged this.

Sullivan's concept of participant-observation can be interpreted in the same way. This view of the role of the analyst grows naturally and inevitably from Sullivan's interpersonal approach. Participant-observation, as Kasin (1977) has pointed out, is not a rule of procedure: it is a statement of fact. It is no more a prescription than is Heisenberg's principle a statement that the physicist ought to be uncertain. One does not *choose* to be a participant with the patient, one *is*, in the nature of things. If one embraces Sullivan's general theory, it is no more possible for him to consider himself a nonparticipant, a blank screen, than it is for a Freudian (in the prestructural model sense of the technical papers) to construe analysis as a dyadic exchange.

As a final example, I take the concept of the working alliance (Greenson, 1967). Did Greenson, who spent so much time talking about the working alliance, do something that Charles Brenner (1976), who spends so much time denying the utility of the concept, does not do? Surely Brenner must do something to convince his patients that he is worth talking to, let's say not being judgmental, but he is not about to tell us what that is, because no activity of the analyst beyond interpretation fits into his theory of the genesis and resolution of psychic conflict. The working alliance is *par excellence* a descriptive and theory-bound concept that has been transformed into a prescription both by its adherents and by its opponents.

Arguments over prescription, and the resultant neglect of description, have, I believe, led to a neglect of investigation of relevant lines of convergence among theories as well as of explication of genuine differences, a fact which is especially important when discussing interpersonal and object relations approaches. It follows from a descriptive perspective that theories which look at personality development similarly necessarily are more alike than different in their understanding of the therapeutic action of psychoanalysis. This will be the theme of the remainder of this paper. But first I must spend a little time on the question of just what an object relations theory is. That the term has been used in any number of ways has frequently been noted, recently by Gedo (1979), Lichtenberg (1979) and Antonovsky (1980). Let me try to suggest a way out of the confusion.

A theory of object relations is necessarily an aspect of every psychoanalytic theory. Every approach draws its data from people's interactions with others, whether these are conceptualized as object relations, interpersonal relations or drive derivatives. Patients, like everybody else, spend a good deal of their time talking about people, and even when their associations run away from explicit concern with others – to dreams, fantasies, symptoms and the like – the presence of other people can always be inferred. Moreover, the patient in analysis talks *to* somebody, a fact which no theory can ignore regardless of the way in which it is construed: blank screen and transference, participant-observer and parataxic distortion, working alliance plus transference and so on. Even at the point in Freud's career at which he focused most on the content of the unconscious at the expense of reality relations – the time between his first postulation of drive theory in the "Three Essays on the Theory of Sexuality" (1905 [1953]) and the prefiguring of the structural model in the metapsychological papers a decade later – the drive's object was, along with its source and aim, proposed as one of its essential characteristics. If the term object relations theory is to have a useful, specific, meaning, we must search for it elsewhere.

So we can turn to an alternate, certainly more specific definition of the term: that it describes not an aspect of all theories but the totality of the work of particular theorists. Here, of course, we run into difficulty, because in this connection the term has been applied to any number of approaches: to Melanie Klein's, to Fairbairn's, to Guntrip's and sometimes to all of them as a group, despite the fact that their kinship is more geographic and fraternal than theoretical. Most recently, and largely by virtue of self-appropriation, it has been applied to the work of Kernberg. Deciding which of these not very similar approaches is to be labeled *the* object relations theory can only be arbitrary and not particularly useful.

In a forthcoming publication, Mitchell and I attempt to clarify some of the confusion to which I have pointed by applying to psychoanalytic theory Kuhn's (1962) concept of scientific paradigms.[2] I don't have time here to go through the entire argument, but the concept of paradigm suggests the compatibility, although by no means the identity, of theories which are in fundamental agreement on such issues as the position of the observer in the observational field, the nature of the subject matter (here, the nature of man), the determinants of motivation, the constituents of regulatory structure and so on. We identify two major competing paradigms which can be considered dichotomous for heuristic purposes but which, in common with paradigms in other fields, allow of accomodation to each other and to newly emerging data. These we have given the not very euphonious but I think quite descriptive labels "drive/structure paradigm" and "relational/structure paradigm." The names point to the origin which theories within each paradigm postulate as accounting for the consistencies and regularities of personality which are embraced by the term "structure," or, in Sullivan's (1953) language, "dynamism." The drive/structure paradigm, which finds its clearest and purest expression in the early work of Freud, takes as its unit of study the discrete individual. Motivation is attributed to the action of discharge seeking drives alone, while regulation evolves as a transformation of the energy of drive. The relational/structure paradigm, which is prefigured to some extent in the early theoretical dissent of Jung and Adler, finds its clearest expression in Sullivan's interpersonal theory and in Fairbairn's later theory of object relations. Both of these theorists find it nonsensical to speak of a person in isolation from his social environment, as in Sullivan's (1953) notion of communal existence and Fairbairn's (1952) belief that an objectless ego is a contradiction in terms. Both attribute motivation to the need to establish or re-establish a particular configuration of the self in relation to a significant other person, and both see regulation as deriving from the sequelae of specific, opposing, self–other configurations.

The concept of paradigms eliminates the necessity to decide among competing aspirants which is to be labeled an object relations theory, and facilitates the comparison of interpersonal theory with other approaches. Theories within a given paradigm approach the question of the therapeutic action of psychoanalysis similarly to other theories with the same paradigm, and quite differently than theories within the opposing paradigm. To take an example, Sullivan's view of the therapy process is quite different from the "object relations theory" of Kernberg, which is demonstrably a drive/structure paradigm approach extending the work of Jacobson and Mahler, and enriched by some emphases borrowed from Fairbairn and especially from Klein. Kernberg, of course, would agree with this statement. In a recent article (Kernberg, 1980), he argues that "[i]n contrast to what might be considered an object-relations approach of Sullivan (1953) and his followers, object relations theory as outlined here has to do not only with interpersonal object relations, but is predominantly a metapsychological approach – an attempt to account for normal and pathological development in terms of structures comprising the psychic apparatus" (p. 209). I don't think that much in this statement bears up well under close analysis; my point in mentioning it is only to indicate that Kernberg accurately, if implicitly (and possibly from political motivations, which is itself a major aspect of the theory of paradigms), recognizes that he and Sullivan are operating out of different underlying conceptual systems.

When we turn to Sullivan's interpersonal theory and the object relations approach of Fairbairn (1952, 1958), however, we reach different conclusions. Sullivan made few summary statements about an underlying theory of therapy; as a number of speakers at the recent Psychoanalysis 1980 conference stated, his concerns were more pragmatic than theoretical. A recent paper by Dyrud (1979), while it is not specifically concerned with the therapy process, offers a concise and accurate summary of what Sullivan thought must happen in treatment. Discussing Sullivan's concept of the illusory other, Dyrud states that:

> [T]he illusory other is part of a dyad made up as much of my version of myself as it is of my version of the other person. This envelope seems to reduce my anxiety by providing a framework of expectations within which I can be comfortable. ... Depending on my ability to tolerate anxiety I may become furious at the failure of fit because I cannot tolerate the disconnectedness of the moment, or I may see a new aspect of our relationship which has the potential of increasing intimacy, reducing loneliness and broadening the range of my self–other constructs. The more new data I am capable of integrating, the more rich, varied and individuated my encounters become. (1979, pp. 190–191)

I think we can agree that this formulation implies a theory of therapeutic change. That it is in fact a critical aspect of Sullivan's approach is underscored by Mary White (1952 [1977]), who points to Sullivan's procedure of actively correcting, rather than interpreting, the patient's parataxic distortions. Sullivan emerges from this presentation as attempting to insert himself, as an actual presence, into the patient's inner world of self–illusory other configurations. White gives the example of a patient who recalled that Sullivan had previously referred to him as "skinny." Sullivan responded that he did not do so, that he had commented on the patient's mother having called him skinny. White goes on to say that, "With this he dropped it. His patients experienced these incidents acutely, and quickly learned to see what had gone on. He used to say that as soon as the patient has recognized and accepted one parataxic distortion there is hope for a successful outcome of therapy" (p. 329).

Now let me turn to Fairbairn's (1958) formulation. He states that:

> [H]owever neutral a role the psycho-analyst may assign to himself therapeutically, he cannot escape from the necessity of becoming an interventionist if he is to be therapeutically effective – and it must be recognized that every interpretation is really an intervention. Thus, in a sense, psychoanalytical treatment resolves itself into a struggle on the part of the patient to press-gang his relationship with the analyst into the closed system of his inner world through the agency of transference, and a determination on the part of the analyst to effect a breach in this closed system and to provide conditions under which, in the setting of a therapeutic relationship, the patient may be induced to accept the open system of outer reality. (p. 385)

I suggest that underneath the dissimilarities of language the two views of the therapeutic action of psychoanalysis are in fundamental agreement. Both understand that change comes about as a result of the analyst's use of himself as a new person to break into the closed inner world of the patient. Sullivan talks of the acceptance by the patient of his parataxic distortions, that is, of learning, while Fairbairn emphasizes instead the substitution of "natural objects" – those of the external world – for pathological internal objects. That Fairbairn's theory is filled with speculation about structures within the mind and the effect upon these of the analytic encounter, while Sullivan eschews such tendencies toward reification in favor of constructs organized around thought processes and the effects of learning, is more the result of philosophical tradition and personal style than of theoretical substance. I will, however, discuss a little later some important differences that derive from these emphases. For the moment, let me add as an aside that these considerations, and the theory of paradigms on which they are based, seem to me to call into question the distinction between "interpersonal" and "intra-psychic" as catch-words for the categorization of theories.

The concept of psychoanalytic paradigms bears directly on the problem of prescription and description. In the paper of Valenstein (1980) to which I referred earlier, the author draws a distinction between what he calls "classical psychoanalysis," in which interpretation is all and insight cures, and the "so-called new … object-oriented psychoanalysis of today, in which the *real* relationship to the analyst as a *real* person is considered to be pivotal." This leads to what he calls "interpersonally promoted experiential effects" (pp. 117–118, italics original), that is, from his drive/structure paradigm approach, to "not-real-psychoanalysis." This to my mind is an excellent example of the confusion of prescription and description. The role of the real relationship to the real analyst, the influence on the patient of interpersonally promoted experiential effects, is not something that can be included in or excluded from the analytic process by technical fiat. Silence, for example, whether it is construed as promoting ego autonomy, as facilitating the development of the transference, as encouraging regression or as abandoning the patient, is an activity whether one likes it or not. One can include the data derived from the study of that activity, and of others, in one's analysis of analysis or not as one chooses; this depends on how one understands the field of study, the relationship of the observer to the observed and so on. In short, it depends on one's paradigm.

Let me emphasize here that the "reality" of the analyst is a descriptive rather than a prescriptive concept; it has nothing to do with how the analyst acts, but rather with how the effects of his actions are understood. In this context it is helpful to recall Fairbairn's statement that "every interpretation is really an intervention." In Guntrip's (1975) account of his analysis with Fairbairn, Fairbairn emerges as a rather austere figure. He did not act like an interventionist (although his extra-analytic meetings with Guntrip cloud the issue). Despite his behavior as an analyst, however, Fairbairn's relational/structure paradigm perspective demands that interpretations be construed as interventions. Neither Fairbairn nor Sullivan can think of the communication of information (interpretation) divorced from its interpersonal context.

Valenstein's "interpersonally promoted experiential effects," his "not-real-psychoanalysis," is for both Sullivan and Fairbairn simply the nature of the case.

I want to stress that I have chosen to compare the approaches of Sullivan and Fairbairn in some detail as exemplars of the relational/structure approach to the theory of psychotherapy, not because they are the only theorists to whom the considerations I have advanced apply. I think similar points could be made with respect to the work of Guntrip (1969, 1971), to some extent to the work of Winnicott (1965), and more recently to that of Kohut (1977). I do believe, however, that there are a few areas in which Sullivan's interpersonal theory conveys a different sensibility than that of some British versions of the relational/structure paradigm. One such area on which I would like to spend some time is Sullivan's (1954) view of the psychiatrist as an expert. The role of the expert is to identify and to rectify, via his presence as a new person, the parataxic distortions of the patient. Sullivan, rather like Freud in some ways, thought that change followed from the patient's increasing awareness of himself. He says in *Conceptions of Modern Psychiatry* (1940) that, "The principal problem of the therapeutic interview is that of facilitating the accession to awareness of information which will clarify for the patient the more troublesome aspects of his life" (p. 185). The therapist/expert uses himself, and especially disjunctions between his awareness of himself and the patient's experience of him as co-determined by the closed world of illusory others, to elucidate distortions which are to be conveyed to and accepted by the patient. Thus, while the psychiatrist participates with the patient, he more or less remains outside of the patient's parataxic distortions: the process of therapy, insofar as it is therapeutic, is construed as a progression from more to less warped ways of conceiving of oneself in relation to others. This emphasis has implications for the role assigned within the therapy process to at least two important phenomena: countertransference and regression. I think the view of the psychiatrist as expert imposes some limitations on Sullivan's approach to countertransference. Mary White (1952 [1977]) notes that Sullivan "cautioned that a therapist who feels actual anger or irritation at a patient needs psychotherapeutic help himself" (p. 321). Something of the same emphasis is apparent in the writings of Clara Thompson, although Thompson (1952) does distinguish between "neurotic" affective reactions of the analyst and those which are triggered by the behavior or personality of the patient.

In light of this, I would like to point to some of the considerations advanced by analysts of the British school who, I believe, construe the participation of the analyst rather differently than do the American interpersonalists. Expertise, by no means overlooked by these theorists, is one among many facets of the analyst's role, as indicated by Sandler's concept of the "role-responsiveness" with which the analyst meets the patient's readiness for transference (Sandler, 1976; Sandler & Sandler, 1978). The concept of role-responsiveness suggests that the analyst is many things for the patient, including, most emphatically, a non-expert (a situation which Epstein [1979] graphically describes in the case of patients dealing with significant amounts of split-off envy), and that he must experience himself as such, possibly for quite some time, before working out of that position. As Khan (1972) puts it, the analyst must have a "dual capacity both to be involved with the patient's illness and [to] distance himself from it for the benefit of both himself and the patient" (p. 134). Racker's (1968) concepts of concordant and complementary identification and Leon Grinberg's (1979) depiction of the process of projective counter-identification are attempts to specify aspects of the analyst's participation sketched broadly by Khan. The convergence of these formulations is that the analyst is seen not only as *participating with* the patient but as, inevitably, *participating in* the patient's illness. The latter would, I think, be seen as neurotically determined countertransference by Sullivan.

The specific mode of the analyst's participation in the patient's illness is, for theorists of the British school, determined by the internal object relations of the patient, that is, by the sequelae of his developmental experiences. If the analyst is a new object he is also, at least for a time, an old one, not only by virtue of the patient's distortions but by virtue of the analyst's own affective and behavioral responses. Therapeutic change depends not only on learning, which has secondary process or syntaxic connotations, but also on growing, which is a broader concept embracing phenomena not accessible to consensual validation or even to conscious awareness. For such growth to take place the point must be reached in analysis at which both patient and analyst abandon their expert–client relationship. From the patient's point of view this is described by Kernberg (1980) as the dissolution of cohesive structure into its constituent primitive self–object representations. From the perspective of the analyst, what is required is a readiness for countertransference (in the non-neurotic sense of the term), an ability to lose one's neutrality transiently and reversibly, similar to Sandler's role-responsiveness. Regardless of whether one accepts Kernberg's specific metapsychological formulation, growing requires regression on the part of the patient and something similar or at least parallel on the part of the analyst. This is, I think, a major point of difference in conceptualizations of the therapeutic action of psychoanalysis within the relational/structure paradigm. This is not to say that regression cannot be encompassed within an interpersonal model – Bromberg (1979) has suggested that it can be – but I do think that the approach of the British school forces regression on the observer in a way that interpersonal theory does not.

Before concluding I would like to make one final point about the paradigm concept. Specifically, I would like to anticipate the objection that it is too dichotomous, that one can, in fact, have it both ways. I have two answers to this objection. First, there are theorists who take extreme positions within each paradigm. Brenner's (1976) view that the real personality of the analyst is an interference in the analytic process and that "for a patient to be in a position to watch his analyst is like introducing extraneous sights and sounds into one's office" (p. 183) is an example of this within the drive/structure paradigm; the articles I have cited by Rangell (1980) and Valenstein (1980) are in similar vein. Secondly, psychoanalytic paradigms, like paradigms in other sciences, do allow of accomodation to each other. In the physical sciences perhaps the clearest example of this is the attempt by Ptolemaic astronomers, after the introduction of the Copernican model of the solar system, to account for new observational data by the addition of epicycles to the presumed motion of the planets. Freud himself consistently responded to paradigmatic alternatives, especially as suggested by Jung and Adler. I believe that it can be demonstrated that much of the history of American ego psychology – I am thinking here of the work of Hartmann, Jacobson, Mahler and most recently Kernberg – is best understood as a series of attempts to adapt the drive/structure paradigm to insights forthcoming from the relational/structure approach. There are drive/structure paradigm theorists who do attempt to account for the relational/structure observation that in every psychoanalytic encounter there are demonstrably two participants. These theorists ground their approach in Freud's (1940) conceptualization of psychoanalysis as "after-education," and in his statement that "We serve the patient in various functions, as an authority, and a substitute for his parents, as a teacher and educator" (p. 181). Stone's (1961) concept of the mature transference, Loewald's

(1960) depiction of psychoanalysis as a developmental experience, Greenson's (1967) idea of the working alliance and more recently Gill's (1980) consideration of the need to relate the patient's transference to the actual relationship between patient and analyst represent attempts at paradigmatic accomodation. Each of these approaches, however, assumes ultimately that analytic change derives from interpretation, from some version of making the unconscious conscious, rather than from aspects of the actual encounter with the analyst. Loewald (in Scharfman, 1979), for example, while recognizing the utility of encouragement and reassurance, makes it clear that these interventions are *not analytic*. Despite the recognition of non-interpretive possibilities, the emphases of each of these accommodating approaches preserves the thrust of the drive/structure paradigm.

At the same time, within the interpersonal school there have been a number of recent attempts to extend the relational/structure paradigm and to bridge the gaps between Sullivan and the British school. I am thinking here of Levenson's (1972) view that therapy consists of the patient's attempt to make the therapist act like significant other people in his history and of the therapist's attempt to "resist transformation." In a similar vein, Feiner (1977) describes "four analysts" who are in the consulting room at any given time. One of these, Number two, is the expert in Sullivan's sense. Number three is "that fantasy analyst who will be created and recreated by the patient into what he or she needs to make the relationship work *at any one moment*" (p. 9, italics original). Thus there is a constant dialectic between transformation in Levenson's sense (or role-responsiveness in Sandler's) and the expertise that permits analysis of these losses of neutrality. Each of these authors extends the perspective of the interpersonal approach, and especially the limitations of Sullivan's concept of the psychiatrist as expert. Not only does the patient attempt to assimilate the therapist's behavior into his inner world of bad objects or illusory others, but he is able actively to influence the behavior of the other. The therapeutic action of psychoanalysis thereby consists not only of the correction of the patient's experience of the analyst, but also of the clarification of the analyst's experience of the patient and his re-finding, in every analytic encounter, of his "real self" to the benefit of both participants. I find in these statements a friendly and compatible extension of the interpersonal approach, one which can be encompassed theoretically by any relational/structure paradigm theory. I have tried to show today that institutional loyalties give rise to arguments over psychoanalytic prescriptions that are inherently meaningless, and that these lead us away from more fruitful examination of our underlying theoretical premises. The events of analysis are like the events of life: the best we can do is to describe what happens, and even this description evolves from the larger context of theory.

Notes

1 This is a slightly modified version of a paper presented at the weekend meeting of the William Alanson White Psychoanalytic Society, Walker Valley, New York, April 13, 1980. Drs. R. Atkins, J. Meltzer and S. Mitchell read drafts of this paper and offered useful suggestions. I owe special thanks to Mr. Kenneth Pierce, who spent considerable time helping me to clarify the points I wished to make.

2 Tentatively entitled *Theories of Object Relations: A Critique*, the book was scheduled for publication in 1982 by the Harvard University Press. A creative application of Kuhn's paradigm concept to psychoanalysis, with a slightly different emphasis than that presented here, can be found in Levenson (1972).

References

Antonovsky, A. (1980). Object relationship or object relations. *Contemporary Psychoanalysis*, 16: 203–210.

Blum, H. (Ed.) (1980). *Psychoanalytic Explorations of Technique: Discourse on the Theory of Therapy*. New York: International Universities Press.

Brenner, C. (1976). *Psychoanalytic Theory and Psychic Conflict*. New York: International Universities Press.

Bromberg, P. (1979). Interpersonal psychoanalysis and regression. *Contemporary Psychoanalysis*, 15: 647–655.

Dyrud, J. (1979). Sullivan's concept of the illusory other. *Contemporary Psychoanalysis*, 15: 190–194.

Epstein, L. (1979). Countertransference with borderline patients In L. Epstein & A. Feiner (Eds), *Countertransference*. New York: Jason Aronson, pp. 375–405.

Fairbairn, W. R. D. (1952). *Psychoanalytic Studies of the Personality*. London: Tavistock.

Fairbairn, W. R. D. (1958). On the nature and aims of psycho-analytical treatment. *International Journal of Psychoanalysis*, 39: 374–385.

Feiner, A. (1977). Countertransference and the anxiety of influence. *Contemporary Psychoanalysis*, 13: 1–16.

Freud, S. (1905 [1953]). *Three Essays on the Theory of Sexuality*, Standard Edition 7. London: Hogarth Press, pp. 125–245.

Freud, S. (1913 [1958]). *On Beginning the Treatment (Further Recommendations on the Technique of Psychoanalysis, I)*, Standard Edition 12. London: Hogarth Press, pp. 121–144.

Freud, S. (1940 [1964]). *An Outline of Psychoanalysis*, Standard Edition 23. London: Hogarth Press, pp. 139–208.
Gedo, J. (1979). Theories of object relations: A metapsychological assessment. *Journal of The American. Psychoanalytic Association*, 27: 361–373.
Gill, M. (1976). Metapsychology is not psychology. In M. Gill & P. Holzman (Eds), *Psychology versus Metapsychology: Psychoanalytic Essays in Memory of George S. Klein*. *Psychological Issues*, 36: 71–105.
Gill, M. (1980). The analysis of the transference In H. Blum (Ed.), *Psychoanalytic Explorations of Technique: Discourse on the Theory of Therapy*. New York: International Universities Press, pp. 263–288.
Greenson, R. (1967). *The Technique and Practice of Psychoanalysis*. New York: International Universities Press.
Grinberg, L. (1979). Projective counteridentification and counter-transference. In L. Epstein & A. Feiner (Eds), *Countertransference*. New York: Jason Aronson, pp. 169–191.
Guntrip, H. (1969). *Schizoid Phenomena, Object Relations and the Self*. New York: International Universities Press.
Guntrip, H. (1971). *Psychoanalytic Theory, Therapy and the Self*. New York: Basic Books.
Guntrip, H. (1975). My experience of analysis with Fairbairn and Winnicott (how complete a result does psycho-analytic therapy achieve?). *International. Review of Psychoanalysis*, 2: 145–156.
Kasin, E. (1977). Some notes on participant observation. *Contemporary Psychoanalysis*, 13: 364–367.
Kernberg, O. (1975). *Borderline Conditions and Pathological Narcissism*. New York: Jason Aronson.
Kernberg, O. (1976). *Object Relations Theory and Clinical Psychoanalysis*. New York: Jason Aronson.
Kernberg, O. (1980). Some implications of object relations theory for psychoanalytic technique In H. Blum (Ed.), *Psychoanalytic Explorations of Technique: Discourse on the Theory of Therapy*. New York: International Universities Press, pp. 207–239.
Khan, M. M. R. (1972). On Freud's provision of the therapeutic frame. In M. M. R. Khan (Ed.), *The Privacy of the Self*. New York: International Universities Press, pp. 129–135.
Klein, G. (1976). *Psychoanalytic Theory: An Exploration of Essentials*. New York: International Universities Press.
Kohut, H. (1977). *The Restoration of the Self*. New York: International Universities Press.
Kuhn, T. (1962). *The Structure of Scientific Revolutions*. Chicago, IL: University of Chicago Press.
Levenson, E. (1972). *The Fallacy of Understanding: An Inquiry into the Changing Structure of Psychoanalysis*. New York: Basic Books.
Lichtenberg, J. (1979). Factors in the development of the sense of the object. *Journal of the American Psychoanalytic Association*, 27: 375–386.
Loewald, H. (1960). On the therapeutic action of psychoanalysis. *International Journal of Psychoanalysis*, 41: 16–33.

Modell, A. (1968). *Object Love and Reality*. New York: International Universities Press.

Racker, H. (1968). *Transference and Countertransference*. New York: International Universities Press.

Rangell, L. (1980). Contemporary issues in the theory of therapy. In H. Blum (Ed.), *Psychoanalytic Explorations of Technique: Discourse on the Theory of Therapy*. New York: International Universities Press, pp. 81–112.

Sandler, J. (1976). Countertransference and role-responsiveness. *International Review of Psychoanalysis*, 3: 43–47.

Sandler, J. & Sandler, A. (1978). On the development of object relationships and affects. *International Journal of Psychoanalysis*, 59: 285–296.

Schafer, R. (1976). *A New Language for Psychoanalysis*. New Haven, CT: Yale University Press.

Scharfman, M. (1979). Panel discussion: Conceptualizing the nature of the therapeutic action of psychoanalysis. *Journal of the American Psychoanalytic Association*, 27: 627–642.

Stone, L. (1961). *The Psychoanalytic Situation: An Examination of its Development and Essential Nature*. New York: International Universities Press.

Sullivan, H. S. (1940). *Conceptions of Modern Psychiatry*. New York: W. W. Norton.

Sullivan, H. S. (1950). The illusion of personal individuality. *Psychiatry*, 13: 317–332.

Sullivan, H. S. (1953). *The Interpersonal Theory of Psychiatry*. New York: W. W. Norton.

Sullivan, H. S. (1954). *The Psychiatric Interview*. New York: W. W. Norton.

Thompson, C. (1952). Countertransference. *Samiksa*, 6: 205–211.

Valenstein, A. (1980). The concept of classical psychoanalysis. In H. Blum (Ed.), *Psychoanalytic Explorations of Technique: Discourse on the Theory of Therapy*. New York: International Universities Press, pp. 113–136.

White, M. (1952 [1977]). Sullivan and treatment. *Contemporary Psychoanalysis*,13: 317–346.

Winnicott, D. W. (1965). *The Maturational Process and the Facilitating Environment*. New York: International Universities Press.

Chapter 8

Psychoanalytic engagement

The transaction as primary data[1] (1982)

Darlene Bregman Ehrenberg

Darlene Ehrenberg explicates a distinctly innovative interpersonal tradition: the use of countertransference experience to shed light not only on the analytic transaction but on the psyche of the patient as well. This tradition was pioneered by the interpersonalists who preceded her, especially Erich Fromm, Benjamin Wolstein, Harold Searles, and Erwin Singer. Ehrenberg also finds herself in accord with what was, at this time, the controversial writing of Merton M. Gill (1982), in particular his readiness to address here and now transference–countertransference experience. Ehrenberg argues convincingly that the strongest analytic work lies in the closest possible examination of the interactions between the two analytic co-participants, both what is obvious and what is subtle – and always what is affective. To the extent that such examination is avoided, she believes the optimal psychoanalytic configuration – the potential for intimacy – goes unrecognized and undeveloped. Ehrenberg believes that working at what she describes as the "intimate edge of therapeutic relatedness" – the careful, verbally articulated scrutiny of analytic process – lies at the heart of psychoanalytic work.

Before some of those analysts identified as interpersonal began sharing their subjective reactions with their patients, analysts were advised to use countertransference feelings only to understand patients, or at most, to direct inquiry. Actually expressing to patients what the analyst perceived in the immediate interaction was generally believed to be intrusive. Perhaps patients were not ready to hear the otherness of the analyst. In conventional psychoanalytic wisdom, the prototypical patient is unlikely to be able to absorb or integrate the experience of the analyst, especially when what the analyst observed was not necessarily admirable, or was discordant with patients' preferred ways of viewing themselves. In a 180-degree turn from this position, Erich Fromm (see

Singer, 1965) argued that patients came to analysis in the first place in order to learn about themselves, and as uncomfortable as it might initially be, they wanted to be seen candidly in the eyes of an analyst who may, indeed, represent the others in the patient's world. Fromm and Singer argued that, although anxiety can be disruptive, it is also a necessary ingredient for change. The view that patients cannot tolerate direct engagement with the analyst can be disrespectful and excessively hierarchical, as if the strong or healthy analyst must "take care of" the weaker patient. Harold Searles, as seen in an earlier chapter of this volume, is the exemplar of this perspective, arguing convincingly that analysts' excessive caution is often iatrogenic, conveying the message that the patient is less than a whole human being.

In this context, Ehrenberg's use of the term "intimacy" to describe optimal analytic engagement is particularly apt. This term is a reflection of the view that the most telling emotional moments in therapy often occur in the immediacy of the two-person transaction. To avoid explication of these moments may be effective in reducing the patient's anxiety – and may reduce the anxiety of the analyst, as well – but at the cost of clarifying to the patient the nature of the troublesome ways that his or her relationships tend to be structured.

Ehrenberg recognized fully the degree to which analytic engagement is mutual – that is, analyst and patient mutually influence one another. This theme lies at the center of the relational theorizing that began to appear within a few years of this article.

In this article and in others, Ehrenberg makes a strong argument for the value of analysts' deliberate disclosure of affective experience. This places her in a position distinct from many who are also identified as interpersonal or relational, and reflects her particular and unique contribution to this literature and, as well, to the ongoing controversy regarding the value of deliberate verbal disclosure of analysts' feeling states.

References

Gill, M. (1982). *The Analysis of Transference*, Volume 1. New York: International Universities Press.

Singer, E. (1965). *Key Concepts in Psychotherapy*. New York: Basic Books.

Psychoanalytic engagement

The transaction as primary data[1] (1982)

Darlene Bregman Ehrenberg

In this paper I would like to address some questions of psychoanalytic technique. My focus will be on those ways in which the analyst can use himself or herself to facilitate the analytic process and analytic possibilities. I will approach this issue, about which there has been some ambiguity, from the point of view of the analytic interaction as an interpersonal field in which the reactions of each participant are significantly influenced by the overt and covert contributions of the other, as well as the way these responses are experienced.

Historically this interactional dimension of the patient–analyst relationship has received considerable attention in the interpersonal literature, particularly in the writings of Sullivan dating from the 1930s (1940 [1953], 1953, 1954, 1956, 1962), Fromm-Reichmann (1950, 1952), J. Rioch (1943), C. Thompson (1950, 1952), M. J. White (1952), Tauber (1954, 1979), Wolstein (1954, 1959, (1971, 1973), Feiner (1970, 1975, 1979), 1982), Singer (1971, 1977), Levenson (1972, 1974, 1981a, 1981b, (1982a, 1982b), Ehrenberg (1974, 1975, 1976), Epstein (1979), and Chrzanowski (1979).

The interactive orientation which is the *sine qua non* of interpersonal psychoanalysis also is important in the writings of others who do not necessarily consider themselves interpersonalists.

It is central in the papers of Lacan (1936, 1952, 1956 [1968], 1961 [1977]), for example, and in the work of Winnicott (1947, 1965, 1971), Little (1951, 1957), Fairbairn (1958), Guntrip (1969), and Searles (1965, 1979).

In the classical literature this view has appeared in essays by Menaker (1942), Gitelson (1952), Anna Freud (1954), Stone (1954, 1961, 1981), Tower (1956), Loewald (1960, 1970), Kernberg (1965), Greenson and Wexler (1969), Viderman (1974), Sandler (1976), Lipton (1977), Gill (1979, 1982, 1983), and Klauber (1981).

Writing from a Kleinian perspective, Heimann (1950) noted the analyst's role in provoking the patient's reactions, and Racker (1957) and Baranger and Baranger (1966) have elaborated field models of the analytic interaction.

Finally, following the Barangers, Langs (1976, 1979, 1981) has made this conception the fundamental consideration in his own extensive publications. It is evident that the interpersonal idea has gained recognition in the thinking of psychoanalysts of all schools. Although these authors differ in terms of their theories of personality, their concepts of health and pathology, their perspectives on technique and their visions of cure, they agree that the analytic interaction constitutes a transactional field.

I believe this has radical implications for a theory of technique. If we accept the concept of the analytic interaction as a transactional field, we are forced to expand the traditional view of the transference as the analytic "playground" (Freud, 1914 [1958]) and as the "point of urgency" (Strachey, 1934) to include all of the transactions in the immediate field of experience as the primary data. Although not all of the above authors would agree, a good number of them explicitly do. Fundamental to this position is a view of transference and countertransference as an interlocking unity, and a recognition that what is structured in the interactional process by both patient and analyst must be analytically addressed. It also follows that in the choice of whether to address the immediate transaction, and to what degree, or not to address it at all, the analyst exerts leverage on the way the relationship will evolve. Since within the transactional framework, whatever we do must be viewed as having impact and consequence, the question I would like to explore is whether there are ways to intervene deliberately to facilitate the work.

In earlier papers (1974, 1975, 1976) I pointed out the value of shifting the analytic focus from content to context. Making explicit the subtle cues sent and received out of awareness and the specific responses to them makes it possible to use the interaction as a diagnostic tool as well as a therapeutic medium. Monitoring transactional nuances becomes a means of minimizing dangers of seduction, coercion, collusion, or of other covert processes being enacted. If the immediate experience is used as the primary data the issues become tangible and emotionally significant associations to the past are elicited as the patient spontaneously produces relevant historical material. Since the goal is to keep the analytic process expanding, as long as affectively charged associations are flowing there often may be no need for the analyst to intervene.

My experience has been that the use of transactions between patient and analyst as primary data makes it possible to document the sequential interactions so that the analyst can clarify to the patient the patient's impact, even delineate the ways in which he structures this with others, as well as his sensitivities and patterns of responsiveness manifested toward the analyst. In this way the analytic work occurs in the transactions between patient and analyst. Styles and patterns of bonding can be studied in process, as expectations and feelings are available for analytic scrutiny. Vulnerability to confusion as to what is self-generated or what may reflect some pattern of unconscious responsiveness also becomes addressable. Limitations in the patient's capacity for mutuality can be clarified as well. Since the patient must be able to use the analysis, difficulties or reluctance to do this can be worked through in the immediate process.It is essential to confront these issues from the beginning of treatment to make the relationship viable. Yet the analyst identifies but does not challenge defenses and resistances. It is the differences in experience that are to be clarified and individual boundaries that are to be delineated. This allows those anxieties and unconscious fantasies which led to the defensiveness to become accessible.

For example[2]: a supervisee related that a patient he had begun to see was reporting self-destructive behavior outside of treatment. This was behavior the patient had never engaged in before. The analytic candidate was eager to arrive at some theoretical formulation based on this information and on historical data he had gathered so that he could make some interpretative intervention.

I suggested that the student consider that the patient's report might have as much to do with the patient's relationship to the analyst and to the treatment as it did to anything else. The following week the supervisee reported with excitement that our discussion had freed him to engage more directly with his patient. When he tried to explore the patient's feelings about the treatment and about himself, the patient became extremely responsive and commented that he felt like crying. The patient was able to articulate specific anxieties about the kind of attachment he believed he might want with the therapist. His fears were that the analyst would find this repellant and he documented evidence based on the therapist's responses to him. He elaborated reactions to experiences of partings and greetings with the therapist, and to experiences of seeing the therapist with other patients who came before or after him that were relevant, and of which the therapist had not been aware. As he described his reactions in the present, there were spontaneous associations to the past. In essence the associational process had been expanded as a result of the therapist's intervention that allowed the anxieties about engaging the immediate experience to be addressed. At this point reactions to the therapist's intervention, and the intense feelings this aroused could also be explored, in an almost limitless progression.

Once the analytic transaction is made the primary data, new questions can be raised. Certainly the ability to talk about the ongoing interaction may constitute a new and corrective experience for the patient. Nevertheless this alone may not be sufficient for transformation. How does one help facilitate those reparative (B. Ehrenberg, 1980) and restorative (Feiner, 1982) experiences that may be necessary for an analytic result to come about? Loewald (1960, 1970), Winnicott (1963 [1965]) and Gill (1983), among others, note that any successful analytic experience is inevitably corrective. Our problem is to maximize the corrective potentialities of the analytic relationship (Alexander, 1956) and maintain, at the same time, the relationship's analytic nature.

Many authors have noted, that with more disturbed or primitively organized patients the analyst's active responsiveness may be essential if any kind of therapeutic change is to be achieved (Bird, 1972; Fromm-Reichmann, 1952; Little, 1951, 1957; McDougall, 1979; Sandler, 1976; Searles, 1965; Singer, 1971; Stein, 1973; Tower, 1956; Winnicott, 1947). I believe the analyst's active responsiveness may be useful in the treatment of less disturbed patients as well. Singer (1971) and Searles (1965) comment on the beneficial consequences a patient derives from the experience of his ability to give to the analyst, to feel useful, relevant, appreciated.

Winnicott (1947) focuses on the importance of knowing one can evoke the analyst's hatred so that one can work through one's own, and of the opportunity to experience that it is possible for the analyst to withstand and survive one's aggressions. I believe that the discovery that neither participant need be damaged or diminished by expressions of positive feelings and experiences of closeness is equally profound. Similarly the opportunity to discover that it is possible to make reparations and to have them be accepted, when one has failed the other in some way (Fromm-Reichmann, 1950), helps contribute to awareness of each individual's interpersonal power and responsibilities. It becomes clear then that one need not be bound by the limitations of the other. Nor can one use the limitations and failings of the other to exempt oneself from responsibility for one's own behavior.

Clarification and resolution of difficulties relating to self and other in the analytic interaction allows for the possibility of new experiences of relatedness in the analytic context. If reciprocity can be achieved in the analytic relationship it may be the first experience of this kind the patient has had, and may become the basis for enabling the patient to engage in more reciprocal ways in all areas of living. Utilization of this therapeutic potential of the analytic relationship often becomes pivotal in facilitating change. With certain patients the analyst's nonresponsiveness may actually have negative consequences and contribute to iatrogenic difficulties and forms of regression (see, for example, Stone, 1954, 1961). Searles (1965) describes how some patients need consensual validation so as to remain convinced of the reliability of their own perceptions (particularly those perceptions of the therapist) and the ego-fragmentation that can occur if this is not provided. Obviously the critical question is what form of responsiveness is most beneficial. In this context it is necessary to recognize that even the more classical forms of interpretation and intervention have definite interactional meaning and consequences. Since there is always transactional meaning to what occurs, it becomes clear that there are ways in which this can be actively utilized, whether one agrees as to what is the most beneficial way to do so or not.

What defines an analytic relationship is that our impact, whether the result of deliberate interventions or the result of inadvertant aspects of our participation, must be explicitly clarified. Gill (1983), citing Freud's stress on the positive transference as the affective factor which opens the patient to influence (Freud, 1916–1917 [1963], pp. 450–453), emphasizes that what distinguishes analysis from suggestive forms of treatment which exploit the positive transference is that in analysis the transference is analyzed. Gill (1982) writes that if an analyst

> intruded himself as a person and did so knowingly and did not make that interaction explicit in the relationship even if he realized that the patient would resist recognizing what had happened he was being non-analytic.

The hallmark of an analytic relationship is that it is essential that there be no covert manipulation and that the patient be cognizant of whatever critical transactions have occurred as well as their impact.

The sense of helplessness the patient experiences when he can't see what the issues are, that is, when he is "mystified" (Laing, 1965), is mitigated as he begins to comprehend the ways in which he participates in and perpetuates his own state of mystification. As interpersonal boundaries become more sharply defined it is no longer possible for him to maintain distortions in perceiving individual responsibilities for what occurs. As repudiated and disavowed experiences are reclaimed perceptual integrity is achieved. It then becomes possible to search for the motivations for the disavowal in the first place in the context of a new sense of choice, competence, and responsibility.

The degree to which the patient experiences increasing trust in his own perceptions and in his interpersonal autonomy and effectiveness, in the analytic interaction, becomes a measure of analytic progress and a basis for new degrees of self confidence and self-esteem. As resistances to functioning autonomously and assuming responsibility in treatment are worked through, resolution of such difficulties in all areas of the patient's life is also facilitated. The analytic transaction, by its very interpersonal nature, thus provides unique opportunities for new experiences. It provides a context in which the patient can work through pathological perceptual patterns with regard to self and other, and become aware of and modify pathological interactions (Rioch, 1943; White, 1952), with awareness.

Some clinical illustrations follow. These examples do not include details of work with dreams. My focus is on the analyst's interventions to explicate the transactional subtleties of the relationship, particularly as these involve some measure of personal responsiveness and active engagement.

Example 1: Ronald, a young man in his twenties, was referred by a colleague after two years of treatment which seemed to have reached a stalemate. Despite acute somatic reactions to stress (including a severe colitis requiring several hospitalizations), and a history of obesity in the past (he was not obese at the time of treatment), Ronald was not aware of great emotional distress except about his physical condition. He was zombielike and detached. He claimed to have "no feelings," had little to say, and wasn't sure why he was coming to treatment. He would miss sessions and acted cynically as though he were saying, "What's the difference anyway?" This was his attitude in general, towards work and towards all relationships. Sessions were characterized by a kind of vapidity when he did come. I tried to convey to Ronald his impact on me.

I insisted that although he seemed to be reluctant to be concerned as to whether our sessions were useful in any way, I was not. I also said that I did not like to feel useless, which is what I did feel in these vacuous sessions. And I wondered if he were aware of his impact on me. He seemed quite surprised by this and became curious. By painstakingly following the minutest vicissitudes of his reactions with me, and mine to him, he seemed to become more responsive. He noticed that his stuporous detachment was itself a reaction to the situation, which instead of making him more invisible had impact on me. This was a revelation as far as he was concerned and affected him greatly. Gradually he began to get in touch with deep feelings of vulnerability, pain, sadness, and anger. This evoked many associations to his childhood which had been extremely traumatic, including memories of scenes of his father, a chronic alcoholic, physically threatening his mother with a knife and the terror the patient had experienced. He was able to experience with me the emotions he had not experienced then, as he told all this to me. At times I commented how painful some of the experiences he reported sounded, when I felt he was glossing over this. He reported that he was touched by the fact I did not accept his own efforts to minimize the extent of his pain. For the first time he could remember he was able to cry and to admit how hurt, hopeless, and desperate he felt.

The man who was untouchable and "did not care" was now very emotional, even passionate. He was able to describe a decision never to be vulnerable again, made out of anger and despair as a child, and a feeling that he would rather be dead. In the context of a growing sense of hope and possibility based on his actual experience of our relationship, he described with great emotion a desire to someday have a family of his own. He contrasted this with how reluctant he had always been to think about having children or a family due to the pain of his own experience and the wish not to inflict anything similar on a child. Three years after termination (treatment lasted about six years), he continues to be free of the somatic symptoms, is successful professionally, and is in a stable and gratifying relationship with a young woman with whom he had become involved during the course of our work.

I believe the fact that I engaged him the way I did and was as responsive as I had been was critical in this treatment. Some analysts fear that active engagement of the patient might foster some kind of pathological dependency. I think this example illustrates that often the analyst's responsiveness can facilitate a turning point in the work. Whatever the analyst's preference for technique, unless he or she can use his or her own aliveness to spark some life into the interaction it sometimes will remain dead. The analyst must engage in some affective way with the patient. If the patient is affectively absent it is essential that this be addressed. What is critical is that the interventions and their impact are made explicit.

Example 2: Dani, a young woman in her twenties, had been anorexic and suicidal. She also suffered from serious colitis and amenorrhea. She was unable to function apart from her family but felt like a "wild maniac" with them. She described experiencing her body as separate from herself, feeling dead inside, like a robot or a machine, unable to enjoy anything including sex, incapable of orgasm, and as experiencing a living death. She was intensely preoccupied with her body, her weight, and exercised fanatically. She described herself as knowing she was extremely beautiful (which she was) but, though obsessed with looking beautiful, spending hours putting on makeup and trying on different clothes, hating how she looked and often unable to go out because she felt ugly and fat. She was five feet six inches tall and weighed one hundred pounds. She would go on eating binges, then starve herself and take laxatives. She would drink herself into oblivion, or eat dog food to make herself sick. She would sleep with men she hated. She would compulsively steal things she did not need or buy things she could not afford. Her explanation was that it was as though forces "beyond her control" took over. She could not distinguish between dreams and hallucinations and found this terrifying. She insisted her behavior had no rhyme or reason and described feeling like a helpless bystander in relation to herself.

Her attitude toward treatment was one of cynicism, pessimism, and despair. She was suspicious about being exploited or manipulated by me. For many months she began every session stating she was going to go to California instead of going through with treatment, but she continued to come three times a week. I focused on the fact that all she felt she was obliged to do was to bring her body to the sessions and the rest was up to me, and how this seemed to characterize her relation to every aspect of her life. This clarified how actively she was attempting to place the major share of the responsibility for the treatment on me and challenged her view of herself as the helpless victim. This made patently clear what she did interpersonally, which she had never grasped before.

As I directed my efforts toward trying to discover the logic of what she experienced as her own incomprehensible radical mood swings I was able to relate these to specific events in our interaction. She was almost embarrassed to be "caught," as her tantrums in relation to me, her threats to destroy my office and attack other patients, and to "do herself in" to get back at me could be clearly seen as the consequence of her acute sensitivity to any lapses in attention or alertness on my part.

The consequence of all of this was that she could no longer argue that she was a hopeless "maniac" whose behavior was beyond comprehension. She described a sense of coming out of a fog, of feeling the veil or cloud she had been submerged in was lifting. There were shifts back and forth from the new level of functioning to the old. When I subsequently was a few minutes late for a session she became distressed and agitated and would not accept my apology. She acted as though I had mortally wounded her in an unforgiveable way and refused to speak the whole session.

When I noted, in the following session, how punitive she had been and expressed my own dislike of being treated that way, she acknowledged that I could have apologized till kingdom come, she would not have yielded. There were associations to hearing her parents in their bedroom and feeling excluded and that was how it felt when she was outside in the waiting room and I was inside my office with another patient. She elaborated how she used to make scenes to keep her parents apart and how painful it was when they were together and she was excluded. She then did apologize to me for not accepting my apology and said it was the way she used to respond to her mother. She described how she used to "get away with murder" by presenting herself as not responsible, and how successfully she had used her tantrums to manipulate and get between her parents. In one session when it was clear that much was still unresolved and the session was about to end, she raged about the fact I would leave her this way before a weekend. She expressed a great deal of anger toward me for opening her up to so much pain. She threatened she would go out and walk in front of a bus and kill herself if I didn't help her that moment. I told her that I did not like to be threatened. I noted also that her inability to endure any frustration seemed to be part of the problem. She became sheepish and said she used to do this kind of thing with her parents and her boyfriends and usually it worked. She reported after the weekend that she held together without causing any catastrophes, but cried that it had been a great strain. She stated that for the first time, however, despite all her prior treatment, she realized she would have to take responsibility for herself.

As we explored further her feelings about our transactions she began to express remorse and regret for how awful she had been to her parents, boyfriends, siblings and me, and to struggle to develop new ways of relating. Her self-esteem increased markedly as she discovered her own capacities to be compassionate and sensitive to me and that I was responsive to her gestures. It also became clear that she had always used herself as an instrument to evoke particular responses from others, often at the expense of her own needs and well-being. We learned, for example, that her body had become a battleground for complicated psychological dramas. Eating and not eating had become ways of pleasing and hurting others. The same applied to sex and to decisions to live or die. These had all been ways of asserting herself, and feeling she had some power. Nevertheless the sense of desperation and impotence she felt otherwise was now clear. She discovered that she could express her feelings more directly, and be even more effective, and avoid the negative repercussions of the acting out.

Her symptoms abated and she stabilized her weight between one hundred ten and one hundred fifteen pounds. She also developed a romantic relationship with a young man and began to establish herself as a freelance professional.

After two years of work on her anxieties about the work and her intensifying relationship with me and with her boyfriend, she felt more confident and less angry and vulnerable. About this time she began to menstruate, and after a long interval of struggling with a decision regarding whether she wanted to live with her boyfriend she decided to live with him.

The new situation of living with a boyfriend intensified all her fears of closeness and of her own vulnerability. She struggled with fears of sexual dependence, fears of orgasm, and was able to link these fears to the dynamics of the anorexia. That is, she resisted taking in anything as a defense against her fear of not being able to control her desires or her dependency needs if allowed expression. Fears of being hurt or disappointed, helplessly at the mercy of the other who might give or withhold, and resentment of her own feelings of intense vulnerability once she allowed herself to care, all surfaced now in relation to me. There were associations to her feelings regarding a recent ski injury

I had suffered that had left me on crutches for an extended period, as to how vulnerable it made her realize she was. The result of being able to acknowledge all of these feelings was that she was also able to realize the ways in which she was not helpless and could survive disappointment. Following this, she reported increasing ability to enjoy sex and to experience orgasm.

At a point when things were going well with her boyfriend she expressed new fears that continued treatment, which had become the metaphor of her right to be her own person, might pose a threat to her love relationship. She was aware of impulses to resort to earlier patterns of sacrificing her own needs to avoid any risks. At the same time she expressed fears that she could not sustain the love relationship without treatment, fears that treatment would go on forever, and awareness of her resentment of her sense of dependence on me. As she articulated all of this she was able to express how she felt stronger, whole, and more independent than she had ever felt in her life.

Example 3: Michael, a young man in his twenties, who also had had prior treatment, suffered from many somatic complaints. These, however, were described as incidental. His presenting complaint was that he had been and continued to be plagued, since his sophomore year in college after his best friend had a breakdown, by gory fantasies of being physically injured, mutilated, or castrated by razor blades. The atmosphere of our sessions was tense and oppressive and dominated by these fantasies, now in relation to me.

He believed his morbid fantasies were unpredictable, had no relation to anything and were proof he was "crazy." He was extremely bright and he felt "different" from other people. Coupled with the feeling that he had to hide what he viewed as his pathological fantasy life from others, he felt a morbid sense of isolation. Being able to tell me all this allowed him to feel more connected and less isolated than he had felt with anyone else.

I struggled to discern some pattern in our interaction and by tracking the most seemingly trivial minutiae was able to point out to him that if I seemed the least bit distracted he was sure to experience a gory fantasy while simultaneously responding in an accepting way. For example, a yawn could set him off. Gradually without either of us being aware of it sessions became less oppressive. We were able to focus on the degree to which he seemed to need to deny his real sensitivities, as he actually became more conscious of them. This was a great relief and he expressed many positive feelings toward me for my role in this development. He was now able to express how vulnerable he felt in relation to me, and there was a flood of memories of childhood fears, dreams, and experiences.

After a long period of work, he began to express intense sexual and murderous feelings towards me and anxiety about these feelings. In the course of all of this there were many associations to his childhood and he described similar sexual and murderous feelings toward his mother which were still current. Eventually we developed a hypothesis that these feelings he experienced toward me (and anticipated from me) might have some basis in his actual experience with his mother. This led him to a courageous and dramatic confrontation with her, in which he reported that she confirmed that she had had suicidal fantasies every day for a period of years and these involved killing her children as well as herself. He also reported that as she related this to him he was aware that she was being very sexually provocative. All of this was a revelation. Over time he became more direct, able to be tender and assertive, and increasingly playful and self-confident. In contrast to his deferential, self-deprecating stance in our early work he now began to enjoy and flaunt his real intelligence and creativity and to challenge or compete with me. In one session he challenged me to read my notes back to him, expressing his surprise and delight when I did. He also proceeded to tell me that I should not forget to write down that I was doing so. He was charming and sessions became a playful, exploratory delight for both of us. This led to a new phase during which he began to be overtly seductive and to vigorously challenge the boundaries of our relationship, with fears that I might respond.

Moments of closeness now aroused fantasies of being murdered or castrated. Following their scrutiny he began to feel more secure with me and to speak about his anxieties about daring to be less than charming, his anxieties about his physical attractiveness, his sexual capacities, and a phobia of having anyone see his naked body. He said he couldn't imagine he could ever feel this free with anyone else, and worried whether I would be jealous if in fact he could. He described feeling more self-confident outside of treatment. He actually looked physically different as he stood straighter and taller. During this period despite a long term preoccupation that he might be homosexual, he began to venture out heterosexually and was successful beyond his expectations.

Example 4: Elizabeth, a young woman in her twenties, was unable to talk to anyone or to manage the simple realities of living at the time we met. She was barely audible in our first sessions, but managed to convey that she wanted to see me once a week and to find a group once a week, and she insisted she would need medication. I said that it seemed to me this plan reflected her anxieties about throwing all her eggs in one basket. She readily agreed this was true. She had had several prior treatment experiences, had been through long periods of inability to function without heavy medication, and had previously been anorexic. Although she felt she had had one positive therapeutic relationship she felt most of her relationships in the past, in and out of treatment, had been destructive and sado-masochistic, and she stated, "Why should I assume this experience will be different from so many others?"

I suggested that if she were going to give our work together a chance she would have to take a risk and not just go through the motions. I encouraged her to come twice a week and forego the group and medication long enough to decide for herself whether working with me could be of any value. She was terrified, skeptical, cynical. We struggled with this over a period of sessions.

I suggested that it was critical to clarify her anxieties about treatment, and her fantasies about how she was planning to use it, before we could expect any meaningful work to be possible. The issue as I saw it was her cynicism and despair about the possibilities of ever changing or of ever getting help. We could easily go through the motions but she had done this enough times before to realize this was not what she needed. In a sense the first issue would have to be how we could work together in a meaningful and productive way, and what was her own reluctance to allow this to happen.

After several sessions she decided to forego the group and medication and we began to meet twice a week. She remained wary. During this time she studied every detail of my behavior, every facial expression, every change in posture, and confronted me with these as evidence of my lack of interest in her. I had to strain to hear her since she was virtually inaudible. I noted how sensitive and vulnerable she obviously felt, but also how challenging and demanding she was being in relation to me; and how she was structuring our interaction as a test of me rather than trying to see if it could really be of use to her. It became clear how this was specifically sabotaging the possibility that treatment could be of any benefit to her. Although it constituted a form of protection it was also self defeating and served to ensure ultimately another disappointment in treatment. It also was clear that the fears she experienced in relation to me and to treatment permeated every aspect of her life and experience.

She was able then to elaborate how she had made it her goal to become impenetrable to defend against dangers of being infiltrated, violated, or destructively influenced and altered. This she saw as a kind of heroic attempt to maintain her own integrity, as was her anorexia. Her fear was that if she were to open herself even a little bit, to be needful or dependent in any way, she would be totally vulnerable and defenseless. She was able to document many painful experiences of hurt and humiliation, and how she had been devastatingly disappointed and betrayed when she had taken risks. She had no sense of what her own participation was in this. Clarifying how she contributed to the perpetuation of these experiences was critical. The fact I was not willing to exploit her was significant but insufficient. What also was required was to help her see what she was doing in specific detail. The experience that something positive could come out of our work in this way was healing in itself and encouraged her to take further risks. Our relationship became increasingly important to her and she decided to come three times a week.

When I had to reschedule a session some time later, she became devastated and felt betrayed. She went into a rage. It was as though all we had achieved was now destroyed. She was unwilling to accept my apology and despite my efforts at opening this for discussion she was absolutely unyielding, unwilling to consider anything I might say. I stated that I understood how painful this was to her, but I also emphasized how inconsiderate and punitive she was being toward me. I insisted that on the basis of our work so far I believed I had at least earned the right for her to forgive me for something I could not help, and that if she would not I felt I had as much right to be angry at her as she felt she had to be angry at me. This seemed to break through the otherwise implacable wall of rage. There was even a hint of a smile as she commented, "If you are poor and starving you can't afford to be generous." This permitted us to explore the extent of her sense of voracious neediness and emotional hunger. There were many associations and memories of how getting close in the past, particularly in relation to her father, had always resulted in devastating betrayals and that that was her fear in relation to me.

She reported the next session that she felt better than she had in weeks after the last session and how touched she was that I was willing to "fight" with her. We were able to see that her usual way of dealing with things was that if she couldn't have all she would take nothing. She began to see how self defeating this inevitably was. In contrast to the desperate starving feeling she had reported earlier, she now began to describe with some embarrassment how "full" she felt in response to our sessions.

All the fears of being at the mercy of others when she felt close to anyone now intensified as she opened herself in treatment. She began to fear that I would make sexual or other claims and that she wouldn't be able to resist. She reported also that she had begun to have sexual feelings for me. She described how this had happened with every therapist she had ever seen, male or female, even those she didn't like and to whom she wasn't attracted. This marked the beginning of a period of work in which we were able to understand that the dangers she feared from the other often reflected her own projected wishes. It became possible to explore also the degree of internal violence and "self annihilation" she was capable of and felt the need to inflict on herself.

Sometime after, she began a session by acting out a pantomime that I could not understand, When I asked her to please explain she continued her behavior and ignored my question. This went on for an extended period during which I felt increasingly uneasy and worried about her state of mind. Finally she stated she had been doing this to test me and to test our relationship. Her fear was that our relationship could only endure if she pleased me. Her wish was to test our relationship, and she felt her behavior was an act of courage and hope. Once this was spelled out I did become irritated at having been played with in this way. At the same time I made it clear that my feeling was independent of my respect for her. I suggested that it had to do with the fact that I cared enough about myself to refuse to accept being treated badly by her. She stated that realizing she could make me angry and create such a distance between us made her aware of how much she valued the closeness between us and how much that was something she had the ability to define. This was a revelation to her. She then described how she finally understood how she always tried to control the other person's responses by trying to please. I replied that I liked her, which I did, and that her efforts to please me were irrelevant to my feelings for her. She started to cry and stated that she was finally beginning to understand, and that she was beginning to recognize that it was possible for people to be angry at each other without necessarily becoming sadistic toward each other or ending the relationship.

She saw too that she had a right to demand that she not be treated sadistically, though not to demand that the other never be angry at her. Her anxieties about standing up for herself, her sense of desperate neediness, and the assumption that her survival required compromising or degrading herself in order to sustain relationships now could be further explored.

Elizabeth spontaneously told me some time later that the fact I had been willing to live through her experiences with her, that she felt treated as a person rather than a "case," is what mattered most to her and made it possible for her to take the risks she did. That I made real demands on her to participate in a constructive and honest way, and expected to be treated decently despite my limitations, forced her to work through her own expectations. By confronting and dealing with the realities of my person and our situation she could begin to work through her intolerance of frustration and disappointment about an imperfect world, and to grapple with her feelings about her sense of her own imperfections as well.

In the context of a view of the analytic relationship as a transactional field in which the contributions of each participant are influenced by the overt and covert reactions of the other, I have emphasized the importance of using the immediate transactional experience as primary analytic data. I have tried to explore additional ways in which the analyst can actively participate to enhance the analytic work.

Illustrations were presented of specific ways of actively engaging with the patient that I have used in my own work in the context of my interest in finding ways to expand the analytic possibilities both in terms of treatable pathology and in terms of achievable results.

Notes

1 I am grateful to Drs. B. Ehrenberg and A. H. Feiner who helped me crystallize the ideas presented in this paper. I also wish to thank Drs. M. Gill, P. E. Gordon, F. Lachmann, E. A. Levenson and E. G. Witenberg for their comments and suggestions. Portions of the material were presented at the New York University Postdoctoral Program in Psychoanalysis and Psychotherapy, December 11, 1981; and at the clinical conference at the William Alanson White Institute, January 19, 1982.

2 This example is based on a patient in psychoanalytic psychotherapy, not in psychoanalysis. For the purposes of my illustration the distinction does not seem relevant. (See Gill, 1982b for a discussion of this issue.)

References

Alexander, F. (1956). *Psychoanalysis and Psychotherapy*. New York: W. W. Norton.

Baranger, M. & Baranger, W. (1966). Insight in the analytic situation In R. E. Litman (Ed.), *Psychoanalysis in the Americas*. New York: International Universities Press, pp. 57–72.

Bird, B. (1972). Notes on transference: Universal phenomenon and hardest part of analysis. *Journal of the American Psychoanalytic Association*, 20: 267–301.

Chrzanowski, G. (1979). The transference–countertransference interaction. *Contemporary Psychoanalysis*, 15: 458–471.

Ehrenberg, B. (1980). The repair of the unconscious. *Contemporary Psychoanalysis*, 16: 249–257.

Ehrenberg, D. B. (1974). The intimate edge in therapeutic relatedness. *Contemporary Psychoanalysis*, 10: 423–437.

Ehrenberg, D. B. (1975). The quest for intimate relatedness. *Contemporary Psychoanalysis*, 11: 320–331.

Ehrenberg, D. B. (1976). The "intimate edge" and the "third area." *Contemporary Psychoanalysis*, 12: 489–496.

Epstein, L. (1979). The therapeutic function of hate in the countertransference. In L. Epstein & A. Feiner (Eds), *Countertransference*. New York: Jason Aronson.

Fairbairn, W. R. (1958). On the nature and aims of psycho-analytical treatment. *International Journal of Psychoanalysis*, 39: 374–385.

Feiner, A. (1970). Toward an understanding of the experience of inauthenticity. *Contemporary Psychoanalysis*, 7: 64–83.

Feiner, A. (1975). The dilemma of integrity. *Contemporary Psychoanalysis*, 11: 500–509.

Feiner, A. (1979). Countertransference and the anxiety of influence. In L. Epstein & A. Feiner (Eds), *Countertransference*. New York: Jason Aronson.

Feiner, A. (1982). Comments on the difficult patient. *Contemporary Psychoanalysis*, 18: 397–411.

Freud, A. (1954). The widening scope of indications for psychoanalysis. *Journal of the American Psychoanalytic Association*, 2: 607–620.

Freud, S. (1914 [1958]). *Remembering, Repeating and Working through*, Standard Edition 12. London: Hogarth Press, p. 154.

Freud, S. (1916–1917 [1955]). *Introductory Lectures on Psycho-Analysis*, Standard Editions 15–16. London: Hogarth Press.

Fromm-Reichmann, F. (1950). *Principles of Intensive Psychotherapy*. Chicago, IL: University of Chicago Press.

Fromm-Reichmann, F. (1952). Some aspects of psychoanalytic psychotherapy with schizophrenia. In E. B. Brody & C. F. Redlich (Eds), *Psychotherapy with Schizophrenics*. New York: International Universities Press.

Gill, M. (1979). The analysis of the transference. *Journal of the American Psychoanalytic Association*, 27: 263–288 (Supplement).

Gill, M. (1982). The distinction between the interpersonal paradigm and the nature of the interpersonal relationship. Paper presented at the William Alanson White Institute, April 2.

Gill, M. (1983). The interpersonal paradigm and the degree of the therapist's involvement. *Contemporary Psychoanalysis*, 19: 200–237.

Gitelson, M. (1952). The emotional position of the analyst in the psychoanalytic situation. *International Journal of Psychoanalysis*, 33: 1–10.

Greenson, R. & Wexler, M. (1969). The non-transference relationship in the psychoanalytic situation. *International Journal of Psychoanalysis*, 50: 27–39.

Guntrip, H. (1969). *Schizoid Phenomena, Object Relations and the Self.* New York: International Universities Press.

Heimann, P. (1950). On countertransference. *International Journal of Psychoanalysis*, 31: 81–84.

Kernberg, O. (1965). Countertransference. *Journal of the American Psychoanalytic Association*, 13: 38–56.

Klauber, J. (1981). *Difficulties in the Analytic Encounter*. New York: Jason Aronson.

Lacan, J. (1936). Au delà du 'Principe de réalité. *L'Evolution Psychiatrique*, 3: 67–86.

Lacan, J. (1952). Intervention sur le transfert. *Revue Francaise de Psychanalyse*, XVI: 154–163.

Lacan, J. (1956 [1968]). Fonction et champ de la parole et du langäge en psychanalyse. *La Psychanalyse.* In A Wilder (trans), *The Language of the Self.*Baltimore, MD: Johns Hopkins University Press.

Lacan, J. (1961 [1977]). La direction de la cure et les principes de son pouvoir. *La Psychanalyse*, 6: 149–206. In A. Sheridan (trans), *The Direction of the Treatment and the Principles of its Power*. New York: W. W. Norton.

Laing, R. (1965). Mystification, confusion and conflict. In I. Boszormenyi-Nagy & J. L. Framo (Eds), *Intensive Family Therapyo.* New York; Harper and Row.

Langs, R. (1976). *The Bipersonal Field.* New York: Jason Aronson.

Langs, R. (1979). The interaction dimension of countertransference. In L. Epstein & A. Feiner (Eds), *Countertransference*. New York: Jason Aronson.

Langs, R. (1981). Modes of "cure" in psychoanalysis and psychoanalytic psychotherapy. *International Journal of Psychoanalysis*, 62: 199–214.

Levenson, E. (1972). *The Fallacy of Understanding*. New York: Basic Books.

Levenson, E. (1974). Changing concepts of intimacy in psychoanalytic practice. *Contemporary Psychoanalysis*, 10: 359–369.

Levenson, E. (1981a). Facts or fantasies: On the nature of psychoanalytic data. *Contemporary Psychoanalysis*, 17: 486–500.

Levenson, E. (1981b). The rhetoric of intimacy. Paper presented to the Eastern Group Psychotherapy Association, October.

Levenson, E. (1982a). Follow the fox. *Contemporary Psychoanalysis*, 18: 1–15.

Levenson, E. (1982b). Playground or playpen. *Contemporary Psychoanalysis*, 18: 365–372.

Lipton, S. D. (1977). The advantage of Freud's technique as shown in his analysis of the Rat Man. *International Journal of Psychoanalysis*, 58: 255–274.
Little, M. (1951). Countertransference and the patient's response to it. *International Journal of Psychoanalysis*, 32: 32–40.
Little, M. (1957). "R" – The analyst's response to his patient's needs. *International Journal of Psychoanalysis*, 38: 240–254.
Loewald, H. (1960). On the therapeutic action of psychoanalysis. *International Journal of Psychoanalysis*, 41: 16–33.
Loewald, H. (1970). Psychoanalytic theory and the psychoanalytic process. *Psychoanalytic Study of the Child*, 25: 45–68.
McDougall, J. (1979). Countertransference and primitive communication. In L. Epstein & A. Feiner (Eds), *Countertransference*. New York: Jason Aronson.
McDougall, J. (1982). From psychosomatosis to psychoneurosis: Reflections on the relationship between psychosomatic and hysterical phenomena. Paper presented at the William Alanson White Institute, February 5.
Menaker, E. (1942). The masochistic factor in the psychoanalytic situation. *Psychoanalytic Quarterly*, 11: 171–186.
Racker, H. (1957). The meaning and uses of countertransference. *Psychoanalytic Quarterly*, 26: 303–357.
Rioch, J. M. (1943). The transference phenomenon in psychoanalytic therapy. *Psychiatry*, 6: 147–156.
Sandler, J. (1976). Countertransference and role responsiveness. *International Review of Psychoanalysis*, 3: 43–47.
Searles, H. (1965). *Collected Papers on Schizophrenia and Related Subjects*. New York: International Universities Press.
Searles, H. (1979). *Countertransference and Related Subjects: Selected Papers*. New York: International Universities Press.
Singer, E. (1971). The patient aids the analyst: Some clinical and theoretical observations. In B. Landis & E. Tauber (Eds), *In the Name of Life*. New York: Holt, Rinehart and Winston.
Singer, E. (1977). The fiction of analytic anonymity. In K. Frank (Ed.), *The Human Dimension in Psychoanalytic Practice*. New York: Grune and Stratton.
Stein, M. (1973). Acting out as a character trait: Its relation to transference. *Psychoanalytic Study of the Child*, 28: 347–364.
Strachey, J. (1934). The nature of the therapeutic action of psyhoanalysis. *International Journal of Psychoanalysis*, 15: 127–159.
Stone, L. (1954). The widening scope of indications for psychoanalysis. *Journal of the American Psychoanalytic Association*, 2: 567–594.
Stone, L. (1961). *The Psychoanalytic Situation*. New York: International Universities Press.
Stone, L. (1973). On resistance to the psychoanalytic process In B. B. Rubinstein (Ed.), *Psychoanalysis and Contemporary Science*. New York: Macmillan, pp. 42–73.
Stone, L. (1981). Some thoughts on the "here and now" in psychoanalytic technique and process. *Psychoanalytic Quarterly*, 50: 709–731.

Sullivan, H. S. (1940 [1953]). Conceptions of modern psychiatry In *Collected Works*, Volume I. New York: W. W. Norton.
Sullivan, H. S. (1953). The interpersonal theory of psychiatry. In *Collected Works*. New York: W. W. Norton.
Sullivan, H. S. (1954). The psychiatric interview. In *Collected Works*. New York: W. W. Norton.
Sullivan, H. S. (1956). Clinical studies in psychiatry. In *Collected Works*. New York: W. W. Norton.
Sullivan, H. S. (1962). Schizophrenia as a human process. In *Collected Works*. New York: W. W. Norton.
Tauber, E. (1954). Exploring the therapeutic use of countertransference data. *Psychiatry*, 17: 331–336.
Tauber, E. (1979). Countertransference reexamined. In L. Epstein & A. Feiner (Eds), *Countertransference*. New York: Jason Aronson.
Thompson, C. (1950). *Psychoanalysis: Evolution and Development*. New York: Hermitage House.
Thompson, C. (1952). Counter-transference. *Samiksa*, 6: 205–211.
Tower, L. (1956). Countertransference. *Journal of the American Psychoanalytic Association*, 4: 224–255.
Viderman, S. (1974). Interpretation in the analytical space. *International Review of Psychoanalysis*, 1: 467–480.
White, M. J. (1952). Sullivan and treatment. In P. Mullahy (Ed.), *The Contributions of Harry Stack Sullivan*. New York: Hermitage House, pp. 117–150.
Winnicott, D. W. (1947). Hate in the countertransference. In *Collected Papers: Through Paediatrics to Psycho-Analysis*. London: Tavistock Publications.
Winnicott, D. W. (1963 [1965]). Dependence in infant-care, in child-care, and in the psychoanalytic setting. In *The Maturational Processes and the Facilitating Environment*. New York: International Universities Press.
Winnicott, D. W. (1971). *Playing and Reality*. New York: Basic Books.
Wolstein, B. (1954). *Transference*. New York: Grune and Stratton.
Wolstein, B. (1959). *Countertransference*. New York: Grune and Stratton.
Wolstein, B. (1971). Human psyche. In *Psychoanalysis*. Springfield, IL: Charles C. Thomas.
Wolstein, B. (1973). The new significance of psychoanalytic structure. In E. G. Witenberg (Ed.), *Interpersonal Explorations in Psychoanalysis*. New York: Basic Books.

Chapter 9

The interpersonal paradigm and the degree of the therapist's involvement[1] (1983)

Merton M. Gill

Beginning in the late 1970s and accelerating in the 1980s, classical Freudian analysts in the United States began to embrace ideas that had been associated for many decades with interpersonal psychoanalysis. For the most part this absorption of interpersonal psychoanalytic theory seems to have taken place without the awareness of the Freudian writers who carried it out. These Freudian writers did not realize the resemblance of their new ideas to an intellectual and clinical tradition that they and their predecessors had dismissed for many years as superficial, unacceptably "environmental," and social-psychological.

Merton M. Gill, a highly prominent and leading thinker in the classical psychoanalytic community for many years, began writing about transference in the late 1970s in a way that reflected an interpersonal sensibility, although he did not actually know about interpersonal psychoanalysis until he was already several years into this phase of his work. A number of psychoanalysts from the William Alanson White Institute wrote to Gill at that point, drawing his attention to the literature on interpersonal psychoanalysis. Gill was receptive, and he embarked on a thorough study of the interpersonal literature. The article we reprint here was the eventual result.

Gill was invited to the White Institute, where he delivered the article to the William Alanson White Society, the society of graduates of the Institute. Gill is actually the only author in this collection who neither felt explicitly identified with the interpersonal tradition nor was trained at a psychoanalytic institute identified with the interpersonal point of view – although, in our opinion, by 1983, the date of the article we reprint here, Gill deserved designation as an interpersonal analyst.

By that time, Gill had already been considered one of the more liberal Freudian theorists for two decades, having been part of a group of analysts (George Klein, Roy Schafer, Robert Holt, and others) who were critical of the centrality of metapsychology and argued for a hermeneutic psychoanalysis. Gill reports in the article we reprint that more and more of his colleagues were telling him during these years that he sounded interpersonal. He seemed to take this news more seriously than any of the other classical writers of his time who were told something similar.

As noted in most of the previous chapters here, Sullivan's introduction of the participant-observation model made it impossible for interpersonalists to believe that the analyst was an objective observer who could position himself outside the analytic process. In the article we reprint, Gill wonders if this characterization of the analyst's role was a prescription for excessive verbal activity on the part of the analyst, or perhaps, for an inclination for the analyst to be especially friendly or to offer the patient counsel. On the basis of his survey of interpersonal writing, Gill answered these questions in the negative, arguing for the conclusion, also reached by Jay Greenberg (see Chapter 7), that participant-observation was a *de*scription, not a *pre*scription. That is, if two people undertake a psychoanalysis, both parties inevitably participate – not only consciously, but unconsciously as well. The analyst cannot possibly be aware of all that he communicates, and so he cannot assume that what the patient observes about him is a distortion based exclusively on projection (i.e., the patient's psychic reality). Gill went so far as to conclude that participant-observation was not a sufficiently radical term to capture the considerable degree of unwitting participation on the analyst's part. Gill preferred a term for the analyst's work that laid more emphasis on the analyst's participation and less on his observation. This had been suggested earlier in this volume by Benjamin Wolstein (see Chapter 2), wherein he characterizes the analyst as far more of an observing-participant than a participant-observer.

In much of his writing during this late period of his work Gill extends the concept of transference into the two-person framework of a transference–countertransference matrix – the interpersonalization of the concept of transference. Embracing many of the contributions of Edgar Levenson, Gill underscores both the inevitability and the therapeutic power of mutual enactments and the necessity to urge patients to articulate consistently their experience of the analytic relationship and of the participation of the analyst.

As described by Wolstein, Levenson, and Ehrenberg, the heart of psychoanalysis lies in the analysis of the analytic interaction. Gill suggests, as did Levenson before him, that the verbal articulation of immediate, here-and-now experience, when linked with an awareness of the patient's historical interpersonal patterning, makes it possible for the patient to internalize new and more salubrious interpersonal configurations.

The interpersonal paradigm and the degree of the therapist's involvement[1] (1983)

Merton M. Gill

I will begin with a brief account of the history of this paper because I believe that will make it more understandable. During the past few years when I have presented my views on the centrality of the analysis of transference and especially on the participation of the analyst in determining how the transference is expressed I have on occasion been asked what was the relation between my ideas and those of Sullivan and later interpersonalists. The question usually implied that there was a strong similarity. Having been reared as a proper Freudian with a more or less unthinking dismissal of Sullivan and interpersonal writings, I was unable to answer. I told myself that I should study these writings, even if I had to risk losing illusions of originality.

What finally forced me to take the question of the relation between my ideas and interpersonal writings seriously was the invitation to present a paper to you. Indeed the invitation referred to a compatibility between my ideas on transference and your views. So I began to read your writings, especially the journal *Contemporary Psychoanalysis*, but also books by Chrzanowski (1977), Levenson (1972), Singer (1965), and Wolstein (1959). What follows is the partial result of reflection on this reading, which naturally was in the context of how it related to my ideas on transference.

I became progressively aware of an important distinction between two cleavages in psychoanalytic thought which had been more or less fused in my mind. It may be that the clarification of this distinction is especially newsworthy for someone trained in the Freudian tradition like myself. Nevertheless I believe it will be worthwhile to state it sharply for this audience too because although it is referred to in various ways in the interpersonal literature I am not aware that it has been explicitly focused upon as a major issue. In any case my experience was that I had to dig it out for myself.

I refer to the distinction between two major cleavages in psychoanalytic thought: one cleavage is between the interpersonal paradigm and the drive discharge paradigm. The other cleavage is between those who believe the analyst inevitably participates in a major way in the analytic situation and those who do not. I came to realize that I had assumed that these two cleavages ran parallel to each other, or at least that those who adhered to the interpersonal paradigm would also ascribe to the analyst a major participation in the analytic situation.

That I had made this assumption implied an intrinsic connection between the interpersonal paradigm and a major participation on the one hand and the drive discharge paradigm and a minor involvement on the other.

To attempt to discover whether the assumption of such intrinsic connections is justified would require an examination and comparison of the interpersonal and drive discharge paradigms. That is an important and difficult task which I am not attempting in this paper. I should say however that I believe it can be demonstrated that there is no such intrinsic connection. I will also say that I suspect that in the course of such an examination it will turn out that the cleavage between interpersonal and drive discharge paradigms will be paralleled by the current controversy between the hermeneutic and metapsychological positions in psychoanalytic theory with the hermeneutic position allied to the interpersonal paradigm and the metapsychological to the drive discharge paradigm. Such a discussion would also have to distinguish between Freud's theories about object relations and an interpersonal paradigm. It would furthermore have to take account of Kernberg's views that the two paradigms are not incompatible (1980). I also suggest that the participant observation theorem may not necessarily imply the interpersonal relations paradigm. I mean that it may be that one can agree that any psychological observation is influenced by the position of the observer without necessarily agreeing that all psychological observations must have interpersonal relations as their basic organizing framework.

My goals in this paper are much more modest than the comparison of the paradigms. I wish to demonstrate first that the cleavages are indeed not parallel in our literature, that is, that an adherent of the interpersonal paradigm need not ascribe a major participant role to the analyst and that an adherent of the drive discharge pattern may ascribe a major participant role to the analyst. Then I will outline some of the implications for technique which I believe follow if one accepts the interpersonal paradigm. I emphasize that I am explicitly distinguishing between the interpersonal paradigm and object relations theory.

First I will show that the paradigms and the quality of participation do not run parallel. The demonstration depends on yet further assumptions, namely that an analyst who calls himself Freudian adheres to the drive discharge paradigm while an analyst who considers himself a Sullivanian adheres to the interpersonal paradigm. I realize that these assumptions may not hold. Indeed it is my hope that the very discrepancies among avowed allegiance to a particular school of psychoanalysis, a particular paradigm, and a particular view of the analyst's participation will suggest that functional groupings which cross cut avowed allegiances tell more about how an analyst works than allegiances do.

I will first quote a statement by Abrams and Shengold (1978, p. 402), two staunch Freudians, to show that they distinguish between themselves and those who ascribe a major participant role to the analyst. The statement occurs in a paper summing up the International Psychoanalytic Congress of 1977. After sketching what would be generally accepted as the Freudian model they say that

> clinical investigation and theory building over the past fifty years have tested and challenged much of this with the result that some analysts have developed substantially different views of the psychoanalytic situation ... in the new model ... the psychoanalytic situation is seen primarily as an *encounter* between two people, rather than as a setting whose purpose is the examination of the intrapsychic processes of one of them.

It was made in a context which implied that the new model is the Kleinian. I leave aside for now the question of whether the Kleinian theory is based on a drive discharge or an interpersonal paradigm. My point here is that these representatives of the Freudian position believe there is a cleavage between themselves and those who see the analytic situation as an encounter, that is, that the latter see the analyst as appropriately significantly involved as a participant in the analytic situation whereas they do not.

My next illustration is an example of a Freudian, presumably an adherent of the drive discharge paradigm, who ascribes a major role to the analyst. James McLaughlin (1981, p. 652), sufficiently respected and trusted by his colleagues that he was chosen to give the final summing up statement at the meeting of the International Psychoanalytic Association (1981), has written recently that several analysts from quite different operational positions, have provided rich data to demonstrate that both parties are caught up in a communicative field of incredible sensitivity and subtlety, with transferential–countertransferential shadings constantly at play in enormous affective intensities – a field in which the possibility of a neutral or catalytic comment, given or received, is remote indeed.

The theme of the paper in which this remark occurs is that it is a mistake to have different terms for the patient's and the analyst's participations in the analytic situation, that is, to distinguish between them by calling them transference and countertransference because such a distinction implies that the two phenomena are significantly different. It is suggested that we therefore should refer to both of them as transference. There is evidence that McLaughlin assumes that his ascription of this major participation to the analyst will be considered to justify classifying him as an adherent of the interpersonal school since he is moved to explicitly disavow such adherence. He writes: "I am not referring to the ever-present alternative of interpersonal psychology, but rather to a closer scrutiny of the verbal intervention–response sequence and patterning of classical technique" (1981, p. 652).

My next illustration comes from Kohut. I believe it can be shown that his self psychology is a significant, though not complete, abandonment of the drive paradigm in favor of an interpersonal paradigm but I am not attempting such a demonstration here. Making that assumption, however, I wish to show that his view of the analyst's participation is that it is a minor one, thus again contradicting the assumption that the interpersonal paradigm is paralleled by the ascription of major participation to the analyst. Kohut writes that in the transference neurosis

> "the analyst, to the extent that he is a transference figure, is not experienced in the framework of an interpersonal relationship" while in the narcissistic disorders the analyst is "introspectively experienced within the framework of an archaic interpersonal relationship." (1959)

One might think that with this view Kohut would see the analyst as making a relatively minor contribution to the interpersonal relationship in the transference neuroses and a relatively major one in the narcissistic personality disorders. One would be right about the former but only partially right about the latter. He writes that in true transference there is "an amalgamation of repressed infantile object strivings with (in the present reality, insignificant) aspects of the analyst" (Kohut, 1959). But in describing a schizophrenic patient who comes to the session in a cold and withdrawn state, he says: "the patient's emotional coldness and his dream are found to be a reaction to an apparently minute, but in reality significant, rejection of the patient by the analyst" (Kohut, 1959). I interpret the distinction between "apparently minute" and "in reality significant" to mean that from the point of view of the analyst or an external observer the involvement is in fact minimal even though to the patient it is significant. I suggest that the position that the contribution is a significant one only from the point of view of the patient, not that of an external observer, is consistent with the position that the contribution of the analyst is minor. In this sense it is wrong to consider that Kohut believes the analyst makes a relatively major contribution to the patient's pathological experience of the relationship in the narcissistic personality disorders. On the other hand Kohut argues in the concept of transmuting internalization that the analyst does play a major role in the "restoration" of a cohesive self.

One of the most illuminating and unexpected jolts I got to my assumption that the interpersonal paradigm goes parallel with the ascription of major participation to the analyst was the complaint by some interpersonalists that Sullivan's concept of participant observation does not make of the analyst as much of a participant as they think he is and should be.

Chrzanowski (1977, pp. 150–151), for example, expresses his dissatisfaction with Sullivan's concept of participant observation by saying that "it is difficult to include the phenomenon of countertransference into the formulation of participant observation because the term does not address itself to emotional components." And, the emotional components of rational and irrational responses to the patient's transferential and actual attitudes to the analyst require broader representation than is possible within the instrumental model of participant observation. My clinical preference is for a different role definition of the analyst, which emphasizes the role reciprocity between patient and analyst while focusing on the analyst's self monitoring and self revealing attitudes.

Levenson (1972) also feels that the Sullivanian concept of participant observer is not adequate. He writes: "the therapist, as an extension of Sullivan's participant observer, becomes a total participant and an observer of his own *experience* of participation" (p. 215). While Sullivan did stress the importance of the analyst being aware of his participation, what Levenson proposes in addition is that the therapist becomes a "total participant."

Greenberg (1981) explicitly contrasts the view of analysts of what he calls the "British school" on the analyst's participations with that of what he calls American interpersonalists. He says that the former see the analyst not only as *participating with* the patient but as, inevitably, *participating in* the patient's illness but then says that the latter view would be considered neurotically determined countertransference by Sullivan (p. 252). The complexity of the possible combinations of views on the paradigm and views on the analyst's participation may be seen in the fact that in referring to the British school Greenberg includes Sandler and Khan, who are not usually considered Kleinians, and Racker and Grinberg, who are. While Racker, a Kleinian, considers the analyst's participation to be a constant co-determinant of the patient's experience of the relationship to varying degrees, the Kleinians are generally criticized for failing to consider the analyst to be a participant as evidenced by their lack of attention to the role he plays in the here-and-now in determining the nature of the transference. Bird (1972), a Freudian, also suggests that a countertransference neurosis may also be a regular phenomenon, at least in an analysis of significant depth. His paper reveals a striking vacillation in the participation he ascribes to the analyst.

My last quotation in this series is from Levenson (1981) again. He writes:

> to give a quick example: that the patient thinks that you are poisoning his soup, the Freudian sees some small and trivial event as having set off a paranoid mechanism of projection. The interpersonalist wonders, what did he *really* do with the patient which cannot be identified or responded to and is therefore amplified in this way? Did he, in the previous session, in some real way, rebuff the patient? For him, the therapy lies in the patient's being able to establish the interrupted threads of connection between the event (unattended) and the symbolism. I consider this to be an absolutely vital distinction, certainly deserving more elaborate documentation. (p. 488)

So Levenson here considers the difference between the Freudian and the interpersonalist to be that the interpersonalist sees the analyst as significantly involved while the Freudian does not. Indeed when he says the Freudian sees some small and trivial event as having set off a paranoid projection he does not even specify that this small and trivial event is something the analyst did. So again, there is an assumption that the interpersonal paradigm is paralleled by significant participation.

The Freudian position

An important gain in stating the distinction between a major and a minor participation by the analyst in the analytic situation is that it will focus on a genuine difference of opinion which is now obscured by a caricature of the position of those who consider that appropriate participation to be minor. I mean the attribution to them of the blank screen or mirror view of the analyst.

If there is any statement which appears in the remarks of almost every author in the Symposium on Participant Observation in *Contemporary Psychoanalysis* (1977), it is to refer to and reject Freud's famous remark that "the doctor should be opaque to his patients and, like a mirror, should show them nothing but what is shown to him" (1912 [1958], p. 118). I believe the remark has been seriously misinterpreted. Certainly Freud didn't behave that way. The remark is made directly after Freud suggests that the analyst might understandably think it might be useful to give the patient "a glimpse of his own mental defects and conflicts and, by giving him intimate information about his own life, enable him to put himself on an equal footing. One confidence deserves another, and any one who demands intimacy from someone else must be prepared to give it in return" (pp. 117–118). It is only as a dramatic antithesis to this understandable but to-be-resisted temptation that Freud makes the mirror remark.

The Freudian considers the attack on the blank screen concept to be directed at a straw man. His rebuttal might run as follows:

> Of course I know that the analytic situation is an interpersonal one, he is likely to say. Isn't the definition of transference that it's a distortion of a real situation? Of course I know that there is a real relationship between patient and analyst but if the patient is not experiencing a transference and the analyst is not involved in a countertransference the relationship is realistic and adapted to the

> current reality. But when he is expressing a transference the patient is incorrectly attributing his experience to the real situation. Indeed it is my experience that if I emphasize what the patient incorrectly considers to be the reality justification for his transference I merely confirm him in his view that it is not transference.

Freud actually cautioned against underinvolvement on the analyst's part. It is true that this caution is not to be found in his published writings but in a letter he wrote to Oskar Pfister on October 22, 1927 [1963]:

> On the question of therapeutic technique I must express myself plainly. You as a minister naturally have the right to call on all the reinforcements that you can command, while we as analysts must be more reserved, and must lay the chief accent on the effort to make the patient independent, which often works out to the disadvantage of the therapy. Apart from that, I am not so far from your point of view as you think. You know the human propensity to take precepts literally or exaggerate them. I know very well that in the matter of analytic passivity that is what some of my pupils do. Of H. in particular I am willing to believe that he spoils the effect of analysis by a certain listless indifference, and then neglects to lay bare the resistance which he thereby awakens in his patients. It should not be concluded from this instance that analysis should be followed by a synthesis, but rather that thorough analysis of the transference situation is of special importance. What then remains of the transference may, indeed should, have the character of a cordial human relationship. (Meng & Freud, 1963, p. 113)

Yet it remains true that Freud's primary concern about the participation of the analyst is the danger of becoming over-involved. The late essay "Analysis Terminable and Interminable" is ordinarily looked upon as relating to the terminability of a patient's analysis, but it includes a sentence which makes clear that the entire essay applies to analyst as well as analysand. He wrote: "This would mean, then, that not only the therapeutic analysis of patients but his own analysis would change from terminable into an interminable task" (1937 [1964], p. 249). Nor does Freud believe that self analysis alone will do the job.

He suggested that "Every analyst should periodically – at intervals of five years or so – submit himself to analysis once more, without feeling ashamed of taking this step" (p. 249). The recommendation might seem to be at odds with the spirit of the essay, for Freud made clear that a latent conflict cannot be analyzed except intellectually. What then would be the use of an analyst entering analysis every five years unless he felt actively conflicted? Perhaps there is a resolution of the apparent paradox which Freud did not make explicit, that is, that a practicing analyst should always be aware that he has active conflicts. The nature of his work will stir up these conflicts in a way which need not be true for persons who are not engaged in daily intense interpersonal interactions. Freud said in the same essay: "It would scarcely be surprising if constant preoccupation with all the repressed impulses which struggle for freedom in the human mind sometimes cause all the instinctual demands which have hitherto been restrained to be violently awakened in the analyst himself" (p. 267). But one must note that Freud spoke of the awakening of instinctual demands, not explicitly about how the analyst would be influenced in his interaction with the patient.

If it be thought that I am being unfair and that Freud obviously meant the interpersonal interaction in what I have just quoted, I add these sentences which he wrote in the same year (1937 [1964]):

> The danger of our leading a patient astray by suggestion, by persuading him to accept things which we ourselves believe but which he ought not to, has certainly been enormously exaggerated. An analyst would have had to behave very incorrectly before such a misfortune could overtake him, above all he would have to blame himself with not allowing his patients to have their say. I can assert without boasting that such an abuse of "suggestion" has never occurred in my practice. (p. 262)

I conclude that the attitude betrayed in this last remark suggests that Freud did not consider that the "instinctual demands" which are "violently awakened" inevitably find expression in the analyst's behavior.

Despite recent emphasis on the real relationship and the various alliances there is no doubt that insofar as there is an official Freudian position, it is to advocate a lesser participation by the analyst than

Freud did. Freud is frequently criticized by Freudian analysts for having been as interactive with his patients as he was. Lipton (1977) agrees that Freud was more manifestly interactive than contemporary Freudian technique would permit but he considers Freud's technique to be preferable. He argues that in addition to his technical relation to the patient an analyst should have a personal relation with his patient too. While his personal relation should be relatively circumscribed, its limits cannot be prescribed. Lipton is careful to emphasize that what one does in this relationship may very well have repercussions on the transference which need then to be drawn into the technical activity of the analyst.

In addition to the blank screen accusation, Freudians believe their position on the participation of the analyst is caricatured as though they do not recognize the importance of object relations. I believe it will be clarifying to distinguish between the drive paradigm within which object relations are important and an interpersonal paradigm. Of course Freud makes much of object relations. Transference and the Oedipus complex are about object relations. It is one of the interesting ironies of psychoanalysis that Freud saw transference as the clinching validation for the drive discharge paradigm. In the Introductory Lectures he writes: "It may be said that our conviction of the significance of symptoms as substitutive satisfactions of the libido only received its final confirmation after the enlistment of the transference" (1916–1917 [1963], p. 445).

Chrzanowski has repeatedly called attention to Freud's statement in the introduction to "Group Psychology and the Analysis of the Ego" from which one would be hard put to deduce exactly how Freud conceived of the connection between object relations and the satisfaction of instinctual impulses, close though the connection must be. Freud wrote:

> The contrast between individual psychology and social or group psychology, which at first glance may seem to be full of significance, loses a great deal of its sharpness when it is examined more closely. It is true that individual psychology is concerned with the individual man and explores the paths by which he seeks to find satisfaction for his instinctual impulses; but only rarely and under certain exceptional conditions is individual psychology in a position to disregard the relations of this individual to others. In the individual's mental life someone else is invariably involved, as a

> model, as an object, as a helper, as an opponent; and so from the very first individual psychology, in this extended but entirely justifiable sense of the words, is at the same time social psychology as well. (1921 [1955], p. 69)

The difference between a psychoanalytic theory which includes theories about object relations and a psychoanalytic theory built on an interpersonal paradigm can be illustrated by the juxtaposition of the following quotations from Stone and Sullivan. Stone (1981, p. 716) writes: "whether or not one is an enthusiastic proponent of "object relations theory" in any of its elaborate forms, it seems self evident that all major developmental vicissitudes and conflicts have occurred in the context of important relations with important objects, and that they or their effects continue to be reflected in relationships with current persons of similar or parallel importance." The reader may not have noticed that the author says that major developmental vicissitudes and conflicts have occurred in the *context* of important relations with important objects. He does not say that major developmental vicissitudes *are* matters of important relations with important objects. I believe that he, wittingly or not, inserts the phrase "in the context of" because he wishes to avoid the implication that the field of psychoanalysis is the field of interpersonal relations. That is, in his view, interpersonal relationships are important in psychoanalysis but they do not constitute the field of psychoanalysis.

Sullivan on the other hand (1954) writes: "the psychiatrist should never lose track of the fact that all the processes of the patient are more or less exactly addressed at him and that all that he offers – his experience – is more or less accurately aimed at the patient with a resulting wonderful interplay" (pp. 19–20).

I summarize then that while it is a caricature of the Freudian view to say that the analyst is a blank screen or a mirror, it is true that the Freudian view sees the analyst as appropriately participating in only a minor way. I allow myself a verbal play by calling the analyst who is considered to be a participant in only a minor way the precipitant observer rather than the participant observer.

I am indebted to Irwin Hoffman for the crucial clarification that the foregoing discussion does not grapple with the distinction between the analyst as a growth promoting participant as in Strachey, Loewald and Kohut and as implicated in the formation of neurotic transferences. He discusses the issue in an important as yet unpublished paper (1983) in terms of the distinction between "conservative" and "radical" critiques of the blank screen view.

Sullivan's position on the analyst's participation

Does Sullivan anywhere suggest that a major involvement with the analyst is a necessary part of the interpersonal view? In fact the theorem of participant observation asserts only that there must be *some* involvement. Sullivan (1954) says this: "There are no psychiatric data that can be observed from a detached position by a person in no way involved in the operation. All psychiatric data arise from participation in the situation that is observed – in other words by participant observation" (p. 57).

The Sullivanian statement which would seem to bespeak the inevitability of a major participation is not the interpersonal paradigm but the one genus statement: "we are all much more simply human than otherwise, be we happy and successful, contented and detached, miserable and mentally disordered or whatever" (1940, p. 7). McLaughlin's (1981) statement quoted above implies the same view of human beings. So does Racker's (1968 [1953]) statement that "'the myth of the analytic situation' is that analysis is an interaction between a sick person and a healthy one" (p. 132).

Sullivan (1954) speaks of the degree of involvement only in a descriptive sense. He alludes to varying degrees of involvement. He says that an inexperienced interviewer may well be more anxious than the patient, that even an experienced interviewer will certainly, particularly if he interviews incipient psychotics, be very acutely anxious in his work now and then and that "in almost everyone, a great deal of anxiety occurs of which the person concerned has no clear awareness" (p. 135). When he asks whether a really skillful psychiatrist "knows just what role to take or just how to behave," he answers: "yes, *but with very great qualifications*. It is more accurate to say that the experience of the psychiatrist is synthesized into *an aptitude to do nothing exterior to his awareness* which will greatly handicap the interview situation, or which will direct its development in an unnecessarily obscure way" (pp. 68–69). The emphasis falls on being aware of what one is doing rather than on what to do. This passage also subtly reveals Sullivan's attitude about what even the skillful psychoanalyst is likely to do and is one of the reasons it is so often a pleasure to read him. It is a variant of "we are all much more simply human than otherwise." He doesn't say "will handicap"; he says "will greatly handicap." He doesn't say "in an obscure way"; he says in an "unnecessarily obscure way." He takes it for granted that there will be handicapping and obscurity. It is true that Sullivan thereby implies that the involvement is unlikely to be merely trivial but he does not make that his explicit and central point.

Prescription versus description

It is important to distinguish between the concepts of how much the analyst ought to be involved and how much he is inevitably involved. This subject has been discussed by Greenberg (1981) in terms of a felicitous distinction between prescription and description. The prescription relates to what is thought to be appropriate whereas the description relates to what is fact. Greenberg correctly says that too much attention to prescription has detracted attention from description and of course that an analyst's concern about conforming to what he considers the proper prescription may be so great that he seriously distorts what is his actual participation, that is to say, the description.

The primary current Freudian position on the analyst's participation is in the prescriptive mode. The analyst is warned against too great participation. The Freudians believe it is important to struggle against involvement and to render it as minimal as possible. Tarachow's (1963) distinction between psychoanalysis and psychotherapy argues, for example, that both participants in the therapeutic situation are constantly tempted to engage in an interaction and that a therapy is psychoanalytic rather than psychotherapeutic only to the extent to which the analyst successfully resists this temptation.

Sullivan's position on the analyst's participation is contradictory. As I have mentioned, and as Greenberg said, he would have regarded a major participation as a pathological countertransference rather than the average expectable variations in countertransference reactions, to use Epstein and Feiner's (1979, p. 20) phrase. That is a prescriptive view. On the other hand the one genus theorem is a descriptive statement about the nature of human beings. It implies that the analyst's *participation* cannot be minor.[2]

Sullivan's position should not be confused with statements by interpersonalists and others which are prescriptive. I refer to the idea that the analyst *ought* to be involved with his patients. A common rationale for this prescription is that one cannot understand another human being unless one is involved to some unspecified degree. Such involvement is sometimes characterized as normal countertransference. There are other prescriptive statements as to the analyst's participation which are based on a conviction that the analyst's participation in a more than trivial way is crucial in bringing about change. Levenson (1972, p. 214) writes, for example: "If the therapist can be loving, because the patient does not impinge on his life in any long-standing meaningful way, it that love worth very much? … [T]his willingness to risk his own identity, to 'trip' with the patient, is the keystone of helpers from shamans to psychoanalysts." I will return to this point when I discuss the implications for technique of the interpersonal paradigm.

It would seem obvious that even within a major or a minor participation the degree to which an analyst participates varies widely. This is true not only as between one analyst and another but also in the different way in which an analyst treats his different patients as well as differences in the analyst's involvement with his patient in different phases of the analysis or on different issues which come up in the analysis.

It would also seem obvious that the analyst's participation is a function not only of his personality but also of the kind of patient he is treating. This is usually formulated in terms of the increasing difficulty of avoiding countertransference concomitant with the increasing pathology of the patient one is treating. In this connection the following admittedly somewhat mocking formulation of analyzability has occurred to me: An analyzable patient is a patient with whom the analyst can maintain the illusion of neutrality. It is important to recognize therefore that the emphasis on inevitable major participation in treating patients with severe pathology can be used to sidestep the question of the average expectable participation in treating the average expectable neurosis – the patient who meets the ordinary criteria for a classical analysis.

It is also worth pointing out that one's view of the countertransference will differ depending on whether one examines an analysis microscopically in isolated sessions or macroscopically in broad longitudinal trends. Presumably a countertransference neurosis will take the form of an organized psychic position over time.

It is also not necessary to assume that a significant participation on the analyst's part will be discernible in any random segment of an analysis and irrespective of the issue under consideration. The analyst's participation will likely wax and wane as the process touches to a greater or lesser extent on issues central in his own psychodynamics.

How to state the degree of participation

I realize that I have contrasted major with minor participation without indicating how one can judge or measure degrees of participation. We have no measures nor are we likely to get any. The terms are qualitative and have only operational significance.

The words employed in discussions of the degree of participation are not only qualitative but their implications are also not usually focused upon. In the example I quoted from Levenson of the patient who says the analyst is poisoning his soup, Levenson asks what did the analyst *really* do with the patient. The word "really" is clearly meant to imply a significant involvement. In discussing a similar issue in another context he uses the word "precipitant" for an unimportant involvement and "genuine" to connote what he considers a significant and appropriate involvement of the analyst (1981, p. 143).

One of the major stimuli which led me to focus as sharply as I have on the distinction between the paradigm and the degree of involvement and which led me to see that I had condensed them is the criticism of my writing on transference for using the words "co-determination" by the analyst and "plausibility" of the patient's experience to refer to the transference because of their connotation of a degree of involvement greater than many analysts consider inevitable or desirable. Clearly my choice of words reflects a belief in the inevitability of significant involvement but that is the very point in question.

Perhaps the decisive question is this: might the patient attribute something to the analyst which is entirely imaginary, which has no basis in anything the analyst has said or done? Does the Freudian conception of transference imply such a possibility?

A Freudian could reply to Levenson's illustration of the patient who thinks the therapist is poisoning his soup on the basis of some "trivial" action on the therapist's part that the patient is responding to something "real," albeit trivial. In discussing ideas of reference Freud states that "sufferers from persecutory paranoia ... cannot regard anything in other people as indifferent, and they, too, take up minute indications with which these other, unknown people present them, and use them in their delusions of reference" (1921 [1955], p. 226). Again, "they do not project it into the blue, so to speak, where there is nothing of the sort already" (ibid). More generally Freud spoke of the nucleus of truth in a delusion.

The paranoid patient will very likely say that the analyst has said or done something which is his justification for the accusation. Must it be true then that the analyst has said or done that of which he is accused? Is it enough to find something that he has said or done which can be misinterpreted to mean what the patient takes it to mean? Does there have to be a meaningful connection between what the analyst has said or done and the patient's interpretation of it? What does it mean in this connection to say a meaningful connection? At least part of the answer lies in considering the range of unconscious meanings that any particular action may have – including, of course, the analyst's actions. The very concept of meaning in this connection relates to the hermeneutic position and the interpersonal paradigm.

I would like to mention a few other words which are used to refer to the analyst's participation to look at this connotation. I have already referred to the word "precipitant." A colleague of mine is willing to go only so far as to say the patient "has a point." Levenson's conviction that the analyst's participation must be more than trivial leads him to reject several terms sometimes used to describe the analyst's participation. He writes: "The therapist does not, as in the machine paradigm, act as the 'servant of the process' as Masud Kahn (1969) puts it. Nor is he midwife at a delivery" (1972, p. 214).

Levenson's effort to answer this question leads him to use several words in addition to "really" which are worth looking at. One is "relevant." He says: "Thus, from the most benign neurotic 'distortions' to the outrageous misrepresentations of the paranoid, one could say that the perception, albeit not literally correct, is a *relevant* conception of the therapist (p. 151). Another word he uses in the same paragraph for the same phenomenon is to call the patient's perception "aesthetically" true.

A clarification of this issue lies in what Levenson calls the perspectivist view. That is, from the patient's perspective the observation is relevant. This may even be a perspective which the patient himself disavows. The disavowal may or may not be conscious. He may recognize that it will not sustain the conclusion he draws, or he may be too distressed to acknowledge what he believes he has seen, or he may feel the analyst would be unwilling or unable to acknowledge what the patient believes he has seen or the conclusion he draws from it. Here perhaps is a place where a distinction between the concepts of participant observer and that of a field constituted by the interpersonal relation – a distinction I earlier alluded to – may have merit. Even if an external observer were to agree with the analyst that what he had done does not justify the patient's conclusion, the fact remains that the patient's organization of the field includes attributing something to the therapist which is relevant to the conclusion, again even if the patient himself does not believe it justifies the conclusion. The event which for the patient is relevant to his conclusion will necessarily be an integral part of an organized position on the patient's part, that is to say, his perspective.

It is now possible to understand the word "relevant" better. It is relevant even if at first the analyst does not recognize that it is. Is this any different from saying that the patient is distorting something because of his own projection? It is because it states the interpersonal paradigm. It changes the question from whether the analyst did anything to justify the patient's experience to the recognition that the patient's perspective always illuminates at least a possible meaning of the analyst's participation, no matter how far-fetched an observer, including the patient in his role of observing participant, may consider this meaning to be. You note that the phrase observing participant for the patient rings another change on the phrase participant observer in addition to Wolstein's (1960) observer participant. Wolstein meant the phrase observer participant to refer to the analyst but it could refer to the patient as well. Wolstein (1981) indicates the analyst's major participation by calling him a co-participant.

The transference–countertransference transaction

I believe the distinction between the degree of the analyst's participation and the interpersonal paradigm will help to clarify a conceptualization and definition of transference and countertransference significantly different from the more generally accepted one, at least in the Freudian literature.

In a research on transference in which Irwin Hoffman and I are engaged (1982b) we have come to the conclusion that the concept of a dichotomy between transference as distortion and non-transference as realistic does violence to the actual nature of the relationship between patient and analyst. Even Langs (1978), whose concept of the bipersonal field places great emphasis on the interpersonal interaction still does not employ the interpersonal paradigm, for he insists that a dichotomy be drawn between transference as distortion and non-transference as realistic, as well as similarly between countertransference and non-countertransference, and between all the other dimensions based on fact and those based on fantasy. Langs' illustration of analytic material invariably includes a major participation by the analyst but it is not clear whether he considers such involvement to be inevitable. Even if he did, that does not constitute the interpersonal paradigm.

Wachtel (1981), who also rejects the dichotomy, has attempted to state a different model by using Piaget's concept of the inevitable coexistence of assimilation and accomodation in the functioning of a schema – in this instance a schema of interpersonal relationship – in however differing proportions. In a recent statement of the issue (1982b), Hoffman and I argued that interpersonal reality is of such a nature that a person's interpersonal motives must always have a degree of ambiguity. Given that this is the fact, the ascription of a particular motive to an analyst by a patient might rest on some subtle item, which only the patient, because of his vested interest in seeing the situation in a particular way, would notice and make much of. We concluded that the patient's experience of the relationship was always plausible in this sense and that we therefore could not accept the view that the patient is distorting the "reality" as perceived by the analyst.

We emphasized that the patient's experience was still transference because it was his past which led him to organize the field as he did, to single out, for example, the particular item which others ignored but to which he attributed an idiosyncratic significance. We recognized that the patient and analyst could differ on their assessment of the situation. We reject the argument that the analyst's view is necessarily the correct one because we reject the view that the analyst can be the arbiter of reality, to use a phrase fairly commonly employed in the analytic literature by those who take the same position. I believe Sullivan's concept of "consensual validation" (1950 [1964], pp. 212–214) stems from a similar rejection of the analyst as the sole judge of external reality. Bromberg (1980, p. 237) has noted that Rapaport (1951, p. 61) pointed out that Sullivan was one of the very few who emphasized the interpersonal context of reality testing. Our argument in effect rests on the ambiguity and relativity of interpersonal reality. We continue to distinguish between transference and non-transference but the distinction is not between realistic and distorted but rather between rigidity and flexibility of an interpersonal attitude, that is, whether it is susceptible to influence from the outside. While we distinguish between the degree of involvement and the interpersonal paradigm we think it likely that any analyst who accepts the interpersonal paradigm is likely to consider the average expectable and acceptable involvement of an analyst to be greater than does an analyst who does not accept that paradigm.

If one holds to the interpersonal paradigm one will hold that transference and countertransference do indeed constitute a transaction rather than countertransference being an occasional regrettable, even if in some ways, useful intrusion into a field essentially determined by the patient's realistic and transferential reactions. The recent book on countertransference edited by Epstein and Feiner (1979) shows a strong contemporary movement among those who call themselves interpersonalists toward such a transactional view of transference and countertransference.

I suggest that the various efforts to spell out a relationship between patient and analyst in addition to transference and countertransference such as a reality relationship and the variously proposed alliances are abortive movements toward the concept of a continuing transference-countertransference transaction.

Because transference continues to be defined by most people apart from the analyst's contribution, anyone who uses the term is considered to be restricting himself to the patient's contribution. I believe this is the reason, for example, that Chrzanowski (1980) believes he is differing with me when he advocates "an exploration of the personal relationship along with the transferential aspects of it rather than primarily in the service of the transference." He is ascribing to me the usual definition of transference and countertransference according to which they are distortions and in which the analyst's appropriate contribution is considered to be only a realistic alliance. I believe on the contrary that the attitudes and responses of each participant are complex unities arising from the transaction, each with its own plausibility. My suggestion that the transference be focused upon includes therefore what Chrzanowski feels is left out if one focuses only on transference. It may be that here indeed lies a justification for coining a term like parataxis to substitute for the term transference. It is not uncommon to hear the two concepts referred to as different names for the same phenomenon. Aside from other differences, however, I believe the true distinction between them lies in Sullivan's use of the concept parataxis to refer to the interpersonal field. He wrote for example: "*parataxic*; that is, when, besides the interpersonal situation as defined within the awareness of the speaker, there is a concomitant interpersonal situation quite different as to its principal integrating tendencies, of which the speaker is more or less completely unaware" (1940, p. 92). I realize that Freud spoke of "situation" too, but he spoke of the analytic situation, while Sullivan spoke of the interpersonal situation. The difference is not merely verbal. Because parataxis is a concept in the framework of the interpersonal field, while transference is not unless it is redefined as in this paper, the concepts are indeed different, despite the fact that both Freud and Sullivan spoke of the patient's distortion of the situation.

The analyst's participation and technique

Levenson has said that "proponents of Sullivan encounter some considerable difficulty, not in explicating the theoretical differences between Freud and Sullivan but in demonstrating the practical consequences for therapy" (1972, p. 181). I believe there are important consequences for therapy and that the difficulty in recognizing them is related to the failure to see clearly the distinction, which is the burden of this essay, that is, between the therapist's participation and the interpersonal paradigm.

An important reason that it is difficult to spell out the technical implications of the interpersonal paradigm is that the paradigm does not have unequivocal implications for technique. I became most clearly aware of this when I realized that the implications which Sullivan draws from it are very different from the ones which I draw from it. Before I was clearly aware that I was working with the interpersonal paradigm I had come to the conclusion that transference, defined as I just have, has to be the primary concern of technique and that therefore the first step in technique should be to clarify the patient's experience of the relationship, while the second should be to discover what is the patient's justification in the analyst's behavior or attitude or even just in a plausible conjecture as to the analyst's subjective feeling for the construction the patient makes of the field. But to clarify the patient's experience and to seek his justification for it means to make the interpersonal interaction in the analytic situation as the patient sees it as explicit as possible.

I turn first to Sullivan's views on the subject. There is no doubt about his belief that the patterns of interpersonal relation need to be made explicit. He said that "one achieves mental health to the extent that one becomes aware of one's interpersonal relations" (1940, p. 102). At the same time he clearly believed there were serious obstacles to doing so in the analytic situation itself, at least for some time. He wrote:

> In general, in the treatment of personality there are three fields of events which are of very great relevance. First of these is the field of current events in the patient's life outside the treatment situation.... The second is his current relations in the treatment situation – that is, his relations with the psychiatrist. And the third field of relevant data is the events of the patient's past.
>
> It is difficult for most people to be straightforward and forthright in discussing their feelings, thoughts, impulses, and so on, with respect to a person with whom they are in the peculiar relationship of patient to a psychiatrist. For a fairly long time at the start of all therapeutic work, most of our field of investigation is concerned with current events outside the treatment situation. ... It is from current events that we move into the current therapeutic relationship between doctor and patient, uncovering both the noted and unnoted emotional problems which constitute the patient's difficulties in living (1954, p. 174, ftn.).

In fact there is abundant evidence in case material, both his own and supervised, that Sullivan did very little in the way of making the relationship in the analytic situation explicit, preferring to deal with it implicitly. This tendency is so marked that a careful study of his work led Havens (1976) to conclude that Sullivan essentially employed a counter-projective technique, that is, "the patient's surmises about the therapist's attitudes, his projections onto the therapist are actively combatted" (p. 15), and I add – by means other than interpretation. An example from Sullivan: The patient hints about thoughts he expects the therapist to find horrible. After eliciting them, Sullivan writes: "One has to be prepared for an eruption of this sort of thing, and probably my response would be, 'well, hell, you must have felt terribly *sore* sometimes in the past.' That proves that I am not horrified and I don't get in too deep. I have tossed out a lifeline, the awful stuff is before us, and we are still there" (Mullahy, 1952, p. 147).

Havens approves and says that Sullivan "has abandoned the parental authoritative position doctors so easily assume" and done something better than saying "I am not one of those who disapproves" (p. 15). An alternative not taken by Sullivan would have been to make the patient's fear explicit and say: "you are afraid I will disapprove."

But that is not Sullivan's way. In fact as a second major difference between interpersonal psychiatry and psychoanalysis, in addition to the idea that transference does not only develop but is present from the start, Havens (1976) concludes that transference cannot always be effectively interpreted, but must often be acted against (ftn., p. 25).

Mary White's (1952 [1977]) discussion of Sullivan's technique and a review of Sullivan's supervisory work in detail in the recent report edited by Kvarnes and Parloff (1976), as well as more globally in the cases treated by Tower (1947) and Cohen (1947), make clear how thoroughly Sullivan avoided making the relationship in the analytic situation explicit. In the case treated by Kvarnes, the rare instances in which the therapist did make the transference explicit were essentially ignored.

Perhaps the extent to which he was involved with sicker patients is responsible for Sullivan's reluctance to make the interaction explicit. Perhaps it reflected his general aversion to interpretation, of which he caustically said the supply far outweighs the demand. Perhaps it was because of his distrust of the magic of words. In the vignette I referred to, for example, he did much more than say that the patient must have been terribly sore. When he suspected that the patient was struggling with the ideas he considered horrible, Sullivan indicated his disrespect for such things by saying for example "God help us, why must we have this hokum when we are doing useful work most of the time? I know something bothers you but does it have to be disguised as a catastrophe?" and so on. His whole attitude was designed to demonstrate that he was not horrified. In his general discussions of communication in "The Psychiatric Interview" (1954) he lays much stress on non-verbal communication. Yet it remains true that he did very little by way of making the interaction explicit, in words at any rate.

In this respect there is an irony in the difference between Sullivan and Freud. Sullivan made the interpersonal paradigm explicit while Freud did not, but Sullivan did much less to make the transference in the analytic relationship explicit than did Freud.

But what was true of Sullivan is not true of present day interpersonalists insofar as I can judge current practice from the literature. Analysis of the transference clearly plays an important role in neo-Sullivanian technique. Even so I believe that a more explicit spelling out of the implications for technique of the interpersonal paradigm would be useful. I will state some of these implications and will illustrate their application by vignettes drawn largely from papers published in *Contemporary Psychoanalysis.*

Before doing so however I want to comment generally on the spirit in which I present this and other vignettes. I ran across a remark by Antonovsky (1980) which almost made me laugh out loud: "when it comes to clinical examples, anyone courageous or foolhardy enough to tell what [she] did invites in a horde of critics eager to explain to the reporting therapist what instead she could have done, should have done, or, worse yet, what she 'really' did do" (p. 208). I am not implying some ideal in which no mistakes are made. I do suggest however that the more clearly and explicitly a principle is stated the more does one increase the likelihood that it will be applied more consistently.

In line with the distinction which is the theme of this paper I emphasize that the implications which I draw for technique are based on the interpersonal paradigm and not on the assumption of a major participation on the analyst's part.

1. The first principle I propose is that because the presenting manifestation of psychopathology lies in the immediate interpersonal interaction, the therapist should be ever ready to inquire into the patient's experience of the relationship. Sullivan said that "[t]he psychiatrist … plays a very active role in introducing interrogations, not to show that he is smart or that he is skeptical, but literally to make sure that he knows what he is being told" (1954, p. 21). The statement does not refer to what he is being told about the patient's experience of the relationship. Indeed one could see the principle that a therapist should make sure that he knows what he is being told as antecedent to the principle that he should make sure that he knows what he is being told about the patient's experience of the relationship.

I will give two examples, one from Levenson and one from Chrzanowski of what I consider to be insufficient inquiry into the patient's experience of the relationship.

The illustration from Levenson occurs in a paper entitled "Facts or Fantasies" (1981), the central thrust of which is to argue that the "data of psychoanalysis are disguised reality, and not autonomous fantasy" (pp. 494–495). Criticizing a vignette offered by Greenson (1976), Levenson writes: "The patient points out that when he expresses political opinions that match the therapist's he gets marginal cues of approval; when he doesn't he is subjected to masked hostile analysis. … [The analyst, that is, Greenson] validates the patient's perception, admits his fault and then asks, why do you feel obliged to satisfy my political views." Levenson assesses this remark by the analyst as playing out exactly the kind of authoritarian inquiry of which the patient complains and recommends instead that patient and analyst should talk about their mutual experience rather than "analyze" the patient's distortions.

I will later refer approvingly to Levenson's application of structuralist thinking to the analytic situation in his emphasis on the isomorphic transformation which leads the patient to hear what the analyst says as though it confirms his preexisting expectations – in this instance, that the analyst is authoritarian. But here Levenson overgeneralizes the principle.

My own criticism of Greenson's question would take a different tack and illustrates a third approach to the issue involved. Not only would it not assume that one knew how the patient experienced this exchange but it would also focus on the most immediate aspect of the patient's experience of it. Does it not seem plausible that if the patient has finally plucked up the courage to complain, the most immediately significant aspect of the exchange to him would be that Greenson validated his perception? Should Greenson not have looked for direct or indirect indications of the patient's response to the fact that the analyst validated his observation?

The illustration points up that one cannot assume that one's view of what is the most immediate here-and-now is the same as the patient's experience of the matter. One might consider it to be why the patient feels obliged to satisfy the analyst's views, or even their mutual experience, meaning by that how it came about that they interacted as they did about political views. Or as I suggest, that it is the complaint and its validation in this instance. One must also recognize that unless one concedes that there is often a time lag between the time something happens in the interaction and when it gets talked about, the patient would be barraged with inquiry and unable to develop a theme.

To take another example of inadequate inquiry, Chrzanowski (1980) tells a vignette of a patient who suggested that the analyst's mind was not functioning well as a result of a recent illness. The analyst calls this a crude attack on his mental faculties, a formulation that suggests to me his feelings were hurt, all the more so perhaps because the patient had expressed solicitude by sending him a get-well card when he was in the hospital. The analyst responded by saying that for all he knew his mind was working well and then he interpreted that perhaps the patient was feeling cut off from him and concealing an element of compassion by his criticism. The patient responded with tears and thanked the analyst the next day which the analyst clearly takes as validation of his interpretation, (pp. 363–364).

Chrzanowski does tell us that the patient felt the analyst was not paying close attention and that he had changed the subject when the patient was in the midst of something he was explaining. I suggest that it is a reasonable hypothesis that the analyst made the interpretation he did to overcome his distress at the patient's criticism and that only further inquiry into the patient's experience would have clarified what was going on.

Chrzanowski uses the vignette as a basis for his argument that there is relational participation as well as transference and countertransference. He calls the former non-technical and the latter technical. I agree that the analyst does much which is not intended as technical but I also suggest that a split between transference–countertransference and participation–relation increases the likelihood that a situation such as the one I described will be dealt with by conjecture rather than inquiry. Levenson correctly says that the "attribution of meaning to behavior is a highly arbitrary business" (p. 197). All the more reason that we should do more inquiring and less interpreting.

2. The second principle I offer is that the analyst should always be ready to consider that associations not explicitly about the relationship may nevertheless be disguised allusions to it. The centrality of the interpersonal relationship and the reluctance to be clearly aware of many aspects of it on the part of both participants – although in this connection I am emphasizing the analyst's participation – is such that there will be ubiquitously present disguised allusions to the relationship in the patient's associations.

I offer a vignette from Chrzanowski (1980) which I think illustrates the failure to employ this principle, though I assume that it is a principle which he accepts. Chrzanowski tells of a situation with a patient who was in serious conflict as to whether to marry a girl from a markedly different background. He feared his loneliness and despair were he not to marry her. At this point he turned to the analyst and asked his opinion. The analyst replied that he was not in a position to tell him what to do but made it clear that he understood his predicament and felt sympathy for his reluctance to get married under the prevailing conditions. Chrzanowski summarizes that he found it compatible with his position as an analyst to show the patient where he stood despite strong emphasis on the subjectivity of his support. Chrzanowski refers to his stance as being a relational participant rather than simply a participant observer. I suggest that the technical implication of the interpersonal paradigm would rather have been to investigate the possibility that the conflict about his relation with the girl – important and even crucial though it be in the patient's life – was being used in the analysis as a disguised allusion to a conflict about his relation with the analyst and that the investigation of this conflict in the transference–countertransference situation would have been more valuable than the stance the analyst took.[3]

Levenson (1972, p. 189) criticizes this view that the patient's associations can be understood as disguised allusions to the transference as subject to the caricature of becoming a therapeutic gimmick in the hands of what he calls "here-and-now" oriented psychoanalytic therapists. That can happen but not for the reason he proposes. It can become a gimmick if the analyst mechanically assumes that anything said must relate to the interaction without making such an hypothesis plausible by relating it to something the analyst has said or done. Levenson says that after all the patient may be talking about an outside relationship, using the analyst as medium. My rejoinder would be that what the patient is talking about is meaningful for *both* his outside relationship and his relationship with the analyst. To focus on the meaning in the analytic interaction is not to deny the significance of the outside meaning but to deal with the interaction in the analytic situation on the assumption that the outside and inside meanings are parallel and that the progress of the analysis is best served by giving priority to clarifying that interaction rather than priority to the interaction in outside relationships. This is not to deny the value in showing the connection between the two.

3. My third and last implication for technique, one which follows only somewhat indirectly from the interpersonal paradigm because it makes an assumption about involvement as well, is that the analyst will inevitably to a greater or lesser degree fall in with the patient's prior expectations. It is well stated in Levenson's (1972) book, *The Fallacy of Understanding*. He says that what makes the therapy is the therapist's "ability to be trapped, immersed and participating in the system and then to work his way out" (p. 174). I had an interesting experience with Levenson's book. It seemed clearly important and insightful to me, so much so that I began recommending it to colleagues. But I kept feeling that some important issue in it was eluding me. I could not clearly understand exactly why he called it the

"Fallacy of Understanding." I think I understand now. As I see it the book makes three main points which are not separated as sharply as they might be. One, which is structuralism applied to the analytic exchange, says that the same theme will be expressed in varied guises in the interaction between the two participants, most notably in the content of their exchange and in the meaning of their behavioral interaction. Two, the analyst always succumbs to a greater or lesser but significant degree to the patient's pressure to experience the interaction according to the patient's prior neurotic expectations. Sandler (1976) calls this the analyst's role responsiveness. Three, the patient interprets whatever the analyst does as evidence for his prior neurotic expectations. Levenson's wish to emphasize this last point leads him to deemphasize insight and to speak of the fallacy of understanding. He pushes the point so far as to call the therapist and patient "each other's creations" (p. 185). He makes what I consider to be the contradictory statements that on the one hand the analyst has to resist transformation and on the other hand that he "acts from within the structure of the patient's transactional field" (p. 214), that he becomes "a total participant" (p. 215), and that intent lies in effect (pp. 76, 203). Hence the "Fallacy of Understanding." Hence the description of therapy as though it is a matter of the "aesthetics of experience ... rather than content and meaning" (p. 211). Hence the conclusion that "neither insight, clarification, nor novel experience will make the difference" (p. 213).

Levenson recognizes that if he leaves his argument at that point, there is no room for the analyst to have an influence on the patient. He makes various attempts to extricate himself from this dilemma in his book. In later papers however he makes what I consider a more balanced formulation. It is that the therapeutic process is both participation and understanding, that is, that the therapist inevitably participates and works his way out of that participation by progressive understanding of the interaction, at the same time communicating that understanding to the patient, who of course plays a role in reaching that understanding too, at least in what he says in response to the therapist's effort to understand what the patient is experiencing and how he accounts for that experience. It is the idea that understanding alone will suffice which is the fallacy because it fails to take account of the inevitable participation on the analyst's part. In a paper published recently (1982), Levenson achieves a view which takes both insight and experience into account. He writes: "*The power of psychoanalysis may well depend on what is said about what is done* as a continuous, integral part of the therapy" (p. 101).[4]

Levenson offers several good examples of the analyst's role responsiveness in his discussion of the case of a young woman he treated (1972). I will give one illustration. She had come home from college because of a sudden panic despite being in supportive psychotherapy. After three apparently good sessions the patient made an abortive suicide attempt. When she came for her next interview she is described as shockingly changed, apparently in a paranoid state. Instead of making the easy assumption that this was a natural progression of her disorder the analyst searched for how he might have been responsible and made a suggestion about that, which led to a marked improvement in her state. The suggestion was that he was so pleased with her cooperativeness and apparent cheerfulness because it was easier to deal with than if he had recognized how terribly upset she was. He fulfilled her expectation that, like her parents, he would prefer not to have to deal with her serious distress (pp. 167–169).

In this instance the analyst was sharp enough to deduce what had happened, but what if he could not come up with a suggestion and still held fast to the assumption which I have stated as the third principle, that he must be contributing to what is happening? The answer would lie in the first two principles I described. He would try to understand her experience of the relationship by careful inquiry and he would assume that associations which are not manifestly about the relationship were nevertheless probably disguised allusions to it.

Should the analyst reveal his feelings?

The conviction that the transference–countertransference interaction is a transaction raises the difficult question of how explicit the analyst should be in revealing how he experiences his own participation. It is clear that there is a major difference of opinion between those who advocate a significant degree of self revelation and those who oppose it. Chrzanowski refers to an atmosphere of "exchanging and documenting mutual impressions, emotions, and observations" (1980, p. 354). Levenson (1979) suggests that one facilitates a shift in the patient's structure "not by interpreting the patient's resistance to one's truth but by reporting one's *own* experience of the transaction" (p. 211). I do not think it is always wrong to report one's own experience, though I believe that when one does so one must be especially alert to how the patient experiences such a report. I realize that often the very inquiry into a particular exchange may be so revealing of something the analyst is experiencing that it would be fatuous to pretend one has not revealed it. Nevetheless, I think it best to be quite chary with such revelations. I believe they have a tendency to shut off further inquiry into the patient's experience, not least because such inquiry might lead to the exposure of something on the analyst's part which he would rather not know about. Furthermore the analyst must recognize that his subjective experience may be as defensive on his own part as he believes the patient's conscious attitudes are. He cannot therefore assume that if he reports his own experience that is the end of the story. But the pursuit of the possible hidden implications of his experience would change the analysis of the patient into a mutual analysis of patient and analyst. Some therapists advocate just that. I assume it is clear that I do not. The position that the analyst makes a major contribution to the transaction does not necessarily mean that a mutual analysis is desirable or perhaps even possible.

My emphasis on the significant role of the analyst in the interaction can be misunderstood to imply a failure to attribute enough importance to the role of fixed patterns of behavior in the patient. I do not intend such an implication. That I may seem to be doing so is an unfortunate result of my emphasis on what I believe is usually not emphasized. The ultimate goal is indeed the exploration and change of the patient's patterns of relationship. The exploration of the analyst's contribution is a prior and necessary means to that end. Such exploration changes the atmosphere of the analysis from one in which the patient is wrong to one in which the patient's point of view gets more respectful hearing. As the patient sees that he is rigidly prone to evaluate and create situations in predetermined terms he can come to see that other evaluations of reality and ways of relating are also possible and is thus embarked on the road to change in his patterns of interpersonal interaction.

The exploration of the past

The great emphasis on the here-and-now which inevitably accompanies the suggestions I have made for the technical implications of the interpersonal paradigm with the possibility of a substantial contribution by the analyst to the transference–countertransference transaction may also seem to imply an underemphasis on the role of the exploration of the patient's past in the analytic process.

Despite wise injunctions to distribute one's attention evenly between past and present there is a reciprocal relationship between emphasis on one or the other, and, as I said, it is inevitable that one will emphasize what one considers to be generally underemphasized. Sullivan (1954), like most Freudians, emphasizes the recovery of the past. He wrote somewhat ambivalently:

> When we locate a problem, identifying something that is impractical, inefficient, and definitely contrary to the achievement of the patient's idealized goals, we have every reason to return to the third field of greatly relevant data – the distant past in which this particular emotional difficulty had its beginning. It is important to notice that finding out how things start often provides a great deal of information as to what they represent, whereas their more sophisticated, more mature manifestations may be very obscure indeed. However, some patients, as I have already said, have a distinct tendency to alter history to suit their wishes or needs; to them, the present has the virtue of being capable of at least some investigation, whereas the past is apt to be pretty heavily colored. From this general standpoint, what is currently going on has a very special significance. (ftn, p. 174)

In another remark he emphasizes the importance of seeing the connection between the past and the present:

> until a patient has seen clearly and unmistakably a concrete example of the way in which unresolved situations from the distant past color the perception of present situations and over-complicate actions in them, there can be no material reorganization of personality, no therapeutically satisfactory expansion of the self, no significant insight into the complexities of one's performances or into the unexpected and often disconcerting behavior of others concerned. (1940, p. 101)

I am not sure that this last is true. In any case I believe the relative importance of present and past and their connection which can best serve an analysis will vary among patients, analysts, and patient–analyst pairs.

The relationship as a factor in bringing about change

I turn to the question of whether the interpersonal paradigm and the view that the analyst may play a substantial role in the transference–countertransference transaction has necessary consequences for the role of the interpersonal relationship between patient and analyst in bringing about change. The question as I have just put it must be differentiated into the role of new experience as such and the role of new experience which is examined and reflected upon.[5] The former may well be relatively ineffective and the latter of central consequence. Without this distinction one could easily misunderstand Levenson, for example, to deny the role of new experience when he writes, as I have already quoted in part: "The therapist's 'new' experience will emerge as stale as yesterday's insight. From the organismic perspective neither insight, clarification nor novel experience will make the difference." One might think that Levenson is even attempting to shame a therapist who believes that new experience in a therapeutic relationship makes a difference by saying that: "the idea that the therapist 'cured' through his kindness, respect for the patient, love, is an incredible conceit considering both the complexity of the patient's needs and the emotional capacity of most psychoanalysts, which largely are no better or worse than most men's" (1972, pp. 213–214).

Levenson perhaps overstates this point. Schafer (1983) has suggested that the analyst, in his role as analyst, is very often able to behave with much more consideration and tact than he is in his life outside, though I realize there are limits to how different he can be. From his writings in general, notably in the concept of resisting transformation, it is clear that Levenson ascribes crucial importance to new experience, but both the old and the new patterns must be explicitly examined.

The distinction I have just offered is ordinarily not made. Instead interpersonalists and Freudians are described as differing sharply in the role ascribed to new experience, with Freudians insisting that insight is the only truly mutative agent.

Greenberg (1981), for example, suggests that despite their differences, Sullivan and Fairbairn agree that "change comes about as a result of the analyst's use of himself as a new person to break into the closed inner world of the patient" (p. 249). He refers to Valenstein's (1980) position that insofar as the "*real* relationship to the analyst as a *real* person is considered to be pivotal" this leads to what Valenstein calls "interpersonally promoted experiential effects," that is, to “not-real-psychoanalysis” (pp. 117–118). Once again there is the implied condensation of degree of involvement and interpersonal paradigm in referring to “real” and “pivotal” effects as “interpersonally promoted.”

One can find here and there in the writing of Freudian analysts references to the significant role of the relationship in bringing about change (Dewald, 1976; Loewald, 1960). But as Greenberg points out these views may be accommodations made by the Freudian paradigm and not a significant change in paradigm.

In addition to the distinction between new experience which is and is not explicitly examined, a discussion of the role of experience in analysis can be clarified by a related distinction between advertent and inadvertent interpersonal influence exerted by the analyst in his interaction with the patient (Gill, 1979b; Reppen, 1982).

I believe the failure to make this distinction leads Greenberg to the mistaken conclusion that there is a contradiction between Loewald’s earlier (1960) depiction of psychoanalysis as a developmental experience and his insistence in a recent statement (1979) that encouragement and reassurance are not analytic.

By an inadvertent interpersonal effect I mean, for example, an analyst making an interpretation which the patient experiences as a criticism when, so far as the analyst was aware, the analyst had no such intent. An advertent interpersonal intervention would be one in which he encouraged, reassured, scolded, or whatever knowing that he was doing something intended to have such an effect. Even then I would say that what is unanalytic would not be that the analyst engaged in such an intervention but only if he failed to look for and make explicit the interpersonal significance to the patient of his intervention.

Here perhaps we come upon a genuine difference of opinion as to what is analytic. I define a non-analytic behavior as one in which the therapist fails to make explicit an interpersonal experience which he knows the patient is having and which he knows the patient would be unable to speak about freely. That means that I would say that if Sullivan attempted to bring about an interpersonal effect knowingly and did not make that interaction explicit in the relationship even if he realized that the patient would resist recognizing what had happened, he was being non-analytic. I do not mean to imply that the analyst would have to interpret his view of how the patient had experienced his intervention as soon as the analyst realized what happened but that his ultimate aim would be to bring inadvertent effects of the interaction to awareness as much as possible.

Greenberg (1981) is of the opinion that my recent paper (1979a) on the analysis of transference remains in the drive paradigm and that, in common with other Freudians who ascribe some significance to the relationship in bringing about change, I assume that ultimately "analytic change derives from interpretation, from some version of making the unconscious conscious, rather than from an aspect of the actual encounter with the analyst" (pp. 253–254). That is not my view (see Gill & Hoffman, 1982b). I believe that Greenberg's position is too dichotomous. Greenberg refers approvingly to Fairbairn's position that every interpretation is really an intervention. I would alter that to read that every interpretation is *also* an intervention. I might note in passing that Kernberg (1980) considers the difference between borderline personalities and transference neurotics to be that the former take an interpretation to be a personal intervention whereas the latter do not. Kernberg therefore advises that the interpersonal significance of interpretation has to be interpreted in borderline personalities. I assume that we would agree that the interpersonal significance of an interpretation would have to be interpreted in the whole range of patients. That is, the interpersonal significance of an interpretation will require an interpretation if there is evidence that the patient experiences it in a way which he is unable either to be conscious of or to freely tell the analyst if he is conscious of it. In that case it is the analyst's job to look for allusions to the interpersonal significance of the interpretation to the patient.

I believe that both insight and new experience play a role in bringing about change in psychoanalysis. I do not believe that the relative role of the two is the same for all analyses. I suspect that the more a result is dependent upon insight alone rather than a new experience as well the less is it likely that it will be maintained in the face of life's vicissitudes. Most of all I believe that the insight into one's patterns of interpersonal relationship at the same time that one is being exposed to a new pattern of interpersonal relationship is the most mutative of all. Especially is this true if the insight is into the comparison between the old and the new at the very moment that the inclination to behave according to the old pattern is being met by an opportunity to relate in a new way.

Concluding statement

I have argued that the interpersonal paradigm does not necessarily imply a conviction that the analyst plays a major role in the analytic interaction even though there is considerable evidence in both Freudian and interpersonal literature that the two are often considered to go together. I have discussed the difficulty one encounters in stating how important a role one is ascribing to the analyst in the interaction and have catalogued a number of terms employed to connote the nature of that ascription. On the basis of a conviction that the interpersonal paradigm is the appropriate one for the therapeutic situation, I have suggested a redefinition of transference. The definition would change from the customary one of transference as a distortion of a reality defined by the analyst to a conception of a transference–countertransference transaction in which from the differing perspectives of patient and analyst each has a view which has its plausibility. I discussed a number of implications of the interpersonal paradigm for psychoanalytic technique. They are: increased attention to the here-and-now patient–analyst transaction including increased attention to the patient's experience of the relationship, to disguised allusions to the transaction in the patient's associations and to the basis in the therapist's behavior on which the patient justifies his experiences, including the assumption that the analyst inevitably responds to a greater or lesser degree to the patient's pressure on him to behave in ways which conform to the patient's prior expectations. I conclude with some comments on the relative roles of the here-and-now and the exploration of the past history and on the relative roles of insight and new experience in bringing about change.

A last word: a response to the idea that the analyst often plays a significantly participant role could well be that it has merit but is overblown. I mean that it could be argued that I have emphasized only the extreme of a continuum of degrees of involvement. It could be conceded that the attitude toward a substantial involvement might well be changed from a rebuke to the analyst for his countertransference to a more relaxed acceptance of our common humanity with the advice to try to work one's way out of the involvement. As matters now stand one's position on the frequency of major involvement is a matter of one's own experience and one's general view of human nature. Only an examination by an external observer of the details of what actually goes on in any particular analysis would show what the analyst's involvement is. I suspect it would very often be significantly greater than he thought it was. One might require a span of sessions to detect the involvement in any particular instance because silence on the analyst's part can hide many qualities and intensities of feelings.

Notes

1 Revised from a presentation to the William Alanson White Psychoanalytic Society, April 2, 1982.

2 Commenting on this paper, Hoffman wrote: "The term 'participation' is ambiguous throughout. It's not clear whether it refers to external *behavior* or to internal emotional *states*. They may correlate but behavior *can* be controlled more than internal states, so behavior can be more readily 'prescribed' although not entirely, of course."

3 If it be countered that one is entitled to conclude only that the patient's manner of relating to the analyst is the issue rather than that there is a specific connection between the *content* of the patient's associations and his relation to the analyst I would reply that in principle they are the same.

4 Compare this statement by Sullivan (1950): "No great progress can be made in this field of study [psychiatry] until it is realized that the field of observation is what people do with each other, what they can communicate to each other about what they do with each other (pp. 220–221).

5 I realize this may seem to threaten an infinite regress. I believe the escape from that conceptual possibility is that it is not necessary for the patient to examine and reflect upon his experience in the relationship unless there is an obstacle to his becoming aware of that experience.

References

Abrams, S. & Shengold, L. (1978). Some reflexions on the topic of the 30th congress: "Affects and the psychoanalytic situation." *International Journal of Psychoanalysis*, 59: 395–407.

Antonovsky, A. (1980). Object relationship or object relations. *Contemporary Psychoanalysis*, 16: 203–210.

Bird, B. (1972). Notes on transference. *Journal of the American Psychoanalytic Association*, 20: 267–301.

Bromberg, P. (1980). Sullivan's concept of "consensual validation." *Contemporary Psychoanalysis*, 16: 237–248.

Chrzanowski, G. (1977). *Interpersonal Approach to Psychoanalysis*. New York: Gardner Press.

Chrzanowski, G. (1980). Collaborative inquiry, affirmation, and neutrality in the psychoanalytic situation. *Contemporary Psychoanalysis*, 16: 348–366.

Cohen, R. (1947). The management of anxiety in a case of paranoid schizophrenia. *Psychiatry*, 10: 143–157.

Dewald, P. (1976). Transference regression and real experience in the psychoanalytic process. *Psychoanalytic Quarterly*, 43: 213–230.
Epstein, L. & Feiner, A. (1979). *Countertransference*. New York: Jason Aronson.
Freud, S. (1912 [1958]). *Recommendations to Physicians Practicing Psychoanalysis*, Standard Edition 12. London: Hogarth Press, pp. 111–120.
Freud, S. (1916–1917 [1963]). *Introductory Lectures on Psychoanalysis*, Standard Edition 16. London: Hogarth Press, pp. 243–496.
Freud, S. (1921 [1955]). *Group Psychology and the Analysis of the Ego*, Standard Edition 18. London: Hogarth Press, pp. 67–143.
Freud, S. (1921 [1955]). *Some Neurotic Mechanisms in Jealousy, Paranoia, and Homosexuality*, Standard Edition 18. London: Hogarth Press, pp. 223–232.
Freud, S. (1927 [1963]). Letter to Oskar Pfister In H. Meng & E. Freud (Eds), *Sigmund Freud: Psychoanalysis and Faith*. New York: Basic Books.
Freud, S. (1937 [1964]). *Analysis Terminable and Interminable*, Standard Edition 23. London: Hogarth Press, pp. 216–253.
Freud, S. (1937 [1964]). *Constructions in Analysis*, Standard Edition 23. London: Hogarth Press, pp. 257–269.
Gill, M. (1979a). The analysis of transference. *Journal of the American Psychoanalytic Association*, 27(Suppl.): 263–288.
Gill, M. (1979b). Psychoanalysis and Psychotherapy 1954–1979. Symposium on psychoanalysis and psychotherapy: Similarities and differences – a 25 year perspective, October 20., Atlanta.
Gill, M. & Hoffman, I. (1982). A method for studying the analysis of aspects of the patient's experience of the relationship in psychoanalysis and psychotherapy. *Journal of the American Psychoanalytic Association*, 30: 137–168.
Greenberg, J. (1981). Prescription or description: Therapeutic action of psychoanalysis. *Contemporary Psychoanalysis*, 17: 239–257.
Greenson, R. (1976). *The Technique and Practice of Psychoanalysis*. New York: International Universities Press.
Grinberg, L. (1979). Projective counteridentification and countertransference. In L. Epstein & A. Feiner (Eds), *Countertransference*. New York: Jason Aronson, pp. 169–191.
Havens, L. (1976). *Participant Observation*. New York: Jason Aronson.
Hoffman, I. (1983). The patient as interpreter of the analyst's experience. *Contemporary Psychoanalysis*, 19: 389–422.
Kernberg, O. (1980). *Internal World and External Reality*. New York: Jason Aronson.
Khan, M. (1972). On Freud's provision of the therapeutic frame. In *The Privacy of the Self*. New York: International Universities Press, pp. 129–135.
Kohut, H. (1959). Introspection, empathy, and psychoanalysis. *Journal of the American Psychoanalytic Association*, 7: 459–483.
Kvarnes, R. & Parloff, G. (Eds) (1976). *A Harry Stack Sullivan Case Seminar*. New York: W. W. Norton.

Langs, R. (1978). The adaptational–interactional dimension of countertransference. *Contemporary Psychoanalysis*, 14: 502–533.
Levenson, E. (1972). *The Fallacy of Understanding*. New York: Basic Books.
Levenson, E. (1979). Language and healing. *Journal of the American Academy of Psychoanalysis*, 10: 271–282.
Levenson, E. (1981). Facts or fantasies: The nature of psychoanalytic data. *Contemporary Psychoanalysis*, 17: 486–500.
Levenson, E. (1982). Language and healing In S. Slipp (Ed.), *Curative Factors in Dynamic Psychotherapy*. New York: McGraw-Hill, pp. 91–103.
Lipton, S. (1977). The advantages of Freud's technique as shown in his analysis of the Rat Man. *International Journal of Psychoanalysis*, 58: 255–274.
Loewald, H. (1960). On the therapeutic action of psychoanalysis. *International Journal of Psychoanalysis*, 41: 16–33.
Loewald, H. (1960). Reflections on the psychoanalytic process and its therapeutic potential. *Pyschoanalytic Study of the Child*, 43: 155–167.
McLaughlin, J. (1981). Transference, psychic reality, and countertransference. *Psychoanalytic Quarterly*, 50: 639–664.
Mullahy, P. (Ed.) (1952). *The Contributions of Harry Stack Sullivan*. New York: Hermitage House.
Racker, H. (1968). *Transference and Countertransference*. New York: International Universities Press.
Rapaport, D. (1951). The conceptual model of psychoanalysis. *Journal of Personality*, 20(1): 56–81.
Reppen, J. (1982). Merton Gill: An interview. *Psychoanalytic Review*, 69: 167–190.
Sandler, J. (1976). Countertransference and role responsiveness. *International Review of Psychoanalysis*, 3: 43–47.
Schafer, R. (1983). *The Analytic Attitude*. New York: Basic Books.
Scharfman, M. (1979). Panel discussion: Conceptualizing the nature of the therapeutic action of psychoanalysis. *Journal of the American Psychoanalytic Association*, 27: 627–642.
Singer, E. (1965). *Key Concepts in Psychotherapy*. New York: Random House.
Stone, L. (1981). Some thoughts on the "here and now" in psychoanalytic technique and process. *Psychoanalytic Quarterly*, 50: 709–733.
Sullivan, H. (1940). *Conceptions of Modern Psychiatry*. New York: W. W. Norton.
Sullivan, H. (1950 [1964]). The illusion of personal individuality In *The Fusion of Psychiatry and Social Science*. New York: W. W. Norton, pp. 198–226.
Sullivan, H. (1954). *The Psychiatric Interview*, edited by H. Perry & M. Gawel. New York: W. W. Norton.
Symposium on Participant Observation. (1977). *Contemporary Psychoanalysis*, 13: 347–386.
Tarachow, S. (1963). *An Introduction to Psychotherapy*. New York: International Universities Press.
Tower, S. (1947). Management of paranoid trends in treatment of a post-psychotic obsessional condition. *Psychiatry*, 10: 137–141.

Valenstein, A. (1980). The concept of classical psychoanalysis. In H. Blum (Ed.), *Psychoanalytic Explorations of Technique*. New York: International Universities Press, pp. 113–136.

Wachtel, P. (1980). The relevance of Piaget to the psychoanalytic theory of transference. *Annual of Psychoanalysis*, 8: 59–76.

White, M. (1952 [1977]). Sullivan and treatment. *Contemporary Psychoanalysis*,: 13: 317–34.

Wolstein, B. (1959). *Countertransference*. New York: Grune and Stratton.

Wolstein, B. (1960). Transference: Historical roots and current concepts in psychoanalytic theory and practice. *Psychiatry*, 23: 159–172.

Wolstein, B. (1981). The psychic realism of psychoanalytic inquiry. *Contemporary Psychoanalysis*, 17: 399–412.

Chapter 10

The intrapsychic and the interpersonal

Different theories, different domains, or historical artifacts? (1988)

Stephen A. Mitchell

Stephen Mitchell is probably best known as the father of relational psychoanalysis, and so it seems fitting to place the article we reprint here, first published in 1988, in the context of that larger effort. *Object Relations in Psychoanalytic Theory*, the highly influential book Mitchell wrote with Jay Greenberg, had been published five years earlier, in 1983. In 1988, the same year the article we reprint here appeared, Mitchell published his first single-authored book, *Relational Concepts in Psychoanalytic Theory*, the text that announced his relational agenda. Over the following twelve years Mitchell published four more single-authored books and one co-authored one (with Margaret Black). In the year 2000, Mitchell died, suddenly and tragically, at the age of 54.

The article you are about to read immediately conveys two things about Mitchell. First, as he himself often said, interpersonal psychoanalysis was the heart of his new relational project. Second, he was an inspired comparative psychoanalyst; he was to return to the comparative study of psychoanalytic theories many times over the coming years.

No one has written comparative psychoanalysis more clearly than Stephen Mitchell. In the article reprinted here, he was invited to address what he believed was too dichotomous a distinction between the intrapsychic and the interpersonal. In a parsimonious and straightforward manner, he conveys the origins and the essences of both the Freudian and interpersonal traditions, while giving readers a taste of self-psychology and object relations theory as well.

For Mitchell, neither classical Freudian nor interpersonal thinkers are monolithic – there is much nuance and difference among those representing each of these traditions. Nevertheless, Mitchell emphasizes the differences between Freud's and Sullivan's philosophical and general intellectual underpinnings. Freud, influenced by Darwin, taught analysts to "think body." The human mind, like our species, originated from the primitive, the lower order. From this perspective, psychoanalysis, both clinical and theoretical, is focused on the struggle to regulate the primitive beast within us, and the inevitable conflict between bestial impulses and civil society. This biological emphasis extended to the psychoanalytic relationship. Patients were seen as responding to the analyst largely from within their own minds – their own intrapsychic worlds – relatively uninfluenced by the social context created by two people being in a room together.

Sullivan's revolution began, Mitchell reminds us, with his work with schizophrenic people, who had been understood to be biologically diseased, their way of being in the world an arbitrary, meaningless jumble having no adaptive function. Sullivan changed all that, focusing his interest on the social/familial circumstances that led to the miserable adaptations of people who are compelled to move as far away from intimate human interaction as possible. As Mitchell describes in this article, where Freud thought body, Sullivan thought parental character: that is, what are the familial circumstances that led each child, whatever they became as they grew older, to develop as he or she did?

Influenced by the field theory of social psychology and by cultural anthropology, Mitchell tells us that Sullivan tried to transform psychoanalysis from the alleged objective and scientific study of the patient *in vacuo* to the study of the patient in the context of that individual's past and current field of others. Sullivan argued that mind is formed in a social context, contrasting his views with the Freudian tradition of the social as the product of more basic, inherent, and universal drive states. Along similar lines he argued that fantasy is a function of what one has gleaned from actual lived experience; it is not *a priori* and driven by universal drive states. And consistent with all of this, in characterizing the psychoanalytic relationship, Sullivan introduced the term *participant-observation*, in the hope of supplanting the concept of the analyst as a blank screen, a person who has no personal or unconscious impact on the patient's transference or the patient's verbal productions.

Mitchell was not unbiased. He tells us that he does not resonate with what he calls the "reckless use of abstractions" and the "clankings" of reified concepts of psychic structure or "psychic apparatus." He refers to the "physics envy" of many of his more conservative psychoanalytic colleagues. It should be noted, however, that Mitchell could also be quite critical of certain Sullivanian traditions, especially Sullivan's contradictory depiction of the analyst as the "expert," and the use of the "detailed inquiry" to find out "what really happened." (Mitchell was a constructivist, and so he could not accept that it was ever possible to know "what really happened," because the idea comes from an objectivist epistemology.) When all is said and done, though, it remains true that nobody has ever captured the differences between the psychoanalytic traditions of his time as clearly and economically as Stephen Mitchell.

The intrapsychic and the interpersonal

Different theories, different domains, or historical artifacts? (1988)

Stephen A. Mitchell

I am relieved to have been asked to discuss the relationship between the "intrapsychic" and the "interpersonal" from *a* Sullivanian perspective, rather than *the* Sullivanian perspective, since Sullivan's work lends itself to many different readings, and various contemporary writers of often dramatically different points of view all identify themselves as interpersonalists and/or Sullivanians. Therefore, I would like to abandon at the start the claim that the following paper is representative in any sense. Rather, I have two more modest goals: first, to consider the manner in which Sullivan himself might have thought about the relation between the "intrapsychic" and the "interpersonal," to reconstruct the context and internal logic of *his* approach; and second, to consider this question through more contemporary interpersonal eyes, my own, taking advantage of the hindsight which nearly 40 years of psychoanalytic thinking has provided since Sullivan's death.

The immediate and quite serious problem in establishing Sullivan's view of the relation between the intrapsychic and the interpersonal is that, although he characterized his own position as "interpersonal" and used that term often, I have found no evidence of any written or spoken statement by him on the "intrapsychic" as such. Even more surprising, neither Freud nor Fenichel used the term "intrapsychic" either. In fact, Grinstein's *Index of Psychoanalytic Writings* (1960, 1966, 1975) has no listing at all under the term "intrapsychic" in the entire psychoanalytic literature before 1952, only one between 1952 and 1960, and four in the decade between 1970 and 1980, while listings under the heading "interpersonal" rose proportionately from 9 to 40 to 80 during those years.

Thus, as far as I have been able to determine, "intrapsychic" seems to be one of those terms, like "classical" psychoanalysis, that was introduced not as early psychoanalytic thinking developed, but much later, retrospectively, to broadly distinguish more traditional psychoanalytic concepts from later schools of thought, like Interpersonal Psychoanalysis, which broke from the mainstream. The term *intrapsychic* was employed by both Sullivan's adherents as well as defenders of traditional psychoanalysis to represent in a broad sense what it was that Sullivan was opposed to.

At first glance, it might seem apparent what is meant by "intrapsychic" and "interpersonal," the former referring to processes within the mind, the latter referring to processes between persons. These are serviceable working definitions, but they don't take us very far if we are trying to distinguish Sullivan's position from classical psychoanalysis, since they clearly do not do justice to either mode of theorizing.

The interpersonal position is sometimes caricatured as a naive environmentalism, a shallow kind of social psychology holding that what goes on "inside" a person's head is either unimportant or else merely a transposition of what took place outside, with no awareness that experiences are processed according to organizational categories effected by desires and fears. Conversely, the intrapsychic position is sometimes caricatured as a naive constitutionalism holding that the constituents of mind are simply generated by the unfolding of inborn ideas, with no awareness that human beings are sensitive to and influenced by their social environment, past and present.

So, within psychoanalytic rhetoric, proponents of each position accuse the proponents of the other of collapsing one realm into the other. Interpersonalists are accused of regarding mental representations as simple derivatives of the "actual"; intrapsychists, to coin a term, are accused of regarding transactions between people as simple enactments of a priori fantasies.

If we are to regard "intrapsychic" and "interpersonal" as topographical realms, one within the mind, the other between people, one private, the other public, psychoanalytic theories cannot be segregated simply into one or the other realm. In philosophy, Kant made obsolete both the naive constitutionalism of Descarte's idealism as well as the naive environmentalism of Hume's materialism. All psychoanalytic theories are necessarily post-Kantian, regarding human experience as constructed out of both sensory data and some sort of a priori organizational principles. Therefore, psychoanalytic theories differ not according to the choice of intrapsychic or interpersonal but as to how they understand the relationship between what happens between people and what takes place in the mind, and vice versa.

Specifying the substantive differences is made more difficult because the terms "intrapsychic" and "interpersonal" have operated like banners representing broad and diverse groupings of ideas that have become clustered together. To separate them out, we need to go back to the point in the history of psychoanalytic ideas when the central contrasts we will be dealing with were drawn.

In 1897, Freud (1887–1902) abandoned the theory of infantile seduction in favor of the theory of infantile sexuality. Before then, he regarded the neurotic mind as one that has been subverted from the outside, by other people, fractured by infantile seductions, operating as pathogenic seeds, lying dormant till puberty, when they germinate into hidden mental recesses of unacceptable memories and affects. In 1897 he decided that his patients' accounts of infantile seductions were not veridical, but the product of fantasy. The pathogenic material is not introduced into the mind of the child through seductions from outside, but evolves from within. The mind contains in itself the seeds of its own fragmentation; children are dominated, independently of precocious and unusual external stimulation, by powerful sexual passions, inevitably conflictual in nature and unable to be contained within a uniform, transparent consciousness.

Thus, in this crucial shift in 1897, Freud replaced one set of ideas, emphases and foci with another, establishing two clusters of dichotomous concepts, which latter became associated with the terms "intrapsychic" and "interpersonal": fantasy vs. perception, psychic reality vs. actuality; inner world vs. outer world, and drive theory vs. a theory of environmental influences. One might argue that Freud's shift in the theory split the different sides of these contrasts from each other and that we have been trying to heal that split ever since. These different contrasts are not at all strictly parallel, but became lumped together because of the broad global shift in theorizing Freud underwent in 1897, leading in the direction of a theory stressing the intrapsychic, i.e.: fantasy, psychic reality, the inner world, and instinctual drives.

Although he was originally steeped in the traditional psychoanalytic thought of his day, Sullivan eventually came to be sharply critical of that tradition. Why?

Sullivan was deeply concerned with treating schizophrenic patients and regarded the greatest obstacle to the understanding and humane treatment of such patients to be the then-dominant Kraepelinian system. Schizophrenics were regarded as victims of a physiologically based, inevitably deteriorative illness, and that belief, Sullivan became convinced, blocked the possibility of ever learning anything about what he felt was the origin of the schizophrenic process within the dynamics of the family or of the schizophrenic's great sensitivity to the social world around him. Sullivan regarded Kraepelin's belief in an invisible morbid process "inside" the patient as akin to a kind of spiritism, blinding meaningful clinical observations, and serving mostly to provide the psychiatrist with a sense of power and pseudocontrol in his dealings with schizophrenic patients.

Sullivan introduced the term "interpersonal" in 1927 not as an alternative to any psychoanalytic concepts, but to Kraepelin's theory of dementia praecox. In the 1920s and 1930s, Sullivan developed his critique of the Kraepelinian approach to schizophrenia into a broad methodological position regarding psychiatric knowledge and clinical practice; the inspiration and rationale for his methodology derived from "operationalism," which dominated the natural and social sciences of Sullivan's day.

Operationalism was an offshoot of the American philosophical tradition of Pragmatism, which offered not so much a philosophy in itself but rather a method, a critical posture, which provides a way of evaluating philosophies, a method of stripping philosophies of their imaginative flights into abstraction, of bringing them down to earth. Bridgeman, the physicist from whom Sullivan borrowed in constructing his methodology, seems to have ventured into the realm of philosophy of science because of the devastating impact of Einstein's discoveries on prior theories in physics. How could we have been so wrong, asks Bridgeman (1927), and his aim is to establish a pragmatist methodology, a way of evaluating scientific postulates and questions that will guarantee that we are never so wrong again. The problem, in Bridgeman's view, lies in a reckless use of abstraction, a proliferation of concepts with no concrete and verifiable referents, leading to entire systems spawned by the imagination, with at best only tenuous connection to actual reality. If concepts are to be scientific, he argues, they must be tied to concrete "operations," to the very activities through which they are defined and determined. In fact, according to Bridgeman, the concept *is* the activity.

Like Bridgeman, Sullivan placed great emphasis on precision of meaning in the use of scientific concepts, and developed an orientation toward particular *kinds* of data, particular *kinds* of issues. Science ought to be concerned with, can meaningfully *only* be concerned with, phenomena that are tangible, engageable through some clearly defined, replicable, concrete operations.

Kraepelin's concept of "dementia praecox" as an invisible, inevitable morbid process, which Sullivan felt was unrelated to clinical observations of the patient's experience and behavior, was just the sort of thinking Sullivan was opposed to. But what of Freudian psychoanalysis? Sullivan was sharply ambivalent. In the 1880s, neurosis had also been regarded as a manifestation of neural degeneracy, and neurotic symptoms as meaningless murmurings and sputterings of a nervous system gone awry. Freud's psychodynamic theory gave meaning to these phenomena, much the same way Sullivan assigned meaning to schizophrenic experience and symptomatology. Thus Freud's depiction of psychic conflict, repression, and unconscious mental processes provided Sullivan with the key conceptual tools he needed to challenge Kraepelin's fatalistic and mechanistic view of schizophrenia as irreversible neurological deterioration.

On the other hand, Freud's 1897 shift away from the impact of actual experience had led him to elaborate a theory of hypothetical, invisible psychodynamic forces. His understanding of schizophrenia as an unanalyzable "narcissistic" neurosis was as clinically pessimistic as Kraepelin's. Further, Freud tended to assume a license for speaking of processes like transformations of libido, life and death instincts, psychic structures, and defense mechanisms, none of which are in any way accessible to observation. His vision of the "psychic apparatus," with its imaginary clanking structures and clashing forces, derives from a sensibility very different from the pragmatism of William James, Bridgeman, and Sullivan.

So Sullivan made the fateful decision not to continue to use Freudian metapsychology as a base upon which to add his own contribution, but to construct a totally different vision of mind and psychopathology. In so doing, he was clearly rejecting some of the features of Freud's work which have become associated with the term "intrapsychic," although he was not at all rejecting others. These need to be sorted out.

Central to Sullivan's critique is Freud's definition of the individual mind as the basic unit of study. This is a crucial, really quite subtle, and very easily misunderstood point. Sullivan felt that traditional psychoanalytic thinking went about studying mind in a fashion that, in its very definition of the object of study, precluded real understanding. We think of ourselves as being or having a mind or self that develops inside our skulls, with as firm a boundary around it as our physical brain. Sullivan suggests that this view of the self as a "self-limited unit that alternates between a state of insular detachment and varying degrees of contact with other people and with cultural entities" (1964, p. 33) is an illusion. What does this mean?

In Sullivan's view, the human mind is inherently dyadic, continually responsive to and in interaction with other minds, much as our physiological systems are in constant exchange with the surrounding physicochemical elements in our environment. Remove a human being from environmental sources of oxygen and other supplies and he quickly dies. Remove a human being from mental contact with the human environment in which he has developed and in which he functions and he is no longer a *human* being in any meaningful sense of the term. "We organize our acquaintance with the world," Sullivan suggests, "in order to maintain necessary or pleasant functional activity within the world with which, whether the objects be manageable or unmanageable, remote or immediate, one has to maintain communal existence – however unwittingly" (1940p, p. 34).

Thus, in Sullivan's view, from the earliest days of infancy, the individual is in continual interaction with others; his very experience is in fact built up out of these interactions. The representation of self which each of us forms is a secondary construction superimposed on this more fundamental and fluid interactional reality.

Sullivan's emphasis on the interpersonal nature of mental states is very much like Stern's recent view culled from current infancy research. "[T]he infant's states of consciousness and activity are ultimately socially negotiated states" (1985, p. 104), suggests Stern. "[T]he infant's life is so thoroughly social that most of the things the infant does, feels, and perceives occur in different kinds of relationships.... In fact, because of memory we are rarely alone, even (perhaps especially) during the first half-year of life ... the notion of self-with-other as a subjective reality is thus almost pervasive" (p. 118).

We discover ourselves in the interpersonal field in which we have long been a participant, and assign ourselves a status and stature outside that field, as if we had developed independently of it, chose to enter it, and could choose to leave. Nietzsche (1872 [1956]) argued that a view of the self as separate is an illusion necessary to human existence. It is not clear the extent to which Sullivan felt the vanity with which we tend to separate and elevate ourselves from our communal existence is an artifact of our particular cultural tradition or endemic to the human condition. Yet he clearly felt that we all tend to superimpose an illusory, impermeable boundary around ourselves, which allows us the illusion of a kind of inviolable and total self-creation.

In his very closely related critique of concepts such as "internalization," "internal objects," and so on, Schafer (1976) argues that many of the ways we think about ourselves derive from the reification of metaphors concerning bodily experiences, particularly in childhood. We put food into our bodies, excretions come out – so we tend to think of our minds as also having inner spaces, an *intra*psychic domain. Substances build up in our bodies and are secreted, excreted, or stored up – so we tend to think of our feelings as substances which are held in, built up, need to get out, and so on. This is the language of experience, but, Schafer argues, it unfortunately became the language of psychoanalytic theory, which employs the reified metaphors not as phenomenological organizers of experience, but as if they were actual places, forces, substances, and so on, within the mind.

Schafer's contemporary action-language critique of psychoanalytic language and drive theory is very much like the one Sullivan developed 50 years ago. Schafer's methodological sources in British analytic philosophy and Sullivan's in American pragmatism were both reactions to the same system – 19th-century European metaphysics. Sullivan is suggesting that the very sense of the individual mind as a separable entity is a reification of the metaphor that is suggested by the seeming separation from the physical environment our skins provide for us.

The view of mind as inherently social rather than composed of a secondary social overlay on top of instinctual drives has developed more recently within several other currents of contemporary psychoanalytic theorizing. Loewald (1980), for example, suggests that mind arises within a matrix of object relations; the conventional sense of separateness, "reality," and "objectivity" are secondary and often depleted constructions, certainly no more "real" in any meaningful sense. The individual self, Kohut (1977, 1984) came to feel, always uses "self-objects" for its own narcissistic supports, no matter how self-sufficient the individual feels himself to be. "[M]an is a social animal," Modell says, "and dependency on another individual or dependency upon the attitudes of a group is testimony to the preeminence of group over individual psychology" (1984, p. 113).

Sullivan's establishment of the interpersonal point of view derives from the same sensibility – the human mind is part of a field, not a self-limited phenomenon in its own right. We are struggling to grasp situations, not individuals.

> To isolate its individual subject-matter, a *personality*, from a complex of interpersonal persons physically exterior to the subject-person, is preposterously beside the point and indicative of more perverted ingenuity than the speaker finds himself possessing ... psychiatry, if it deals with anything, must deal with disordered living of subject-persons in and within their *personal complexes*. It is not an impossible study of an *individual* suffering mental disorder; it is a study of disordered interpersonal relations nucleating more or less clearly in particular persons. (1962, p. 258)

Let us say we want to understand the functioning of the left arm. We block out everything else, shine a spotlight on the arm, and follow its movements over the course of a day. Now it moves this way, now that way. How can we explain this? By defining the unit of study erroneously, we preclude the most compelling and economical grasp of the movements, which are suddenly quite simple if the illumination is broadened to include the entire body and its daily situations. We would have to posit internal forces within the arm itself, moving it this way and that, perhaps a complex system of drive – vertical, horizontal, sideways – pushing and pulling the arm in various directions. Sullivan felt that the traditional psychoanalytic framework made just as serious a mistake in defining the field for studying human emotional life and difficulties. By isolating the individual mind from its interpersonal context, this framework blackens out the very sources and context from which that mind draws its content.

To say that the arm functions in the context of bodily activities does not suggest that the arm lacks its own internal structure. Neither did Sullivan naively believe that interpersonal interactions could be experienced and/or stored in an unmediated fashion, without a priori organizational structures. His concepts of needs for satisfaction and security, personifications, security operations, and so on serve this function within his theory. But Sullivan did feel that the psychoanalytic theory of instinctual drive as generating from within the organism itself all the basic constituents of experience was erroneous and a result of isolating the person from the interpersonal field: "everything that can be found in the human mind has been put there by interpersonal relations, excepting only the capabilities to receive *and elaborate* the relevant experiences. This statement is also intended to be the antithesis of any doctrine of human instincts" (1964, p. 302).

Is Sullivan being fair to Freud to say that in postulating his theory of instinctual drive he isolated the individual personality from the interpersonal field? In some sense he is not, or is at least selective in his reading of Freud, who clearly granted importance in many places in his work to real events between real people. Yet the central thrust of drive theory is to grant causal weight to universal issues in a way that often seems to make actual events and the parents as people insignificant. The individual mind creates its own world out of the material provided by experience, but the composition of that world is preset. Interpersonal experiences are slotted into the categories generated inevitably by the drives and their vicissitudes. Actual experience and events are not unimportant, but are appropriated for the construction of the inevitable universal longings, fears, and dramas that are extensions of the child's nature, like the mosaic artist placing shards and fragments into a predesigned pattern.

Freud suggests that "these events of childhood are somehow demanded as a necessity.... If they have occurred in reality, so much to the good; but if they have been withheld by reality, they are put together from hints and supplemented by phantasy.... Whence comes the need for these phantasies and the material for them? There can be no doubt that sources lie in the instincts" (1916–1917, p. 370).

So, part of what passes under the banner of the term *intrapsychic*, the motivational theory of drive, Sullivan clearly objected to. What of the other meanings? Did Sullivan also object to including or granting a central place to: fantasy as opposed to perception? psychic reality as opposed to actuality? the inner world as opposed to the outer world? No, he didn't object to any of these principles, although his way of thinking about them has its own distinctive features.

Sullivan's respect for the importance of fantasy is evident in his very understanding of "interpersonal" situations. He defines psychiatry as the "study of the phenomena that occur in configurations made up of two or more people, all but one of whom may be more or less completely illusory" (1964, p. 33). Although Sullivan regards the individual as highly sensitive and responsive to the current interpersonal situation, that situation is coterminous with and filtered through images of fantastic others which are residues of earlier interpersonal integrations. The schizophrenic represents the extreme version of a fantasy-dominated subjective reality, in that, in Sullivan's vivid description, he "no longer amalgamates readily in ordinary social activities but instead finds himself surrounded by extraordinary caricatures of other people, engaging in bizarre activities more or less definitely injurious to him, the whole of his interpersonal relations resembling the phantasmagoria of the nightmare" (1962, pp. 218–219).

But it is not only the schizophrenic that lives in a world of fantastic others. "As a matter of brute fact," Sullivan suggests, "these bilateral parataxic interpersonal situations are the rule rather than the exception among us, and the average person magically stripped of his illusions about his friends and acquaintances would find himself surrounded by strangers" (1964, p. 24). The crucial difference between Sullivan's understanding of fantasy and some versions of the more traditional psychoanalytic approach is that, for Sullivan, fantasies, illusory others, personifications, and so on are always composed of pieces of lived experience with actual others. They are never simply a derivative or projection of some constitutional, a priori, "primal fantasy."

On the closely related issue of psychic reality vs. actuality, we would have to say that Sullivan had a deep respect for the importance of the subjective meanings of all experiences. Michels (1985) has pointed out the variability in usage of the term *psychic reality*. If what is meant is unconscious fantasy derived from drives, Sullivan is clearly opposed. But if psychic reality is defined as the patient's subjective experience, the personal meanings he attaches to past and present events, consciously and unconsciously, Sullivan would be all for it.

Probably the closest term in Sullivan's lexicon to "psychic reality" would be "parataxic integrations," which he defines as follows: "when, beside the interpersonal situation as defined within the awareness of the speaker, there is a concomitant interpersonal situation quite different as to its principal integrating tendencies, of which the speaker is more or less completely unaware" (1940, p. 92). An inquiry into the realm of parataxic integrations and illusory others is clearly central to Sullivan's approach to the psychoanalytic process, but, unlike Schwaber and others influenced by self psychology, Sullivan would also include the importance of what he termed "syntaxic" experience, the correction of parataxic distortions through consensual validation. Once again, Sullivan's position is quite close to that of Schafer, who argues for an oscillating balance between a point of view within the patient's psychic reality and one he terms a "developmental-environmental-functional approach," which introduces other, consensually held considerations.

What of "intrapsychic" meaning "inner world" as opposed to public, observable events? This concept is a bit trickier to position Sullivan in relation to, since it depends very much on what one means by "inner world." Sullivan repeatedly distinguished between the patient's subjective experiences that are able to be articulated and those which are not, which he termed the "immutably private." The former domain of the patient's inner life Sullivan regards as, in fact, interpersonal, since it translates into language that makes it communicable to another. "Human behavior," Sullivan suggests, "including the verbal report of subjective ... [phenomena], is the actual matter of observation" (1964, p. 34).

It is crucial to note that Sullivan doesn't assume that what the patient reports gives the analyst a direct glimpse into the patient's experience, a clear window into the patient's inner world. Rather, since verbal reports always take place within an interpersonal situation, they are always directed toward and involve the analyst as participant. Freud sees so-called free-associations as shaped by unconscious dynamic factors, the patient's conflictual struggles with the contents of his own mind. Sullivan sees "free-associations" as also shaped by the particular situation with the particular analyst. In Sullivan's view, the patient would not associate in precisely the same way with a different analyst. Therefore the associations are not pieces of the patient's experience unfolding in a neutral medium, but to some degree derivative of the interaction itself. "The processes ... that make up the data which can be subjected to scientific study occur," Sullivan suggests, "not in the subject person nor in the observer, but in the situation which is created between the observer and his subject" (1954, p. 3).

Hence Sullivan's position is very close to Spence's (1982) critique of Freud's "archaeological metaphor" and his (Freud's) assumption that the fragments of the patient's inner life are exposed in the free-associations, intact, just as they were experienced, rather than selected and composed in the context of the transference relationship with the particular analyst at any given time.

What of the patient's *unconscious* subjective experience? Here Sullivan was very cautious. It is sometimes said of Sullivan that he did not believe in the "unconscious"; although his rhetoric sometimes suggests this disclaimer, this is very misleading. Sullivan clearly believed that all of us are up to much more than we know about consciously. He spoke of "prehension" (as opposed to perception), selective inattention, dissociation, covert processes – all these involve phenomena generally considered to be unconscious (although sometimes partly preconscious).

If the patient doesn't know what is going on, he can't translate it into language to communicate it to the analyst. How can the analyst know? In Sullivan's view, the analyst really can't. He can generate hypotheses based on what the patient actually does and says, which *is* observable even though the patient may inattend to it, and he can hypothesize about unconscious aspects of the patient's experience based on theories of development, motivation, and so on, all of which point him toward what might be missing in the patient's account. But he really can't know. This is why Sullivan felt we can be both totally convinced that there is something going on, but necessarily wary about how much we assume we know about it. Sullivan puts it as follows:

> The unconscious ... is quite clearly that which cannot be experienced directly, which fills all the gaps in the mental life. In that rather broad sense, the postulate of the unconscious has, so far as I know, nothing in the world the matter with it. As soon as you begin to arrange the furniture in something that cannot be directly experienced, you are engaged in a work that requires more than parlor magic and you are apt to be embarrassed by some skeptic. (1964, p. 204)

By translating structural metaphors into process or action terms, Schafer has similarly "operationalized" the unconscious in a fashion strikingly reminiscent of Sullivan:

> Putting the concept of self-deception this way also invites investigation of the modes of action by means of which people can act in selectively inattentive and selectively ignorant modes, especially with regard to personal matters of great moment. *The investigation of these reasons and of these actions and their modes is what the metapsychologist would call the investigation of "the dynamic unconscious."* (1976, pp. 243–244)

Many contemporary interpersonalists feel that Sullivan's strict operationalist methodology led him to be too cautious in developing hypotheses about the structure of the "inner world." Many of us find complementary and useful the theories of the British school, like

Fairbairn's and Winnicott's, whose basic motivational and developmental theories are, like Sullivan's, fundamentally interpersonal, but who have elaborated a vision of the organizational principles of the "inner world."

Let us review the ground we have covered. I have suggested that the terms *intrapsychic* and *interpersonal* have been used loosely in the literature as banners representing clusters of different kinds of concepts and emphases, and I have broken the dichotomy down into four contrasts: fantasy vs. perception, psychic reality vs. actuality, inner world vs. outer world, and drive theory vs. a theory of environmental interaction. We noted that Sullivan gave great prominence to both fantasy and psychic reality in general, and that, although tentative, he used concepts referring to the patient's inner world. Only on Freud's concept of drive per se, do we find Sullivan uncompromisingly opposed, since drives are, by definition, understood to be sheltered from the interpersonal field, arising independently in the id and encountering the actual world only through the mediating activities of the ego.

It is important to note that the way in which Freud derived the content of the intrapsychic, largely from a priori, body-based instinctual sources, was very much consistent with the time in which Freud lived and wrote.

Throughout the many centuries of western civilization prior to Freud's day, human beings were understood to have originated in a fall from a higher state. Plato saw human experience, indeed all life in time, as a descent from an eternal world of ideal forms, and the Judeo-Christian tradition portrayed man as fallen from a paradisal harmony designed by a divine creator. Freud was three years old when Darwin's *Origin of Species* was published. The evolutionary perspective that Darwin introduced, and which dominated the scientific *Zeitgeist* of Freud's day, was an abrupt reversal of prior centuries of Platonic-Christian thought. Man had not stumbled from above, Darwin argued, but had gradually evolved from below. Man was not a fallen angel, a chip off the divine block gone astray, but a more or less refined beast.

This reversal provided a fresh and exciting vista on human nature and experience, and Freud was very much a beneficiary of this novel perspective. In the broadest sense, Freud regarded the intrapsychic, the inner world of each individual, as providing a window into man's phylogenetic history. Freud's drive theory of motivation is a brilliant analogue, in a theory of the evolution of human motives, of the structure of Darwin's theory of the evolution of the human species. Just as lower organisms evolve into higher forms of life, bestial sexual and aggressive impulses are transformed into the entire array of civilized human activities. "Primitive" impulses bubble up from the id, a "cauldron full of seething excitations", and are worked over by a "secondary" process concerned with adaptation to external reality, to fuel "higher" functions. Phylogeny is recapitulated not only in ontogeny, but in the very process of thought itself.

The general strategy of finding meanings in the present by uncovering a *prehistory* of the individual in a remote ancestral past dominated the natural sciences in the second half of the 19th century, inspired not only by developments in biology, but by advances in geology as well. Preceeding the development of Darwin's theory of bestial prehuman ancestors was the discovery of what McPhee (1980) has called "deep time." Contrary to the biblical account, which dates mankind from the very beginning of things, geologists in the first half of the 19th century were beginning to grasp what a small fragment of the vast age of the earth coincides with human history. The present, the surface, what is manifest, somehow pales in significance to what has gone before. What Berlin refers to as the "historicism" of the 19th century reflects this tendency to look for answers in the remote past. "History alone – the sum of empirically discovered data – holds the key to the mystery of why what happened happened as it did and not otherwise (Berlin, 1953, p. 11).

Thus Freud's sense of what it means to really "explain" something was greatly influenced by the Copernican discovery of deep space, the geological discovery of deep time, and the Darwinian discovery of man's remote, prehuman ancestry. Explanation for Freud means going beneath the present, the surface, the manifest. The intrapsychic realm, the derivatives of which bubble up in free-associations, offers a window into the well of the past, where he felt the deepest truths about human experience are to be found.

Sullivan's sensibility, honed by operationalism, was very different and very much in tune with 20th-century movements like structuralism and hermeneutics. Here meaning is to be found not in underlying or remote "causes," but in an understanding of the structure of things, the way in which they are put together. For Sullivan, the intrapsychic, the inner world, although he would hate to use such language, is inextricably intertwined with what is actually going on. The intrapsychic, for Sullivan, *is* intrinsically interpersonal, deriving from interactions occurring in the interpersonal field.

What would Sullivan have to say about later developments in drive theory within Freudian ego psychology? In the contributions of Jacobson, Kernberg, Loewald, Sandler, and others, drives have been gradually more and more interpersonalized, viewed as appearing not preformed within the organism itself, but as arising and shaped in interaction between the infant and the mother and as therefore inherently dyadic. Here language becomes very tricky, and exactly what is meant by "drive" often difficult to pin down. However, Sullivan presumably would have found such an approach considerably more amenable.

We began with definitions of "intrapsychic" and "interpersonal" as locations, the former "in" the mind, the latter "between persons," and have argued that any sophisticated psychoanalytic theory must encompass both realms. What are some of the key differences in the way this is done? I'll conclude with a brief consideration of different ways of approaching two separate but closely related facets of the relationship between the intrapsychic and the interpersonal: of what is experience composed? and where is it heading?

We suggested earlier that all psychoanalytic theories regard experience as a mixture of something brought to the experience by the subject and actual phenomena in the real world. No one believes in a totally naive observer simply recording actuality; no one believes in a totally programmed observer only projecting his internal reality. But there are many differences in how one sees the ratio between these two factors in the construction of subjective experience.

What generates the major features of the child's emotional life? A more intrapsychic position stresses pre-set categories, metaphors, universal themes. Traditionally drive theory has provided the theoretical underpinnings for such an understanding. But Schafer is an interesting example of a theorist who is heavily intrapsychic in this sense but eschews the concept of drive. For Schafer, the body doesn't generate drives, but provides metaphors. Bodily structures and events are fundamental in the child's reality, and therefore all experiences are encoded in terms of metaphors borrowed from the body.

A more purely interpersonal position, by contrast, stresses the formative input of parental character. The child becomes human by making contact with parenting figures. One cannot be human in some generic sense, but only through dyadic exchange, and therefore the emotional life of the child is filled with and shaped by the contours of parental character and is constructed out of actual interactions. The parents' issues become the child's issues; the kinds of interaction they make possible determine the metaphors. Of course, as soon as interpersonal interactions are registered and stored in memory, they become intrapsychic phenomena and are part of the set which the child brings with him to the next interaction.

Kuhn (1962) has described the differences between paradigms in scientific theorizing as different kinds of "thinking caps." A supervisee of mine trained in the classical tradition once told me he felt he was taught to listen to clinical material and "think body." The interpersonal tradition, it seems to me, teaches one to listen and "think parental character." Of course, no good clinician keeps these questions in the forefront of his mind; we all try to be as good phenomenologists as possible and let the material shape itself. But there is no unmediated listening, and these differences in premises as to the balance between intrapsychic and interpersonal factors in the origins of experience go a long way in determining how one hears the patient.

The same kind of contrast can be drawn at the level of the patient's experience of the transference and the analytic situation. Does the patient experience the analyst in terms of the past, what Freud (1912 [1958]) called "earlier editions," or is the transference at least partially a response to actual input from the analyst? Here the "intrapsychic," what the patient brings to the experience, includes the residues of the past, whether based on drives or childhood interpersonal experiences, and the ratio between intrapsychic and interpersonal factors concerns itself with the question of how one regards the interaction between past experience and current perceptions.

Arlow, for example, regards the actuality of the analyst as operating like the day residue in the dream, an inconsequential trigger allowing a smuggled access into the preconscious, making possible the emergence of unconscious fantasy. "[T]he persistent influence of unconscious fantasy creates the mental set against which the data of perception are perceived, registered, integrated, remembered and responded to. The patient literally misses the actual, or what we might call the 'interpersonal,' because he is living subjectively in the past, or, in the context of the analytic situation, the 'intrapsychic.' The neurotic process and transference may be understood as representing how the individual misperceives, misintegrates, and misresponds to, the data of perception, in terms of the mental set created by persistent unconscious fantasies" (1985, p. 526).

Hoffman (1983) has contrasted this approach with what he terms a "relativistic-social view" of the analytic situation, as developed most radically by writers like Racker, Levenson, and Gill. Here the patient is regarded as building subjective reality in the transference out of a "plausible," to use Gill's term, interpretation of what is actually going on. One can understand the analyst's participation variously as the analyst inevitably bringing to the field his own character and individuality, or the analyst as transformed through induced countertransference, by the patient's transference; what these more interpersonal approaches have in common is the assumption that the patient's subjective experience of the analyst is open to, and to a large extent shaped by, the actual interactions with the analyst.

Abrams and Shengold (1978) contrast the view of the analytic situation as an "encounter" with the view of the analytic situation as an examination of intrapsychic processes. From the traditional "intrapsychic" point of view, there is no encountering the analyst except as a screen for the patient to encounter himself. From the interpersonal point of view, there is no examination of intrapsychic processes except as they are transformed and in a sense uniquely created in the encounter with the analyst.

The self psychology approach, certain developmentally oriented versions of ego psychology (Stone, Loewald), and some of the British object relations writers (especially Winnicott and Guntrip) present a mixture of perspectives. The child's early experience tends to be regarded as heavily influenced by the child's interpersonal world, resulting in a developmental arrest, which is reexperienced in the analytic situation. But the patient's experience of the analyst is understood to be largely intrapsychically determined, and merely released by the nurturing presence of the analyst. Goldberg notes the contrast between this and a more fully interpersonal position:

> Self psychology struggles hard not to be an interpersonal psychology not only because it wishes to avoid the social psychological connotations of the phrase but also because it wishes to minimize the input of the analyst into the mix.... Since self psychology is so preeminently a developmental psychology, it is based on the idea of a developmental program (one that may be innate or pre-wired if you wish) that will reconstitute itself under certain conditions. (1986, p. 387)

Here again, is the assumption that there is an "inside" to the patient which can manifest itself largely independently of the interpersonal situation in which it appears. Gill has noted that in such formulations, the analyst is not so much a fully interpersonal "participant observer" as a "precipitant observer," a simple trigger for processes inside the patient.

Thus, all experience, whether in childhood or in the analytic situation, is composed of a complex mixture of what the subject brings to the experience, either constitutionally or from past interactions, and what he encounters in real transactions with others. Psychoanalytic theories differ on how they conceive of the ratio between these ingredients. Gill has argued for an integration which grants a central role to each set of determinants:

> The individual sees the world not only as his intrapsychic patterns dictate, but also as he veridically assesses it. Furthermore, the two kinds of determinants mutually influence each other. The intrapsychic patterns not only determine selective attention to those aspects of the external world which conform to them, but the individual behaves in such a way to enhance the likelihood that the responses he meets will indeed confirm the views with which he sets out. This external validation in turn is necessary for the maintenance of those patterns.... The unique contribution of psychoanalysis is the demonstration of the power and persistence of the intrapsychic determinants. But these determinants become only artificial abstractions if they are dealt with in isolation from the interpersonal context in which they find expression. (1982, p. 92)

A second issue concerns motivational thrust. One way to think about motivation is in terms of the regulation of internal, intrapsychic states. What people are generally up to is the establishment of some sort of internal, homeostatic equilibrium, and this can be viewed variously in terms of drive regulation, affective states, a sense of identity, self-cohesion, and so on.

Another way to think about motivation is in terms of the regulation of the interpersonal field. What people are generally up to is the establishment of patterns of integrating relationships with others that provide them with some sense of familiarity, safety, control, and so on.

One can distinguish specific interpretations in terms of the contrast between intrapsychic and interpersonal with respect to where you think the scene of the action is motivationally. If you regard homeostatis, self-regulation, or self-definition as of deepest dynamic significance, you will view the analytic situation as a space within which the patient's internal world is altered; changes in lived reality with other people would follow as a matter of course. On the other hand, if you regard patterns of connection and transaction as of deepest dynamic significance, you will view the analytic situation as a space within which the patient learns to be with other people in a different way; changes in the inner world will follow as a matter of course.

One could contrast classical drive theory and classical interpersonal theory generally on this basis. Self psychology, although similar in many respects to interpersonal theory, is like classical drive theory in regarding motivation as involved essentially with self-regulation. Concepts like Sandler and Rosenblatt's (1962) "representational world" or Racker's (1968) world of "internal object relations" might be located at the midpoint on this continuum in a way that bridges the two sides, since they refer to phenomena within the mind and therefore involved in self-regulation, but phenomena drawn directly from the interpersonal field and in continual interchange with that field.

Consider the following description of Sullivan's work with a patient who has an intrapsychic understanding of her symptomatic nail-biting: "one patient described nail-biting as an expression of anxiety. Dr. Sullivan acted puzzled; he wanted to know more about it. By the time the patient had spent five minutes trying to prove that point, the fallacy was apparent. They could agree that it was 'acting uncomfortable to impress other people with how uncomfortable they make one'" (White, 1952, p. 127).

Sullivan understands the nail-biting in terms of its organizing impact on the interpersonal field; it could also be understood in terms of the regulation of internal states, discharging drives, soothing tensions, and so on. A third alternative would be to regard the nail-biting as an *interpersonal* act between characters in an *internal* drama, expressive of an internal object relationship.

It is not necessary to cast one's lot always at the same point in locating the motivational thrust of any piece of clinical data. One might regard motivation as having, simultaneously, two different thrusts, self-regulatory and field-regulatory, with one or the other sometimes being more prominent. In this view, the intrapsychic and the interpersonal are continually interpenetrating realms, each with its own set of processes, mechanisms, and concerns.

The history of psychoanalytic ideas has developed not smoothly and linearly but in jumps and lurches in a dialectical field of conceptual possibilities created by sets of polarized concepts: fantasy/reality, insight/relationship, conflict/developmental arrest, oedipal/preoedipal, and intrapsychic/interpersonal. They arise as dichotomies, but, particularly at this point in the history of psychoanalytic ideas, it seems to me that we are gradually learning to regard many of them not as mutually exclusive. Freud's drive theory is a particular intrapsychic theory which *is* incompatible with radically relational theories like Sullivan's and Fairbairn's. The distinction between the intrapsychic (taken more broadly than drive theory) and the interpersonal, however, represents complementary views of a common analytic experience whose richness and complexity always eludes the efforts we make to grasp it through the inevitable limitations of our language and our ideas.

References

Abrams, S. & Shengold, L. (1978). Some reflexions on the topic of the 30th congress: "Affects and the psychoanalytic situation." *International Journal of Psycho-Analysis*, 59: 395–407.

Arlow, J. (1985). The concept of psychic reality and related problems. *Journal of the American Psychoanalytic Association*, 33: 521–535.

Berlin, I. (1953). *The Hedgehog and the Fox: An Essay on Tolstoy's View of History*. New York: Simon & Schuster.

Bridgeman, P. W. (1927). *The Logic of Modern Psychics*. New York: Macmillan.

Freud, S. (1887–1902). *The Origins of Psycho-analysis*. New York: Basic Books.

Freud, S. (1912 [1958]). *The Dynamics of Transference*, Standard Edition 12.London: Hogarth Press.

Freud, S. (1916–1917[1963]). *Introductory Lectures on Psychoanalysis*, Standard Edition 15. London: Hogarth Press, p. 16.

Gill, M. (1982). *Analysis of Transference*, Volume 1. New York: International Universities Press.

Goldberg, A. (1986). Reply to discussion by P. Bromberg of "The wishy-washy personality." *Contemporary Psychoanalysis*, 22: 387–388.

Grinstein, A. (1960, 1966, 1975). *Index of Psychoanalytic Writings*, Volumes 5, 9, 14. New York: International Universities Press.

Hoffman, I. (1983). The patient as interpreter of the analyst's experience. *Contemporary Psychoanalysis*, 19: 389–422.

Kohut, H. (1977). *The Restoration of the Self*. New York: International Universities Press.

Kohut, H. (1984). *How Does Analysis Cure?* Chicago, IL: Chicago University Press.

Kuhn, T. (1962). *The Structure of Scientific Revolutions*. Chicago, IL: Chicago University Press.

Loewald, H. (1980). *Papers on Psychoanalysis*. New Haven, CT: Yale University Press.

McPhee, J. (1980). *Basic and Range*. New York: Farrar, Strauss & Giroux.

Michels, R. (1985). Introduction to panel: Perspectives on the nature of psychic reality. *Journal of the American Psychoanalytic Association*, 33: 515–520.

Modell, A. (1984). *Psychoanalysis in a New Context*. New York: International Universities Press.

Nietzsche, F. (1872 [1956]). *The Birth of Tragedy*, trans. F. Golffing. New York: Doubleday Anchor.

Racker, H. (1968). *Transference and Countertransference*. New York: International Universities Press.

Sandler, J. & Rosenblatt, B. (1962). The concept of the representational world. *Psychoanalytic Study of the Child*, 17: 128–145.

Schafer, R. (1976). *A New Language for Psychoanalysis*. New Haven, CT: Yale University Press.

Spence, D. (1982). *Narrative Truth and Historical Truth*. New York: W. W. Norton.

Stern, D. (1985). *The Interpersonal World of the Infant*. New York: Basic Books.

Sullivan, H. S. (1927). The common field of research and clinical psychiatry. *Psychoanalytic Quarterly*, 1: 276–291.

Sullivan, H. S. (1940). *Conceptions of Modern Psychiatry*. New York: W. W. Norton.

Sullivan, H. S. (1954). *The Psychiatric Interview*. New York: W. W. Norton.

Sullivan, H. S. (1962). *Schizophrenia as a Human Process*. New York: W. W. Norton.

Sullivan, H. S. (1964). *The Fusion of Psychiatry and Social Science*. New York: W. W. Norton.

White, M. (1952). Sullivan and treatment. In *The Contributions of Harry Stack Sullivan: A Symposium*. New York: Hermitage House, pp. 117–150.

Chapter 11

Countertransference and participant-observation (1990)

Irwin Hirsch

Irwin Hirsch notes the very different geographies and cultural eras involved at the time of Freud's development of psychoanalysis and Sullivan's emendations a half-century later. Freud was raised in conservative, turn-of-the-century Vienna. Society was hierarchical and formal, and this was reflected in the attitude toward authority, in and out of the sciences. The disciplined scientist, restrained and rational, was celebrated. The heroic scientist could isolate the specimen (and, by extension, the patient) for intensive, objective study, like a cell on a microscope slide. Principles of uncertainty and relativity had not yet been introduced in physics.

Sullivan's early professional career, on the other hand, was spent in the chaotic Depression years in Chicago, where dire economic conditions and radical social flux drew attention to the role of social relations in the development and psychology of the individual. Sullivan became involved in the new fields of anthropology and social psychology, in both of which the individual was studied not in isolation, but in the context of an interactive field. It was the era of gestalt psychology and Kurt Lewin's field theory. The positivist model of research science that had been idealized in Freud's culture was replaced by a kind of socially responsible pragmatism. The question was how to apply science to help the world emerge from its misery. In Sullivan's world, the ideal was not so much the discovery of universal theoretical certainties about human beings, but the assertion of a more contextual reality. The individual, in this frame of reference, needed to be studied in the context of his field, and the subjective, observing scientist was understood to be a part of that field.

Freud's more formal psychoanalysis was brought to America by European immigrant analysts. They knew well, as Freud had learned in Vienna, to avoid allegations of prurience the investigation of sexuality must appear to be objective and scientific. By the time Sullivan entered the psychoanalytic picture, psychoanalysis in this country was dominated by a mainstream that was conservative and classically Freudian. Sullivan and his radical left wing colleague Erich Fromm took on the role of the opposition.

Freudian psychoanalysis in the USA was ego psychology, a clear technical theory and procedure in which the objective scientist/analyst studied the patient without interacting with that patient and without participating in the creation of data that evolved from the process. Interpersonal psychoanalytic thinking, on the other hand, situated the analyst in a field of forces with the patient. The patient could not be understood in isolation from that two-person environment. In this more mutual and less-controlled context, there came to exist less of a hierarchy between an allegedly objective analyst and a non-rational patient. As the interpersonal perspective evolved, patients were understood to be capable of actually seeing the subjectivity of their flawed and subjective analysts. To the extent that analysts embraced their inevitably unconscious participation in the dyad, the study of countertransference assumed primary significance. No longer viewed as an expression of the analyst's unanalyzed neurosis, countertransference took its place, with transference, as the central ingredients in the field of psychoanalytic engagement. Since the late 1980s, previously disparate traditions have converged around the inevitability of countertransference. Eventually, this attitude grew to include the acceptance of inevitable mutual enactment between patient and analyst. Transference and countertransference were no longer conceived separately, but instead were understood to form, together, a matrix. Today, in many orientations, including the classical Freudian, the analysis of mutual enactments has become the central ingredient of therapeutic action.

Countertransference and participant-observation (1990)

Irwin Hirsch

The study of countertransference experience as potentially useful data logically follows from participant observation as a psychoanalytic model. It is inherent in a model in which the physical science base is relativity theory and the principle of uncertainty. Harry Stack Sullivan (see Perry, 1982), not formally analytically trained and largely a self-educated intellectual, reflected the prevailing culture of his time and place. Chicago, during and post-World War I, was apparently the setting for Sullivan's possible schizophrenic break as well as for his personal and conceptual rejuvenation. He was a farm boy from the East and was exposed for the first time to a middle-American, urban, immigrant city. In contrast with the longstanding traditions and values in Freud's conservative, turn-of-the-century Vienna, Chicago appeared disorganized, without tradition, and in total flux.

For Freud, embedded in his time and place, science was hard science and the researcher sought absolute and indisputable truth. He believed that he studied from objective distance, controlled most of the variables, and if operating properly was not affected by his own person or his own biases. To think otherwise would undermine the validity of the findings and raise the specter of anarchy. Grey (1979) refers to Freud's research approach as reflecting the principle of isolates: "The most reliable way to acquire information about a phenomenon is to examine it in vacuo, in a test tube in its purist and most simple form" (p. 473).

Sullivan, on the other hand, in a new and developing society (and new to himself), resonated toward the theories of relativity and uncertainty and toward field theory, all of which throw into question the notion of absolute truth in the basic sciences, much less the social sciences. The scientist as personal researcher interacts with the data under study. Everything is contextual. What one sees is at least somewhat dependent on who one is and where and when one looks. The observer and the idiosyncratic conditions of observation are inevitably reflected in the findings. The researcher/observer is part of the observed. Absolute truth is elusive.

In addition to the trends in the physical sciences, Sullivan as a developing thinker was influenced by and much interested in the nascent social sciences. Freud, though far more formally educated than Sullivan, had no opportunity for such exposure. Anthropology and sociology were beginning American disciplines, directly relevant to the new urban world. The prevailing philosophy, pragmatism, lined up well with uncertainty and relativity. The social scientist was called upon to be of practical value to a society in some turmoil. Pure, in contrast with applied, research was a bit too esoteric for this unsophisticated culture. The charge was for the researcher to affect his subjects and not simply study them. Practical outcome had more value than the discovery of universal principles. Large or small group interactions (or even dyads) are to a large extent each unique and encompass their own particular forces of interaction. What produces an effect in one field may not be duplicated in another.

Sullivan, a bit later, became interested in another new discipline: social psychology. Field theory was a dominant early force in social psychology and its object of study was interactions within a field. The interactive focus was consistent with Sullivan's emerging scientific orientation. It provided a sharp contrast to Freud's natural science emphasis: the isolation and pure study of one variable. The study of interactions on the one hand and the study of solitary subject on the other lead to contrasting psychoanalytic philosophies.

Clear, easily repeatable and exquisite technique has never been the hallmark of interpersonal psychoanalysis. There are far too many uncertainties, relativities, subjectivities, and uncontrolled forces. This apparent systemic deficiency, however, can be turned to advantage or advance in analytic technique, which is precisely what Sullivan, Clara Thompson, Erich Fromm, and Freida Fromm-Reichmann tried to initiate in their shift of psychoanalysis from a purely "intra" subject matter to an "inter" focus. Interpersonal psychoanalysis studies the intrapsychic as it is manifested in the analytic dyad while classical psychoanalysis tries to isolate and study the individual in vacuo (Barnett, 1980a; Greenberg & Mitchell, 1983). Objectivity and notions of absolute truth are possible when the analyst is a natural scientist studying the data (the patient) from outside the dyadic system. If the analyst is viewed as inside the system he too must be the object of study for he inevitably influences the data (the patient) and in fact becomes part of the data. In the interpersonal model, participant observation, the study of countertransference is inherent in the system.

This notion has never generated popular appeal within the American psychoanalytic community and until quite recently only a small minority of trained analysts have worked within this framework. One reason for this situation, not *directly* relevant to the main theme of this paper, is the notion that when the dyad is studied the individual gets lost. The dyad has been viewed by many as a superficial focus and a study of social relations and not individual, depth psychology. It is often said that the internal life of the patient gets short shrift. It has been the subject of much accusation and defense and I believe the best interpersonal retort is that the inner world of the patient *is* studied but in the context of the dyadic field. The internalized self is based on past interpersonal experience and lived out in all current interactions (Barnett, 1980b). There is no more logical and sensible way to study the inner world of the individual. Of course, one never knows for certain what is purely intrapsychic since interpersonal data are always influenced by both participants. The recent infant observation research of Stern (1985) supports the long-held minority argument that social interaction is the primary determinant of psychological development every step of the way. The individual cannot be studied apart from the social context. Actually, Winnicott (1965) said something quite a while back when he spoke of not studying infants but infant and mother pairs.

A second reason for the lack of wide appeal for the participant observation model is directly related to its (by definition) more subjective, less systematic procedure. In classical theory of therapy, objectivity and neutrality are felt to be reasonably reachable ideals. By operating from outside of the patient's system one can ostensibly achieve clarity without getting caught up in the patient's world. To most analysts this position has been clearly preferable. It presumes to be a cleaner method that keeps the patient and the analyst each in their own separate tracks. It is assumed that the patient's perceptions of the analyst are usually projections and/or distortions. The analyst, unless he is not working properly, does not have to be concerned about how he is influencing or affecting the patient. It is allegedly not happening. There is only one person to examine: the patient who is projecting his inner world on to a relative blank screen.

A third reason for the recoil from participant observation is directly related to countertransference (Epstein & Feiner, 1979). The participant observation model is one that acknowledges mutual influence. The analyst observes but is also an unwitting participant. Contrary to some criticism of this orientation, the analyst does not consciously *try* to participate or to influence the patient or even to be more verbally active than the classical analyst. Just as in classical technique the analyst attempts to primarily listen, inquire, make observations, and interpret. How quiet or active one is, is an individual variable for analysts of all persuasions.

The participant observation analyst is primarily an observer but one who recognizes that the observer inevitably becomes part of the observed. It is not as if this recognition is a virtue to strive for but simply a human given. When not ignored it becomes an essential part of analytic data. As many current authors have noted (e.g., Gill, 1982; Langs, 1976; Levenson, 1983; Racker, 1968; Searles, 1965), the patient is quite capable of picking up the analyst's errors, attitudes, values, feelings, anxieties, and personal characteristics. The philosophy behind the participant observation model is such that it invites the patient to address these observations. Parenthetically, though Sullivan developed this model, he personally avoided examination of the transference–countertransference interaction in the here and now.

According to Gill, a major advocate of encouraging patients to point out the analyst's unconscious participation, the analyst must view these observations as at least plausible, not simply as projections or distortions. The analyst is made aware of often uncomfortable countertransference enactments and attempts to use these to deepen the understanding of the patient's patterns of interaction. The nature of the traditional classical model is such that the patient's observations about the analyst are less likely to be viewed as plausible. If the patient were deemed accurate and not seen as distorting, the strict orthodox position would view this situation as excessive analytic engagement: a countertransference problem. In a sense, the analyst who acknowledges inevitable countertransference and the patient's ability to read it is aware of more nakedness. There is little anonymity (Singer, 1977). There is much appeal in the relative blank screen, for the concept can be used to reduce the anxiety of exposure and provide the analyst with a sense of more rigorous, scientific boundaries. Such boundaries help quell fears of acting out and provide a shield of safety behind which the analyst may operate with a feeling of greater comfort and precision.

Despite this long history of these and other reservations, there is increasing evidence that the participant observation model is gaining wider acceptance in the psychoanalytic mainstream in the United States. In the same vein, much significant current writing on countertransference, though often not labeled as countertransference literature, has been penned by classically trained analysts. Cooper (1985), past president of the American Psychoanalytic Association, describes an increasing convergence between historically disparate psychoanalytic models. He states, "A portion of the growth of psychoanalytic theory can be seen as the effort to incorporate, often without acknowledgment, the valid aspects of the critique of oppositional schools. Recently, for example, Sullivan's work has increasingly reappeared in mainstream psychoanalysis, not always with attribution" (p. 11).

Probably for the first time, the *Journal of the American Psychoanalytic Association* (1986) has devoted a significant portion of an edition to the subject of countertransference. In one of these articles, Blum (1986), the former editor of the journal, states, "Present-day interest in a two-person, analytic field of forces and the analyst as participant observer has many ramifications. One of these ramifications has been the vast broadening of the concept of countertransference to take into account the entire emotional set of conscious and unconscious reactions that analysts have to a patient" (p. 34). Illustrative of a point that Cooper and I (Hirsch, 1985) have both made, there is no reference to Sullivan or other interpersonal literature. Cooper discusses this situation largely as a function of Freud's dominance and the degree of organizational disruption over the early deviations of Alfred Adler and Carl Jung. Freud's attitude forced other significant ideas on to "oppositional" schools or on to sidetracks where they could not interact with the main directions of psychoanalytic development. Cooper sees this situation as just now beginning to shift; that is, formerly "oppositional" schools (e.g., interpersonal) are starting to be acknowledged as contributors to what is considered mainstream psychoanalysis.

I have suggested that the classical veering toward a more field theoretical participant observation approach has come about largely through Freudian analysts, like Blum, introducing or reintroducing other conceptions without recognizing that they represent already developed thinking and an already published body of literature. When introduced from within, these ideas are more acceptable and then perhaps, as Cooper notes, the formerly "oppositional" schools may be acknowledged. Loewald (1986), in the same *JAPA* volume devoted to the examination of countertransference, notes that countertransference as a concept was particularly difficult for Freud to integrate partially because he analyzed himself. More specifically, Freud never viewed psychoanalysis as a mutual relationship. The notion of mutuality is inherent in the participant observation model as well as in conceiving of countertransference experience as inevitable and potentially useful.

The manner in which the American mainstream psychoanalytic body is becoming increasingly interested in countertransference and concepts of the self, and is converging with the participant observation model, is based more on personal and political matters than on scientific advance. In addition to what Cooper has discussed, classical analysts have been gradually assimilating the contributions of the British and South American object relations groups (e.g., Heimann, 1951; Little, 1951; Racker, 1968; Winnicott, 1947) and the more recent developments of Kohut (e.g., 1977, 1984) and the self psychologists. Though not everyone would agree, I believe that most object relations analysts and self psychologists are closer to interpersonal than to classical thinking in their theories of development, their notions of the self, and their acknowledgment of the analyst's strong participation in the analytic process. Although the specifics of development and the exact nature of analytic participation may be quite different from those of the interpersonalists, both reject the blank-screen, natural science methods of investigation and both see countertransference as having a potentially productive role in technique. Most of the leading contributors of these schools have been trained originally as classical analysts or have had mixed training. By and large they all maintain a tie to Freudian theory through at least an allegiance to the *language* of drive theory, even though they may indeed reject drive theory entirely (Greenberg & Mitchell, 1983). Their early training, their psychoanalytic language, and the access they have to mainstream psychoanalytic journals have led to influence and acknowledgment not shared by analysts of the interpersonal school.

I believe that these trends, in part, have influenced perhaps the most powerful new voices of participant observation. I refer to a group of liberal classical analysts who, except for Gill (1983, 1984), are unaware of or have not acknowledged their harmony with the participant observation model and the centrality of countertransference, per se, in their thinking. Recent contributions of Schafer (1983) and Spence (1982) are most widely known though less-known authors (e.g., Bird, 1972; Jacobs, 1986; McLaughlin, 1981; Tower, 1956) have contributed significantly.

Schafer and Spence take the notion of participant observation to an extreme that Sullivan and a number of interpersonal writers (e.g., Levenson, 1983) have addressed but never spelled out so thoroughly. They, as well as Jacobs, are saying that literally every aspect of what analysts do is affected by the analyst as person. This action includes the choice of theory the patient may be fit into and the understanding of the patient's allegedly veridical life history. According to Schafer, one's psychoanalytic theory is his "story line." It is what makes sense to an analyst based on who he is, who was his analyst, and who were his teachers. When an analyst interprets analytic material he is placing it in a framework that belongs to his own being and into a theory that makes personal sense to him. Different analysts, with the same patient, will develop different recountings of history and offer different interpretations based on disparate theories. There is not an objective theory, an objective history, or an objective interpretation. Everything can be countertransference-based, an interaction between the person of the analyst, his belief system, and the object of study: the patient. Participant observation is total.

Spence speaks to much the same issue, emphasizing efforts at historical reconstruction and explanatory interpretations. He states, given that early history is not truly available for recall and certainly not verifiable in the analytic dyad, that analysts help patients construct fictional narratives that satisfy requirements of "making sense." These narratives may be based on theoretical biases, personal idiosyncrasies of the analyst, and so forth. Nonetheless, if they generate a good explanatory accounting they can provide historical coherence and be helpful to the patient. He is, of course, saying that analysts, based on their own countertransference inclinations, unwittingly participate with patients in making up stories. These stories may have only minimal relation to the elusive truth. The observer is intimately a part of what is observed. This notion is also central in Jacobs' documentation of how generally accepted technique can serve as a guise for countertransference enactments.

McLaughlin (1981), also from within the classical school, objects to the terms *transference* and *countertransference* as too biased in the direction of the patient as primary distorter. He believes that transference is the better term for what occurs with both patient and analyst since he views both parties in this mutual process as reflecting their own subjective or psychic reality. It is not necessarily the patient who does it first (transference) and provokes the analyst (countertransference). Along somewhat similar lines, Tower (1956) and Bird (1972), in two widely cited older articles, speak of a countertransference neurosis in conjunction with transference neurosis. They observe, in what they call the eye of the storm of transference neurosis, a shared countertransference neurosis. In the midst of the most intense analytic moments the analyst is just as lost in subjectivity and repetition as is the patient.

Hoffman (1983) summarizes what is the logical extreme of the participant observation model and the ubiquity of countertransference. He integrates the work of leading thinkers from varying analytic schools (Gill, Levenson, Racker, Sandler, and Searles) and refers to them as the "radical social paradigm." Hirsch (1987) has referred to this group as the "observing participants," borrowing the term from Fromm (1964) and Wolstein (1964), who elaborated on it. The emphasis is on participation, with *observing* as the modifying adverb. From the perspective of these authors the analyst inevitably becomes thoroughly enmeshed in the interactional world of the patient. It is not by premeditated intent but occurs as a natural process during the normal analyzing function of observation.

The analyst, in trying to minimize the intrusion of his own person, lends himself to the influence of the patient and over time becomes drawn into the patient's characteristic interpersonal patterns. These patterns most likely conform to the patient's early significant interactions with family members and to the patient's current way of forming relationships with others. Each individual analyst brings his own unique personality and theory to the situation and will not engage in precisely the same way as any other analyst. According to the point stressed by these thinkers, however, the analyst will enter the patient's interactional field in some way that resembles those of significant early others. It is like what Bird and Tower describe in their concept of countertransference neurosis, though it does not necessarily reflect only one intense period in the analysis. The analyst is trying to be an observer but has unwittingly become a co-participant (Wolstein, 1975). It is usually the patient who conveys this to the analyst in a direct or disguised manner. In Hoffman's (1983) and Searles' (1979) terms, the patient interprets the analyst's experience and wakes up the analyst to what is happening between them.

In Levenson's (1972) language the analyst had been "transformed," and in Sandler's (1976) dialect he had been "nudged into role responsiveness." Gill in particular stresses how crucial it is to listen for the patient's observations about the participation of the analyst. He makes the strongest case of all for the ubiquity of analytic influence and the effects on the process when the analyst remains unaware.

According to Gill, if the analyst is not helped to become aware of his unwitting participation, two serious dangers occur. The first is the loss of the ability to make explicit and to analyze the patient–analyst interaction. The second is the likelihood that the analyst will influence the patient without this being clear to either participant and what could potentially evolve to analytic change could dissolve into a transference cure. Gill has been criticized for implying that the patient is always right. Indeed, he does believe, as do others who emphasize the validity of the patient's psychic reality (e.g., Schawber, 1983), that all of the patient's perceptions are plausible and that the analyst does not have the corner on objective reality. From this perspective both parties participate with their subjective selves and the patient cannot be assumed to be projecting or distorting.

One of the values of working from this theory of therapy lies in the way observations may be made from direct and potent experience in the immediacy of the analytic exchange. Like with transference neurosis, what is addressed are the essential life patterns of the patient as they are actually being lived out with the unwitting, observing participant analyst. The patient repeats early experience and tries to shape his current relationships to conform to this experience. When the analyst is sensitive to the patient's countertransference interpretations he can more readily focus on these transference–countertransference enactments at the point of urgency.

The patient is more easily able to see how the analytic interaction lines up with other significant patterns of engagement and how consistent are his patterns of living. The emerging clarity and explicitness of the analytic relationship, in conjunction with the awareness of how it parallels both historical and current extratransference patterns, combines the value of insight, on the one hand, and formation of a new relationship or corrective experience, on the other. Sullivan's introduction of the participant observer analyst has been pushed to its logical extreme by analysts from within and outside of the school he initiated.

References

Barnett, J. (1980a). Self and character. *Journal of the American Academy of Psychoanalysis and Dynamic Psychiatry*, 8: 337–352.

Barnett, J. (1980b). Interpersonal processes, cognition, and the analysis of character. *Contemporary Psychoanalysis*, 16: 397–416.

Bird, B. (1972). Notes on transference: Universal phenomenon and hardest part of analysis. *Journal of the American Psychoanalytic Association*, 20: 267–301.
Blum, H. (1986). Countertransference and the theory of technique: Discussion. *Journal of the American Psychoanalytic Association*, 34: 309–327.
Cooper, A. (1985). A historic review of psychoanalytic paradigms. In A. Rothstein (Ed.), *Models of the Mind*. New York: International Universities Press.
Epstein, L., Feiner, A. (1979). *Countertransference*. New York: Jason Aronson.
Fromm, E. (1964). *The Heart of Man*. New York: Harper and Row.
Gill, M. (1982). *Analysis of Transference*, Volume I. New York: International Universities Press.
Gill, M. (1983). The interpersonal paradigm and the degree of the therapist's involvement. *Contemporary Psychoanalysis*, 19: 200–237.
Gill, M. (1984). Psychoanalysis and psychotherapy: A revision. *International Review of Psycho-Analysis*, 11: 161–179.
Greenberg, J. & Mitchell, S. (1983). *Object Relations in Psychoanalytic Theory*. Cambridge, MA: Harvard University Press.
Grey, A. (1979). Countertransference and parataxis. *Contemporary Psychoanalysis*, 15: 472–483.
Heimann, P. (1951). On countertransference. *International Journal of Psycho-Analysis*, 31: 81–84.
Hirsch, I. (1985). The rediscovery of the advantages of the participant observation model. *Psychoanalysis and Contemporary Thought*, 8: 441–459.
Hirsch, I. (1987). Varying modes of analytic participation. *Journal of the American Academy of Psychoanalysis and Dynamic Psychiatry*, 15: 205–222.
Hoffman, I. (1983). The patient as interpreter of the analyst's experience. *Contemporary Psychoanalysis*, 19: 389–422.
Jacobs, T. (1986). On countertransference enactments. *Journal of the American Psychoanalytic Association*, 34: 289–307.
Kohut, H. (1977). *The Restoration of the Self*. New York: International Universities Press.
Kohut, H. (1984). *How Does Analysis Cure?* Chicago, IL: University of Chicago Press.
Langs, R. (1976). *The Therapeutic Interaction*, Volume II. New York: Jason Aronson.
Levenson, E. (1972). *The Fallacy of Understanding*. New York: Basic Books.
Levenson, E. (1983). *The Ambiguity of Change*. New York: Basic Books.
Little, M. (1951). Countertransference and the patient's response to it. *International Journal of Psycho-Analysis*, 32: 32–40.
Loewald, H. (1986). Transference–countertransference. *Journal of the American Psychoanalytic Association*, 34: 275–287.
McLaughlin, J. (1981). Transference, psychic reality and countertransference. *Psychoanalytic Quarterly*, 50: 639–664.
Perry, H. S. (1982). *Psychiatrist of America*. Cambridge, MA: Harvard University Press.

Racker, H. (1968). *Transference and Countertransference*. New York: International Universities Press.
Sandler, J. (1976). Countertransference and role-responsiveness. *International Review of Psycho-Analysis*, 3: 43–47.
Schafer, R. (1983). *The Analytic Attitude*. New York: Basic Books.
Schawber, E. (1983). Psychoanalytic listening and psychic reality. *International Review of Psycho-Analysis*, 10: 379–392.
Searles, H. F. (1965). *Collected Papers on Schizophrenia and Related Subjects*. New York: International Universities Press.
Searles, H. F. (1979). *Countertransference and Related Subjects*. New York: International Universities Press.
Singer, E. (1977). The fiction of analytic anonymity. In K. Frank (Ed.), *The Human Dimension in Psychoanalytic Practice*. New York: Grune and Stratton.
Spence, D. (1982). *Narrative Truth and Historical Truth*. New York: W. W. Norton.
Stern, D. (1985). *The Interpersonal World of the Infant*. New York: Basic Books.
Tower, L. (1956). Countertransference. *Journal of the American Psychoanalytic Association*, 4: 224–255.
Winnicott, D. W. (1947). Hate in the countertransference. *International Journal of Psycho-Analysis*, 30: 69–74.
Winnicott, D. W. (1965). *The Maturational Process and the Facilitating Environment*. New York: International Universities Press.
Wolstein, B. (1964). *Transference*. New York: Grune and Stratton.
Wolstein, B. (1975). Countertransference: The psychoanalyst's shared experience and inquiry with his patient. *Journal of the American Academy of Psychoanalysis and Dynamic Psychiatry*, 3: 77–89.

Chapter 12

Courting surprise

Unbidden perceptions in clinical practice[1] (1990)

Donnel B. Stern

In this article Donnel Stern writes about analytic process and the ideal conditions for fruitful psychoanalytic work. What is most important to him in analytic work grows from his own experience with the patient, not from pre-existing theories and formulations and expectancies with regard to how people develop and what generally motivates behavior. What he does with the patient is not necessarily suggested by the patient's life history, nor does he derive his interventions from the formulation of current personality configurations. He refers to fiction writers who do not plan or know what is coming next in their work. Instead, the next words and scenes come in a way that is unbidden, a favorite word of Stern's, used throughout his writing.

In a psychoanalytic context, he argues, most of the analyst's most significant perceptions (and the patient's) arise without conscious intention. He observes that we do not learn what we set out to discover, and what we do discover is not necessarily what we expect to learn. Openness to surprise is key.

Stern (1997) has written a theory of unconsciousness as *unformulated experience*, by which he means that unconsciousness is not fully formed meaning hidden away in the mind, but potential experience, a vaguely organized, global, nonideational, affective state. The eventual, articulate meaning that arises from unformulated experience is not entirely predetermined. There is always "wiggle room." The particular articulate experience that comes into being depends on the nature of the interpersonal field existing when the process of articulation comes about.

Like Edgar Levenson and other interpersonalists, Stern resists the closure of too readily making sense of the clinical data. Our theories will always provide answers and reasonable narratives, though these do not necessarily lead to new ways of experiencing the world. Stern argues in this article that we serve our patients best when we are able to perceive the difference "between experience and expectation." If what we experience is nothing more than what we expect, we learn nothing, because experience just "keeps on keeping on," repeating itself in the same way. But if we can grasp the difference between what we expect and what we actually meet in the clinical interaction, then the possibility of new understanding and new experience stays alive. These ideas reflect what Stern has learned from the writings of hermeneutic philosopher Hans-Georg Gadamer, and this article is intended to be a companion piece to a paper by Stern (1991) on the psychoanalytic application of Gadamer's thought.

Stern follows Sullivan's dictum that good questions are more important than answers. Questions that emerge from genuine curiosity are perhaps the psychoanalyst's most powerful tool or skill. In addition, questions serve the valuable function of deconstructing what may be too familiar to reveal new meaning. But the asking of questions is not the essence of curiosity. Curiosity, says Stern in this article, is "an active attitude of openness," not "mere inquisitiveness." The acceptance of familiarity, Stern says elsewhere, which dampens curiosity, often serves defensive purposes because it prevents uncertainty.

Stern does not depend for his understanding of the patient on explicit, conscious dependence on theories of development or technique. Instead, when he is with the patient, what is central for him is the unique, lived experience of the psychoanalytic hour. In this, he carries forward in his own way a theme developed over many decades by earlier interpersonal analysts. Stern argues that for clinical experience to be richest, the analyst must be free to engage the patient with a spontaneity that allows for the emergence of unbidden perceptions that may be completely unexpected.

References

Stern, D. B. (1991). A philosophy for the embedded analyst: Gadamer's hermeneutics and the social paradigm of psychoanalysis. *Contemporary Psychoanalysis*, 27: 51–80.

Stern, D. B. (1997). *Unformulated Experience: From Dissociation to Imagination in Psychoanalysis*. Hillsdale, NJ: Analytic Press.

Courting surprise

Unbidden perceptions in clinical practice[1] (1990)

Donnel B. Stern

> *[W]e must simply wait until what we desire appears, because that is all we can do. We have no means of getting exactly what we wish from ourselves.*
> – *Paul Valéry*, 'The course in poetics: First lesson' (1940 [1952])

The arrival of thought

Knowing that we author even the most startling of our own thoughts does nothing to demystify that common experience of merely recording them. The unexpected thought or image or feeling seems to come to us; one feels like a conduit. The experience is ubiquitous enough to have spawned myriad descriptions. Most of this remarkably common and consistent testimony has come from artists, especially and not surprisingly from writers. Here is Joyce Carol Oates: "If I say that I write with the enormous hope of altering the world – and why write without that hope? – I should first say that I write to discover what it is *I will have written*" (1982, p. 1). Gabriel García Márquez: "I'm very curious, as I'm writing this book, to see how the characters go on behaving. It's a true investigation. I could almost say that one writes the novel to see how it will turn out. And to be able to read it" (quoted by Simons, 1985, p. 18). And here is Raymond Carver, convincing and a little touching in his surprise at discovering he is not alone in not knowing what he will write: "[Flannery] O'Connor says she most often did not know where she was going when she sat down to work on a short story. … When I read this some years ago, it came as a shock that she, or anyone for that matter, wrote stories in this fashion. I thought this was my uncomfortable secret, and I was a little uneasy with it. For sure I thought this way of working on a short story somehow revealed my own shortcomings. I remember being tremendously heartened by reading what she had to say on the subject." In the passage which heartened Carver, O'Connor (says Patricia Hampl [1989], from whose essay the quotations from both writers are drawn) was discussing her story, "Good Country People." When she began the story, she did not know "there was going to be a Ph.D. with a wooden leg in it. I merely found myself one morning writing a description of two women I knew something about and before I realized it, I had equipped one of them with a wooden leg." Then, also with no particular plan in mind, she invented and introduced a Bible salesman. "I didn't know he was going to steal that wooden leg," continues O'Connor, "until ten or twelve lines before he did it, but when I found out that this was what was going to happen, I realized it was inevitable." Apparently the conscious application of technique is no more responsible for good fiction than it is for good psychoanalysis!

And then there are the many famous examples of nocturnal illuminations seemingly foisted upon their sleeping discoverers, such as Coleridge's "Kubla Khan," and Hilprecht's sudden comprehension of Sumerian cuneiform writing. Mathematicians, scientists, painters, sculptors, composers, choreographers, and no doubt others, have all contributed accounts of discoveries coming together seemingly without the thinker's participation.[2] And last come prophecy and madness: the list could not be ended without citing the unbiddenness of visions and delusions.

This notion that ideas simply arrive in the minds of the genius and the madman is familiar.[3] But the possibility that everyone thinks this way is not. Though it has indeed been creative people who have most often captured and conveyed the experience, the phenomenon of finding oneself faced by one's own thoughts is by no means limited to exalted or otherwise altered states of consciousness. Thoughts need not be sublime, nocturnal, or psychotic to be unbidden. As a matter of fact, surprise is not the exception, but the rule. The "unconscious thought" revealed in inspirations and creative dreams is not as unusual or mysterious as it seems. These events are best understood as particularly graphic and dramatic instances of a process that occurs with regularity, and in waking hours as well as sleep. All thought, in this sense, is unconscious thought. It happens, in Heidegger's phrase, "behind one's back." We are onlookers at the outcome of our own ways of grasping the world. My purpose in the present paper is to introduce a version of this view and to point out some clinical ramifications.

Much of this paper is the result of reading the philosophical hermeneutics of Hans-Georg Gadamer (1960 [1975], 1976) and finding in his ideas possibilities for clinical psychoanalytic thinking. Gadamer's work has been referenced here and there, but a more focused discussion of Gadamer's relevance for psychoanalysis appears in a separate paper, intended as a companion to this one (Stern, 1991).

Patient and analyst work with unbidden perceptions routinely. Most significant perceptions of others – of ourselves, too – arise without conscious intention. They come from elsewhere, unbidden as symptoms or dreams. They are events falling outside expectation, though seldom startling and not infrequent. Often they are the outcome of many small and half-noticed perceptions, the accretion of which, if it is noted at all, may be seen only in retrospect. Because the experience occurs spontaneously – that is, it is not consciously constructed – it is inevitably authentic. It may be a distorted or ambiguous expression of whatever truth it contains, but it cannot be simply wrong. An unbidden thought can be no more wrong than a dream. The problem is to discover how it is right. How does the thought embody a real observation (Fromm, 1951; Levenson, 1981; Tauber, 1954; Tauber & Green, 1959)? Once such a thought – perhaps merely an inclination to think, a protothought – has arrived, conscious, willful effort is usually essential in evaluating it, honing it, and developing its ramifications. But the original, to be a real contribution, must arise from an intention so much of a piece with living that it is outside the bounds of reflection or control. Authentic perceptions are not uncovered or figured out. The experience of the perception is that one simply knows something or sees something – something about how the other experiences the world, about how the other feels, about one's own experience of the other, etc. This reactive experience is the most common method of interpersonal perception, unpurposeful and prelogical in nature (Tauber & Green, 1959). And though psychoanalysts may sometimes learn about patients in more consciously designed ways (e.g., conscious extrapolation from theory or developmental expectations), the great proportion of analytic observations, and all the most significant ones, are of the common human variety.

Take something as simple as suddenly knowing that the patient is sad. Seldom does this occur solely as the result of seeing the patient's tears and making an inference. When it does happen that way, the observation is liable to feel forced and unnatural, intellectualized. It feels like a lack of contact; patient and analyst are out of touch. The more usual course is that one simply finds oneself in possession of the information, along with some kind of responsive feeling. How the information has come into one's possession is seldom considered.

And if the observation were then mentioned to the patient, and the patient were to deny it, one would not simply conclude that an error had been made. Rather, and again without having to wrangle over the decision, it would be natural to try to discover alternative ways the perception might be meaningful. Perhaps the perception represents a sense of something nascent or dissociated in the patient's experience. Or perhaps sadness is a common human expectation under the circumstances, in which case it is significant that the patient did not feel it. Or perhaps the analyst concludes the observation is just "wrong." Even in this last case, though, the analyst is unlikely to conclude that the mistake is meaningless. Instead, the experience is treated as if it were a dream, an indirect representation.

When a perception arrives unbidden, one seldom questions its veracity. One assumes there is truth in it; it is just not immediately clear what that truth is. Misperception of the patient is not based on putting too much faith in one's unbidden perceptions. That faith is justified. The failure lies in assuming that the truth in the unbidden perception is there at face value.

If the most important of the analyst's gleanings in the consulting room are unbidden, are strenuous efforts to understand misplaced? Should analysts resign themselves to a role as conduits for the wiser perceptions of their unconscious selves? Obviously not. Just because the experience of being a conduit sometimes accompanies the feeling of being deeply involved does not mean involvement can be artificially recreated by playing the part, clearing one's mind and waiting for inspiration to strike. This would not be what Freud (1912 [1958]) meant by evenly-suspended attention; it would be what Primo Levi (1989, p. 173) calls "lazy abandonment to the flow of the unconscious," or what Patricia Hampl (1989) refers to as "the lax habits of the free imagination."

It is easy to agree on this point. But it is not immediately apparent what the meaning of curiosity is in a world in which we have no means of getting exactly what we want from ourselves. Isn't the essence of curiosity the search within oneself for whatever one needs to know? How can that be so if there is no choice but to wait for our most salient thoughts to float into view? How can we look for that which must surprise us?

The fallacy here is the suggestion that unbidden learning is passive learning, that there is no way to influence what arrives in one's mind without conscious intention. Put this way, controversy again evaporates: though one cannot orchestrate one's own dreams, no one else is responsible for them. To accept the centrality of unbidden observations takes nothing away from the significance of precision, rigor, and curiosity in psychoanalytic inquiry. As a matter of fact, as a later section of this paper ("The Problem of Curiosity") will suggest, holding the conviction that learning occurs in this way requires giving these attributes of our work even more emphasis than they already receive.

But before that point can be considered, the logic of unbidden learning must be established. How can it be that there is only an indirect relationship between the analyst's efforts and what is eventually understood? And for that matter, what is the evidence that most important understanding occurs in this way?

The answer to the latter question is simpler than it might seem. For in a careful analytic inquiry, what is learned must come unbidden. If it did not, if the analyst knew beforehand what could be expected as a result of questions and interpretations and the patient's responses to them, the work would be stale and intellectualized. Everyone is familiar with sessions like that. They are unsatisfying at best, often dispiriting, usually a reflection of some poorly comprehended aspect of the interpersonal field. When inquiry is more successful, it is because the question is clear and the answer is not. There is no way to know what will come next. This attitude is reflected in the way clinicians talk to one another, or put together a case report. When describing how a new thought about the patient or the field arose, for instance, an analyst is unlikely to say, "I figured out that ..." or, "I reasoned that. ...." Instead the passive voice tends to be used, indicating that one has received these thoughts, that one lacks a clear feeling of agency. One says, "It occurred to me that ..." or, "It struck me that. ...." Even when the manner of expression is more consistent with awareness of personal agency, such as, "I saw that ..." or, "It seemed to me that ...," upon closer inspection it very often turns out that the sequence of cognitive events that led up to the observation cannot be recreated. It is sometimes possible to do so after the fact, and at times, in order to clarify the origin of a conclusion or speculation, the analyst makes a point of telling the patient as much of the thought process as can be recaptured. But this is the exception, not the rule. Most of the time the whole process takes place unnoticed. It is so natural for clinicians to practice this way – it is so natural for *all* humans to go about their living in this way – that little or no attention is paid to how seldom what one sets out to discover is what one ends up learning.

And yet there is no particular distinction in merely not knowing what will happen next. By itself, this is simply lack of discipline, Levi's lazy abandon. And – the other side of the coin – it would be absurd to discount the necessity for consciously designed effort from patient and analyst, as if psychoanalysis, like an adolescent's notion of true love, were only genuine when it comes like a bolt out of the blue. Thus, there still needs to be a conceptual link drawn between the analyst's efforts in the inquiry – that is, expertise – and the eventually productive outcome. How does the inquiry result in observations which could not have been suspected?

Ernest Schachtel's answer to this question would probably be that the truth, unexpected or not, appears as soon as inquiry reveals one's incapacity and unwillingness to perceive the unfamiliar. For Schachtel (1959), truth is the spontaneous apprehension of the world as it really is, stripped of prior interpretations. One opens oneself to this truth through acts of existential courage, blazing a path beyond the socially sanctioned forms of "an already labelled world." Schachtel refers to the attitude within which such openness is possible as allocentricity. In the allocentric attitude one has no particular use or purpose for the other and is therefore free to see him as he is. Elsewhere, I have described how the analyst, breaking the grip of the interpersonal field on his perceptions and regaining the allocentric attitude, articulates in language his unformulated experience of the patient (Stern, 1989). The present paper takes up this thread, describing in more detailed terms the formulation of experience in psychoanalysis.

Although Schachtel was one of the first to see that experience is not a given, but a construction, he believed, in accordance with the existential tradition to which he belonged, that the constructed aspects of experience were false, obscuring a truth which would otherwise be obvious. Allocentricity is a kind of innocence, more characteristic of what Schachtel understood as the pristine (though by no means sweet) perceptions of childhood than of the "closed world" of adulthood. Today this view is less compelling, primarily because of fundamental developments in the understanding of the nature of language. Even in childhood, experience is an interpretation. There was never a raw form. All experience, even pre-reflective experience, can be constructed only according to the possibilities and limitations of language. There is no experience possible outside this range. Humans live within the world language encompasses, and it is meaningless, a misuse of language actually, to make reference to meaning beyond this boundary.[4]

As a result, the existential call to throw off our shackles and accept the burden of freedom cannot be heeded with the same fervor and simplicity. It is not that the struggle for liberation means any less; rather, freedom now seems relative, and it is a more complicated thing to reach what can be had of it. The radical choice and risk that were the core of the existential project are harder to believe in. No one can be rid of the assumed roles and received categories of thought that both Fromm (e.g., 1941, 1947) and Schachtel tried to see past. These same categories of thought, because they are embedded in language itself, become the very objects of study. Truth in this view is not understood as a correspondence between one's belief and an entity or principle with an independent existence in the external world. New truths cannot be approached directly, but only by exposing limitations in the understandings we already have.

Thus, contrary to what has been until recently the accepted view, the analyst's observational powers in the consulting room cannot be so simply directed at an unknown presumed to have been already present "in" the patient, independent of any structure contributed by the analyst. Because it cannot be assumed that there is a single truth, it cannot even be claimed that the patient could see it if his eyes were not blinkered by convention. What the patient does not yet know can no longer be portrayed as substantive unconscious content, but instead must be understood as unformulated, partially indeterminate, and actually absent (Bollas, 1987; Spence, 1987; Stern, 1981, 1985, 1989; Stolorow, 1988). Its possibilities are the possibilities of language, and its formulation is an event which will be participated in by both patient and analyst. The unconscious can no longer be conceived as a container. It is more consistent with current practice to say, in line with Heidegger and those who followed him, that for something to be unconscious is for it to be so much present that we live in it instead of seeing it. To describe something as unconscious is to say that it is outside the range of explicit reflection.

In modern hermeneutic views of understanding, of which this line of thought is an example, interest is directed at what is already known, with the intention of stating explicitly the implicit assumptions underlying its construction.[5] Once these assumptions have been specified, gaps in the material become evident, and phenomena that have fallen through the cracks of the implicit interpretive scheme may become visible. The analyst pursues an awareness of absence by focusing the most detailed attention on what is present. The emphasis shifts from imposing yet another interpretation to specifying the schemes according to which the material has already been interpreted. Thus the method is usually called deconstruction.[6] Levenson (1988) presents such a view, concluding that, "the real task in therapy is not so much making sense of the data as it is, but resisting the temptation to make sense of the data!" (p. 5). Elsewhere, describing what he believes is the algorithm of psychotherapy, he has this to say: "the therapist listens to the patient's story, gets a background, looks for what are essentially the lacunae – the holes in the Swiss cheese, the gaps in the continuity and coherence of the patient's life story" (1982, p. 9). No less, as Levenson indicates later in the same paper, the analyst looks for lacunae in the continuity and coherence of the story of the treatment itself. The vital question here is how analysts come to an awareness of these gaps.

Between experience and expectation

How do unbidden perceptions come about? It will be useful to approach this question from the other direction, with an examination of the circumstances in which experience is not known – in which the possibility of lacunae has not even become relevant yet. In this situation experience disappears as fast as it takes place. There is no memory. Nothing can be reflected on because, at least in memory, nothing happened. There is only a present. These are the circumstances within which we live most of the time, as Schachtel saw. But it is a rare event to tune out completely, to remember nothing afterward, as in a fugue state. Rather, one is aware of experience of one kind, one is capable of reflecting on it, while experience of a different kind just keeps going past, unnoted. For instance, most analysts would probably agree that they are involved in unseen patterns of interaction with the patient even during the moments when they are making progress on sorting out something else. Let us say, for example, that the analyst is laying out the details of the patient's relationship with Aunt Agatha in precisely the interactive style of this important person. (This is an instance of Levenson's [1983] dictum that what patient and analyst talk about and how they talk about it are transforms of the same content.) And then, as the analyst eventually clarifies with the patient how the two of them are playing the Aunt Agatha scenario, perhaps something else remains unformulated – for instance, how the analyst may now be replicating the way the patient's mother, reacting to feeling deprived by Aunt Agatha, bitterly criticized the aunt, leaving the patient feeling disloyal whether she protested or assented. At this point, the analyst notices that the patient is suddenly in what seem to be low spirits, and he is mystified. What the analyst cannot see, of course, and probably the patient, too, cannot yet see, is that the patient is reacting to finding herself in the no-win situation he is presenting her with. Eventually this interaction, too, is untangled. Maybe it becomes clear, for instance, that the analyst was more proud than he realized about having been able to see himself playing the Aunt Agatha role, and the patient, reacting to this pressure to accept the new clarification, felt resentful but helpless, not being any more willing to hurt the analyst's feelings than her mother's. But as quickly as this is discovered, something else needs to be understood.

It is even simpler to say the same thing about content not explicitly concerned with the transference. That is, becoming able to reflect on one aspect of living does not necessarily raise the likelihood of being able to reflect upon another.

What happens, then, when experience does not register? What was going on when the analyst was acting out Aunt Agatha's part of the interaction? Why is it that the analyst often doesn't see what he is doing even though he is sitting there with the express purpose of understanding?

At these times experience and expectation are indistinguishable. When nothing is learned, when things just happen, when experience passes by without being noted, it is because there is no space between what is (unconsciously) anticipated and what is (consciously) experienced. There is no gap between them. As long as that is so, experience disappears as fast as it takes place. It is invisible not because it makes no impression on one's mind, but because the impression it makes coincides exactly with expectations one does not even know one has. One cannot spell it out because one has no reason to. It is taken for granted. There is no memory of it because whatever did happen had happened before in such a way that events will now be noticed only if they deviate. And generally, as Schachtel (and Bartlett [1932] before him) taught, the mere existence of expectations tends to preserve the status quo. Paradoxically, though the perception of deviations from expectation is the source of new experience, such perceptions are unlikely precisely to the extent that expectations have gelled. Once in place, anticipations influence the future to conform to their shape. We see what we expect to see – and we actually construct, too, what we expect to see. In interpersonal terms, this means that transference is not only an experience and a set of perceptions, but an influence which is quite often effective in provoking the anticipated response from the analyst. Even when the provocation is not so devastating in its effect that every observer would agree on its impact, the events of the analytic interaction, being as ambiguous as any other social intercourse, can usually be plausibly understood in this way (Gill, 1982; Hoffman, 1984; Levenson, 1972, 1983). Patient and analyst create expectations in interaction with each other, and responses to these expectations, and it is then the most significant task of the analysis to discover them.

Learning, in the form of an unbidden perception, is what happens when a space appears between experience and expectation. This is true, separately, for analyst and patient. New experience does not arise *de novo* – it emerges from what has come before, it becomes visible as a contrast to what is already known, against the background of the familiar. Gadamer, for whom this is central, says it succinctly: "Only the support of familiar and common understanding makes possible the venture into the alien, the lifting up of something out of the alien, and thus the broadening and enrichment of our own experience of the world" (1966 [1976], p. 15). It is from this vast fund of familiar and common understanding that unconscious expectations are drawn, and it is the articulation of these unformulated expectations that makes it possible to broaden and enrich our experience of the world. Learning is impossible precisely to the extent that expectations cannot be brought into language.

The identification and explicit description of expectations is the major task of the analysis. Analyst and patient find their way to speaking the familiar, and then find in what has been spoken other gaps which can be worded, so that the description of experience moves always toward a greater degree of precision and subtlety. New experience emerges naturally and inevitably in the form of alternatives to the familiar.

Clinical illustration

The process of making expectations visible is not routinely difficult. The usual instances are the everyday bits of learning that go on between any two people, such as the earlier illustration of the sad patient. In that example the expectation did not have to remain unformulated. To detail that very simple interaction will sound awkward and artificial, but with that proviso, perhaps the sequence went something like this: the analyst entered the moment with an expectation born of what had just happened. He simply expected, without conscious consideration, that the patient would feel as he had a moment before. There was no reason to expect otherwise. Suddenly the analyst saw tears, and the patient's tone of voice lowered and softened. His expression changed. Without explicit recognition of the event, the analyst now eased into a position in which his expectation was no longer valid. Immediately and naturally, the current expectation was as much taken for granted as the old one had been a moment before.

In this instance there was no interference in the analyst's awareness of his expectation, i.e., neither the analyst nor the patient had any reason to object to the analyst knowing it. The expectation could be disconfirmed and discarded quite automatically: the patient had not been feeling anything obvious; suddenly he was. Seldom would one be directly aware of a preconception of this kind. It isn't necessary. Explicit reflection would quite often be a cumbersome intrusion into otherwise smoothly flowing experience. The important thing is whether one could be aware. Is the expectation knowable? Could it be seen if one had a reason to see it? This is the primary differentiation between those expectations which are problematic and those which are not.

Everyday examples of successful understanding do not draw clinical attention, though. Accounting for these events is primarily an epistemological problem, more properly the business of philosophers than psychoanalysts. Analysts are most interested in the pathology of understanding, especially those instances in which the analyst and the patient cannot see their expectations of one another, as in the following example.

A professional woman in her late twenties sought treatment because of depression over the death of an elderly relative, but it was soon clear that she had been depressed much of her life. We began psychoanalytic work. During the first several months of the treatment, as I got to know her and she got to know me, she relaxed – or so I thought – and a delightful, playful, mildly flirtatious kind of interaction began, and then became more frequent. I noted it, but did not try to say anything about it. It was a delicate and intimate way of relating, and I feared that I could not call attention to it without being clumsy, and that talking about it, at least at this point, could only be experienced by the patient as humiliating and rejecting. Perhaps, I thought, it was the kind of relatedness she needed in order to establish a reliable therapeutic situation with me. (This, incidentally, was not necessarily wrong, despite the later events I shall describe.) I felt I was participating in something that would eventually become clear – or perhaps it would not. Most of the time I was not aware enough for it to matter. I do recall having a suspicion from time to time that perhaps there was some reason to address the subject, a reason I ought to be able to think of and could not. I think this had less to do with an understanding of the field, though, than it did with a worry that I really should hold myself in check, since I was responding in kind without having thought through why.

In describing the interaction to this point, I may be making it sound as if my behavior was the result of conscious decision more often than was the case. It is true that I reflected on the interaction enough to gain the impression that there was nothing actively destructive about it. That much most analysts are able to do most of the time, even when they are caught in the grip of the field. The interaction was also in my focal awareness at those few moments during which I have described feeling a bit suspicious of my compliance – but even then, I did not see what I later learned was most relevant. Other than these partial exceptions, though, and a general attitude of tolerance about it, this aspect of what transpired between us became part of the unformulated background of the sessions, the medium within which we spent the hours. The experience was inattended. I was not curious about it at that time, for I was embedded in it, living it, taking it for granted. The work went on more or less unremarkably about one thing and another, including the patient's fear that I was critical of her and dissatisfied with her, just as she felt her highly accomplished, self-involved, and emotionally distant father was. The patient was well aware that she wanted to appeal to me, and on the one or two occasions when I was able to gently draw attention to the bantering between us, she said that indeed she derived some reassurance from this kind of interaction. It was also clear to her, as I had suspected, that she would be hurt if I did not respond in kind.

For my own part, I looked forward to the patient's hours. I felt helpful and appreciated. The inquiry seemed to be moving along smoothly. I assumed that eventually, after learning enough to make it safe to do so, we would be able to address the bantering more directly and thoroughly. In fact, at that time I am sure I would have guessed, if I had been asked to consider the question explicitly, that the patient probably even shared this prediction about the future course of the treatment.

Then, in the midst of such gentleness and good humor, the patient began to face me with complaints. She wondered whether she should have seen someone more "serious," perhaps someone who insisted on interrupting her playfulness. She was having too good a time. *I* was having too good a time. There was not enough going on in the treatment. Things should have been more solemn. Even if she initiated the interactions, she said, I should have refused to respond to them.

My first reaction was to feel that it was obvious she was right. How could I have gone along with this? I was chagrined and somewhat guilty, feeling that my behavior had not been appropriate. And yet I could not see clearly how to handle the situation. The inconsistency between the patient's current attitude and her previous conviction that she wished me to respond to her playfully, that in fact she needed such reassurance, did not occur to me yet. Whether or not I knew the very best thing to do, though, I decided that at the least I had to rein myself in.

This decision about my conduct was based upon the guilty application of a rule: do not respond reciprocally to the transference. I do not even believe one can realistically adhere to this dictum. That is, my decision was (for me) not a sensible one, but a fallback position born of the wish to be a good and useful analyst. It may have relieved me of anxiety about the patient's sudden lack of appreciation of me, but it was not based upon an understanding of my part in the interpersonal situation. In retrospect it is therefore not particularly surprising that it failed. I was merely continuing my participation in another guise, though of course this was completely beyond me at the time. To my horror, and despite my best intentions, I kept making slyly humorous remarks – inhibited and subtle enough to allow them to pass my lips before I really noted what I was doing, but unmistakably playful – especially in the newly sensitive ambiance of our sessions. The patient did not miss my gaffes, either, and let me know that her unhappiness with me was mounting. I began to learn that she felt not only that I was not serious enough, but that I was not taking her seriously enough. I also saw that sometimes I had begun to initiate these playful sequences myself, not waiting for the patient, and that, in fact, I had been participating in this way for some time now. For instance, I might say, on seeing her, with a grin and an exaggerated sweep of the arm, "Well, come on in!" Or she might say she had a bad day, with a shake of her head and humorous overdone woe, and I would say – in tune with the tone of her remark, but with more expressiveness than was really necessary – "A real lulu, huh?" The patient felt this conveyed that I was altogether too ready to have a nice time discussing events which were essentially miserable for her. Another time she was describing a frightening incident with a psychotic cabdriver. She told me how menacing he was. "He was so *big*," she said, wide-eyed. As was often the case, there was in her tone a kind of innocent wonder that usually struck me as intentionally cute, though not objectionable. I think – again in retrospect – that I enjoyed it. In this instance I responded by saying, in the same tone, "And you're so *little*!" Now, this was not completely out of tune. It did convey an understanding of her feelings. But it is not the way I generally talk to patients. In fact, it is not the way two adults usually converse about a matter of gravity. It certainly is not what one would call sober. And, to her, it was therefore one more piece of evidence that I did not take her seriously.

However, I did not agree with the patient that my behavior had to mean that I was taking her lightly. Why did these bon mots of mine have to be interpreted in only this one way? I felt quite sure that I did take her seriously, no less seriously than I took any other patient.

As it turned out this was wrong, and she was right. On a Friday night, after emitting one of these distressing remarks in a session with the patient, I consulted a colleague whose judgment I respect. I told her the story with the aim of understanding how I could help the patient to look into the problem. My colleague's unexpected response, though, was, "Has it occurred to you that she might have a point?" That was enough to turn my perception of the situation on its head. Quite suddenly I saw that in a very important sense I was not taking the patient seriously, just as she said. The truth of this was underscored by the fact that I had seen the point immediately when my respected colleague had said it, but had not been able to accept the same thing from the patient.

Over that weekend something else occurred to me, and it helped explain what I was doing. I saw that I had come to enjoy the patient's response to my humor, even to look forward to it. This was largely why I had enjoyed the patient's sessions so much. When she had begun to complain, I had felt deprived, a little betrayed, as if the rug had been pulled out from under me. It had felt a bit like being lured into a trap. Everything had been going so swimmingly, so pleasantly! She had been so appreciative!

There was no question that I now saw something I had not seen before about the grip of the field on us both. Since I had to explain the change in my views to the patient, I elected in the next session to lay out everything I had learned about how we had both participated in the establishment and maintenance of the problematic interaction. The patient, sensing my conviction, was greatly relieved. I had no doubt that I would now be able to change the nature of my participation, and in fact I did. It would now have been uncomfortable not to have participated differently (see also Stern, 1989).

It was possible, too, for the patient to participate differently. Perhaps it was even as necessary for her as it had become for me. In short order, she and I discovered that indeed she did encourage me to continue bantering with her, that she had developed with her father the capacity to be the unusually gratifying audience I had found her to be, but that she had done so only out of a sense that this was her sole possibility. She could not be taken seriously by the men she wanted, and I, like her father, was one of that kind. Her bid for my attention had therefore been accompanied by resentment, and her expressions of delight and appreciation had been humiliating. Yet she had been no freer to present herself seriously than I had been to take her that way.

I had been operating on the implicit assumption that my claim to take the patient seriously was based on all the relevant data. I had been assuming (also implicitly) that I maintained this attitude only because it was true and reasonable, and that I disagreed with the patient only because her take on the situation was wrong. It might be said, then, that these assumptions constituted the unseen expectation. The problem with that interpretation is that it can be made in retrospect about any bind that analyst and patient work their way out of. The analyst (and the patient) always assume, incorrectly and without reflecting on it explicitly, that they are taking advantage of all relevant data. The unseen expectation needs to be stated more specifically in terms of the unformulated images the participants had of one another, such as the following: like the father, I was treating the patient (to a degree) as if she were there to appreciate me, to be delighted by me. I was assuming, it turns out, that there was no good reason why she should object to being my audience. She, on the other side of this, was assuming that I was so self-involved that the only way she could make contact with me was by playing up her delight in me and encouraging me to behave in precisely the way she complained about. When these assumptions became visible – that is, once she and I gained the capability to see that we *had* expectations of one another – a series of new experiences occurred.

The problem of curiosity: Seeing what is questionable

In this particular example I could point to the event – the consultation with my colleague – that allowed me to identify my expectation and formulate an alternative. Ongoing peer supervision is vital for analysts who believe they have no choice but to be embedded, since colleagues seldom have the same reasons to be buried in the interaction and may therefore be able to occupy that uninvolved position which the analyst simply cannot locate.[7]

But not always is it even clear which details to tell one's consultant, nor are colleagues always able to see the problems as clearly as mine did. And of course, even if the analyst knows what to describe, it is unfeasible to consult someone else every time it might be helpful to do so. Most of the time analysts fly solo, relying upon the desire to know, a desire which everything that has been said to this point leads one to believe is only dubiously reliable. And thus the problem of curiosity reappears. For if we have no means of getting exactly what we want from ourselves, if we must doubt that the truth even exists prior to the wish to know it, how does it make sense to think of curiosity?

To be curious is to be determined to know what is already there – what one is already aware of being confronted with – in the most detailed and complete way possible. It is receptivity to questions about matters which, on the face of it, may already seem fully understood. Curiosity means being in the process of differentiating whatever perceptions one has already identified; the unbidden emerges from that which has been meticulously described. The more fine-grained the grasp of what is already visible, the smaller the unexplained blip that can be noticed passing across it. When the analyst questions what he thinks he already knows about the patient, and about his reactions to the patient, uncertainty is preserved. It becomes harder to feel convinced of any single answer. These conditions constitute the climate in which unbidden perceptions flourish. In trying to create them, the analyst is doing what is possible to court surprise.

Harry Stack Sullivan probably would have believed it was not only unnecessary, but undesirable, to depend on perceptions arising outside volition. At the same time, though, he was very interested in meticulous description. He was committed to the idea that the treatment should assume the shape of a detailed inquiry. His method amounts to a continuous, long-term effort to drive a wedge between experience and expectation.[8] This way of conducting treatment depends less than classical technique on interpretation and more on finding good questions. The analyst seldom thinks he has an answer to offer. Previous understandings are continually subjected to study and review. Sullivan's procedure is today as easy to state, and as difficult to practice, as it was when he described it. Good questions are still harder to come by than good answers:

> [T]he psychiatrist listens to all statements with a certain critical interest, asking, "Could that mean anything except what first occurs to me?" He questions (at least to himself) much of what he hears, not on the assumption that the patient is a liar, or doesn't know how to express himself, or anything like that, but always with the simple query in mind, "Now, could this mean something that would not immediately occur to me? Do I know what he means by that?" (Sullivan, 1954 [1970], p. 19)[9]

Curiosity is the imagination and discipline which lead to seeing what is questionable. To be curious is to be sensitive to the possibility of a question. It is the constant suspicion that one's own capacity for thought is woefully inadequate in ways which will eventually become painfully clear. It is a respect for particularity, a respect which for some attains the dimensions of love, or even reverence. For Mies van der Rohe, "God is in the details." Vladimir Nabokov admonishes writers to "Caress the detail, the divine detail."[10] Patricia Hampl (1989) comments that, "If, as Nabokov says, the detail is divine, there's nothing much to do but give yourself over to it as one properly does in worship. If there's any question about the divinity of detail, by the way, think of that *one thing* that you can explain to no one but which is precious beyond expression. That is a divine detail. It is also a literary opportunity" (p. 38). Need it be added that it is an analytic opportunity as well?

When a guiding intelligence accumulates details, the result is clarity; and thus clarity is the result of curiosity. But clarity and curiosity bear a reciprocal relation to one another, so that curiosity is also the result of clarity. To the extent that one cannot cite particulars about something – an event, a person, an interaction – one does not know how to be curious about that thing. Not knowing how to be curious, though, is not worthy of condemnation, at least not when it occurs, as it so frequently does, in the experience of someone who is dedicated to understanding. Often the closest one can come to being curious is wanting to be. Or being puzzled about why one cannot be. The state of being unable to see what is questionable is a way station on the path to an open question. To be unclear can be as much an opportunity as a liability. Primo Levi (1989) tells us, "It is obvious that perfectly lucid writing presupposes a totally conscious writer, and this does not correspond to reality. We are made up of ego and id, spirit and flesh, and furthermore nucleic acids, traditions, hormones, remote and recent experiences, and traumas; therefore we are condemned to carry from crib to grave a doppelganger, a mute and faceless brother who nevertheless is co-responsible for our actions, and so for all our pages" (p. 170). And so, too, responsible for all our psychoanalytic work. Curiosity is the never satisfied insistence on knowing the doppelganger, the unknown psychoanalyst who is there in the room, too, and who will always be just beyond acquaintance, forever moving and forever still, occupying the same shadows on the far side of every new understanding. No writer knows deeply what he has written, Levi tells us; and no analyst, we can echo, thoroughly understands the course of an analysis.

It should also be emphasized what curiosity is not: it is not mere inquisitiveness, the asking of questions. Questions are the most visible evidence that curiosity is operative, but they are an outcome and not the phenomenon itself. The answers given by the patient to the spoken questions in a detailed inquiry, for example, are not themselves the most interesting understandings. The most interesting and significant observations arrive unbidden following the answers to questions. They become possible because of what is brought to light in the patient's response, but exactly how they are related to these concrete and volitional responses very often remains unknown.

Contrast all this to the conventional view of curiosity derived from the epistemology of correspondence: if the truth is out there somewhere, or maybe "in there" somewhere, curiosity is the desire to look for it, or at least the willingness to trip over it. Understanding should not depend on expectations, but on a direct link between what is perceived and what is actually out there. Expectations are not considered the soil in which understanding must root, but the source of distortion and error. They are to be exposed, excised, and cleanly done with, returning us to that unprejudiced state of being in which we can be inscribed by the impressions of the world around and within us. And when a very good and plausible explanation for something has been spoken, it can be said that curiosity has been satisfied. The truth is like buried treasure, and it has been found. We can stop looking. We can trust ourselves, actually, in a way that modern hermeneutic epistemology forever deprives us of. If preconceptions are ubiquitous, and if the greatest clinical necessity is constantly to question them, then there is no final answer to any question that arises in the course of the treatment. Since each understanding is contextual, what Issacharoff and Hunt (1978) call a "new truth," it will be displaced by fresh understanding as the work proceeds. There is an excitement to this, but also a kind of sadness, because every new truth becomes a prejudice.

Every understanding is eventually a betrayal. Analysts are always on the verge of relinquishing their proudest moments, understandings that sometimes have been hoped for and awaited over long periods of time. It is no accident that Gadamer often refers to disconfirmations as disappointments.

The innocent analyst

It is painful enough not to be able to believe any longer in the simplicity of the existential call to freedom. But what of the clinical values, anchored in those same existential views, that have guided the practice of generations of analysts? What of openness to the other? What of the authentic intention to see the other clearly? If human beings can never be rid of so-called distorting influences, if the patient's truth can never simply impress itself on the listening analyst, then is it realistic to maintain the ideal of the analyst's openness to the patient? Must we conclude that Schachtel's allocentric attitude and Buber's I–Thou are romantic illusions, the naive expressions of an outmoded epistemology?

If openness is illusory, it is not only Schachtel and Buber whose work will have to be dismissed. Other artists, philosophers, and critics have proposed similar ideas, each attempting to describe what Shattuck (1984) calls "a subtle mental operation which seeks to achieve freshness and particularity of attention" (p. 416). Shattuck's list of these writers includes Keats ("Negative Capability"), Bergson ("a more direct vision of reality"), Ruskin ("innocence of the eye"), Laforgue ("the natural eye"), Husserl ("bracketing"), Shklovsky ("defamiliarization"), Brecht ("distancing"), Rilke ("let each germ of feeling come to completeness quite in itself"), and Heidegger ("releasement"). To be required to discard all these ideas in the service of the vision of some brave new epistemological world would be a good reason to throw out the vision instead. We know we experience openness to our patients, as these writers knew they experienced openness to the world around them. There are times that the patient's experience is as clear as one's own, and the more this happens (as long as the treatment bears out that one's grasp was accurate) the more effective the treatment. How can this be reconciled?

If there is a way to understand openness as an achievement, a result of knowledge and effort and not just a return to an imagined state of unfettered perception, then the clinical experience and the epistemology cease to be contradictory. And there is such a way. It requires, though, that the analyst give up any vestigial belief in being a sensor, in being capable of registering the truth merely by being receptive. It requires sacrificing the reassuring view that the truth is really there behind the veils. If openness is redefined according to hermeneutic views, it becomes a more complex and uncomfortable matter, an accomplishment for which innocence is not required, at least not innocence as it is most commonly understood.

Roger Shattuck (1984), though addressing himself to literature and not to psychoanalysis, takes on similar questions in the same recent essay in which he cited the writers listed above:

> By the time we can talk seriously about literature, it is too late to find a natural starting point in any direct, spontaneous response to the act of reading. … We live all our lives in the prison house of language, from whose codes and conventions no particle of our experience can escape. … The armed vision is the only vision. (p. 413)

Similarly, it is always too late to find a response to the patient which is not rooted in preconception. Is innocence, then, the illusion it seems? Is the innocent analyst a myth?[11] Shattuck continues:

> Yes, of course [it is a myth], as long as that term is construed to mean not damaging falsehood but useful fiction. We have a whole set of such devices that allow us to live beyond our immediate experience – the state of nature in philosophy, the corporation in economics and law, infinity in mathematics, salvation in religion. … We are dealing with the most subtle of all hermeneutics. Candor is a goal, not a given … the attitude does not result from a lapse back into inexperience, a newly costumed anti-intellectualism. On the contrary, the "new" in Rilke and the "remaking" in Laforgue point toward an advance beyond experience, an ulterior innocence derived from and building on our encounter with life, not know-nothingism, but a tolerant wisdom in the face of what we both know and don't know. (p. 416)

Innocence does not have to be pristine to be meaningful. It is not a return to a child's-eye view of the world, as in the romantic conception. On the contrary, it is the result of learning. The capacity for innocence is an accomplishment. To psychoanalysts, whose work and commitment require constant exposure to the difficulty of self-knowledge, this way of understanding openness is not only fitting but just. Analytic ideals survive intact. As a matter of fact, bringing together faith in the value of openness with the respect for learning that runs so deep in psychoanalysis actually strengthens the ideal.

Openness is that same ongoing willingness to question everyday expectations that has come up over and over again in this paper, a state of explicit familiarity with, and acceptance of, the strictures of one's own character and culture. Openness is, in a word, wisdom. This is obviously not to claim that analysts qualify as wise just because analytic work requires the formulation of expectations. But clinical practice does demand a high level of openness. The analyst develops a "work ego" in the course of treatment and training, a capacity for self-containment and self-reflection which may originally have been the training analyst's, but which is now the analyst's own, and which will become the patient's (though most patients will never have reason to employ it as consistently as the analyst needs to during sessions). Analysts are at their best in the office. There is a minimum of interruption in the capacity to disconfirm the preconceptions emerging in interaction with the patient. The freedom to disconfirm varies, of course – with the mood one brings to the hour, the content under discussion, and most of all, with the vagaries of the interaction. But the foundation of psychoanalytic competence is that analysts are relatively free, within the special analytic setting, to allow themselves the unbidden experience that marks the formulation of expectations.

Notes

1 I am grateful for careful readings and criticism of the manuscript by Kathe Hift, Ph.D., Emmanuel Kaftal, Ph.D., and Barry Protter, Ph.D.

2 The dream of "Kubla Khan" appears in Coleridge (1816 [1941]); Hilprecht's dream can be found in Newbold (1896 [1947]). Other examples are the dreams in which Robert Louis Stevenson regularly received completed stories from the "Brownies" (Stevenson, 1925, p. 44), the process of copper engraving bequeathed in a dream to William Blake by his dead brother (Raine, 1971, p. 43), and Kekulé's dream image of the molecular structure of benzene (MacKenzie, 1965, p. 135). Also see Garfield (1974) and Woods (1947). There are probably innumerable compendia of references to accounts of unbidden discoveries from artists of various kinds, scientists, and mathematicians. Those I have come across include Bruner, (1979),

Burnshaw (1970), Ghiselin (1952), Hadamard (1945 [1954]), Hampl (1989), Kris (1952), Poincaré (1952), Raft and Andresen (1986), Rosner and Abt (1974), Rothenberg (1979), and Shattuck (1984).

3 Familiar not only from our implicit acceptance of the widespread images of our culture, but also from the literature of psychoanalysis – cf. Fingarette's (1963) discussion of philosophy and psychoanalysis, Kris's (1952) classic and deeply influential essays on art and creativity, and Reik's (1937) work on surprise. Kris, though he proposed a creative synthesis linking artistic creation and psychoanalytic insight, did not take the next step. Unbidden experience remained for him the stuff of inspiration, the exception in thinking, not the rule. Fingarette and Reik, on the other hand, imply that unbidden experience, wondrous as it may be, is routinely the channel through which something new comes to be. Georg Groddeck's (1923 [1961]) conception of "the It" also deserves mention, since for Groddeck we "are lived" by this force, of which we are entirely unaware. We are unconscious of most of our being, which is not experienced as our own, but as coming from somewhere or something else. Groddeck intends his idea to be a description of all living, not only art or psychosis, and in that sense his book is germane. However, Groddeck's animism, his concretization of the unknown into an actual life force, makes his work of more historical than conceptual significance in the present discussion.

4 Any number of writers have adopted this point of view. An inventive and readable account is the widely known one by Rorty (1979).

5 The reader interested in hermeneutics in psychoanalysis should consult Protter's work (1985, 1988a), (1988b), which is notable for its integration of philosophy and psychoanalysis and for the breadth of its scholarship.

6 Despite being new and modish, deconstruction has a history in psychoanalysis. One of Freud's most significant imaginative leaps, his recognition of transference (1905 [1953]), was a deconstructive one. Transference (and, it is now clear, countertransference as well) is certainly one of the more important assumed roles, or received categories of thought. What Freud understood was that far from being the obstacle he first took it to be, transference was the single most important object of clinical study. It was not to be excised, but grasped. By seeing the limitations of understanding as an opportunity, Freud committed the first deconstructionist act in psychoanalysis.

7 Adherents of the concept of parallel process in supervision would have it otherwise, claiming that the supervisor is often buried in an analogue of the therapeutic situation which is unconsciously created between therapist and supervisor. This view, so popular a few years ago that almost every article on supervision referred to it, seems already to have faded in significance. It makes better sense to argue, as Bromberg (1982) and Grey and Fiscalini (1987) have, that when supervisor and therapist become

embedded, it is in a mire of their own making – a separate relationship, independent of the therapy being supervised.

8 This is not to say that Sullivan would have agreed with the emphasis here. In fact he would have argued, and emphatically, that one helps one's patients precisely to the extent that one *does* perform a directed search for the truth. Sullivan had a deep conviction about the accuracy of positivism. Thus it may seem contradictory to cite him in support of the view being developed here. To this objection the best reply is that Sullivan's clinical attitude and his ideas retain liveliness and relevance even in a different epistemology. Sullivan's interest in the complexities of the clinical interaction, which he focused on because of his belief in the significance of the observable, happens to be the same emphasis one has to take from a hermeneutic view (see text).

9 While Sullivan would not agree with Gadamer's epistemology, there is a close correspondence between the two writers' understanding of the significance of questioning. Each insists on finding a grip from which to continue expanding thoughts which already seem complete. It is partly because of the centrality of inquiry to the conduct of Interpersonal Psychoanalysis that Gadamer has much to offer the Interpersonalist (see Stern, 1991). As illustration of this correspondence, compare the following quotation to the quotation from Sullivan in the text:

> As a student of Plato I particularly love those scenes in which Socrates gets into a dispute with the Sophist virtuosi and drives them to despair by his questions. Eventually they can endure his questions no longer and they claim for themselves the apparently preferable role of questioner. And what happens? Nothing at all occurs to them that is worth while going into and trying to answer.
>
> I draw the following inference from this observation. The real power of hermeneutical consciousness is our power to see what is questionable (Gadamer, 1966 [1976], p. 13).

10 Van der Rohe is quoted by Bruner (1987), Nabokov by Hampl (1989). See Levenson (1988) for an emphasis on particularity in psychoanalysis which is also derived from a hermeneutic view. Levenson concludes that it is in "asking some good questions" that the therapist has the best opportunity to be helpful.

11 Spence (1987) examines some of the same questions from a hermeneutic point of view which is in most ways consistent with the one I am presenting. As a matter of fact, he entitles one of his chapters "The Myth of the Innocent Analyst," by which he means that anyone, analysts included, in order to understand, must work from a prior commitment to some grasp of the material to be interpreted. Ergo a loss of innocence, at least in the blank-slate sense. But Spence does not then go on to redefine innocence in terms consistent with his hermeneutic point of view. He really does mean that the innocent analyst must now be considered a myth. As the following text indicates, I believe the description of the analyst as innocent remains meaningful.

References

Bartlett, F. C. (1932). *Remembering*. Cambridge: Cambridge University Press.

Bollas, C. (1987). *The Shadow of the Object: Psychoanalysis of the Unthought Known*. New York: Columbia University Press.

Bromberg, P. M. (1982). The supervisory process and parallel process. *Contemporary Psychoanalysis*, 18:92–111.

Bruner, J. (1979). The conditions of creativity. In *On Knowing: Essays for the Left Hand*, Expanded Edition. Cambridge, MA: Harvard University Press, pp. 17–30.

Bruner, J. (1987). Foreword. In *The Freudian Metaphor: Toward Paradigm Change in Psychoanalysis*. New York: W. W. Norton, pp. ix–xvi.

Buber, M. (1965). *The Knowledge of Man: A Philosophy of the Interhuman*, Trans. M. Friedman & R. G. Smith. New York: Harper and Row.

Buber, M. (1957 [1970]). *I and Thou*, 2nd Edition, trans. W. Kaufmann. New York: Charles Scribner's Sons.

Burnshaw, S. (1970). *The Seamless Web*. New York: Braziller.

Coleridge, S. T. (1816 [1941]). Kubla Khan: Or a vision in a dream. A fragment. In D. Stauffer (Ed.), *Selected Poetry and Prose of Coleridge*. New York: Modern Library, pp. 43–45.

Fingarette, H. (1963). *The Self in Transformation: Psychoanalysis, Philosophy and the Life of the Spirit*. New York: Basic Books.

Freud, S. (1905 [1953]). *Fragment of an Analysis of a Case of Hysteria*, Standard Edition 7. London: Hogarth Press, pp. 3–122.

Freud, S. (1912 [1958]). *Recommendations to Physicians Practicing Psychoanalysis*, Standard Edition 12. London: Hogarth Press, pp 109–120.

Fromm, E. (1941). *Escape from Freedom*. New York: Rinehart and Co.

Fromm, E. (1947). *Man for Himself*. New York: Rinehart and Co.

Fromm, E. (1951). *The Forgotten Language*. New York: Rinehart and Co.

Gadamer, H.-G. (1960 [1975]). *Truth and Method*, Trans. G. Barden & J. Cumming. New York: Seabury Press.

Gadamer, H.-G. (1966 [1976]). The universality of the hermeneutical problem. In D. E. Linge (Trans./Ed.), *Philosophical Hermeneutics*. Berkeley, CA: University of California Press, pp. 3–17.

Gadamer, H.-G. (1976). *Philosophical Hermeneutics*, Trans. D. E. Linge. Berkeley, CA: University of California Press.

Garfield, P. (1974). *Creative Dreaming*. New York: Simon and Schuster.

Ghiselin, B. (1952). *The Creative Process*. Berkeley, CA: University of California Press.

Gill, M. R. (1982). *The Analysis of Transference*, Volume 1 *Psychological Issues*, Monograph 53. New York: International Universities Press.

Grey, A. & Fiscalini, J. (1987). Parallel process as transference–countertransference interaction. *Psychoanalytic Psychology*, 4: 131–144.

Groddeck, G. (1923 [1961]). *The Book of the It*. New York: Mentor Books.

Hadamard, J. (1945 [1954]). *The Psychology of Invention in the Mathematical Field*. New York: Dover.

Hampl, P. (1989). The lax habits of the free imagination. *New York Times Book Review*, March 5, pp. 1, 37–38.
Hoffman, I. Z. (1983). The patient as interpreter of the analyst's experience. *Contemporary Psychoanalysis*, 19: 389–422.
Issacharoff, A. & Hunt, W. (1978). Beyond countertransference. *Contemporary Psychoanalysis*, 14: 291–310.
Kris, E. (1952). *Psychoanalytic Explorations in Art*. New York: International Universities Press.
Levenson, E. A. (1972). *The Fallacy of Understanding*. New York: Basic Books.
Levenson, E. A. (1981). Facts or fantasies: The nature of psychoanalytic data. *Contemporary Psychoanalysis*, 17: 486–500.
Levenson, E. A. (1982). Follow the fox – an inquiry into the vicissitudes of psychoanalytic supervision. *Contemporary Psychoanalysis*, 18: 1–15.
Levenson, E. A. (1983). *The Ambiguity of Change*. New York: Basic Books.
Levenson, E. A. (1988). The pursuit of the particular. *Contemporary Psychoanalysis*, 24: 1–19.
Levi, P. (1989). On obscure writing. In *Other People's Trades*, Trans. R. Rosenthal. New York: Summit Books, pp. 169–175.
MacKenzie, N. (1965). *Dreams and Dreaming*. London: Aldus Books, p. 135.
Newbold, W. R. (1896 [1947]). A dream detective solves Professor Hilprecht's famous dream. In R. L. Woods (Ed.), *The World of Dreams*. New York: Random House, pp. 525–530.
Oates, J. C. (1982). Stories that define me. *New York Times Book Review*, July 11, pp. 1, 15–16.
Poincaré, H. (1952). *Science and Method*, Trans. F. Maitland. New York: Dover.
Protter, B. (1985). Toward an emergent psychoanalytic epistemology. *Contemporary Psychoanalysis*, 21: 208–227.
Protter, B. (1988a). Some reflections. *Contemporary Psychoanalysis*, 24: 142–155.
Protter, B. (1988b). Ways of knowing in psychoanalysis. *Contemporary Psychoanalysis*, 24: 498–526.
Raft, D. & Andresen, J. (1986). Transformations in self-understanding after near-death experiences. *Contemporary Psychoanalysis*, 22: 319–346.
Raine, K. (1971). *William Blake*. New York: Praeger, p. 43.
Reik, T. (1937). *Surprise and the Psychoanalyst*, Trans. M. R. Green. New York: E. P. Dutton and Company.
Rothenberg, A. (1979). *The Emerging Goddess: The Creative Process in Art, Science and other Fields*. Chicago, IL: University of Chicago Press.
Rorty, R. (1979). *Philosophy and the Mirror of Nature*. Princeton, NJ: Princeton University Press.
Rosner, S. & Abt, L. E. (Eds). (1974). *Essays in Creativity*. Croton-on-Hudson, NY: North River Press.
Ryle, G. (1949). *The Concept of Mind*. New York: Barnes and Noble.
Schachtel, E. G. (1959). *Metamorphosis*. New York: Basic Books.
Shattuck, R. (1984). The innocent eye and the armed vision. In *The Innocent Eye: On Modern Literature and the Arts*. New York: Washington Square Press, pp. 413–424.

Simons, M. (1985). Love and age: A talk with Garcia Marquez *The New York Times Book Review*, April 7, pp. 1, 18–19.
Spence, D. P. (1987). *The Freudian Metaphor: Toward Paradigm Change in Psychoanalysis*. New York: W. W. Norton.
Stern, D. B. (1983). Unformulated experience. *Contemporary Psychoanalysis*, 19: 71–99.
Stern, D. B. (1985). Unformulated experience and transference. *Contemporary Psychoanalysis*, 23: 484–491.
Stern, D. B. (1989). The analyst's unformulated experience of the patient. *Contemporary Psychoanalysis*, 25: 1–33.
Stern, D. B. (1991). A philosophy for the embedded analyst: Gadamer's hermeneutics and the social paradigm of psychoanalysis. *Contemporary Psychoanalysis*, 27: 51–80.
Stevenson, R. L. (1925). A chapter on dreams In *Memories and Portraits, Random Memories, Memories of Himself.* New York: Charles Scribner's Sons.
Stolorow, R. D. (1988). Intersubjectivity, psychoanalytic knowing, and reality. *Contemporary Psychoanalysis*, 24: 331–338.
Sullivan, H. S. (1954 [1970]). *The Psychiatric Interview*. New York: W. W. Norton.
Tauber, E. S. (1954). Exploring the therapeutic use of counter-transference data. *Psychiatry*, 17: 332–336.
Tauber, E. S. & Green, M. R. (1959). *Prelogical Experience*. New York: Basic Books.
Valéry, P. (1940 [1952]). The course in poetics: First lesson, trans. J. Mathews. In B. Ghiselin (Ed.), *The Creative Process*. Berkeley, CA: University of California Press, pp. 92–106. Date of original publication unknown.
Woods, R. L. (1947). *The World of Dreams: An Anthology*. New York: Random House.

Chapter 13

"Speak! that I may see you"

Some reflections on dissociation, reality, and psychoanalytic listening (1994)

Philip M. Bromberg

Philip Bromberg is one of the preeminent writers in psychoanalysis today. Along with Jay Greenberg, Stephen Mitchell, and Donnel Stern, Bromberg has, on one hand, shown the degree to which interpersonal and relational psychoanalysis coincide, and on the other, drawn attention to the central contribution of interpersonal psychoanalysis to relational psychoanalysis. Among analysts identified with relational psychoanalysis, Bromberg, Greenberg, Mitchell, and Stern share a special emphasis on the analysis of the interpersonal field.

Bromberg begins by making dissociation central to unconscious process. He extends Sullivan's emphasis on "not me," which is that part of subjectivity that exists outside the self and that therefore has never been given symbolic representation. These dissociated states cannot be thought; they are lived out in the interpersonal world through a combination of self-fulfilling prophecies and expectancies, and cannot be integrated or successfully bridged with the states that are recognized as "me." In this way, mind is protected; one can avoid having to acknowledge that one is someone other than the person one recognizes oneself to be. The cost is fragmentation – of experience, of mind, of self.

The primary value of the psychoanalytic enterprise lies in the ability of the analyst to see and to engage patients' range of states, including and especially, of course, those that have been dissociated. Patients cannot put dissociated states into words – they emerge as subtly and mutually lived out only in the context of the transference–countertransference relationship, which for Bromberg must be personal and affectively alive. Reaching psychoanalytic goals cannot be planned, and prescribed technical procedures are more likely to thwart treatment than enhance it. Bromberg explains in this article that productive psychoanalytic process is inherently nonlinear and chaotic.

For Bromberg, successful analytic work depends on engaging with patients in a way he describes as "authentic." This requires the analyst to convey whatever it is that she sees in a genuine way. The patient must feel "seen" (recognized) by the analyst. This involves acute attention to patients' and analysts' shifting self-states as they emerge in interaction with one another. In the tradition of Harold Searles and Benjamin Wolstein, Bromberg advises us to take the risk of speaking what we see and what we experience. Following Edgar Levenson, he underscores that what is being discussed is also being lived out in the transference–countertransference. Addressing this intersubjective field becomes the very heart of therapeutic action. One can also see here the legacy of Erich Fromm and Erwin Singer, in their emphasis on sharing countertransference experience with patients. Bromberg, in common with Singer and Fromm, holds the position that it is important to share with patients perceptions of what they are like in the field of others.

Though it is possible to trace certain aspects of Bromberg's views to his interpersonal heritage, his voice is unique. No one has conceptualized an intrapsychic world composed of internalized self–other states as clearly as he has, and no one else has defined troubled living as the result of failure to bridge self states – a failure, in Bromberg's wording elsewhere, to "stand in the spaces" between these states. For Bromberg, therapeutic action arises from the events of the patient–analyst relationship – which means that the analyst's way of being or engaging with a given patient always carries more weight than interpretation in the conduct and outcome of treatment. If an analysis falls short, it is likely to be because the analyst has not been sufficiently affectively present, by resorting to prescribed technique or avoiding authentic engagement with the patient in some other way.

"Speak! that I may see you"

Some reflections on dissociation, reality, and psychoanalytic listening (1994)

Philip M. Bromberg

The new emphasis on nonlinear dynamics in psychoanalytic thinking is rapidly changing our view of both psychological structure and psychological growth. The conceptualization of psychoanalytic listening and technique as therapeutically mediating the lifting of repression and the resolution of intrapsychic conflict is reexamined here in terms of new types of questions having to do with such concepts as "self-organization," "states of consciousness," and "dissociation." This paper presents the view that dissociation is as basic as repression to human mental functioning and as central to the stability and growth of personality. Even in the most resilient personality, an analyst will always encounter domains of dissociated experience that have weak or nonexistent linkage to the experience of "me" as a communicable entity. Before these "not-me" states of mind can be taken as objects of analytic self-reflection, they must first become "thinkable" while becoming linguistically communicable through enactment in the analytic relationship. This depends on the analyst's ability to acknowledge the divergent realities held by discontinuous self-states in the patient while simultaneously maintaining an authentic dialogue with each. By "unfreezing" the concrete, literal quality of a patient's discontinuous states of consciousness, the patient is able to embrace the full range of his perceptual reality within a single relational field, so that the process becomes a dialectic between *seeing and being seen*, rather than simply being seen "into." It is through this that intrapsychic bridges are built between a patient's self-experiences that could not formerly be contained in a relationship with the same object, and a transition begins to take place from enacted dissociative experience to interpretable intrapsychic conflict.

To thine own selves be true

The following clinical vignette was not written by a therapist but by a physicist. It is from a book entitled *Einstein's Dreams* (Lightman,

1993), which has to do with the many possible natures of time and the many possible natures of reality that depend on how we experience past, present, and future.

> Every Tuesday, a middle-aged man brings stones from the quarry east of Berne to the masonry on Hodlerstrasse.... He wears a gray wool coat in all seasons, works in the quarry until after dark, has dinner with his wife and goes to bed, tends his garden on Sundays. And on Tuesday mornings, he loads his truck with stones and comes to town.... And as he passes people on the street, his eyes are on the ground. Some people know him, try to catch his eye or say hello. He mumbles and walks on. Even when he delivers his stones to Hodlerstrasse, he cannot look the mason in the eye. Instead, he looks aside, he talks to the wall in answer to the mason's friendly chatter, he stands in a corner while his stones are weighed.
>
> Forty years ago in school, one afternoon in March, he urinated in class. He could not hold it in. Afterwards, he tried to stay in his chair, but the other boys saw the puddle and made him walk around the room, round and round. They pointed at the wet spot on his pants and howled.... A clock with big red hands read 2:15. And the boys hooted at him, hooted at him as they chased him around the room, with the wet spot on his pants....
>
> That memory has become his life. When he wakes up in the morning, he is the boy who urinated in his pants. When he passes people on the street, he knows they see the wet spot on his pants. He glances at his pants and looks away. When his children visit, he stays in his room and talks to them through the door. He is the boy who could not hold it in. (pp. 167–170)

What if this man were in analysis! How would we see the nature of his problem? What happened to him that day in school? Is he psychotic? After all, he does hide from his children. Is he "borderline"? Is the therapeutic issue one of shame and pathological narcissism? If so, what is the process through which we might hope to comprehend what he feels as an adult, much less know what he felt as a child? What kind of transference can we expect? I am starting here, because I want gradually to approach the topic of what we imagine we are doing when we do psychoanalysis; what our image is of the human being we are listening to; and what our conception is of the mental apparatus and the personality structure that we are applying our technical skills to engage. In what way was this man's emotional response adaptive to the event, how did it become pathological, and how does one listen to such a man so as to determine why his emotions overwhelmed him and to find a way to help him? Consider what Nesse (1991) has to say about emotions:

> [E]motions are set to maximize Darwinian fitness, not happiness, and ... natural selection has molded each kind of bad feeling to help protect against a specific threat.... Emotions adjust a person's response to the task at hand. In that sense they are similar to computer programs, which adjust the setup of the computer to carry out a certain kind of task.... The behavioral, physiological and cognitive responses that help a person elude a tiger are different from those that help woo a lover or attack a competitor. Thus, fear, love and anger are highly distinct psychological subroutines gradually shaped by natural selection to improve the person's ability to cope with each challenge.... When a tiger bounds towards you, what should your response be? Should you file your toenails? Do a cartwheel? Sing a song? Is this the moment to run an uncountable number of randomly generated response possibilities through the decision rule? ... How could you compute which possibility would result in more grandchildren? The alternative: Darwinian algorithms specialized for predator avoidance ... and upon detecting a potential predator, constrain your responses to flight, fight, or hiding. (p. 33)

But human relationships, especially for the young, are sometimes not that simple. What of situations where there are competing algorithms at the same moment? What of a moment when your mother bounds toward you with fangs bared? Or a moment when your father approaches you with penis bared? Or, as in this man's case, where your peer group suddenly becomes a pack of hyenas, stripping *you* bare while you are still alive? The algorithm of flight, fight, or hiding pertains only to escape from predators. What does someone (particularly a child) do when there is another strong algorithm already operating, such as "obedience to a parent or an adult," or "love of one's caretaker," or "being accepted by one's peers"? This is the situation, I suggest, that, at least from an evolutionary standpoint, defines the meaning of trauma, and may explain why natural selection seems to have endowed the human mind with a Darwinian algorithm that helps us cope with trauma by providing what Putnam (1992) has called "the escape when there is no escape" (p. 104) – the mechanism of dissociation. Where drastically incompatible emotions or perceptions are required to be cognitively processed within the same relationship and such processing is adaptationally beyond the capacity of the individual to contain this disjunction within a unitary self-experience, one of the competing algorithms is hypnoidally denied access to consciousness to preserve sanity and survival. When ordinary adaptational adjustment to the task at hand is not possible, dissociation comes into play. The experience that is causing the incompatible perception and emotion is "unhooked" from the cognitive processing system and remains raw data that is cognitively unsymbolized within that particular self–other representation, except as a survival reaction. Thus, the person retains the capacity to survive by preserving the dissociated "predator" experience in its pure form of deadly assault (or in contemporary terms, "abuse") and also retains the original self–other representations organized by obedience, love, and friendship, but without the capacity to modify them by appropriate courses of action that take self-interest into account.

Dissociation is not inherently pathological, but it can become so. The process of dissociation is basic to human mental functioning and is central to the stability and growth of personality. It is intrinsically an adaptational talent that represents the very nature of what we call "consciousness." Dissociation is not fragmentation. In fact, it may be reasonably seen as a defense against fragmentation, and in this regard, Ferenczi's (1930a [1980], p. 230) struggle with whether fragmentation is merely a mechanical consequence of trauma or may actually be a form of adaptation to it was brilliantly ahead of its time. The answer to his question, however, took 60 years to appear. *There is now abundant evidence that the psyche does not start as an integrated whole, but is nonunitary in origin – a mental structure that begins and continues as a multiplicity of self-states that maturationally attain a feeling of coherence which overrides the awareness of discontinuity* (Bromberg, 1993, p. 162). *This leads to the experience of a cohesive sense of personal identity and the necessary illusion of being "one self."* One of the major reasons that this understanding of the normal mind has taken so long to reach full scientific consciousness is that changes of state are, for the most part, difficult to perceive in normal adults. The developmental process that eases the transitions across states of consciousness typically results in a healthy person being able to smooth out awareness of the changes, an achievement that is greatly facilitated by caretakers who, through a process of mutual regulation, help the child attain nontraumatic state transitions by appropriate interactive responsiveness to the child's subjectivity.

For psychoanalysts, this view of the mind has been supported by psychoanalytically oriented infant studies such as those by Emde, Gaensbaure, and Harmon (1976), Sander (1977), Stern (1985), Wolff (1987), and Beebe and Lachmann (1992), but the most direct support has come from nonanalytic empirical research into normal and pathological adult mental functioning – research representing a wide range of disciplines and research centers. The director of the Dissociative Disorders Research Unit of the NIMH, in a seminal paper discussing nonlinear state changes as a developmental paradigm (Putnam, 1988), speaks to the fact that the most central property of states is that they are discrete and discontinuous. Asserting that "states appear to be the fundamental unit of organization of consciousness and are detectable from the first moments following birth," he describes them as

> self-organizing and self-stabilizing structures of behavior. When a transition (switch) from one state of consciousness to another state of consciousness occurs, the new state acts to impose a quantitatively and qualitatively different structure on the variables that define the state of consciousness. The new structure acts to reorganize behavior and resist changes to other states.... [S]witches between states are manifest by non-linear changes in a number of variables (Wolff, 1987). These variables include: 1) affect; 2) access to memory, i.e., state-dependent memory; 3) attention and cognition; 4) regulatory physiology; and 5) sense of self.... *Changes in affect and mood are, however, probably the single best marker of state switches in normal adults.* (p. 25, italics added)

Nonlinear switches in discontinuous states of consciousness! The implications are profound. A case could be made, for example, that the reason a state such as depression is difficult to alleviate even with medication is that it is not simply an "affective disorder" but an internally coherent aspect of the self. For many people, it is a self-state with its own narrative, its own memory configuration, its own perceptual reality, and its own style of relatedness to others. It is not simply something one feels – it is who one *is*, at least at certain times. There is, therefore, as much of a need to preserve self-meaning in this state of being as in any other, despite its painful, guilt-ridden, and often suicidal nature – to not allow any domain of one's personal reality to be destroyed as though it were meaningless simply because it is painful. The resistance to losing one's depressive reality is greatest where personality is organized more by a dissociative mental structure than by conflict, because the importance of the feeling of selfhood attached to a given state of mind is greatest when there is least simultaneous access to alternative self-states with other potential perceptual realities and internal self-narratives. So the "curing" of depression must be a process that does not become an effort to cure the patient of "who he[1] is." Thus, the analytic exploration of the suffering in depression, before it can become accessible to a mutual cognitive perspective in the analytic relationship, must be in a dialectic with a multiplicity of different self-narratives, perceptual realities, and adaptational meanings to the patient, each of which speaks with its own voice. To put it a bit more poetically, an analyst must be constantly negotiating with a range of self-states with different voices, even when the voice of pain is louder than the others.

"Speak! that I may see you"

"Speak, in order that I may see you," Socrates is alleged to have said (Reik, 1936, p. 21). Speak, that I may see the speaker hidden in his words. Freud (1913 [1955]) implied almost the same thing in formulating his basic rule of the free association method. Speak everything that comes to mind, and I will discover the person you wish to hide. But the process of being seen "into," no matter how benign or well-meaning the motive, evokes what analysts' traditionally have called "resistance." Socrates, in fact, was invited by the Athenians to retire permanently, and though the descendents of Freud haven't yet been offered the hemlock, most psychoanalysts are wearily familiar with the image of the "headshrinker" – the dangerous "truthsayer" holding a special power to discern hidden secrets inadvertently revealed by the other's unguarded speech.

Here I present an argument that both supports and challenges this image. I hold that when psychoanalysis is successful as a method of psychotherapy, the reason is indeed to be found in Socrates's words, but that in any successful analysis the process is a dialectic between *seeing and being seen*, rather than simply being seen "into." That is, when optimally effective, analysis simultaneously frees our patients to do unto us, with equivalent perceptiveness, what we are doing unto them, to see us as part of the act of listening to us.

Words begin as carriers. In early childhood they are vocal carriers of personal feeling – an articulated form of a cry (Sullivan, 1953, p. 185). With the onset of communicative speech they are more than carriers; they are also building blocks in the relational construction of personal meaning. They shift from a sophisticated vehicle for relatively autistic expression of what one feels and what one needs, to the primary modality for the interpersonal creation of who one *is*. Relationally, words in themselves do not exist in time or space. Only the speaker's meaning exists in time and space; and the speaker's meaning is constructed from a perception of his words framed by the immediacy of the context in which they are spoken. Speaking is an action in an interpersonal context (real or implied). Schafer's (1976) concept of "action language" partly addresses this fact, but words – even "action words" – simply point in the direction of the speaker. Ultimately, the speaker must be seen if the words are to achieve meaning.

"Speaking," in psychoanalysis, is thus not simply a process of delivering content. It is also a relational act that shapes the content of what is spoken about. For patients dealing in a primary way with dissociative experience, this point comes into particularly high relief because words themselves feel more or less meaningless. The person carries a sense of internal isolation as his natural state, and trying to convey this in words is experienced as an exercise in futility. But, in analysis, because he is expected to speak, a communicative route can potentially be constructed, sometimes painfully, through the relationship. In the interplay of silence and words, a patient can, at least potentially, force the analyst to give up his attempts to "understand" his patient and allow himself to "know" his patient – to know him in the only way possible – through the ongoing intersubjective field they are sharing at that moment. It is through this medium that an act of recognition can take place in which words and concepts can symbolize instead of substitute for experience. The analyst has an opportunity to recognize (personally know) the thing that cannot be said in words – the quality of subjective experience that makes verbal communication feel artificial and meaningless. But this can take place only if the analyst does not too quickly attempt to translate recognition into understanding, that is, if he does not substitute interpreted meaning for experientially symbolized meaning.

I recently listened to a case being presented to me in ongoing consultation. It may illustrate what I mean. The patient was a woman who had been in treatment for quite a few years and who had made major changes in her life and her self-experience, except with regard to the thing that had brought her into treatment in the first place, her obesity. She felt her weight as a burden that she would carry unto death, with no hope of relief. At the point I entered the case it was her analyst who was feeling no hope of relief, and that was a major reason for the consultation. The situation was quite an extraordinary one and impressed me once again with the fact that when it comes to certain kinds of enactments, it's really a lot more pleasurable to be the consultant than the analyst. As a consultant I'm spared the experience of being personally dismantled by the patient, a fact I feel is critical to comprehend in working as a therapist from this frame of reference. The analyst's willingness to participate in an enactment does not begin as "willingness" in the usual meaning of the term. It is not something the analyst does voluntarily, nor is it something over which he even has much control. It is, in fact, the opposite of what is usually meant by "technique" (something that one "applies" and has command over). The analyst's initial experience of his participation is much closer to the consternation that accompanies projective identification, and the two at times may actually be the same phenomenon with different names. The person "who you are" is perceived as seriously lacking in some way, with regard to the patient, and the more you try to incorporate what your patient is saying about you and use it within your current stance, the more evidence you seem to be supplying of your deficiencies. What the patient is saying in words does not carry the message; the message is carried by the relationship between the words and the experiential context in which they are heard – the way an analyst begins to feel about himself and about his patient as his position feels more and more uncontainable within his natural stance and sometimes within his self-definition as an analyst.

This phase is not (and should not be) a pleasant experience for the analyst. If it is – if the analyst is feeling satisfaction from his willingness to be "used as an object" (Winnicott, 1969 [1971]) – he is not really being used at all, at least not yet. The patient's need is to perceive and confront the analyst with what is perceived that has been known but unthought. This process involves a dismantling of aspects of the relationship that patient and analyst have used to define who they are to each other. In effect, it means that the patient is "destroying" aspects of the analyst's identity, who he is to himself, as defined through that relationship. Loewald (1979) calls it "emancipatory murder" (p. 758).

In the case of the patient I mentioned, whose treatment I had been following, the dismantling took place around the analyst's "failure" to mention the patient's weight when she herself wasn't mentioning it. "*You* ought to know," the patient insisted, "that when I'm talking about anything else as long as I'm still fat, it's only my good self that's talking and that I'm doing something self-destructive that you're not even caring about." In fact, the analyst cared a great deal about it, as you might well imagine. It was the one painfully overt sign that something still needed to be "cured" and that talking hadn't helped. So the analyst had decided (on his own) to stop addressing it because he was tired of getting nowhere (kind of "fed up," you might say) and hoped that the patient would then bring it up herself. He allowed long silences to develop in which he hoped that she might ultimately put what she was feeling into words. Well, she did, but not in the way that he had hoped. As he was finding the silences increasingly hard to tolerate, she, without the least regard for logic, told him he had no right to stop trying to find out what she was feeling, and "what did he think he was doing?" This is not a situation in which a therapist can just sit back and comfortably do his work (at least, he *shouldn't* be able to). It was in the course of their dealing with the apparent "no-win" quality of his "failure" that he was able to begin to find a small island of shared experience on which he could plant at least one of his feet. It was at this point that the patient began to be able to "back off" from her concrete state of consciousness and to develop a cognitive perspective through which the "unthought known" (Bollas, 1987) became the thought known and through which the analyst could authentically experience himself as a willing participant.

"Only in my silence," the patient stated, "do I feel real. The only way I can get out of here is to be silent for a year." What she meant consciously by "here" was "here" meaning her inner world, and, unconsciously, meaning the analysis. But let's stay with what, at that moment, she was able to render conscious. How could it make any sense that the only way she recognized that she could release herself from the trap of her dissociated mental structure was without words, by remaining silent for a year? The point she was making was not that silence itself mattered, but silence in the presence of her analyst. Why? Because her silence in his presence could have a communicative impact – *as long as he hadn't given up trying*. This is the essence, I think, of the "projective identification" phase of enactment. The analyst has to get fed up; it is important that he get fed up; he should get fed up. But he shouldn't get so detached from his own "fed-upness" that he cannot perceive the retaliatory component of his behavior. If he is open to that, he will feel the communication from the patient as it is pressed into his soul through her silence as well as into his brain through her words. The patient was ultimately able to put into words this remarkable insight:

> When I'm not talking to you and you don't realize that my silence is talking, I feel like I'm hurting myself and you don't care. I hurt myself by being fat in order to call attention to the inside "me." And if you don't notice or seem not to, it's like you're mad that I'm still fat and will let me hurt myself because I'm fat instead of putting why I'm fat into words. But if I do talk, it's not my fat self that's talking. So you have to find her by noticing the fat and not pretending you don't. If I get thin, no one will ever look for her because if I stop calling attention to her existence you will settle for my good self, which looks healthy because it is thin, and you will never know it isn't real to me. I'm like Dr. Jekyll and Mr. Hyde. [Shortly, the HYDE/H-I-D-E pun became clear.] Or, like with Clark Kent and Superman, the two parts never get into the same room at the same time because they're the same person.

In other words, by "noticing," through the impact of forced involvement with what the patient needs to call attention to without communicative speech, the dissociated self can start to exist, and a transition begins to take place to what this patient so evocatively described as a growing awareness of "Mr. Hyde." But the success of the transition depends on the ability of the patient to destroy successfully the analyst's conception of "what this is really all about" and thus destroy the analyst's image of the patient in which Mr. "Hide" is imprisoned. The analyst's own self-image, which is a part of all this, is also destroyed, and it is this destruction he must "survive" in Winnicott's (1969 [1971]) conceptualization of object usage.

In this context, analytic listening might be compared to approaching a patient's words in the same manner that Henry Adams (1904 [1986]) advocated in appreciating medieval architecture – as if one were approaching medieval poetry in the troublesome "roughness" of the original language in which it was written. Adams wrote, in his delightful book *Mont Saint-Michel and Chartres*:

> Translation is an evil chiefly because anyone who cares for mediaeval architecture ... ought to care still more for mediaeval English.... Anyone who attacks them boldly will find that the [verses] run along like a ballad, *singing their own meaning*, and troubling themselves very little whether the meaning is exact or not. One's translation is sure to be full of gross blunders, but *the supreme blunder is that of translating at all when one is trying to catch not a fact but a feeling*. If translate one must, we had best begin by trying to be literal, under protest that it matters not a straw whether we succeed. (pp. 18–19, italics added)

An interpretation is a translation, and what is reflected in an interpretation is the analyst's personal view of the patient, which is one of many possible realities. At the moment the patient is looking at himself through the analyst's eyes, he's also looking at the analyst in a very personal way. The ability of the patient to accept the image of himself that the analyst is offering is directly influenced by his ability to trust his perception of the person presenting it. So his rejection of the interpretation is not only a rejection of a view of himself but also a rejection of an unpalatable view of the analyst – a view in which he experiences the analyst as asking him to substitute, without sufficient negotiation, the analyst's subjectivity for his own. Within normal limits, this is simply part of the natural process of "trying to stay the same while changing" (Bromberg, 1991), but if the analyst's interpretive posture attempts to conceal his own subjectivity while simultaneously attempting to deny that there is anything there to see, a collusive masquerade takes place. The patient seemingly accepts or resists as objective "reality" the language into which the analyst has chosen to translate the patient's original "verses" (the analyst's personal view of the patient), under the guise of its being a reflection of what is "really there" that the patient does or does not want to see.

Dissociation, enactment, and reality

I have essentially been arguing for an interpersonal and intersubjective listening stance, a viewpoint that many analytic writers, myself included, have passionately advanced for some time. In the remainder of this paper I would like to try to develop this position along somewhat different lines and present a few ideas that may help its progress toward what I feel is its most likely next step. To do that I want to return in greater detail to the phenomenon of the human mind as a complex system of discontinuous and shifting states of consciousness and examine the impact of this nonlinear model of the mind on the way we think about psychoanalysis as a theory and the way we think about psychoanalysis in "how we listen and what we do" while with our patients. As will be clear from the following anecdote, I personally find the normal nonlinearity of the human mind a mystery that continues to amaze me.

I recently took a cab ride that, among other things, cured me forever of complaining about taxi drivers who can't speak English. The driver, who was listening to a radio station broadcasting a soap opera in Spanish, would at each red light pick up a newspaper from the seat next to him and start to read, while at the same time clearly following what was happening in the soap opera. I had just begun to feel irritated that he wasn't even pretending to concentrate on what I was paying him for, his driving, when I looked at the newspaper and saw that it was in French. My irritation was replaced by a combination of envy and disbelief. "Is the human mind really capable of simultaneously processing different content, through different perceptual channels, in different languages? And even if it were, wouldn't it be more natural (not to mention easier on the brain) to choose one or the other?" So I asked him about it, in English. He replied – in English easily as fluent as mine – that he never thought about it before. He's lived in different places and speaks different languages; that's all. He definitely didn't want to get into a discussion about what language he thinks in, what language he dreams in, and whether he could do the same thing if the radio program or the newspaper were in English. He didn't really want to "speak so that I might see him." I think he had too many other things to do, but also he was afraid I was going to try to nail him for reading while he was driving. So I lost a potentially valuable informant, but I continue to wonder about it.

A recent paper in the *American Psychologist* (Barton, 1994) starts with the statement that "a new paradigm for understanding systems has been gaining the attention of psychologists from a wide variety of specialty areas" (p. 5). The paradigm, which describes the behavior of complex systems, is known as nonlinear dynamics, or Chaos Theory. It is a science without an implication of "prescribed" sequences, but rather with *a set of necessary and sufficient conditions to allow the construction of something different from the past pattern, but unpredictable as a future event*. It postulates that complex systems (like the human mind) have an underlying order, but that simple systems (like a human interaction) can produce complex behavior. In theory, you could predict the course of an interaction far into the future, but in fact you can't, because almost immediately very small effects start to make a difference and will eventually lead to unpredictable behavior. Gleick (1987) described the heart of the discovery as revealing that "chaos and instability ... were not the same at all. A chaotic system could be stable if its particular brand of irregularity persisted in the face of small disturbances" (p. 48). He went on: "[C]haos brought an astonishing message: simple deterministic models could produce what looked like random behavior. The behavior actually had an exquisite fine structure, yet any piece of it seemed indistinguishable from noise" (p. 79).

The new emphasis on nonlinear dynamics in psychoanalytic thinking is particularly well captured by a changing view of mental structure, both normal and pathological. The conceptualization of personality growth as therapeutically mediated by the lifting of repression and the uncovering of unconscious conflict is being reexamined in terms of new types of questions – questions that have to do with such concepts as "self-organization," states of consciousness, dissociation, and the readiness of the human personality to exhibit, in Barton's (1994) words, "multiple self states that can change suddenly from one to another when a parameter value crosses a critical threshold" (p. 8).

Even in the most resilient personality psychic structure is organized by trauma as well as by repression, and an analyst will always encounter domains of dissociated experience that have weak or nonexistent links to the experience of "me" as a communicable entity. Before these "not-me" states of mind can be taken as objects of self-reflection, they must first become "thinkable" while becoming linguistically communicable through enactment in the analytic relationship. Until this happens, neither genuine repression nor the experience of intrapsychic conflict can take place, because each state of consciousness holds its own experientially encapsulated "truth" that is enacted over and over again without the availability of the necessary conditions for cognitive resolution. Chu (1991) has described the issue vividly and succinctly. He states that trauma that has been dissociated is repeated with a compulsive quality that takes on an almost biological urgency, and that

> patients are thrust back into the traumatic events both in their dreams and while awake.... The reliving of the trauma is experienced as a real and contemporary event. That is, the patient does not talk about feeling as if he or she remembers the experience; rather, he or she feels the experience in the present.... *Therapists are all too familiar with the difficult task of attempting to help patients keep one foot in current reality at the same time as they experience the past.* (p. 328, italics added)

In analytic listening, regardless of whether we use the term "reliving" or "enactment," each state of consciousness is signified by its own relational context. While one narrative is being "told," another is being played out between patient and analyst while the telling goes on. Levenson (1982) has gone as far as to state that "analyzing the relationship between what is talked about and the behavior that goes along with what's talked about *constitutes* the psychoanalytic process ... and is what *distinguishes* it, essentially, from all other forms of psychotherapy" (p. 11, italics added). This, to me, is also what Winnicott's (1967 [1971]) concept of "potential space" is all about – the interpersonal construction of reality in which playing with meaning (deconcretizing it) becomes possible. It is why parapraxes are so wonderful! Not because they provide a window into what a patient "really" believes, but because they allow opposing realities held by different self-states to coexist, and mutuality can increase simultaneous access to a fuller range of self through the analytic relationship.

For example: a 40-year-old male patient, a widower early in life, was furious and self-righteous because his current girlfriend had refused to accept his claim that he could not marry again because of his religious conviction that his original marriage was a holy covenant. "She won't believe," he shouted, "that I really care about preserving the '*sanctimony*' (sic) of marriage." Did this delightful slip lead him to replace his religious conviction with a new image of it being nothing but self-serving and hypocritical? No! But it was funny enough to each of us that we could work with both words in a way that produced another "slip," which led to the emergence of a dissociated self-state that held the memory of why the religious conviction was so important. The second parapraxis was: "When I think of forgetting my wife, I feel so selfish that I'm afraid God is going to punish me. The world feels like it will come to an end, so I can't cut the "*un-biblical cord* (sic)." As we "played" with this one together, he became in my presence the traumatized five-year-old boy whose world had felt as if it were ending when he was sadistically punished by his mother for wishing to leave her in order to live with his beloved aunt. To "teach him to be good," he had been placed in a children's home overnight, having been told he would have to stay there "for as long as it took to learn his lesson." He relived, in interaction with me, the terror of this dissociated experience and the pact he had made with God never to be bad again if God would only let him come home. For the first time in his treatment, this 40-year-old man was able to meet the frightened five-year-old who accompanied him to every session and for whom the therapy itself was nothing more than a different version of the children's asylum from which he was waiting to be released.

If an analyst thinks of a person as speaking from different self-states rather than from a single center of self, then the analyst will inevitably listen that way. It demands an overarching attunement to the speaker, an attunement that addresses the same issue described by Schafer's (1983) mode of listening and interpreting in which "the analyst focuses on the action of telling itself … [and] telling is treated as an object of description rather than … an indifferent or transparent medium for imparting information or thematic content" (p. 228). From a nonlinear perspective, however, this means a special attunement to both the impact the speaker is having on you at any given moment and the *shifts* in that impact as close to the time they occur as possible. Obviously I am looking at these shifts as representing shifts in states of self that are to be held by the analyst as an *ongoing* focus of attention. It is a way of listening different from that of hearing the person feel differently at different moments. The latter takes the switches in states of consciousness as more or less normal background music, unless they are particularly dramatic. The former takes them as the primary data that organize everything else you are hearing and doing, including how you approach the issue of unconscious fantasy and the reconstruction of personal narrative. We speak of a person as being in different "moods," or as being emotionally "labile," or as not being "himself." These metaphors are useful, particularly with certain patients at specific moments. But because they are based on a conception of affective shifts as emanating from a unitary, centered self that is temporarily decentered, an analyst's traditional posture and listening stance has tended to focus on the *content* of mental states without particular regard for the basic discontinuity in structural *context* – the states themselves. What an analyst hears has thus tended to be organized by a search for continuity between conscious and unconscious meaning rather than by a dialogue between discontinuous domains of self-meaning held by a multiplicity of states of consciousness, some of which can be told and some only enacted. I am offering the view that for any human being, feeling differently at different moments about the same thing, or "getting into a mood," represents a shift to a state of consciousness with its own internal integrity, its own reality, and sometimes its own "truth."

The challenge for an analyst is in being aware that with every patient some state shifts have minimal or no link to other states of consciousness, even to those that may have just preceded the change. The change points are moments that sometimes may indeed signify the presence of an interpretable state of conflict and at other times may herald the emergence of a dissociated domain of experience. In a personality that is significantly organized by dissociative protection against trauma, there is, of course, a greater likelihood that an affective shift signals the presence of a self-state that not only is disjunctive with the one preceding it, but also is relatively inaccessible to it. But even in a patient without a diagnosed dissociative disorder, a shift in self-state may signify the absence rather than the presence of a state of conflict even though the patient may appear conflicted because the content has remained the same. In such instances, what the analyst may be conceptualizing as "externalization of conflict" is often precisely the opposite – the presence of a dissociated self-state that cannot yet *experience* intrapsychic conflict, much less externalize it. From a nonlinear listening stance, shifts in states of consciousness are firstly viewed by the analyst as moments of recognition, exploration, and potential negotiation within the transference–countertransference field and only through this process as genuine windows for conflict interpretation and resolution.

Once again, language does not merely carry meaning, but constructs it as a relational process. The analyst's goal is not to bring the patient to a point where he can eventually accept a "delivered" interpretation and to assume that, if such a point is in fact reached, it means that the interpretation has already been made. It was "made," in the sense that it was "constructed," in interactive exploration of the multiple realities of opposing self-states held by patient and analyst, rather than "made" (as in "delivered") by the analyst. The result is not literally a "new" reality and most definitely not the correction of a faulty or distorted "old" reality. It represents a linking of opposing subnarratives held by different states of consciousness that have been dissociatively inaccessible to an experience of internal conflict. Psychological integration, as I have suggested elsewhere (Bromberg, 1993), does not lead to a single "real you" or "true self." Rather, it "is the ability to stand in the spaces between realities without losing any of them … the capacity to feel like one self while being many" (p. 166).

The patient's ability to move from dissociation to conflict depends on the analyst's ability to relate to several selves simultaneously while maintaining an authentic dialogue with each. It is through this process that relational bridges are built between self-experiences that could not formerly be contained in a relationship with the same object. Because, however, the conception of the human mind has been anchored in linear, rather than nonlinear, dynamics, each major school of thought has had its own emphasis in accounting for the therapeutic action of psychoanalysis. One could say that, despite the effort of every experienced analyst to maintain a clinical balancing act, the stance of any given analyst has tended to slant toward one of three postures partly organized by individual differences in metapsychology – interpretation of conflict, detailed inquiry, or empathic attunement. It is interesting to observe, however, that built into each posture, regardless of differences in theory, is an acceptance, based on its own clinical logic, of the fact that the transference–countertransference field is where the action takes place. In other words, any analysis from any theoretical context that has as its goal enduring and far-reaching characterological growth is grounded in this understanding. Why?

Clinically, the transference–countertransference field is characterized by its vividness and its immediacy. But why is this fact so important that it is able to transcend metapsychology in the best utilization of this field? My own answer is that, regardless of individual metapsychologies of therapeutic action, every school of thought *clinically* attempts either explicitily or implicitly to enhance *perception*, to facilitate a patient's access to the broadest possible range of consciousness by reducing the use of dissociation. The patient, through one technical approach or another, must be freed to see the analyst while the analyst is seeing the patient. "Speak!, that your patient might see you," in order that his dissociated states of mind may find access to the analytic relationship and be lived within it. Dissociated domains of self can achieve symbolization only through enactment in a relational context because *experience becomes symbolized not by words themselves but by the new relational context that the words come to represent.* Judith Peterson (1993) has addressed this in her cogent observation that

> many steps are necessary in order to move someone from a dissociative state to an integrated one.... However, the therapy [does] not consist of Freud and Breuer's definition of abreaction, nor of discharging emotional energy to release repressed ideas.... The focus is not on abreaction but on the change points or moments in therapy where cognitive insights, reconstruction or blending and integration occur. (pp. 74–75)

Particularly illustrative of this focus in my own work (Bromberg, 1984, 1991) has been the direct appearance in sessions of the Isakower phenomenon (Isakower, 1938), a dissociated autosymbolic hallucination that typically occurs in the twilight state of falling asleep. When it appears, it is most often reported as a soft, white, amorphous bubble descending slowly upon the person's face and threatening to engulf him. My first experience with it was in treating a man whose schizoid personality encompassed all the elements of an extreme dissociative disorder. Other patients like this man have also sometimes had in sessions with me dissociated experiences similar to the Isakower phenomenon itself. I believe that all these perceptual events, including the Isakower phenomenon, may represent an effort to restore a developmentally normal process that was traumatically impaired early in life – the process of perceptual transition to linguistic symbolization of experience. The hallucinatory experience, when it has appeared in my own patients, was at times "blank," at other times "gridlike," and at still other times, imagistic. It is my hypothesis that in the process of moving from dissociation to conflict, the use of language in the act of constructing cognitive meaning from experience is first represented schematically through perception, and this is sometimes manifested by the degree of articulation that occurs in transitional perceptual experience when the individual is neither fully awake nor fully asleep. It is a state of consciousness that bridges both and is notably similar to the trance and fugue-like states preceding major dissociative episodes. The early literature on the Isakower phenomenon is suggestive in this regard. Depending on an author's perspective as to whether the person was believed to be more asleep or more awake when the phenomenon occurred, the event is written about as either a form of dream or an autosymbolic hallucination. Thus, it has been interpreted by Lewin (1946, 1948, 1953) as what he calls "the dream screen" and by Stern (1961) as what he has labeled "blank hallucinations." I think it is not unreasonable to suggest that the hallucinations may be a kind of "way-station" on the road to the use of language, the individual's attempt actively to restore the linkage of his creative and his adaptational capacities. One of my patients (Bromberg, 1991) actually reported that his earliest childhood memory of the Isakower phenomenon was of trying to cope with it by attempting to write into it, but the bubble was so soft and mushy that his hand went into it and left no impression – a description remarkably similar to that of his early experience with his mother (pp. 406–407). Treating this kind of patient, one can often see a structural resonance between the autosymbolic visual imagery and the simultaneously occuring enactment in the transference–countertransference field, particularly during phases when dissociative structures are being surrendered.

Trauma and technique

What about the issue of "technique"? It is in my view too linear a concept; if you do "this" correctly now, then "that" will follow later. It feels too overly based on an "If this, then that" model that looks for linear causes for events, with individuality seen as random "noise" in the system. From the vantage point of nonlinear dynamics, it is the unpredictability that is the very nature of the event, and *proper analytic technique lies in the analyst's ability to beware of its presence*, to be as attuned as possible to those moments when application of "technique" has replaced a stance centrally organized by ongoing involvement with the patient's experience. A pattern of pointless retraumatization in analysis can take as many forms as there are analytic techniques, and any systematized analytic posture holds the potential for repeating the trauma of nonrecognition, no matter how useful the theory from which the posture is derived. Nonrecognition is equivalent to relational abandonment, and it is that which evokes the familiar and often bewildering accusation "you don't want to know me." In other words, it is in the process of "knowing" one's patient through direct relatedness, as distinguished from frustrating, gratifying, containing, empathizing, or even understanding him, that those aspects of self which cannot "speak" will ever find a voice and exist as a felt presence owned by the patient rather than as a "not-me" state that possesses him.

Areas of personality that are organized by conflict are always interwoven with areas organized by trauma. Trauma produces dissociation, and dissociation creates retrospective falsification of the past and retrospective falsification of one's ability to predict the future. The linear sequence of time experience is altered as a protective device. Amnesia is produced, at least for the perceptual memory of the events, but experiential memory remains relatively intact. It is as if the person "feels" something happened to him because "he just feels it," but he can't remember it as a perceptual event – an image that can be processed cognitively – and thus, temporally, as a piece of the past.

What takes the place of the memory is a "time condensation," a reliving of the past as a frozen replica that structures the person's image of the future and of the present. Instead of being able to deal with "what happened to me," the person enters therapy in order to deal with what he is sure *will* happen to him and what is happening to him now. Terr (1984) has discussed this issue in the context of her research into the aftermath of various traumatic events, including the kidnapping and burying alive of a busload of schoolchildren in Chowchilla, California:

> Following psychic trauma, disorders of time sequencing may assume various guises: (1) condensations of contiguous events into simultaneity; (2) time-skew; (3) retrospective significances (including omens); and (4) the sense of prediction. These post-traumatic distortions of ordering require sizeable suspensions of reality sense, and they may lead the psychiatrist or psychoanalyst erroneously to conclude that the psychically traumatized patient suffers from a "borderline" or worse condition. (p. 644)

The difficulty for psychoanalysts is that they do not have a strong theoretical model to deal with the implications of this phenomenon because Freud, abandoning trauma theory, replaced it with a conceptual system leading to the belief that, except for the most seriously disturbed patients, interpretation of intrapsychic conflict (with or without "parameters") should be sufficient. In fact, trauma and dissociation breed discontinuous realities in *every* human being that are not amenable to interpretation. Even though a patient's bleak view of the future is a psychodynamic issue based largely on something that really happened in the past, because of the nature of dissociation, he often has minimal perspective on his pain or his dread. It is an experiential truth that he lives with. Thus, the more an analyst pursues his interpretations, the more a patient frequently feels that the analyst really doesn't want to know him. The "him" that he feels the analyst doesn't want to know is the dissociated self-state holding the experience of trauma that can't be processed as a memory. So the analyst is right but wrong, and in being wrong he is presented with a context to discover the speaker hidden in the words. It is an opportunity for an analyst to live with his patient through an inevitable enactment of the original trauma, thus providing the best chance to have the unprocessed experience become a real memory. How does this occur? There is no answer to that because it takes place differently for every unique patient–analyst dyad. But the approach and the principle can at least be stated.

The essential nature of trauma is that because the person is not prepared to cope with it, the integrity of the ego is passively overwhelmed, and the experience of "being oneself" begins to fragment and depersonalize. It is in this sense that dissociation protects against self-fragmentation and restores personhood and sanity by hypnoidally unlinking the incompatible states of consciousness and allowing access to them only as discontinuous and cognitively unrelated mental experiences. It works, but *the basic problem for the traumatized individual then becomes his own self-cure*. The living present and the image of the future serve largely as warnings designed to protect the person against trauma that has already occurred. The capacity for imagination is perverted into a way of making sure that the unanticipated quality of the unremembered original event cannot be repeated. By consistently mobilizing for disaster, the person is unwittingly contributing to its likelihood, and no matter how bad it turns out to be, the person is already prepared for it and his ego is set to master it. To deal with the original trauma, a dissociated state of consciousness is created that holds the experience as a terrifying, but retrospectively falsified temporal event. The nature of the fear is real enough, but the mind retains it as a dread of what can happen or is happening rather than as a memory of what has happened. The result is that the person, through continual enactment of the experiential memory, creates a world of miniature versions of the original situation and lives in that world as a reality that continues to be substantiated through his ongoing relationships. It is as though he is not to be allowed any peace. Around each corner is potential trauma; peace is simply the calm before the storm, and if he goes too long without verification of the reality of his dread, he needs to find some event that provides evidence that justifies his felt need for vigilance in a world of traumatic reality.

The "truth" that is held by a dissociated state exists as an experiential memory without an accurate perceptual memory of its traumatic origin. It will remain untouched unless a new perceptual reality is created between patient and analyst that has some impact on altering the narrative structure that maintains dissociation as though the past were still a present danger. The quality of the relationship between patient and analyst at any given moment will thus determine the degree to which the content of an interpretation will be heard *as* an interpretation rather than as a verbal disguise for what is experienced as the analyst's repetition of the original abuse or neglect. In other words, for traumatic experience to be cognitively symbolized it has to be reenacted in a relationship that replays the interpersonal context without blindly reproducing the original outcome. If the analyst includes this fact in his working stance, then he is more likely to be attuned to the shifts in states of consciousness – *his own as well as his patient's* – that signal when an enactment is taking place and that a modification in approach is required which may or may not include verbally addressing the enactment at that moment.

All in all, I think the patient's dilemma has been particularly well described in a four-line poem by Emerson (1851 [1945]) that is in its own way a kind of tribute to the patient. Unfortunately, you can't read it to your patient because he will not only deny its validity but will take it as further evidence that you don't want to know his pain. The poem, called "Borrowing," reads

> Some of the hurts you have cured,
> And the sharpest you still have survived,
> But what torments of grief you endured
> From evils which never arrived!

The uses and abuses of self-disclosure

With regard to how one approaches analytic intervention with this frame of reference in mind, probably the prime clinical issue that addresses the difference between linear and nonlinear thinking in technique is that of self-disclosure by the analyst. Like any other choice an analyst makes with a given patient, self-disclosure derives its meaning from the ongoing context of the relationship in which it takes place, not from its utility as a "technique." Its usefulness to the analytic process is organized by the quality of its genuineness as a human act, particularly the degree to which the analyst is free of internal pressure (conscious or unconscious) to prove his honesty or trustworthiness as a technical maneuver designed to counter the patient's mistrust. The analyst's self-disclosure must be what Symington (1983) calls an "act of freedom" in which the analyst comfortably retains his right to not disclose or, if he does choose to disclose, to claim his own privacy and set his own boundaries. If it is not an "act of freedom" then it also loses its potential as an "act of meaning" in Bruner's (1990) terms, a relational act through which personal narrative is reconstructed as a perceptual event in a context of interpersonal authenticity.

The subjective experience of freedom to say "no," or the absence of such freedom, inevitably informs the way in which the patient's self-disclosure is shaped, and this is equally true for the analyst. His motivation and affective state become as much a part of what is disclosed as the intended content. In other words, if the analyst's choice is motivated by his need to be seen in a certain way by his patient (such as honest, accommodating, unsadistic, or innovatively "free" as an analyst) then self-disclosure becomes a technique and as a technique is as instrumentally linear as any other intervention based on an "if I do this, then the patient will do that" model. Like any human quality that is "packaged," self-disclosure too can lose its primary relational ingredient (mutuality) and become what Greenberg (1981) has called "prescriptive." When it fails in its purpose, it is usually for that reason. It lacks the authenticity, spontaneity, and unpredictable impact on the future that makes analytic growth possible.

A colleague of mine (Therese Ragen, personal communication) has commented that my viewpoint implies a distinction between genuineness and honesty, and I agree. Genuineness is a human attribute only in a relational context. If you try to turn it into a technique, it loses mutuality and becomes a personal instrumentality called "honesty." Any attempt to turn a therapeutic discovery that emerges from a relational context into a technique that can be "applied" to other patients is an illustration of what I believe to be the single most ubiquitous failing in all analytic schools of thought as methods of therapy, and the shared blind-spot in each of their creators (including Freud, Ferenczi, Sullivan, and Kohut).

For example, Ferenczi's failure with "mutual analysis" as a technique (Dupont, 1988) occurred not because what he did was wrong, but because it failed to be right. What I mean by this is that an analyst who systematically attempts to gratify needs fails the patient, not because gratification is "wrong" or intrinsically harmful, but because it is a form of nonrecognition and for that reason fails, just as does systematic *frustration* of needs. Both are evidence to the patient that the analyst is unable or unwilling to authentically "live with" the patient's state of mind in whatever form it presents itself and attempt to know it without surrendering his right to "be himself" as part of the process. I believe this to be a more accurate assessment than Ferenczi's own statement of his disillusionment, in which he concludes (Dupont, 1988) that "mutual analysis is merely a 'last resort' made necessary by insufficiently deep analysis of the analysts themselves [and] 'proper analysis by a stranger, without any obligation, would be better'" (p. xxii). Ferenczi's concept of "mutual analysis" was based on something he originally percieved as demanded of him by certain patients, particularly by his famous patient Elizabeth Severn, known as RN. At that point, his approach to his patient was genuinely mutual – it was not Ferenczi's technical creation but a cocreation of that particular patient and analyst dyad. Following that, Ferenczi turned it into a technique he called "mutual analysis," at which point, like any other technique, it was no longer a cocreation and, I submit, was in fact no longer mutual. It was something, for better or for worse, applied prescriptively, and it failed because of that.

In fact, the way Ferenczi discovered this "technique" reminds me a bit of the old joke based on Charles Lamb's (1822 [1948]) essay about the farmer in ancient China whose house burned down with his pig in it. While removing the dead animal, the farmer scorched himself, and when he put his finger into his mouth to cool it, he became so thrilled with the exciting new taste that he called all his neighbors to try it. And so, the joke goes, roast pork was discovered, and on the same day each year until the farmer's death he would gather his neighbors together for a feast and burn down his new house with a pig in it. My own addendum would be that perhaps that joke isn't really about the discovery of roast pork but the discovery of "technique."

I am suggesting, in other words, that the reason Ferenczi was successful with Elizabeth Severn (and perhaps a few other patients later on) when he attempted "mutual analysis" was not because patients in general need soul-searching emotional openness from their analysts, but because that patient at that moment in Ferenczi's work was able to confront his inauthenticity with regard to her. She settled for "mutual analysis" because she could not hope to change his personality. In an ironic way, she asked for what she knew he might be able to give, not for what she really needed. She asked for a demonstration of honesty rather than an effort at mutuality because there was no way to get the real thing. In his own way, of course, Ferenczi did ultimately respond with genuine mutuality even though, ironically, he missed her real message – "I need you to be yourself while recognizing what I am feeling, but since you haven't yet been able to do both, let's see what you can do if I push you to the edge." His courage to try self-disclosure at that point came mostly from his need to control what was going on between himself and his patient, and because it "worked" it prevented him from potentially experiencing and recognizing the complex interplay between what his patient was saying to him and what she was doing with him while saying it. Ferenczi could not register, as part of a single configuration, the controlling and intrusive way she was behaving toward him while she was talking about "mutual" analysis as the only way she could "protect herself" *from* him. But he could experience in himself at that immediate moment the presence of the very kinds of feelings toward her that she was accusing him of harboring. He could feel what she was saying about him as accurate – his reaction to what he called in his clinical diary her "terrorism of suffering" (Dupont, 1988, p. 211) – and he turned toward what she insisted was the only possible path that could validate her feelings and enable her to trust him: that of self-disclosure equivalent to hers. It "worked." And *because* it "worked," he came to believe it was the technique that accounted for the improvement in the treatment relationship. In my terms, he confused authenticity with self-disclosure and kept burning down the house to get the roast pork. But unlike the farmer in the joke, he didn't even end up getting the pork again. His subsequent patients, for the most part, kept reacting as though he were doing something bad to them, and I would have to agree; he was inadvertantly retraumatizing them to no immediate therapeutic purpose. All this could have turned out much better if he had adhered to what he had already written about the importance of trauma in personality development. Don't just attend to the words; try to see the dissociated speaker who is relating to you at that moment, the part of the self that "lives on, hidden, ceaselessly endeavoring to make itself felt" (Ferenczi, 1930b [1980], p. 122).

All this having been said, I must admit that Dupont's (1993) statement that "gratifications should only be granted to demands aiming at recognition" (p. 154) doesn't provide much of a place to anchor oneself when a patient is rocking the couch and insisting with absolute conviction that you are depriving him of the one thing he needs to get better. At such a moment an analyst is often floundering and not at all sure of what he thinks. There are very few external guidelines, and it's very lonely with only your doubts to keep you company. All I can say is that, while I do believe that gratification is most often experienced by patients as an empathic abandonment because it is typically a substitute for the more painful effort at recognition, there are in my experience certain patients for whom some directly gratifying response by the analyst is the only way they can trust the analyst's concern for them, at least for a period of time. With such an individual at such a moment, I sometimes find myself making some compromise that is invariably not satisfying to either of us but almost always seems to move the work ahead. Over the years I've come to believe that it may be the *limitation* in my flexibility – the fact that I do implicitly draw a line in the sand – that has the most impact because it emanates from relational authenticity. If I do ultimately move the line, *the process through which that happens is at least as important as the accommodation itself.* It carries the fact that what I'm doing is not a technique but a personal effort I am willing to make as long as it does not exceed the limits of what I establish as my personal boundaries and is thus part of a genuine relational negotiation. So, all in all, I could probably say that my position on technique feels compatible with Kaiser's (1965) observation that "whenever you feel the need to do something, or to refrain from doing something for the purpose of showing [a patient] your concern, you can be certain that your concern is lacking" (p. 170).

Many different analytic concepts have, each in its own metaphor, addressed the fact that the aesthetics of analytic communication is an ineffable coming together of two minds in an unpredictable way, from which something "new but not new" is constructed. Michael Balint's (1968) "new beginning," Winnicott's (1967 [1971]) "potential space," and Sullivan's (1953) "parataxic mode of experience" are just a few of the more influential examples. I believe that the logic of conceptualizing the intersubjective field in these ways is strongest in the context of a nonlinear view of mental structure and the discontinuity of self-states. The ability of a patient to take in and seriously consider the analyst's perception of him is possible only if another reality (or truth) being held in a dissociated state is not being invalidated as a tradeoff. The patient doesn't need to be "agreed with" or need a heroic attempt at self-disclosure by the analyst. What is required is that the multiple realities being held by different self-states find opportunity for linkage. The most powerful medium through which this takes place is the analyst's ability to recognize that his feelings about his patient are not his personal property, and that his own feelings and his patient's are part of a unitary configuration that must be linked in the immediacy of the analytic relationship in order for the multiple realities within the patient to become linked through cognitive symbolization by language. Peterson (1993), whom I quoted earlier, referred to the "change points" or moments in therapy where cognitive insights occur. My view is that these change points occur when an enactment is serving its proper function and the patient's dissociated experience that the analyst has been holding as part of himself is sufficiently processed between them for the patient to begin to take it back into his own self-experience little by little. It is a change point because the patient's processing of the experience continues internally as a state of conflict rather than intersubjectively. In other words, the use of language, instead of being a substitute for experience, allows a new self-narrative to be created. It moves a new experience of reality that begins as perceptual and interpersonal to its most mature level of mental processing by the use of thought and intrapsychic conflict resolution. Put most simply, *"unfreezing" the concrete, literal quality of a patient's states of consciousness allows him to embrace the full range of his self-narratives by first embracing the full range of his perceptual apparatus within a single relational field.* All in all, perhaps Socrates would not mind if the title of this paper were changed to "Speak! that I may see both of us."

Note

1 I have used the male gender designation in this paper for convenience of exposition. Unless I am referring to a specific individual, it is intended to represent male or female interchangably.

References

Adams, H. (1904 [1986]). *Mont Saint-Michel and Chartres*. New York: Penguin Classics.

Balint, M. (1968). *The Basic Fault*. London: Tavistock.

Barton, S. (1994). Chaos, self-organization, and psychology. *American Psychologist*, 49: 5–14.

Beebe, B. & Lachmann, F. M. (1992). The contribution of mother–infant mutual influence to the origins of self- and object representations. In N. J. Skolnick & S. C. Warshaw (Eds), *Relational Perspectives in Psychoanalysis*. Hillsdale, NJ: Analytic Press, pp. 83–117.

Bollas, C. (1987). *The Shadow of the Object*. London: Free Association Books.

Bromberg, P. M. (1984). On the occurrence of the Isakower phenomenon in a schizoid disorder. *Contemporary Psychoanalysis*, 20: 600–624.

Bromberg, P. M. (1991). On knowing one's patient inside out: The aesthetics of unconscious communication. *Psychoanalytic Dialogues*, 1: 399–422.

Bromberg, P. M. (1993). Shadow and substance: A relational perspective on clinical process. *Psychoanalytic Psychology*, 10: 147–168.

Bruner, J. (1990). *Acts of Meaning*. Cambridge, MA: Harvard University Press.

Chu, J. A. (1991). The repetition compulsion revisited: Reliving dissociated trauma. *Psychotherapy*, 28: 327–332.

Dupont, J. (Ed.) (1988). *The Clinical Diary of Sándor Ferenczi*. Cambridge, MA: Harvard University Press.

Dupont, J. (Ed.) (1993). Michael Balint: Analysand, pupil, friend, and successor to Sándor Ferenczi. In L. Aron & A. Harris (Eds), *The Legacy of Sándor Ferenczi*. Hillsdale, NJ: Analytic Press.

Emde, R. N., Gaensbaure, T. J. & Harmon, R. J. (1976). Emotional expression in infancy: A biobehavioral study. *Psychological Issues*, 10, Monograph 37. New York: International Universities Press.

Emerson, R. W. (1851 [1945]). Borrowing. In D. McCord (Ed.), *What Cheer*. New York: Coward-McCann, p. 321.

Ferenczi, S. (1930a [1980]). Notes and fragments II. In M. Balint (Ed.), *Final Contributions to the Problems and Methods of Psycho-Analysis*. New York: Brunner/Mazel, pp. 219–231.

Ferenczi, S. (1930b [1980]). The principles of relaxation and neo-catharsis. In M. Balint (Ed.), *Final Contributions to the Problems and Methods of Psycho-Analysis*. New York: Brunner/Mazel, pp. 108–125.

Freud, S. (1913 [1955]). *On Beginning the Treatment*, Standard Edition 12. London: Hogarth Press, pp. 121–144.

Gleick, J. (1987). *Chaos*. New York: Viking.

Greenberg, J. (1981). Prescription or description: The therapeutic action of psychoanalysis. *Contemporary Psychoanalysis*, 17: 239–257.

Isakower, O. (1938). A contribution to the patho-psychology of phenomena associated with falling asleep. *International Journal of Psycho-Analysis*, 19: 331–345.

Kaiser, H. (1965). The universal symptom of the psychoneuroses: A search for the conditions of effective psychotherapy. In L. B. Fierman (Ed.), *Effective Psychotherapy*. New York: Free Press, pp. 14–171.

Lamb, C. (1822 [1948]). A dissertation upon roast pig. In E. Bernbaum (Ed.), *Anthology of Romanticism*, 3rd edition. New York: Ronald Press, pp. 385–388.

Levenson, E. A. (1982). Follow the fox. *Contemporary Psychoanalysis*, 18: 1–15.

Lewin, B. D. (1946). Sleep, the mouth, and the dream screen. *Psychoanalytic Quarterly*, 15: 419–434.
Lewin, B. D. (1948). Inferences from the dream screen. *International Journal of Psycho-Analysis*, 29: 224–231.
Lewin, B. D. (1953) Reconsideration of the dream screen. *Psychoanalytic Quarterly*, 22: 174–199.
Lightman, A. (1993). *Einstein's Dreams*. New York: Pantheon Books.
Loewald, H. (1979). The waning of the Oedipus complex. *Journal of the American Psychoanalytic Association*, 27: 751–775.
Nesse, R. M. (1991). What good is feeling bad?: The evolutionary benefits of psychic pain. *The Sciences*, Nov/Dec: 30–37.
Peterson, J. (1993). Reply to Van der Hart/Brown Article. *Dissociation*, 6: 74–75.
Putnam, F. (1988). The switch process in multiple personality disorder and other state-change disorders. *Dissociation*, 1: 24–32.
Putnam, F. (1992). Discussion: Are alter personalities fragments or fictions? *Psychoanalytic Inquiry*, 12: 95–111.
Reik, T. (1936). *Surprise and the Psycho-Analyst*. London: Kegan Paul.
Sander, L. (1977). The regulation of exchange in the infant caretaker system and some aspects of the context–content relationship. In M. Lewis & L. Rosenblum (Eds), *Interaction, Conversation, and the Development of Language*. New York: Wiley, pp. 133–156.
Schafer, R. (1976). *A New Language for Psychoanalysis*. New Haven, CT: Yale University Press.
Schafer, R. (1983). *The Analytic Attitude*. New York: Basic Books.
Stern, D. N. (1985). *The Interpersonal World of the Infant*. New York: Basic Books.
Stern, M. M. (1961). Blank hallucinations: Remarks about trauma and perceptual disturbances. *International Journal of Psycho-Analysis*, 42: 205–215.
Sullivan, H. S. (1953). *The Interpersonal Theory of Psychiatry*. New York: W. W. Norton.
Symington, N. (1983). The analyst's act of freedom as agent of therapeutic change. *International Review of Psycho-Analysis*, 10: 283–291.
Terr, L. C. (1984). Time and trauma. *Psychoanalytic Study of the Child*, 39: 633–665.
Winnicott, D. W. (1967 [1971]). The location of cultural experience. In *Playing and Reality*. New York: Basic Books, pp. 95–103.
Winnicott, D. W. (1969). The use of an object and relating through identifications. In *Playing and Reality*. New York: Basic Books, pp. 86–94.
Wolff, P. H. (1987). *The Development of Behavioral States and Expression of Emotion in Early Infancy*. Chicago, IL: University of Chicago Press.